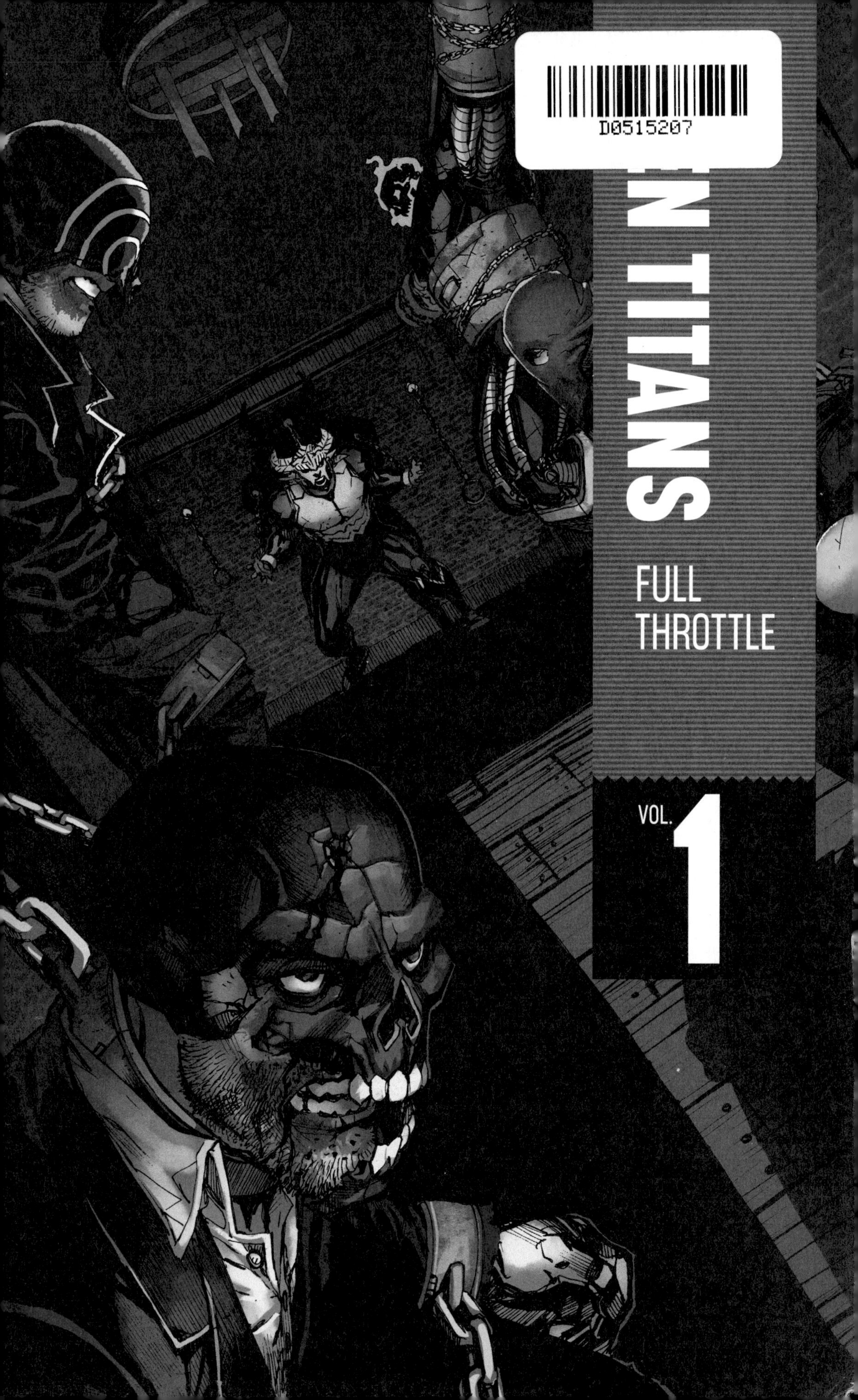
N TITANS
FULL
THROTTLE
VOL. 1

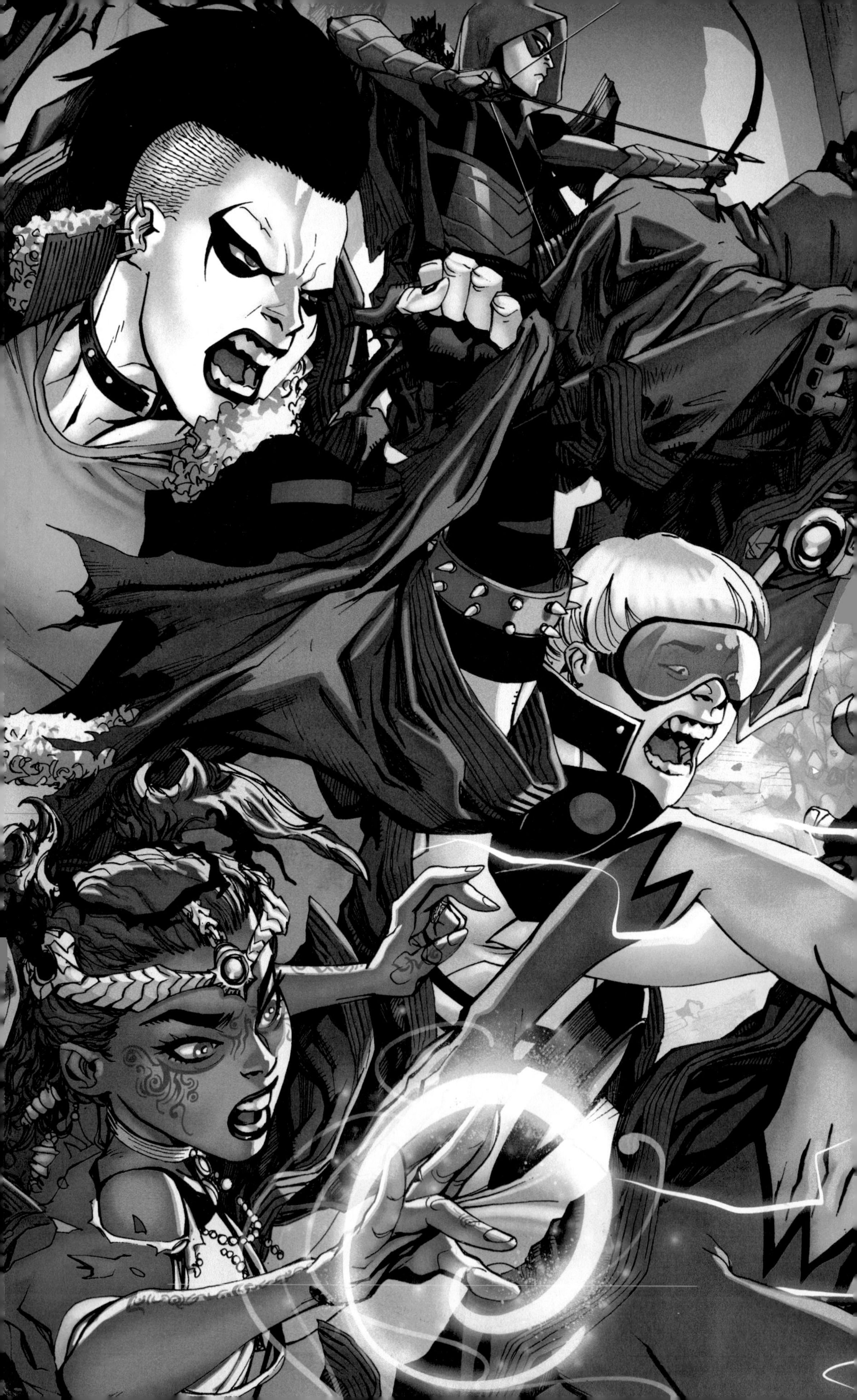

# TEEN TITANS
## FULL THROTTLE

writer

**ADAM GLASS**

artists

**BERNARD CHANG**
ROBSON ROCHA
DANIEL HENRIQUES
SCOTT HANNA

colorists

**MARCELO MAIOLO**
**SUNNY GHO**
**HI-FI**

letterers

**ROB LEIGH**
**DERON BENNETT**

collection cover artists

**BERNARD CHANG and WIL QUINTANA**

VOL.
# 1

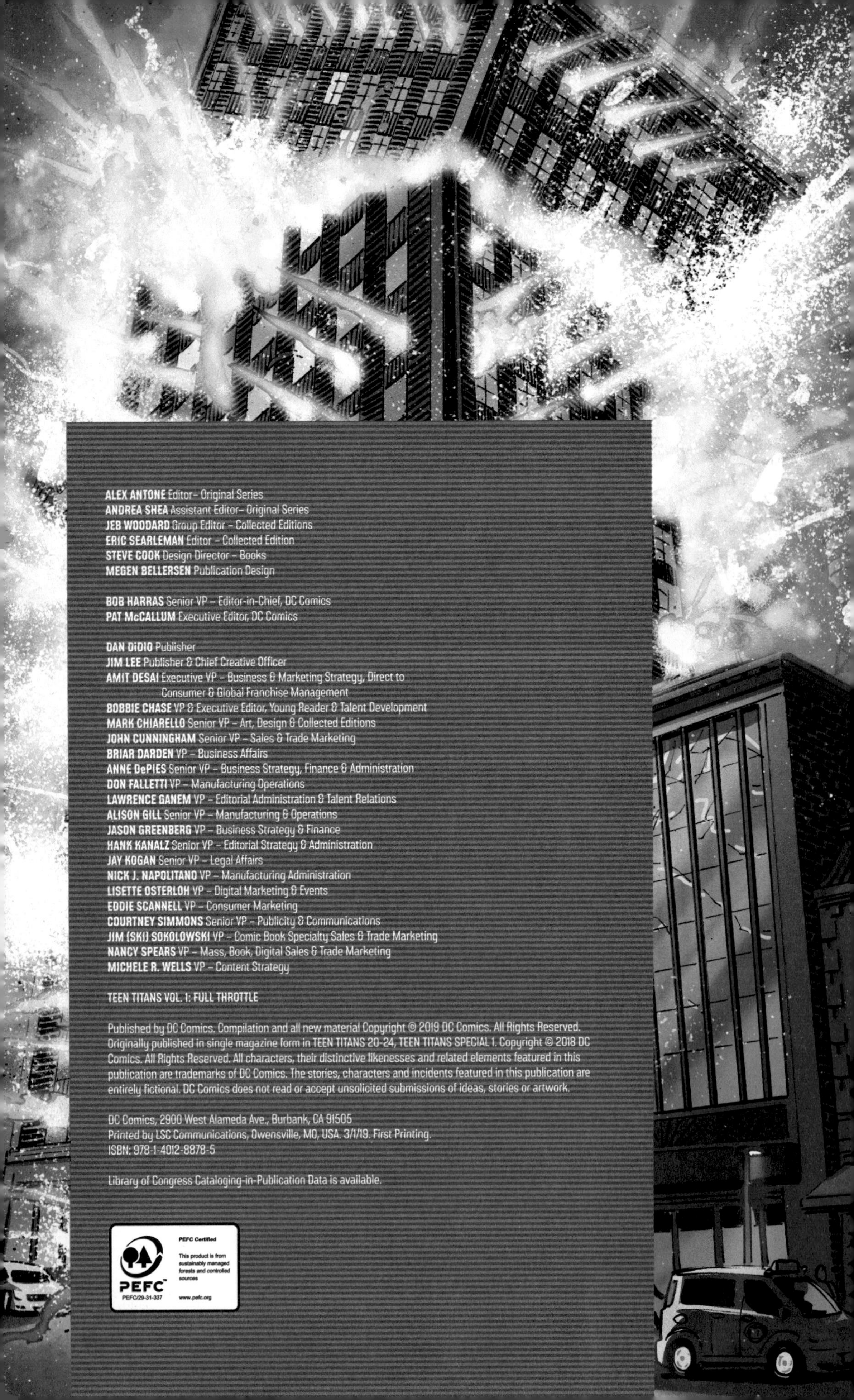

**ALEX ANTONE** Editor– Original Series
**ANDREA SHEA** Assistant Editor– Original Series
**JEB WOODARD** Group Editor – Collected Editions
**ERIC SEARLEMAN** Editor – Collected Edition
**STEVE COOK** Design Director – Books
**MEGEN BELLERSEN** Publication Design

**BOB HARRAS** Senior VP – Editor-in-Chief, DC Comics
**PAT McCALLUM** Executive Editor, DC Comics

**DAN DiDIO** Publisher
**JIM LEE** Publisher & Chief Creative Officer
**AMIT DESAI** Executive VP – Business & Marketing Strategy, Direct to Consumer & Global Franchise Management
**BOBBIE CHASE** VP & Executive Editor, Young Reader & Talent Development
**MARK CHIARELLO** Senior VP – Art, Design & Collected Editions
**JOHN CUNNINGHAM** Senior VP – Sales & Trade Marketing
**BRIAR DARDEN** VP – Business Affairs
**ANNE DePIES** Senior VP – Business Strategy, Finance & Administration
**DON FALLETTI** VP – Manufacturing Operations
**LAWRENCE GANEM** VP – Editorial Administration & Talent Relations
**ALISON GILL** Senior VP – Manufacturing & Operations
**JASON GREENBERG** VP – Business Strategy & Finance
**HANK KANALZ** Senior VP – Editorial Strategy & Administration
**JAY KOGAN** Senior VP – Legal Affairs
**NICK J. NAPOLITANO** VP – Manufacturing Administration
**LISETTE OSTERLOH** VP – Digital Marketing & Events
**EDDIE SCANNELL** VP – Consumer Marketing
**COURTNEY SIMMONS** Senior VP – Publicity & Communications
**JIM (SKI) SOKOLOWSKI** VP – Comic Book Specialty Sales & Trade Marketing
**NANCY SPEARS** VP – Mass, Book, Digital Sales & Trade Marketing
**MICHELE R. WELLS** VP – Content Strategy

**TEEN TITANS VOL. 1: FULL THROTTLE**



DC Comics, 2900 West Alameda Ave., Burbank, CA 91505
Printed by LSC Communications, Owensville, MO, USA. 3/1/19. First Printing.
ISBN: 978-1-4012-8878-5

Library of Congress Cataloging-in-Publication Data is available.

PEFC Certified
This product is from sustainably managed forests and controlled sources
PEFC/29-31-337
www.pefc.org

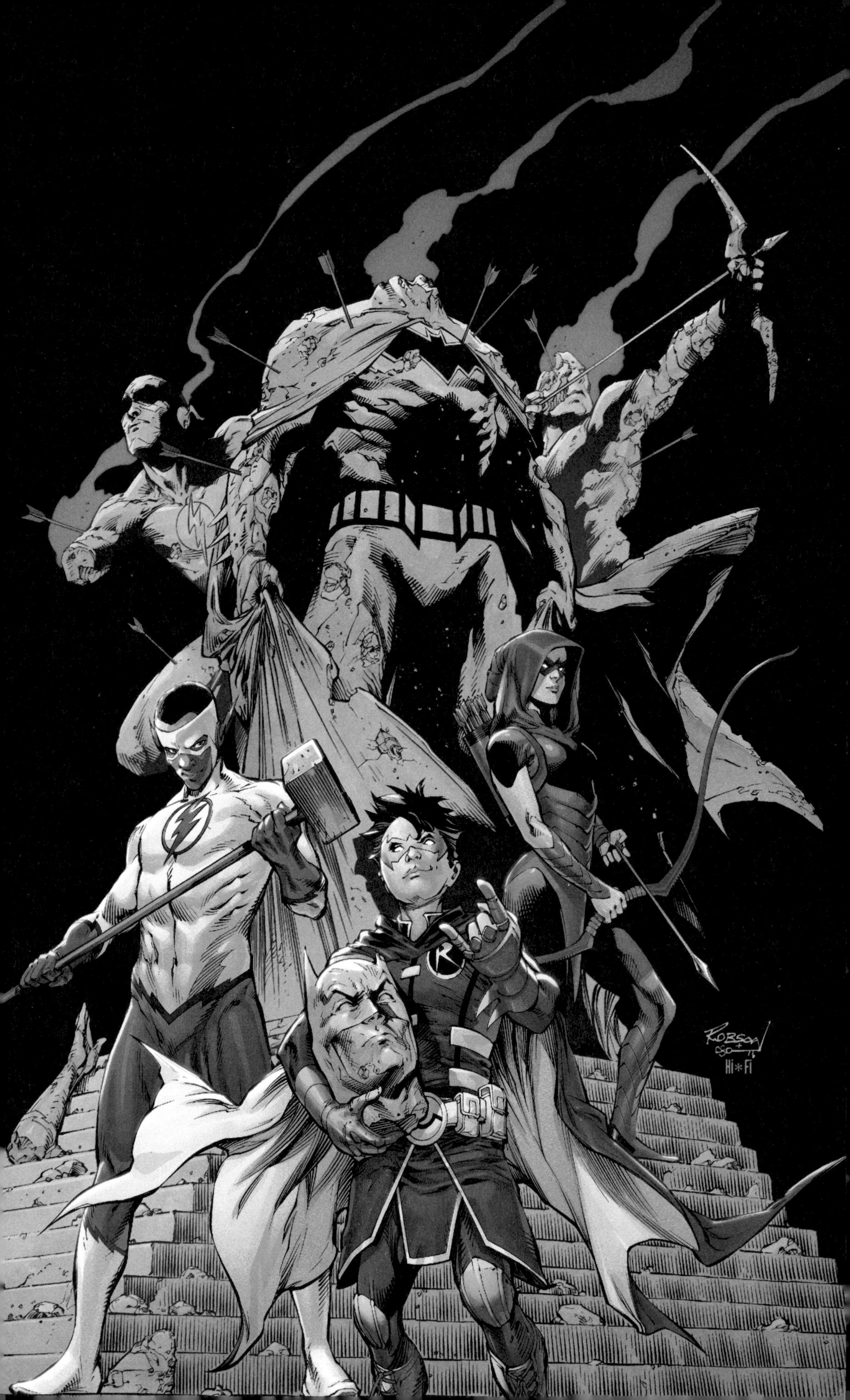
ROBSON
Hi*Fi

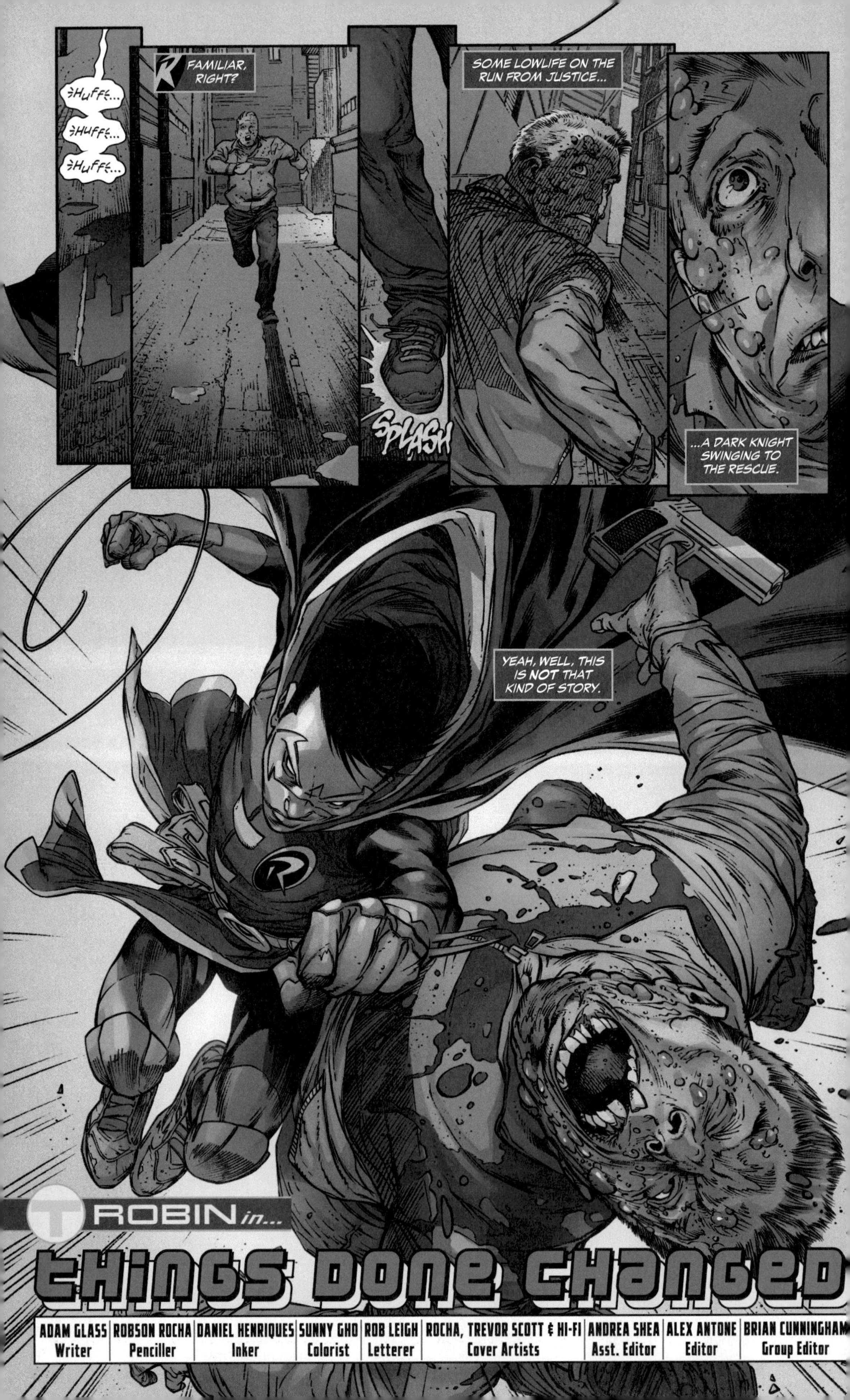

HUFF...
HUFF...
HUFF...
FAMILIAR, RIGHT?
SPLASH
SOME LOWLIFE ON THE RUN FROM JUSTICE...
...A DARK KNIGHT SWINGING TO THE RESCUE.
YEAH, WELL, THIS IS **NOT** THAT KIND OF STORY.
ROBIN in...
THINGS DONE CHANGED
ADAM GLASS Writer
ROBSON ROCHA Penciller
DANIEL HENRIQUES Inker
SUNNY GHO Colorist
ROB LEIGH Letterer
ROCHA, TREVOR SCOTT & HI-FI Cover Artists
ANDREA SHEA Asst. Editor
ALEX ANTONE Editor
BRIAN CUNNINGHAM Group Editor

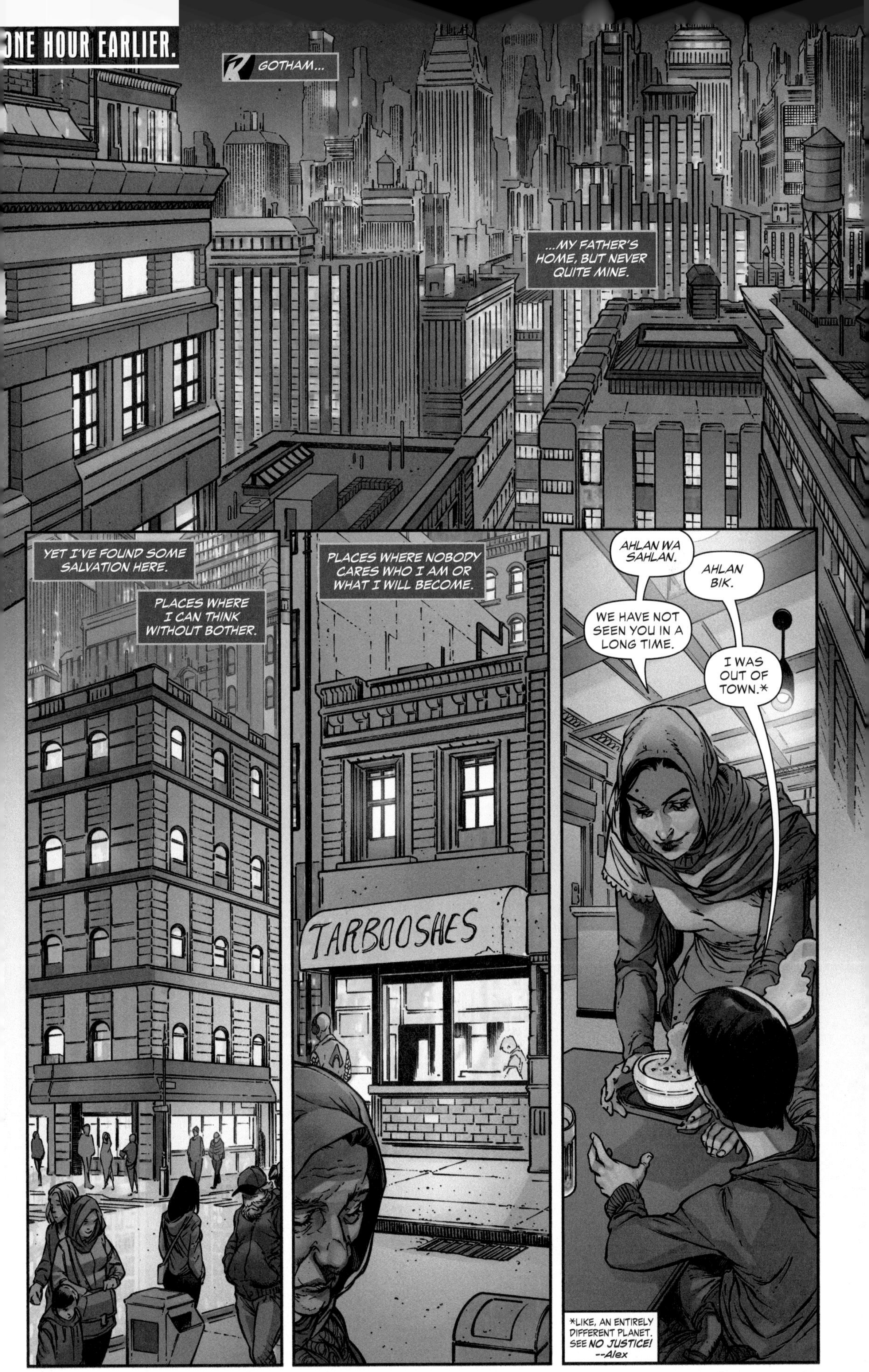
ONE HOUR EARLIER.
GOTHAM...
...MY FATHER'S HOME, BUT NEVER QUITE MINE.
YET I'VE FOUND SOME SALVATION HERE.
PLACES WHERE I CAN THINK WITHOUT BOTHER.
PLACES WHERE NOBODY CARES WHO I AM OR WHAT I WILL BECOME.
TARBOOSHES
AHLAN WA SAHLAN.
AHLAN BIK.
WE HAVE NOT SEEN YOU IN A LONG TIME.
I WAS OUT OF TOWN.*
*LIKE, AN ENTIRELY DIFFERENT PLANET. SEE NO JUSTICE! --Alex

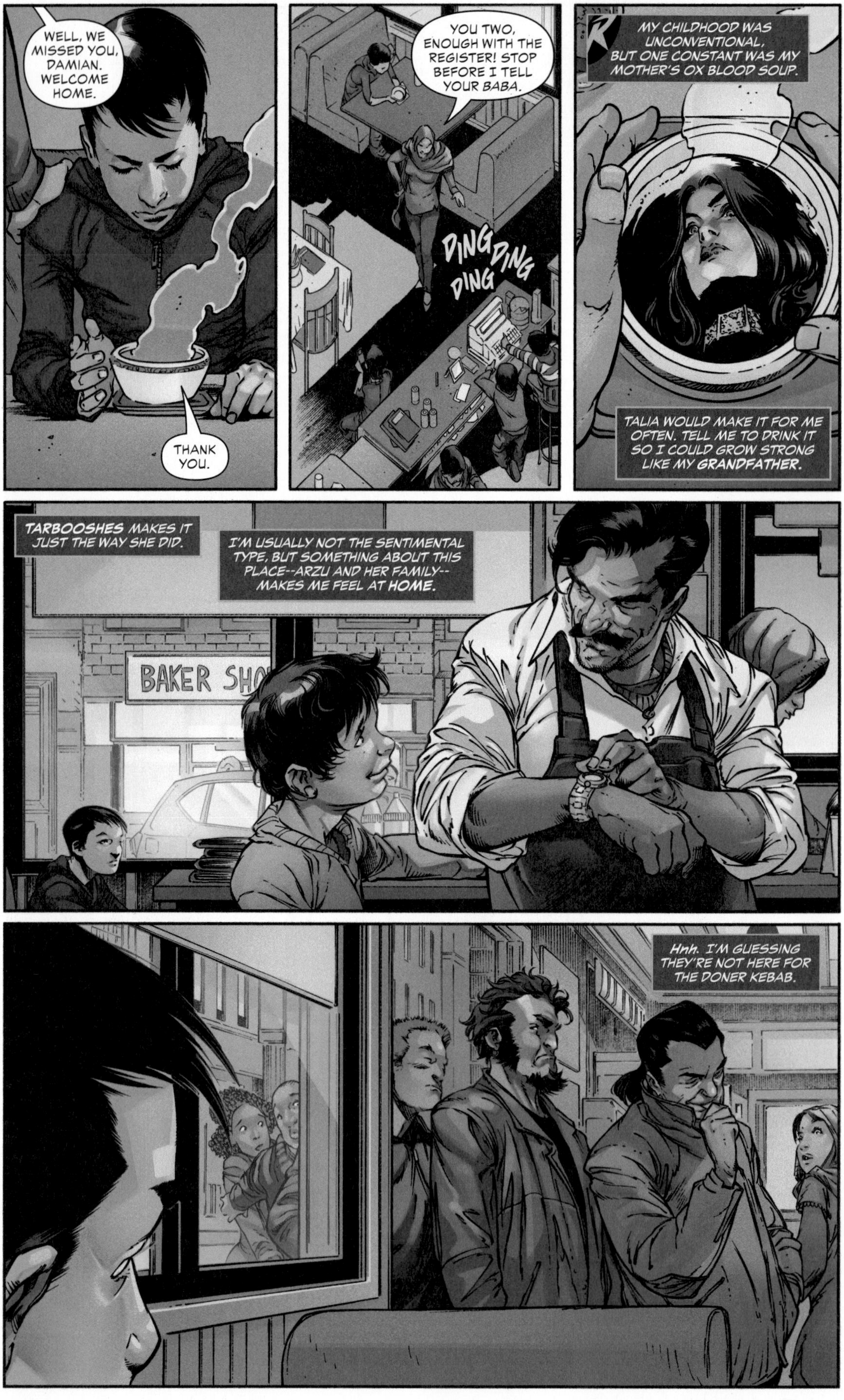
WELL, WE MISSED YOU, DAMIAN. WELCOME HOME.
THANK YOU.
YOU TWO, ENOUGH WITH THE REGISTER! STOP BEFORE I TELL YOUR BABA.
DING DING DING
MY CHILDHOOD WAS UNCONVENTIONAL, BUT ONE CONSTANT WAS MY MOTHER'S OX BLOOD SOUP.
TALIA WOULD MAKE IT FOR ME OFTEN. TELL ME TO DRINK IT SO I COULD GROW STRONG LIKE MY GRANDFATHER.
TARBOOSHES MAKES IT JUST THE WAY SHE DID.
I'M USUALLY NOT THE SENTIMENTAL TYPE, BUT SOMETHING ABOUT THIS PLACE--ARZU AND HER FAMILY--MAKES ME FEEL AT HOME.
BAKER SHO
Hnh. I'M GUESSING THEY'RE NOT HERE FOR THE DONER KEBAB.

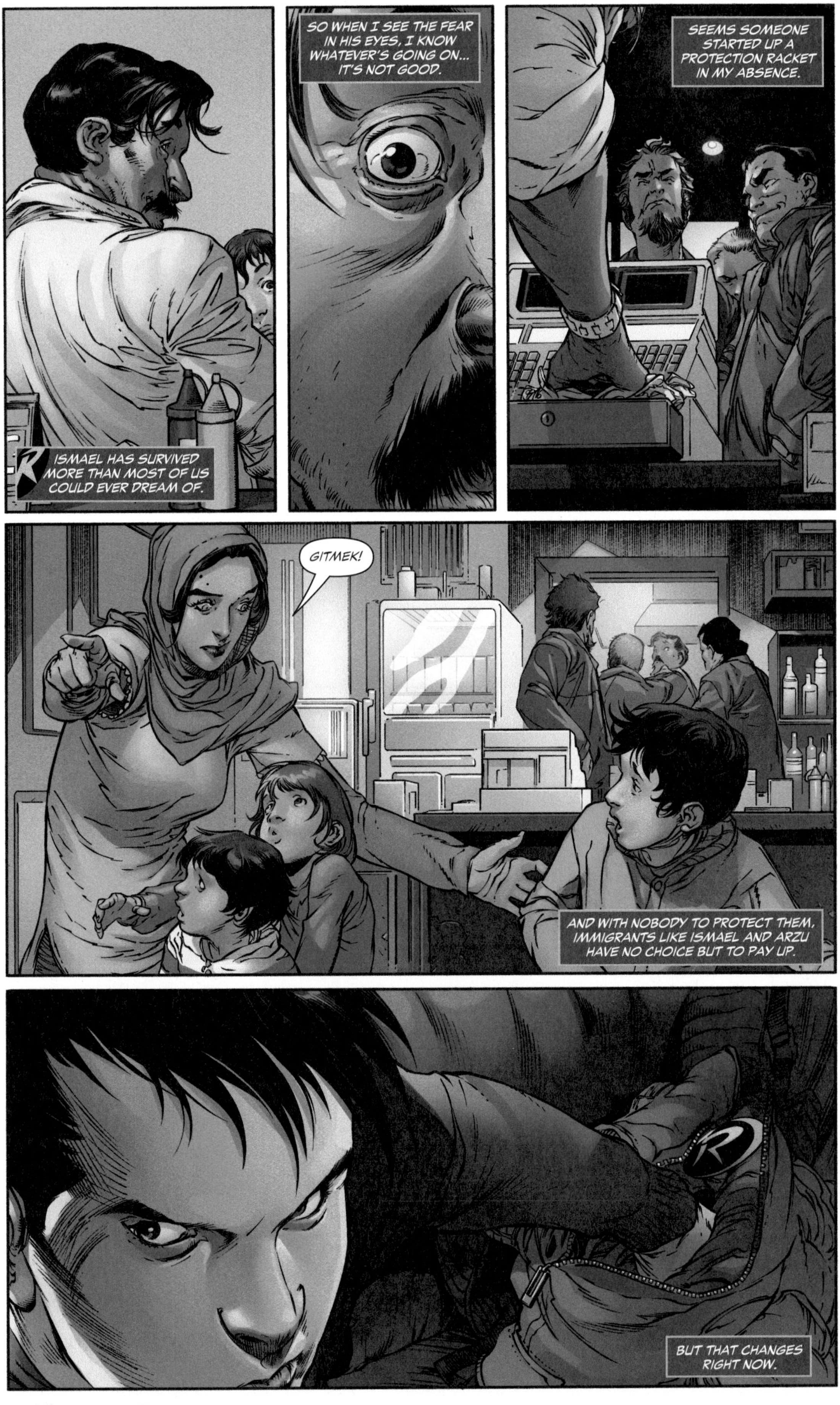
ISMAEL HAS SURVIVED MORE THAN MOST OF US COULD EVER DREAM OF.
SO WHEN I SEE THE FEAR IN HIS EYES, I KNOW WHATEVER'S GOING ON... IT'S NOT GOOD.
SEEMS SOMEONE STARTED UP A PROTECTION RACKET IN MY ABSENCE.
GITMEK!
AND WITH NOBODY TO PROTECT THEM, IMMIGRANTS LIKE ISMAEL AND ARZU HAVE NO CHOICE BUT TO PAY UP.
BUT THAT CHANGES RIGHT NOW.

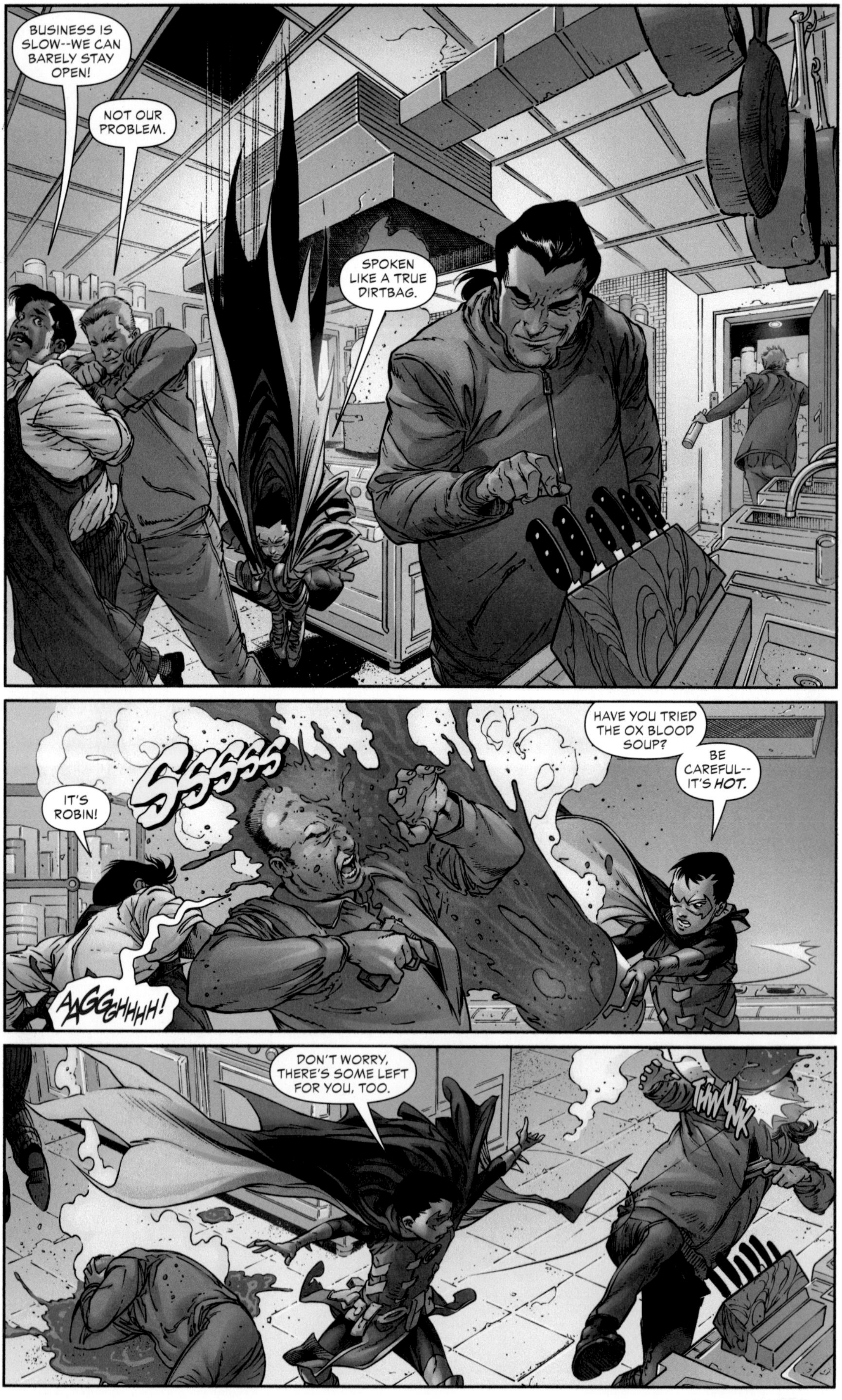
BUSINESS IS SLOW--WE CAN BARELY STAY OPEN!
NOT OUR PROBLEM.
SPOKEN LIKE A TRUE DIRTBAG.
SSSSS
IT'S ROBIN!
HAVE YOU TRIED THE OX BLOOD SOUP?
BE CAREFUL-- IT'S HOT.
AAGGHHHH!
DON'T WORRY, THERE'S SOME LEFT FOR YOU, TOO.
THWUNK

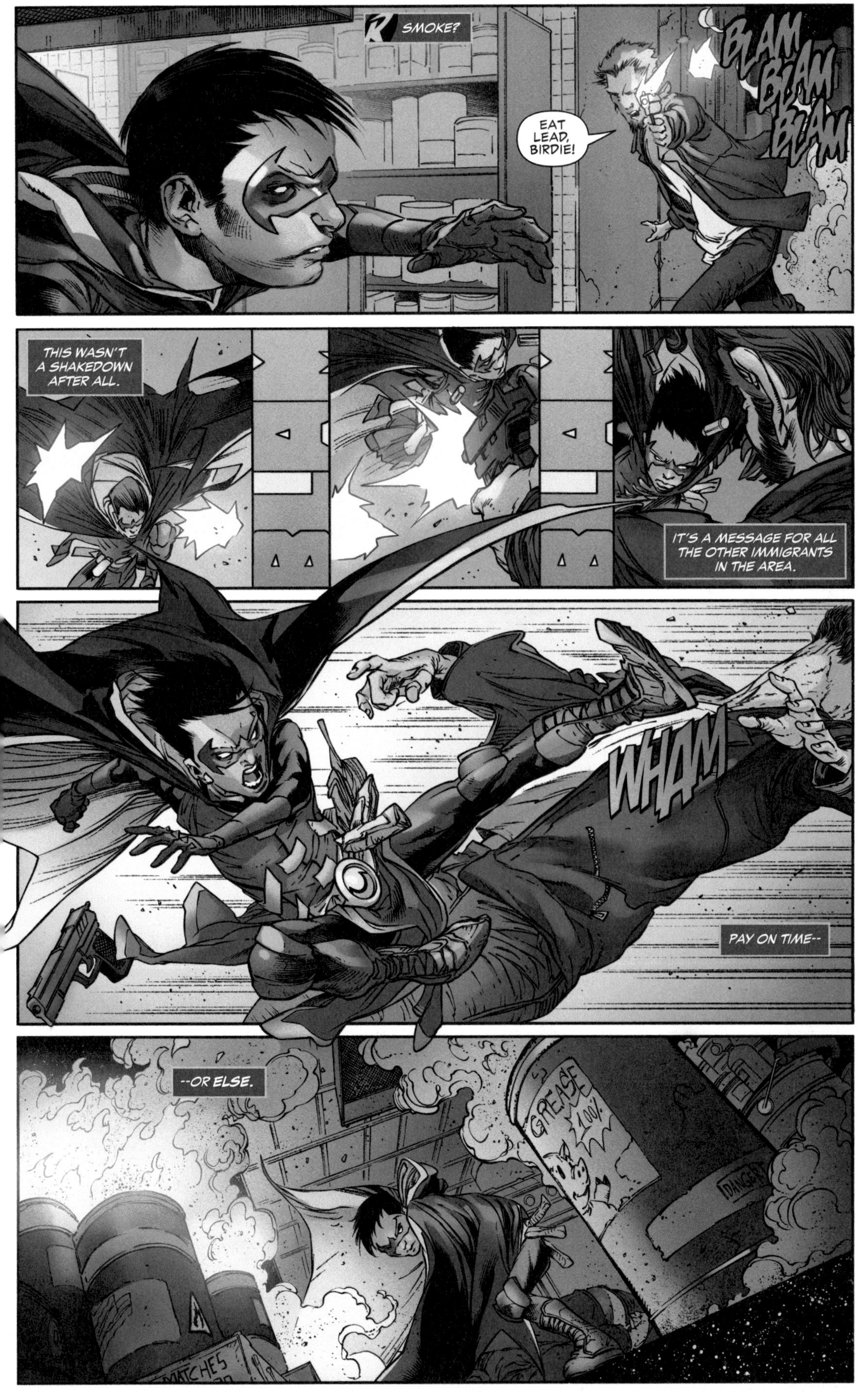
SMOKE?
EAT LEAD, BIRDIE!
BLAM BLAM BLAM
THIS WASN'T A SHAKEDOWN AFTER ALL.
IT'S A MESSAGE FOR ALL THE OTHER IMMIGRANTS IN THE AREA.
WHAM
PAY ON TIME--
--OR ELSE.
GREASE
100%
DANGER
MATCHES

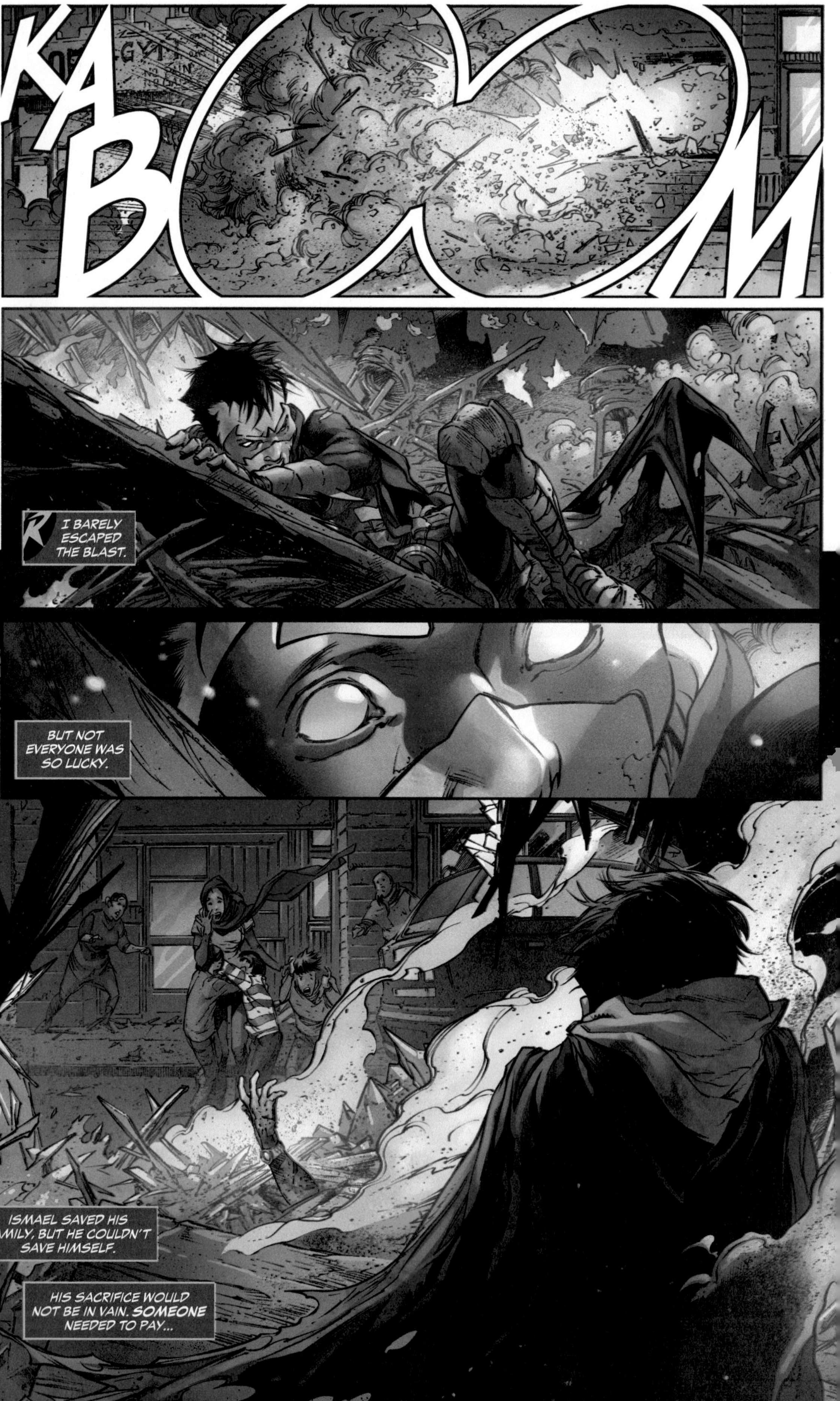
KABOOM
I BARELY ESCAPED THE BLAST.
BUT NOT EVERYONE WAS SO LUCKY.
ISMAEL SAVED HIS FAMILY, BUT HE COULDN'T SAVE HIMSELF.
HIS SACRIFICE WOULD NOT BE IN VAIN. SOMEONE NEEDED TO PAY...

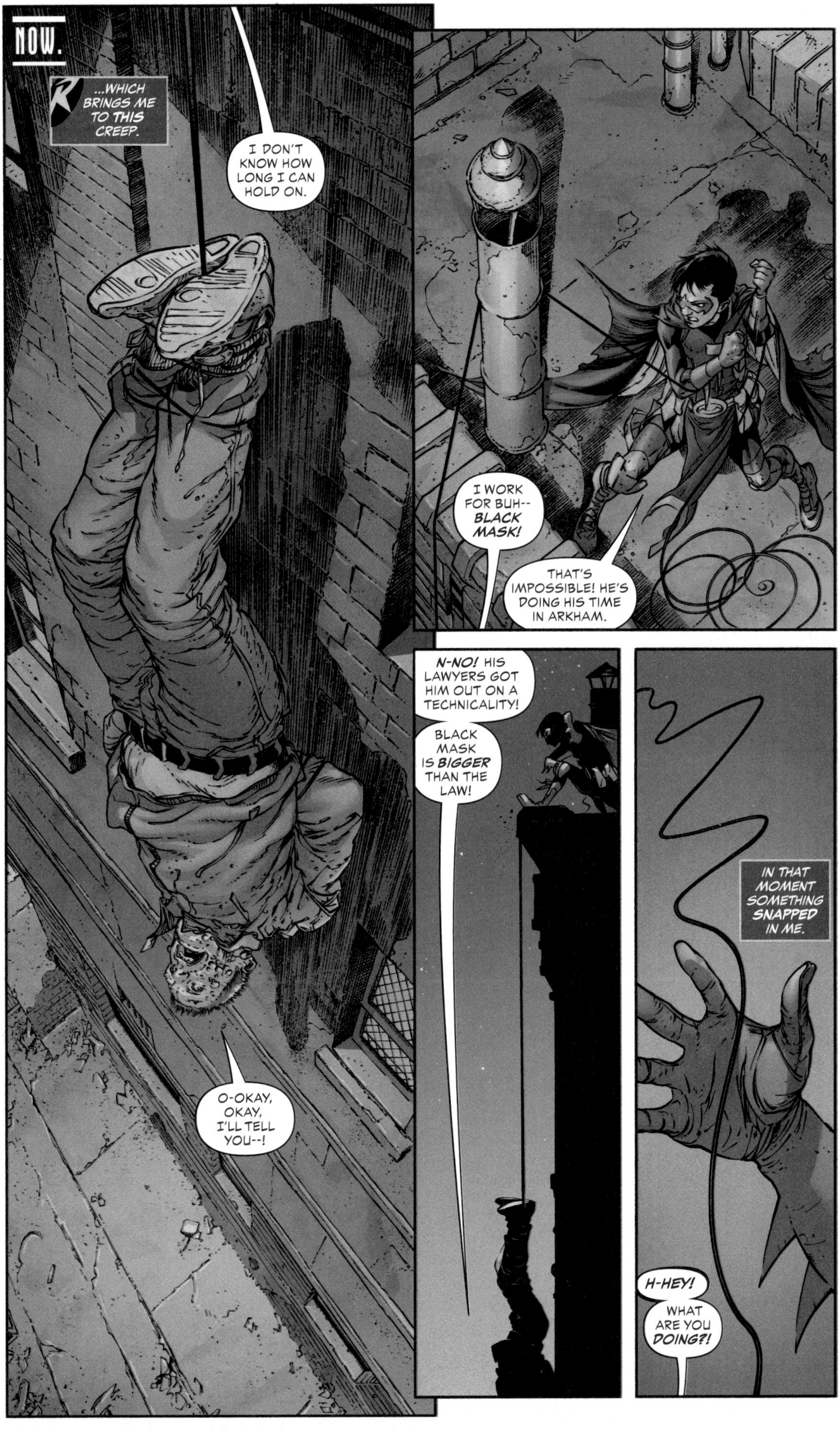
NOW.
...WHICH BRINGS ME TO THIS CREEP.
I DON'T KNOW HOW LONG I CAN HOLD ON.
O-OKAY, OKAY, I'LL TELL YOU--!
I WORK FOR BUH-- BLACK MASK!
THAT'S IMPOSSIBLE! HE'S DOING HIS TIME IN ARKHAM.
N-NO! HIS LAWYERS GOT HIM OUT ON A TECHNICALITY!
BLACK MASK IS BIGGER THAN THE LAW!
IN THAT MOMENT SOMETHING SNAPPED IN ME.
H-HEY!
WHAT ARE YOU DOING?!

MAYBE I WAS STILL REELING FROM WATCHING AN ENTIRE PLANET GET DESTROYED.*

OR MY RAISON D'ÊTRE JUST BECAME CLEAR.

NOOO!!!

PLEASE!!!

*IN *NO JUSTICE!* --Alex

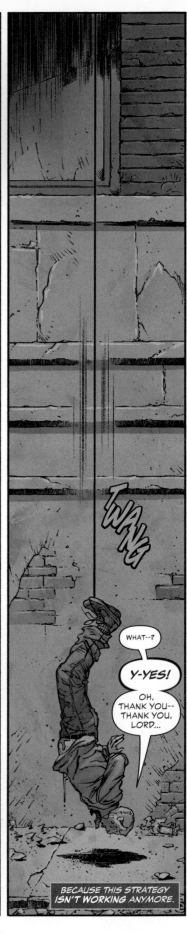

TWANG

WHAT--?

Y-YES!

OH, THANK YOU-- THANK YOU, LORD...

BECAUSE THIS STRATEGY ISN'T WORKING ANYMORE.

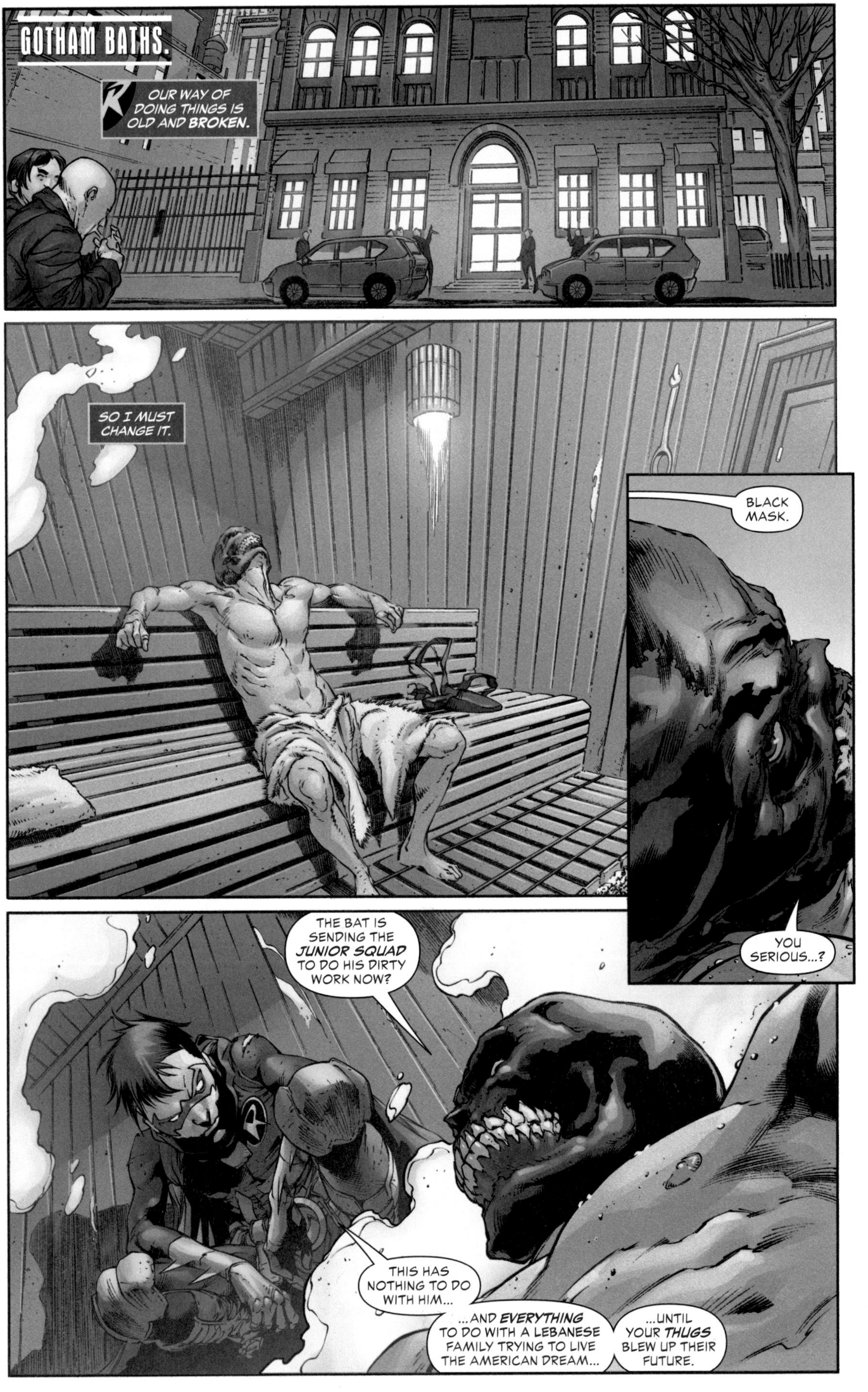
GOTHAM BATHS.
OUR WAY OF DOING THINGS IS OLD AND BROKEN.
SO I MUST CHANGE IT.
BLACK MASK.
YOU SERIOUS...?
THE BAT IS SENDING THE JUNIOR SQUAD TO DO HIS DIRTY WORK NOW?
THIS HAS NOTHING TO DO WITH HIM...
...AND EVERYTHING TO DO WITH A LEBANESE FAMILY TRYING TO LIVE THE AMERICAN DREAM...
...UNTIL YOUR THUGS BLEW UP THEIR FUTURE.

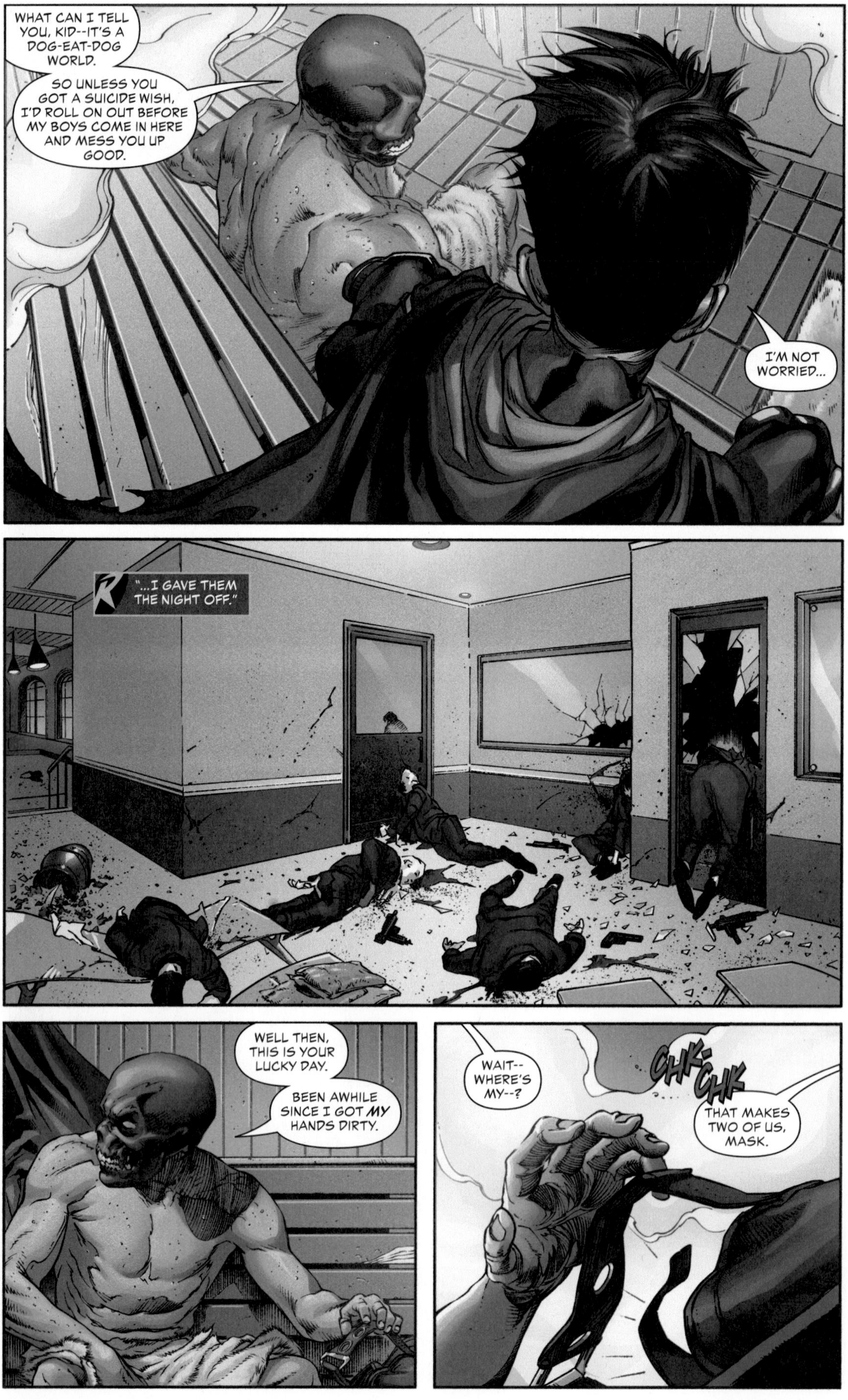
WHAT CAN I TELL YOU, KID--IT'S A DOG-EAT-DOG WORLD.
SO UNLESS YOU GOT A SUICIDE WISH, I'D ROLL ON OUT BEFORE MY BOYS COME IN HERE AND MESS YOU UP GOOD.
I'M NOT WORRIED...
"...I GAVE THEM THE NIGHT OFF."
WELL THEN, THIS IS YOUR LUCKY DAY.
BEEN AWHILE SINCE I GOT *MY* HANDS DIRTY.
WAIT-- WHERE'S MY--?
CHK-CHK
THAT MAKES TWO OF US, MASK.

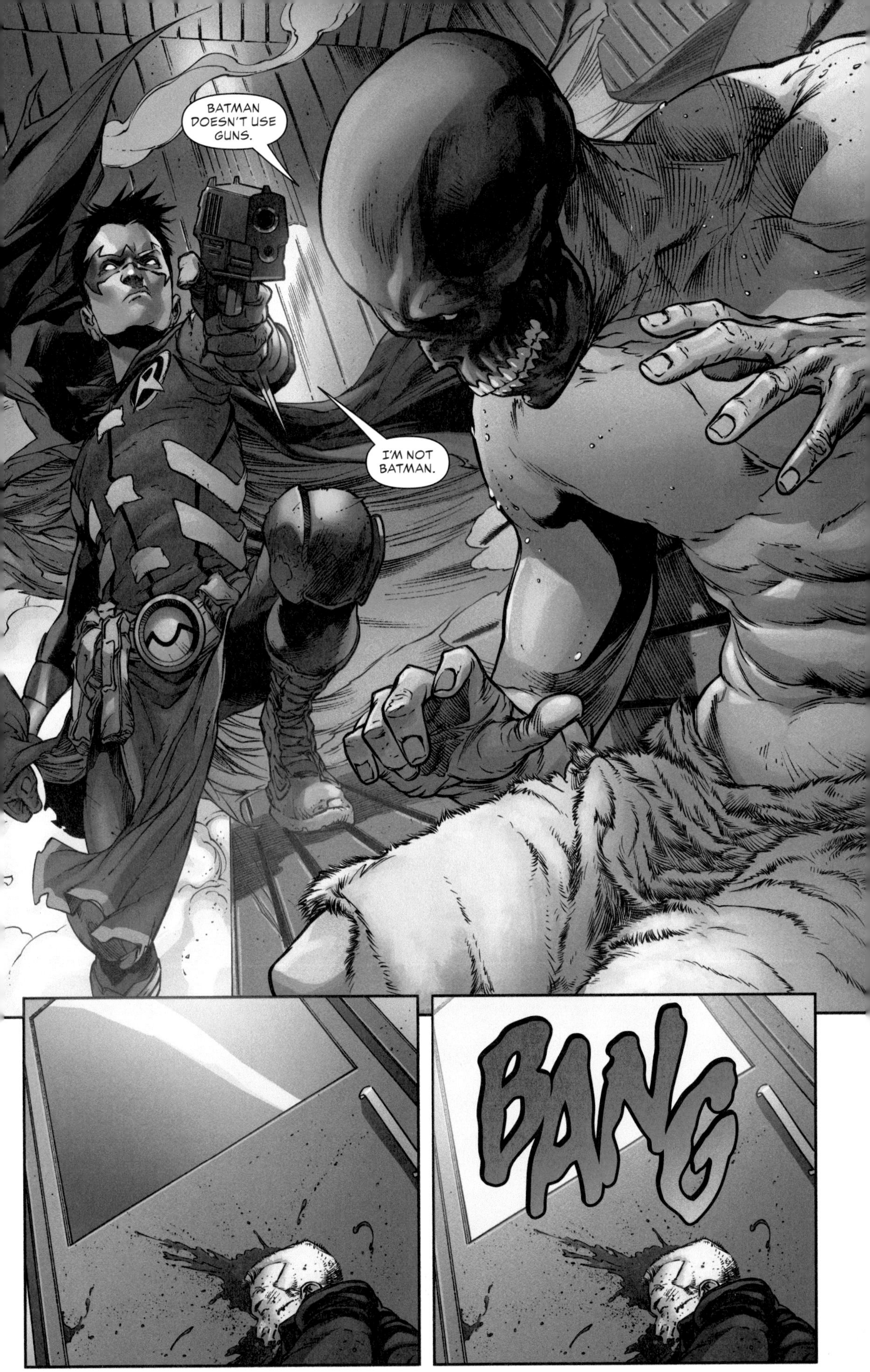
BATMAN DOESN'T USE GUNS.
I'M NOT BATMAN.
BANG

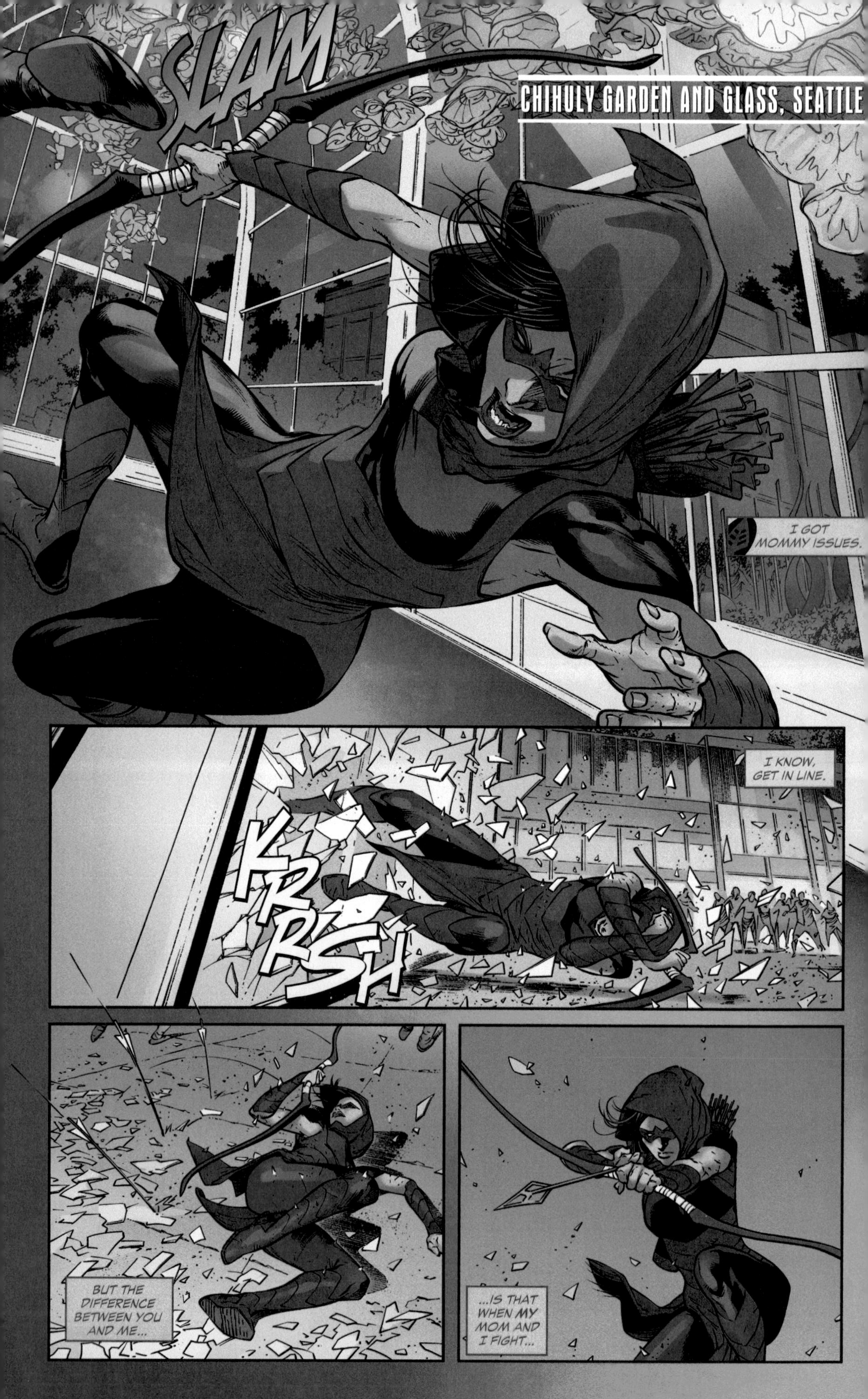
SLAM
CHIHULY GARDEN AND GLASS, SEATTLE
I GOT MOMMY ISSUES.
I KNOW, GET IN LINE.
KRRSH
BUT THE DIFFERENCE BETWEEN YOU AND ME...
...IS THAT WHEN MY MOM AND I FIGHT...

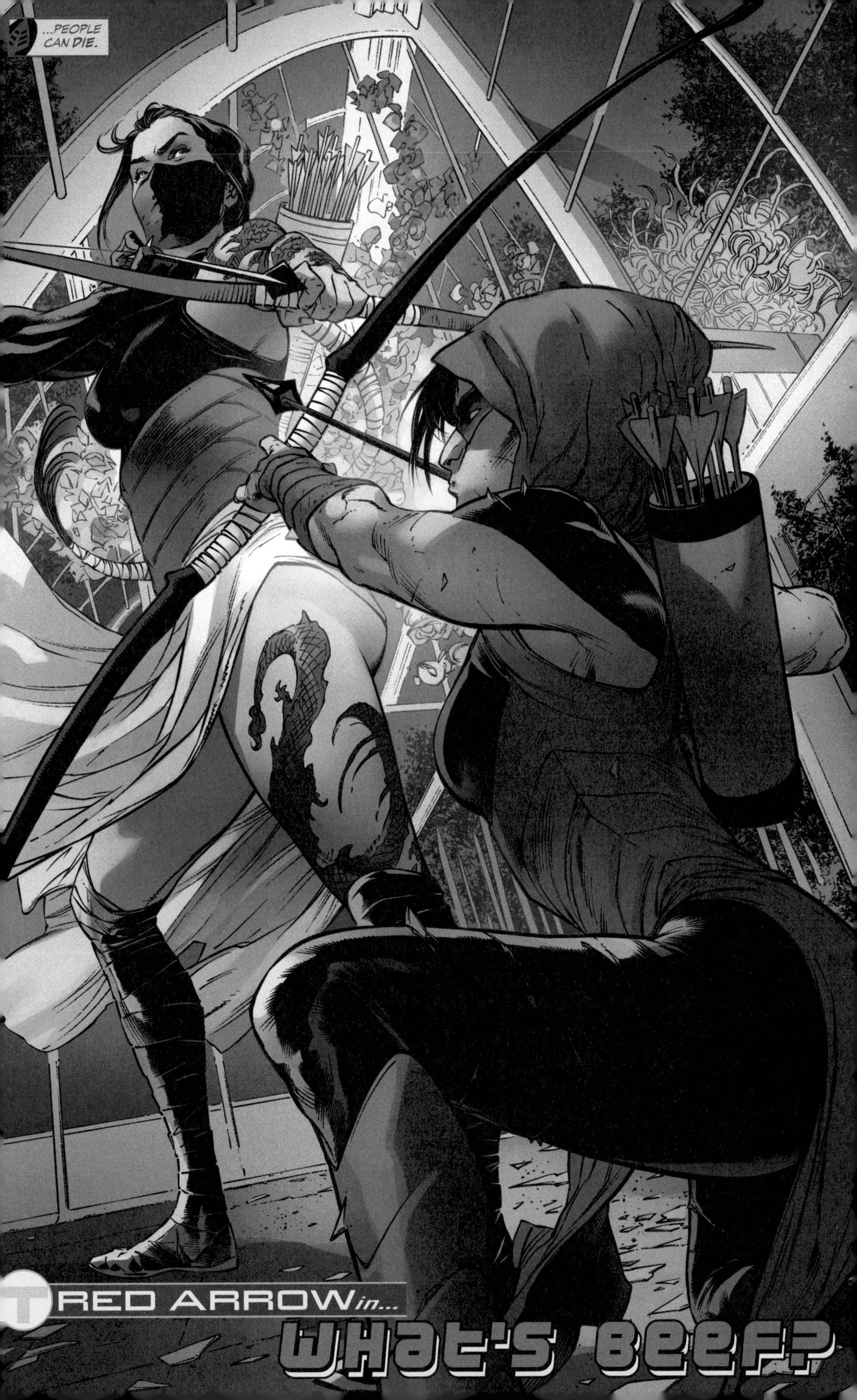
...PEOPLE CAN DIE.
RED ARROW in...
WHAT'S BEEF?

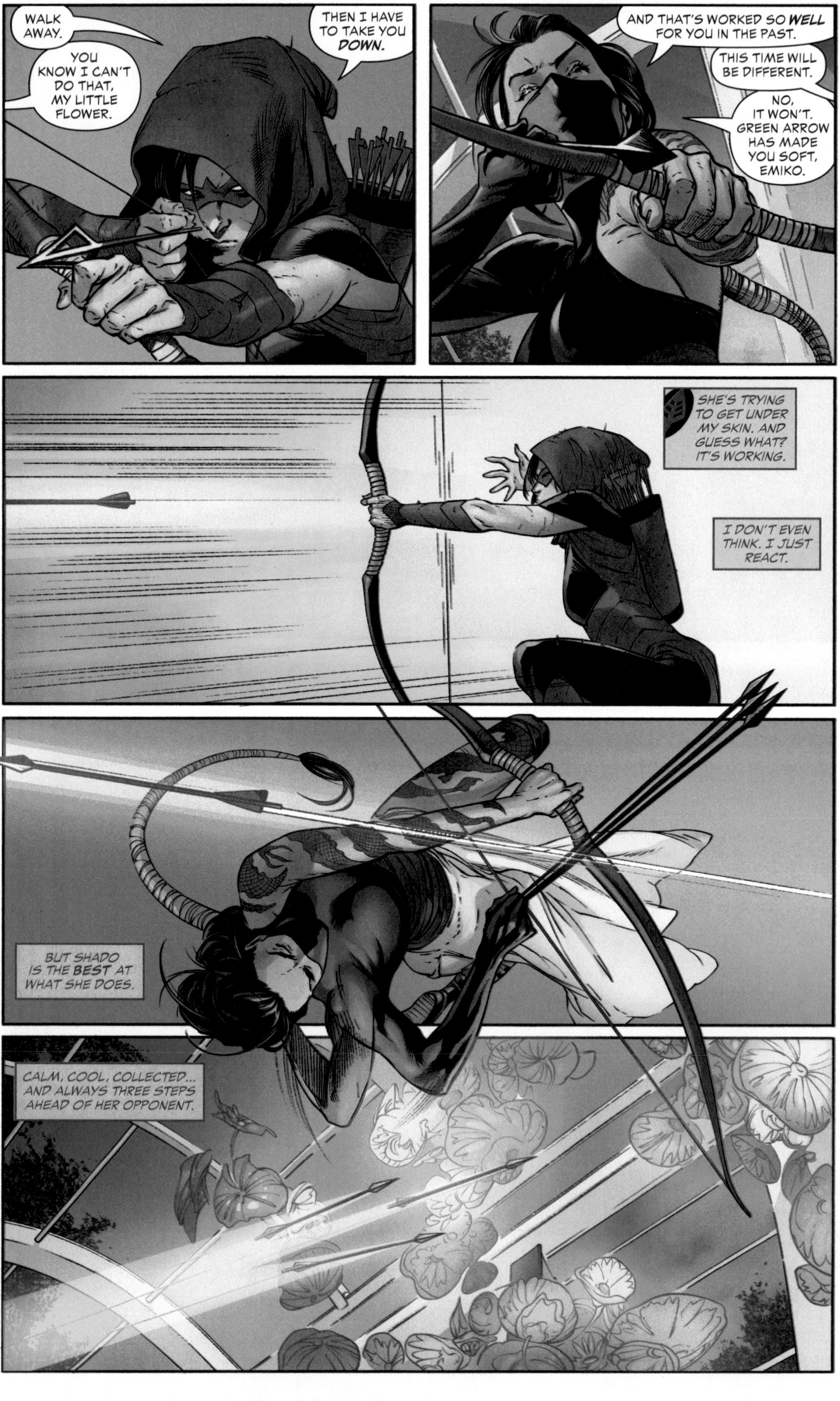

WALK AWAY.
YOU KNOW I CAN'T DO THAT, MY LITTLE FLOWER.
THEN I HAVE TO TAKE YOU DOWN.
AND THAT'S WORKED SO WELL FOR YOU IN THE PAST.
THIS TIME WILL BE DIFFERENT.
NO, IT WON'T. GREEN ARROW HAS MADE YOU SOFT, EMIKO.
SHE'S TRYING TO GET UNDER MY SKIN. AND GUESS WHAT? IT'S WORKING.
I DON'T EVEN THINK. I JUST REACT.
BUT SHADO IS THE BEST AT WHAT SHE DOES.
CALM, COOL, COLLECTED... AND ALWAYS THREE STEPS AHEAD OF HER OPPONENT.

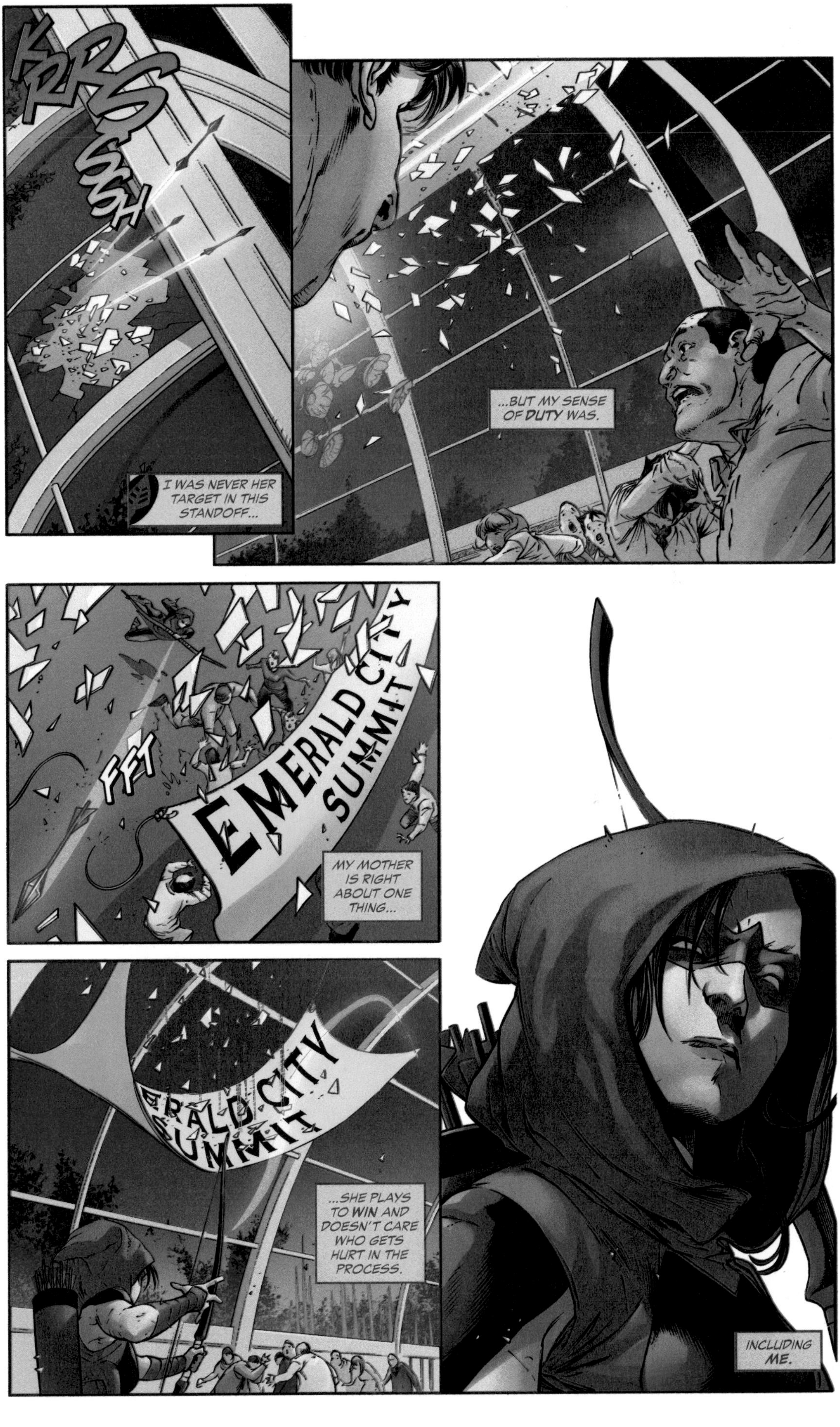
KRRSSSH
I WAS NEVER HER TARGET IN THIS STANDOFF...
...BUT MY SENSE OF DUTY WAS.
FFT
EMERALD CITY SUMMIT
MY MOTHER IS RIGHT ABOUT ONE THING...
...SHE PLAYS TO WIN AND DOESN'T CARE WHO GETS HURT IN THE PROCESS.
INCLUDING ME.

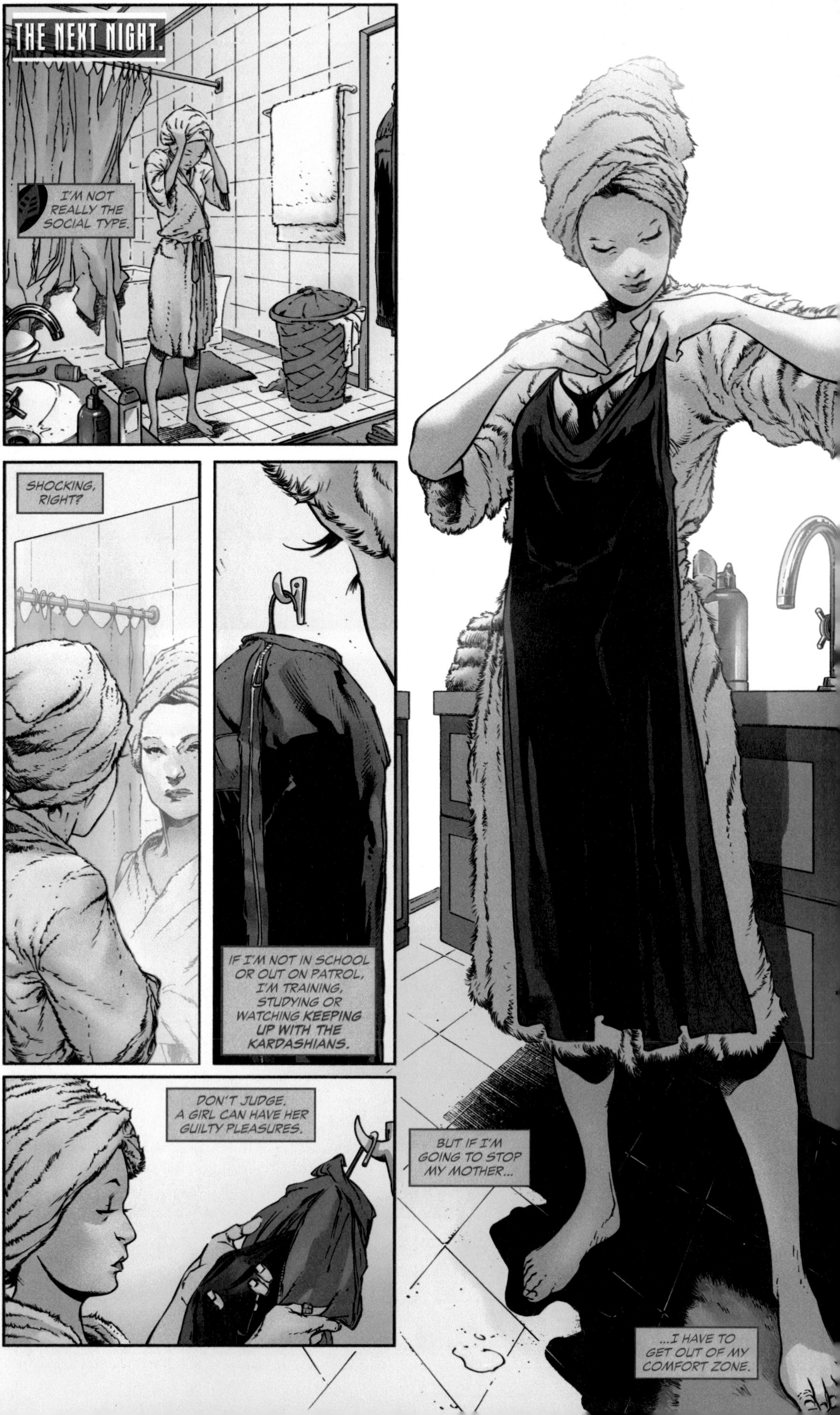
THE NEXT NIGHT.
I'M NOT REALLY THE SOCIAL TYPE.
SHOCKING, RIGHT?
IF I'M NOT IN SCHOOL OR OUT ON PATROL, I'M TRAINING, STUDYING OR WATCHING KEEPING UP WITH THE KARDASHIANS.
DON'T JUDGE. A GIRL CAN HAVE HER GUILTY PLEASURES.
BUT IF I'M GOING TO STOP MY MOTHER...
...I HAVE TO GET OUT OF MY COMFORT ZONE.

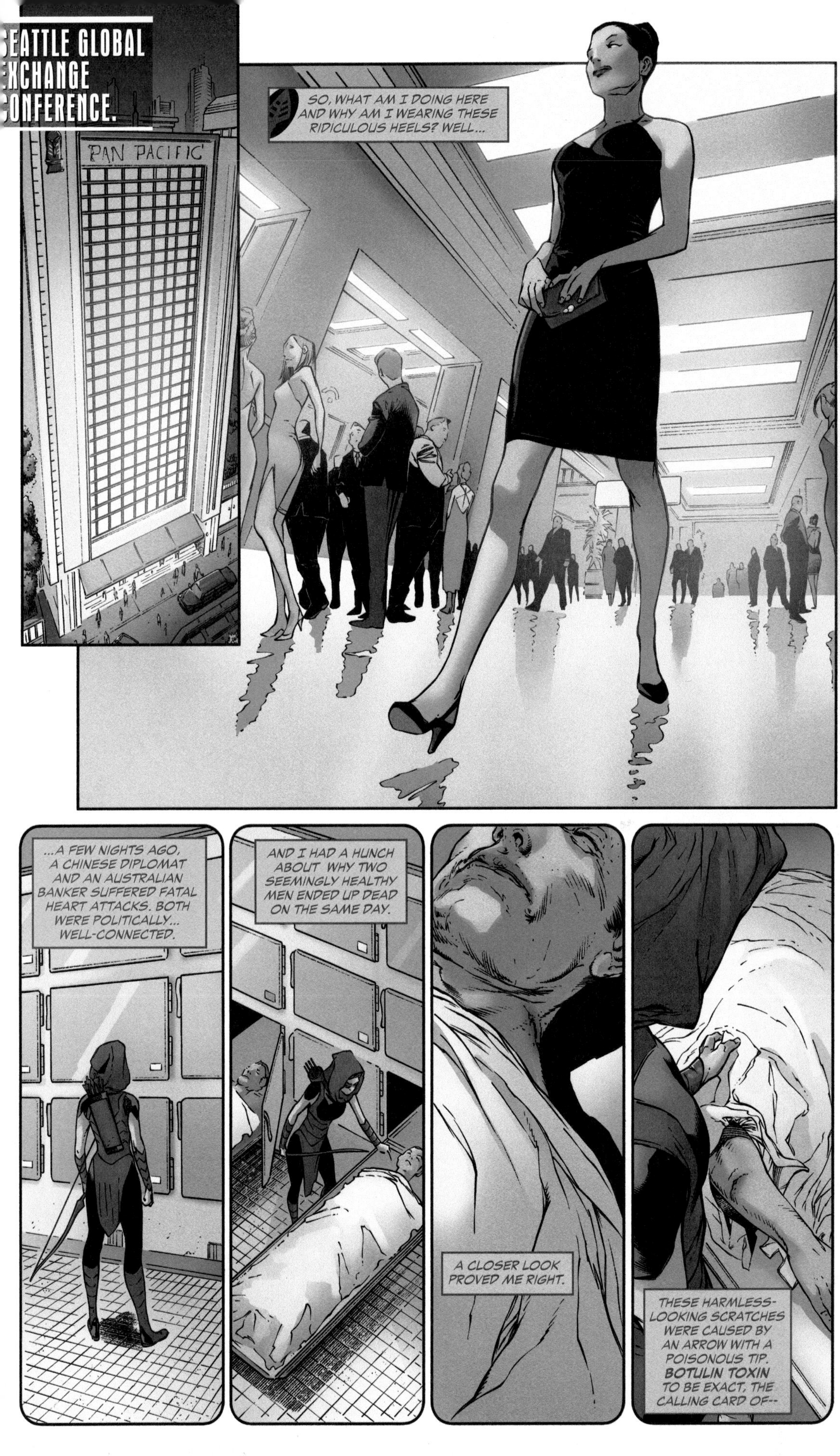
SEATTLE GLOBAL EXCHANGE CONFERENCE.
PAN PACIFIC
SO, WHAT AM I DOING HERE AND WHY AM I WEARING THESE RIDICULOUS HEELS? WELL...
...A FEW NIGHTS AGO, A CHINESE DIPLOMAT AND AN AUSTRALIAN BANKER SUFFERED FATAL HEART ATTACKS. BOTH WERE POLITICALLY... WELL-CONNECTED.
AND I HAD A HUNCH ABOUT WHY TWO SEEMINGLY HEALTHY MEN ENDED UP DEAD ON THE SAME DAY.
A CLOSER LOOK PROVED ME RIGHT.
THESE HARMLESS-LOOKING SCRATCHES WERE CAUSED BY AN ARROW WITH A POISONOUS TIP. BOTULIN TOXIN TO BE EXACT, THE CALLING CARD OF--

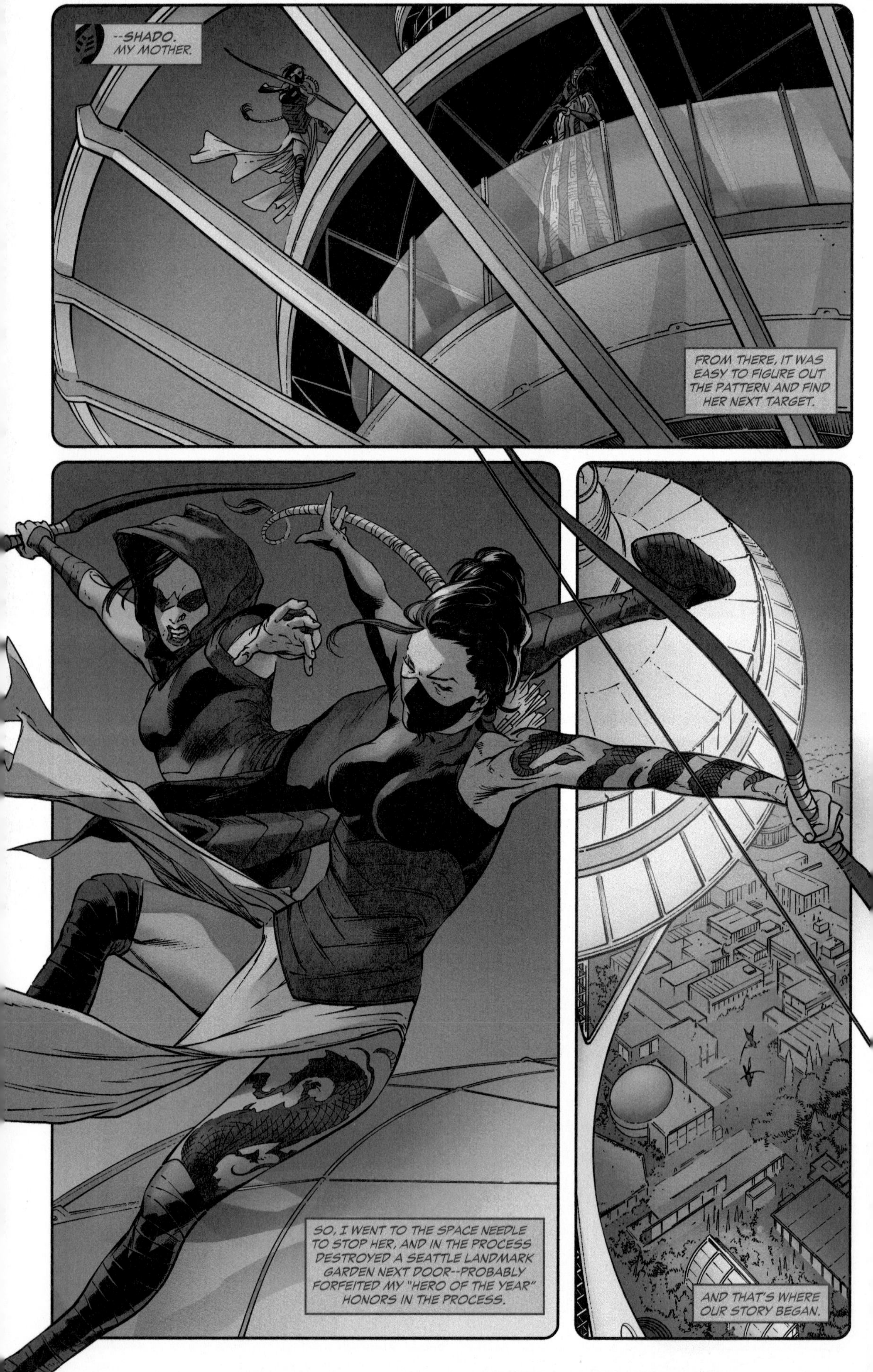
--SHADO. MY MOTHER.
FROM THERE, IT WAS EASY TO FIGURE OUT THE PATTERN AND FIND HER NEXT TARGET.
SO, I WENT TO THE SPACE NEEDLE TO STOP HER, AND IN THE PROCESS DESTROYED A SEATTLE LANDMARK GARDEN NEXT DOOR--PROBABLY FORFEITED MY "HERO OF THE YEAR" HONORS IN THE PROCESS.
AND THAT'S WHERE OUR STORY BEGAN.

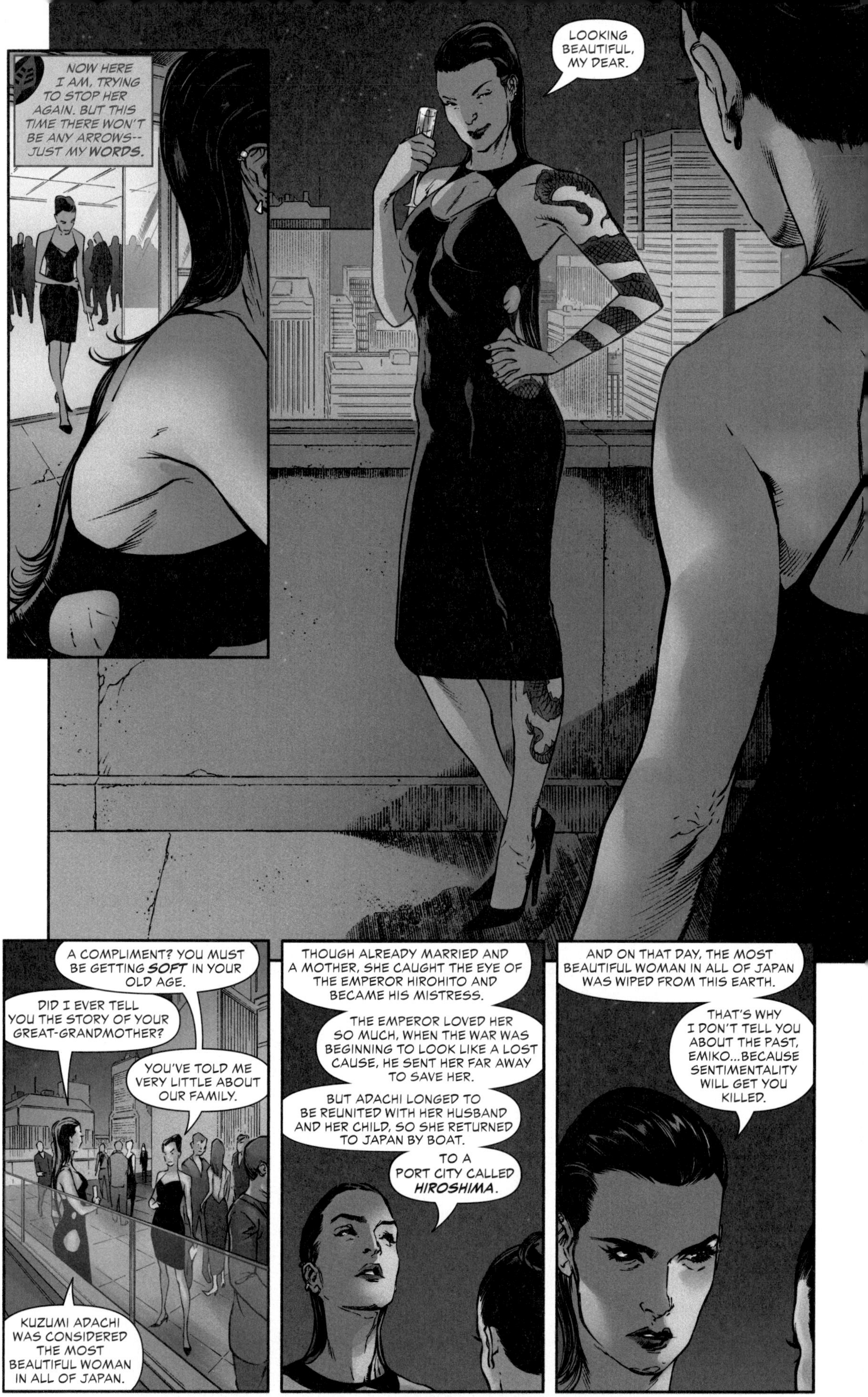
NOW HERE I AM, TRYING TO STOP HER AGAIN. BUT THIS TIME THERE WON'T BE ANY ARROWS-- JUST MY WORDS.
LOOKING BEAUTIFUL, MY DEAR.
A COMPLIMENT? YOU MUST BE GETTING SOFT IN YOUR OLD AGE.
DID I EVER TELL YOU THE STORY OF YOUR GREAT-GRANDMOTHER?
YOU'VE TOLD ME VERY LITTLE ABOUT OUR FAMILY.
KUZUMI ADACHI WAS CONSIDERED THE MOST BEAUTIFUL WOMAN IN ALL OF JAPAN.
THOUGH ALREADY MARRIED AND A MOTHER, SHE CAUGHT THE EYE OF THE EMPEROR HIROHITO AND BECAME HIS MISTRESS.
THE EMPEROR LOVED HER SO MUCH, WHEN THE WAR WAS BEGINNING TO LOOK LIKE A LOST CAUSE, HE SENT HER FAR AWAY TO SAVE HER.
BUT ADACHI LONGED TO BE REUNITED WITH HER HUSBAND AND HER CHILD, SO SHE RETURNED TO JAPAN BY BOAT.
TO A PORT CITY CALLED HIROSHIMA.
AND ON THAT DAY, THE MOST BEAUTIFUL WOMAN IN ALL OF JAPAN WAS WIPED FROM THIS EARTH.
THAT'S WHY I DON'T TELL YOU ABOUT THE PAST, EMIKO...BECAUSE SENTIMENTALITY WILL GET YOU KILLED.

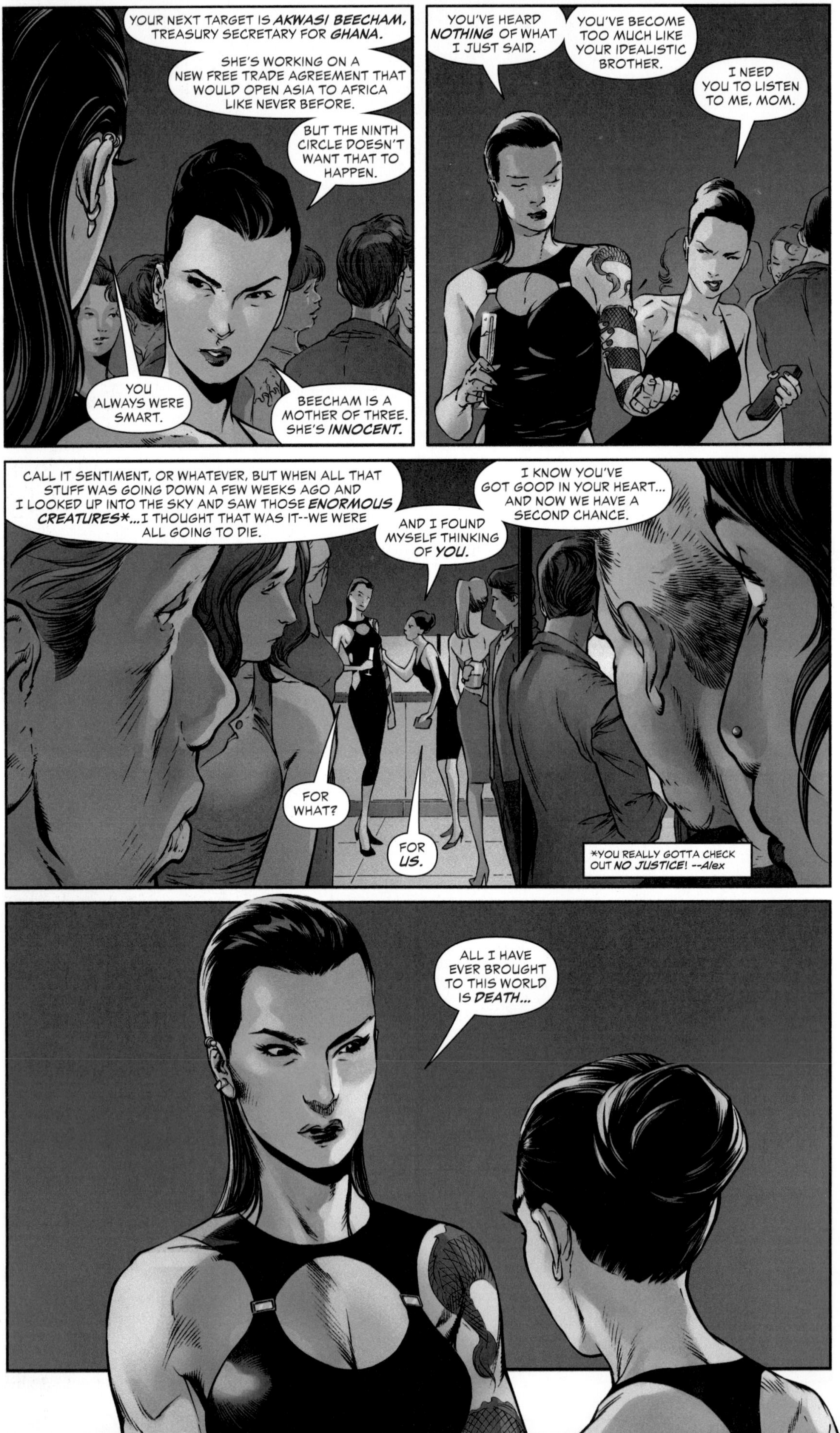

YOUR NEXT TARGET IS AKWASI BEECHAM, TREASURY SECRETARY FOR GHANA.
SHE'S WORKING ON A NEW FREE TRADE AGREEMENT THAT WOULD OPEN ASIA TO AFRICA LIKE NEVER BEFORE.
BUT THE NINTH CIRCLE DOESN'T WANT THAT TO HAPPEN.
YOU ALWAYS WERE SMART.
BEECHAM IS A MOTHER OF THREE. SHE'S INNOCENT.
YOU'VE HEARD NOTHING OF WHAT I JUST SAID.
YOU'VE BECOME TOO MUCH LIKE YOUR IDEALISTIC BROTHER.
I NEED YOU TO LISTEN TO ME, MOM.
CALL IT SENTIMENT, OR WHATEVER, BUT WHEN ALL THAT STUFF WAS GOING DOWN A FEW WEEKS AGO AND I LOOKED UP INTO THE SKY AND SAW THOSE ENORMOUS CREATURES*...I THOUGHT THAT WAS IT--WE WERE ALL GOING TO DIE.
AND I FOUND MYSELF THINKING OF YOU.
I KNOW YOU'VE GOT GOOD IN YOUR HEART... AND NOW WE HAVE A SECOND CHANCE.
FOR WHAT?
FOR US.
*YOU REALLY GOTTA CHECK OUT NO JUSTICE! --Alex
ALL I HAVE EVER BROUGHT TO THIS WORLD IS DEATH...

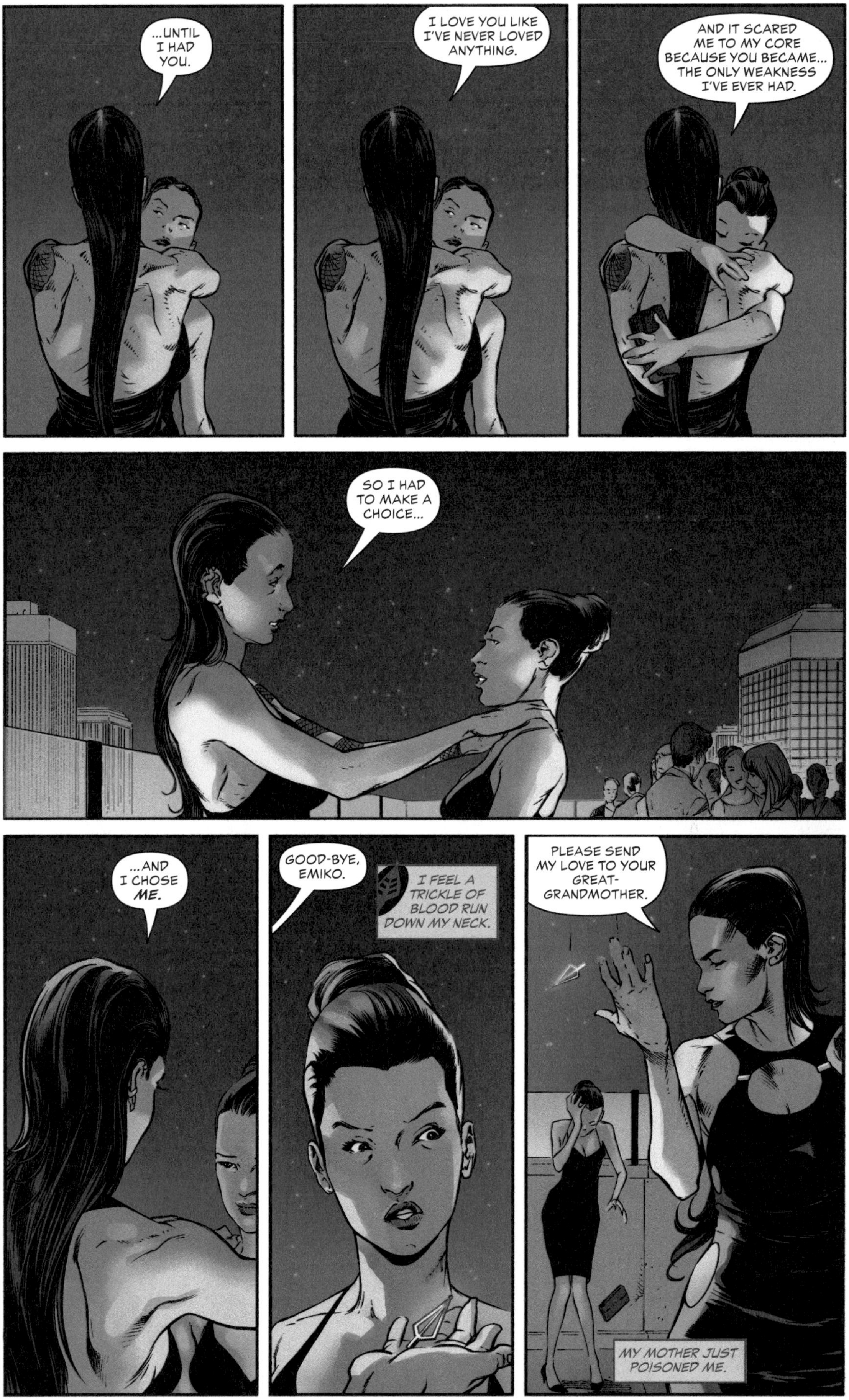

...UNTIL I HAD YOU.
I LOVE YOU LIKE I'VE NEVER LOVED ANYTHING.
AND IT SCARED ME TO MY CORE BECAUSE YOU BECAME... THE ONLY WEAKNESS I'VE EVER HAD.
SO I HAD TO MAKE A CHOICE...
...AND I CHOSE *ME.*
GOOD-BYE, EMIKO.
*I FEEL A TRICKLE OF BLOOD RUN DOWN MY NECK.*
PLEASE SEND MY LOVE TO YOUR GREAT-GRANDMOTHER.
*MY MOTHER JUST POISONED ME.*

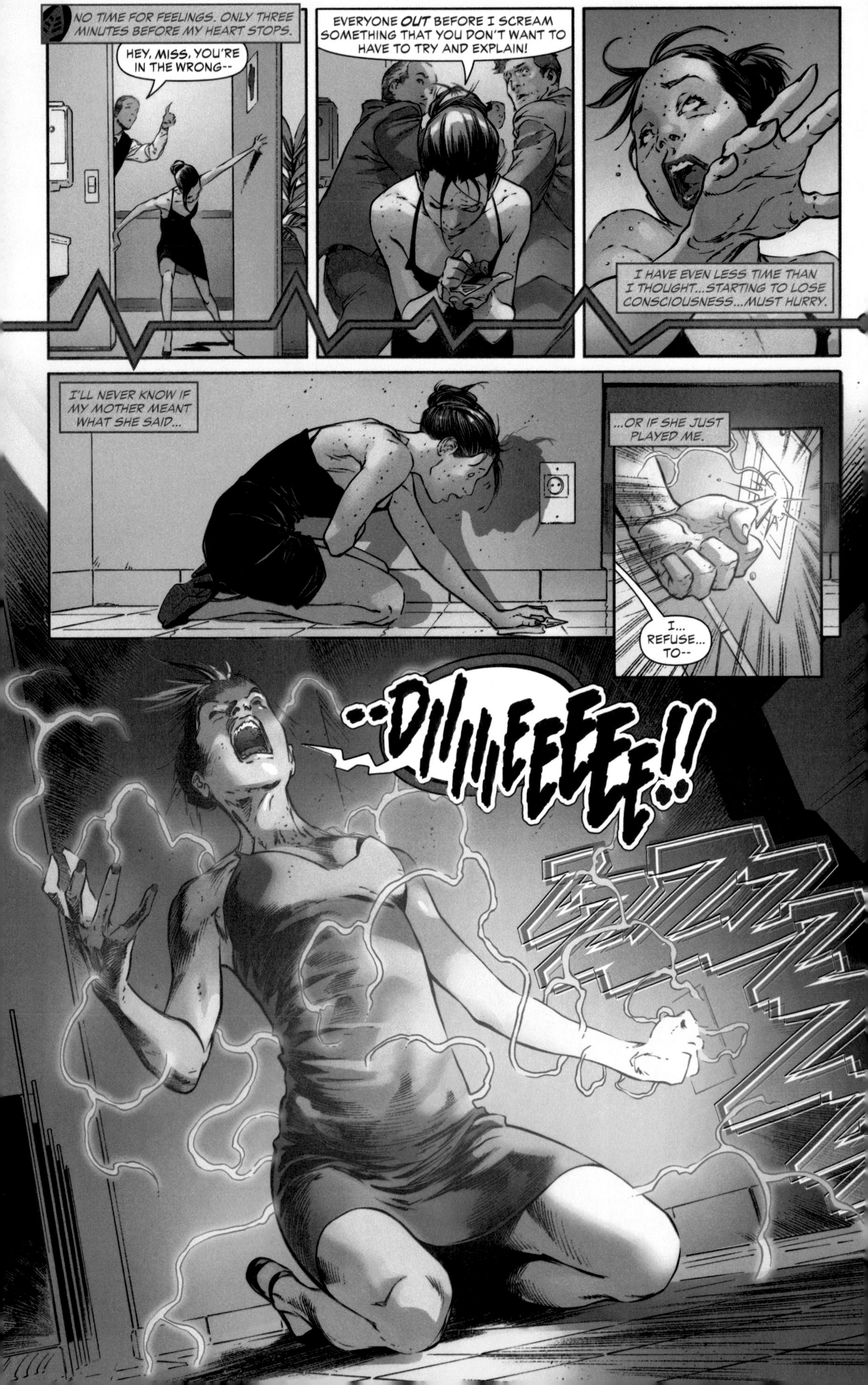
NO TIME FOR FEELINGS. ONLY THREE MINUTES BEFORE MY HEART STOPS.
HEY, MISS, YOU'RE IN THE WRONG--
EVERYONE OUT BEFORE I SCREAM SOMETHING THAT YOU DON'T WANT TO HAVE TO TRY AND EXPLAIN!
I HAVE EVEN LESS TIME THAN I THOUGHT...STARTING TO LOSE CONSCIOUSNESS...MUST HURRY.
I'LL NEVER KNOW IF MY MOTHER MEANT WHAT SHE SAID...
...OR IF SHE JUST PLAYED ME.
I... REFUSE... TO--
--DIIIIEEEEEE!!

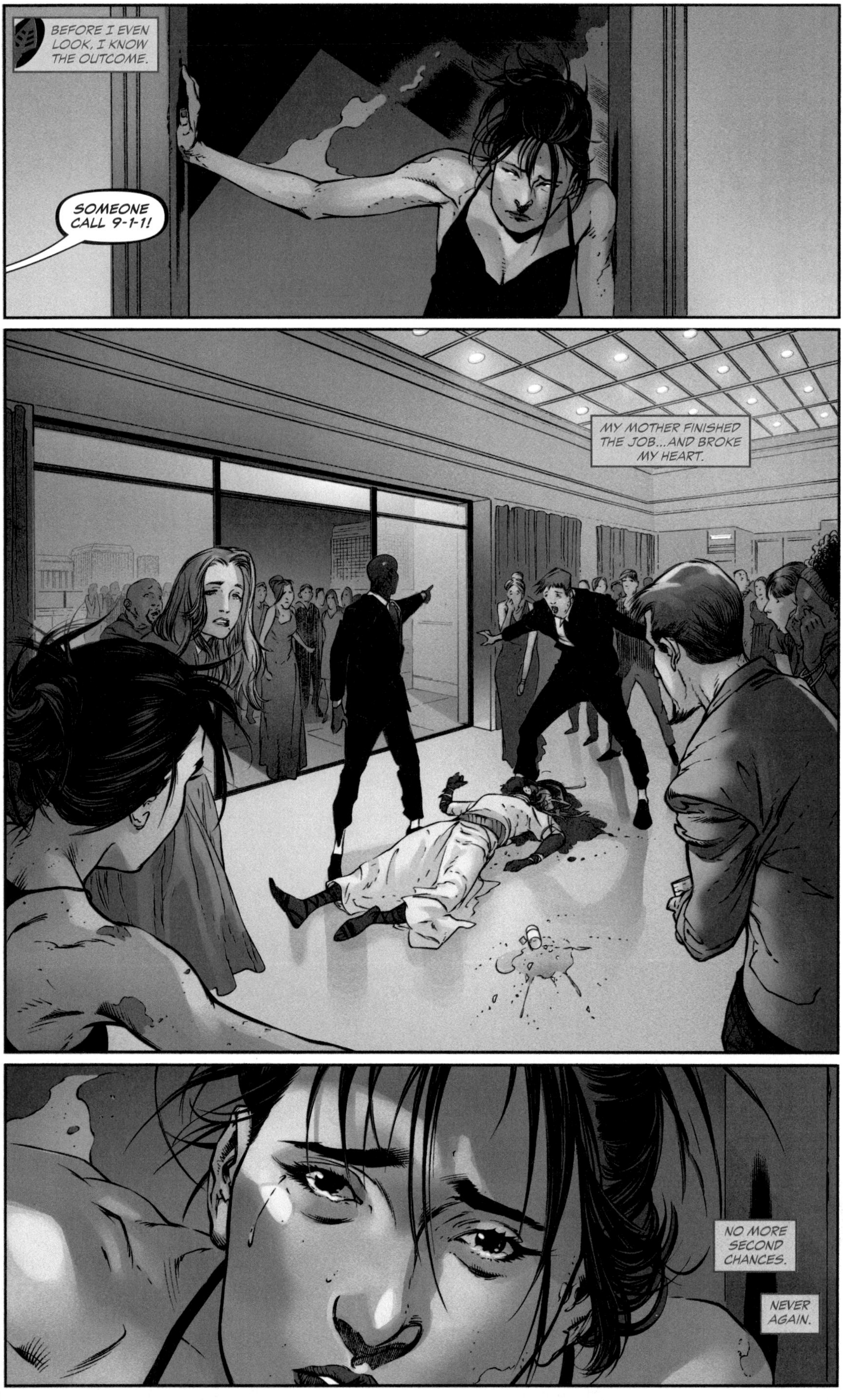
BEFORE I EVEN LOOK, I KNOW THE OUTCOME.
SOMEONE CALL 9-1-1!
MY MOTHER FINISHED THE JOB...AND BROKE MY HEART.
NO MORE SECOND CHANCES.
NEVER AGAIN.

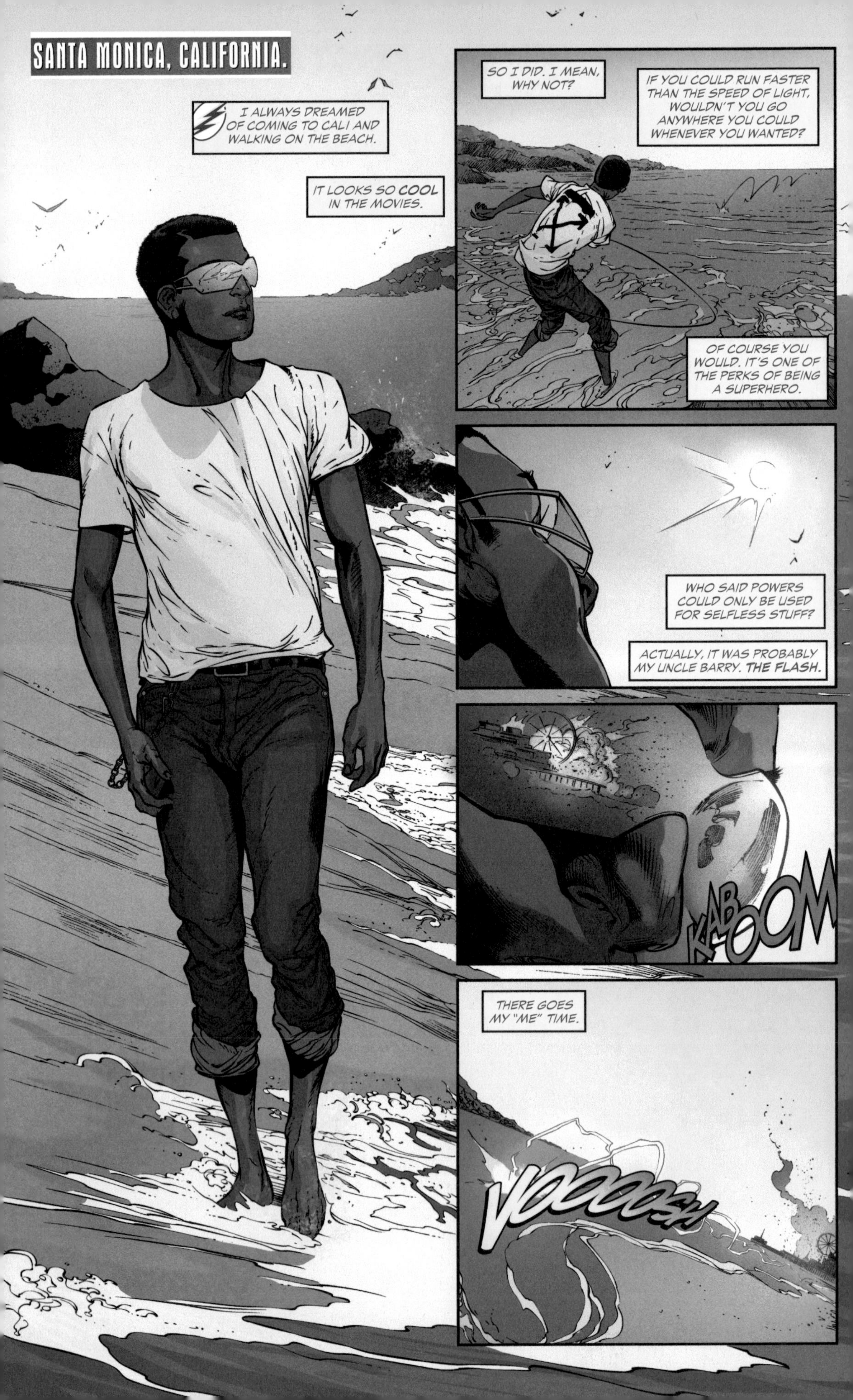
SANTA MONICA, CALIFORNIA.
I ALWAYS DREAMED OF COMING TO CALI AND WALKING ON THE BEACH.
IT LOOKS SO COOL IN THE MOVIES.
SO I DID. I MEAN, WHY NOT?
IF YOU COULD RUN FASTER THAN THE SPEED OF LIGHT, WOULDN'T YOU GO ANYWHERE YOU COULD WHENEVER YOU WANTED?
OF COURSE YOU WOULD. IT'S ONE OF THE PERKS OF BEING A SUPERHERO.
WHO SAID POWERS COULD ONLY BE USED FOR SELFLESS STUFF?
ACTUALLY, IT WAS PROBABLY MY UNCLE BARRY. THE FLASH.
KABOOM
THERE GOES MY "ME" TIME.
VOOOOSH

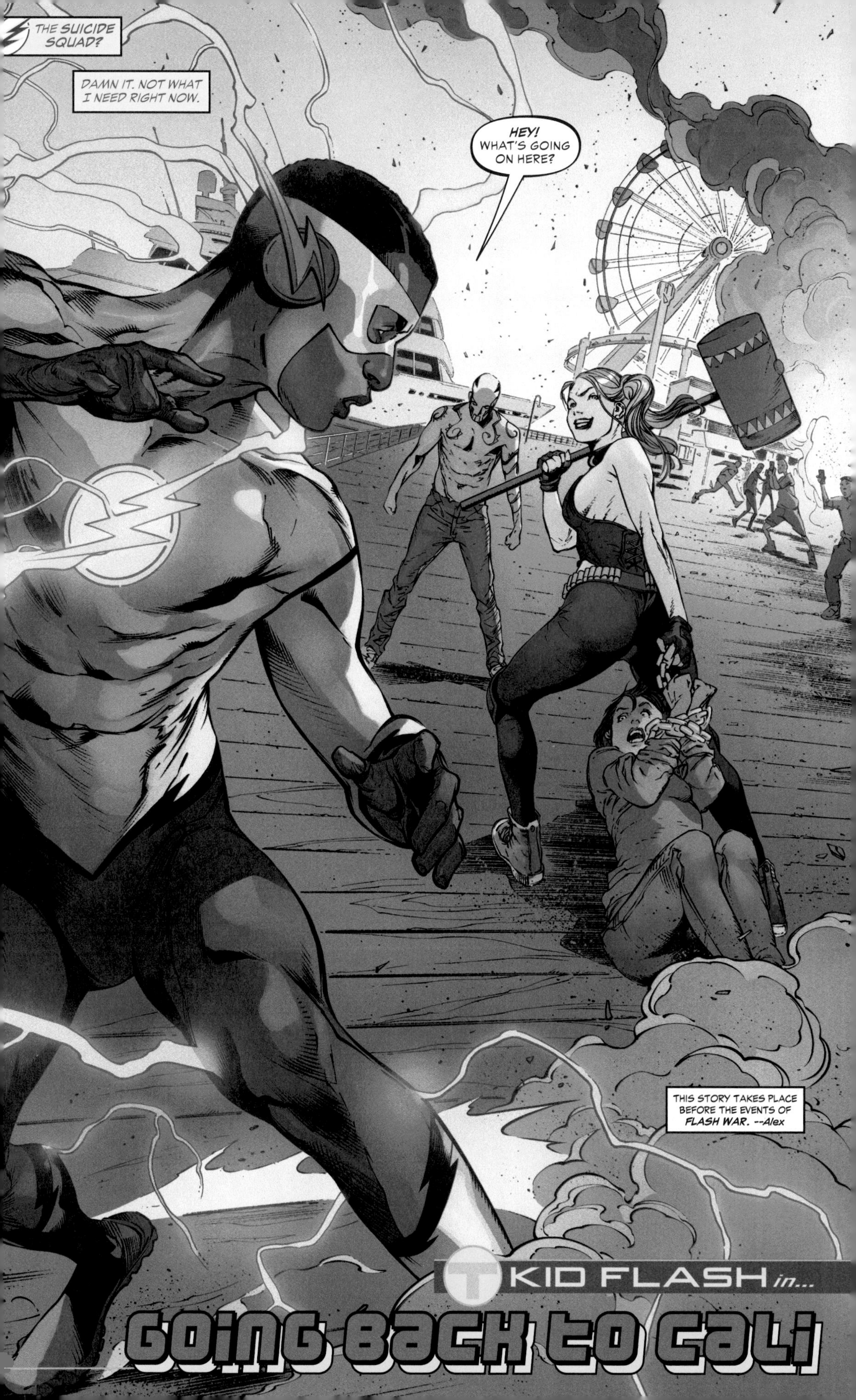
THE SUICIDE SQUAD?
DAMN IT. NOT WHAT I NEED RIGHT NOW.
HEY! WHAT'S GOING ON HERE?
THIS STORY TAKES PLACE BEFORE THE EVENTS OF FLASH WAR. --Alex
KID FLASH in...
GOING BACK TO CALI

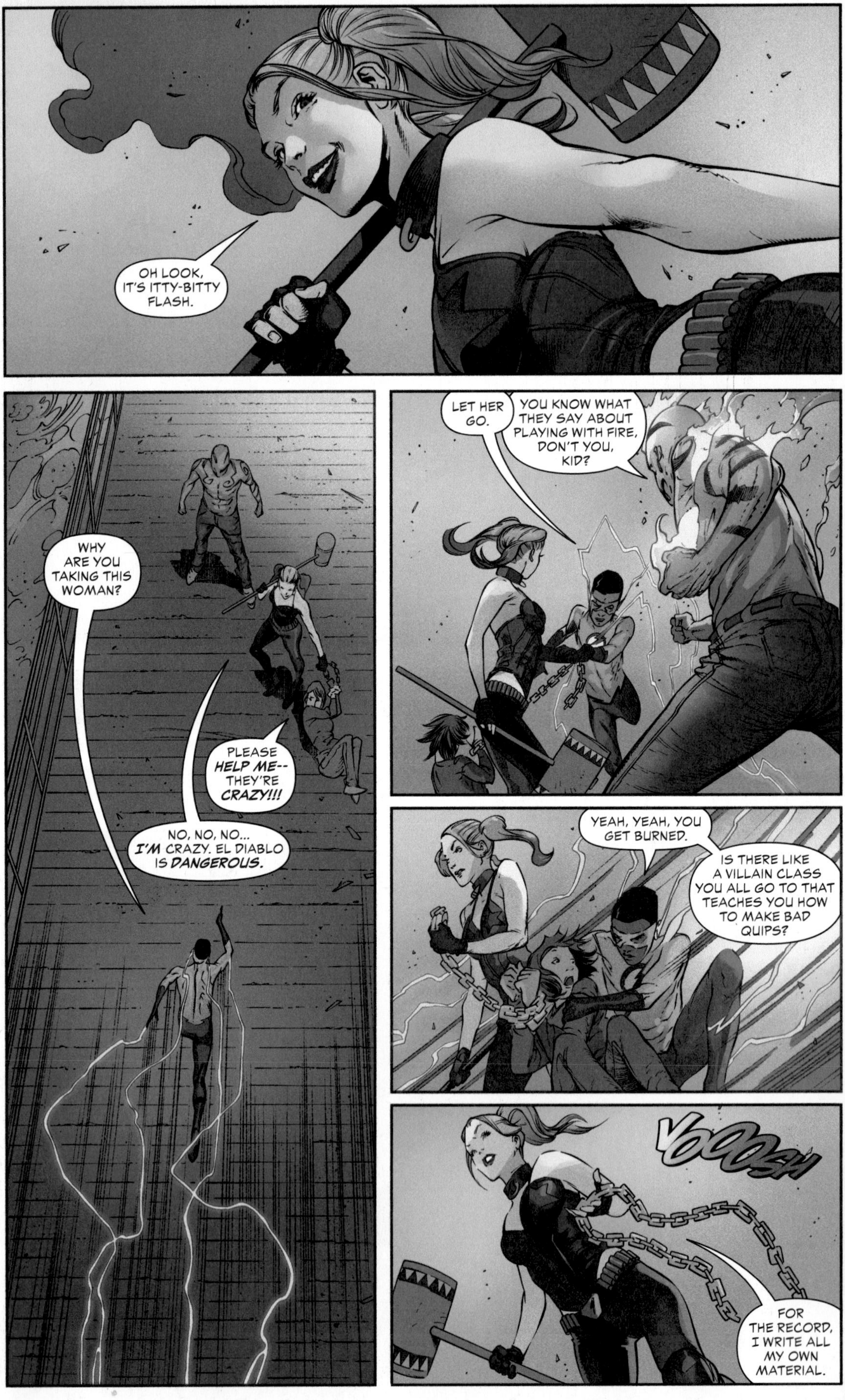
OH LOOK, IT'S ITTY-BITTY FLASH.
WHY ARE YOU TAKING THIS WOMAN?
PLEASE HELP ME-- THEY'RE CRAZY!!!
NO, NO, NO... I'M CRAZY. EL DIABLO IS DANGEROUS.
LET HER GO.
YOU KNOW WHAT THEY SAY ABOUT PLAYING WITH FIRE, DON'T YOU, KID?
YEAH, YEAH, YOU GET BURNED.
IS THERE LIKE A VILLAIN CLASS YOU ALL GO TO THAT TEACHES YOU HOW TO MAKE BAD QUIPS?
VOOOSH
FOR THE RECORD, I WRITE ALL MY OWN MATERIAL.

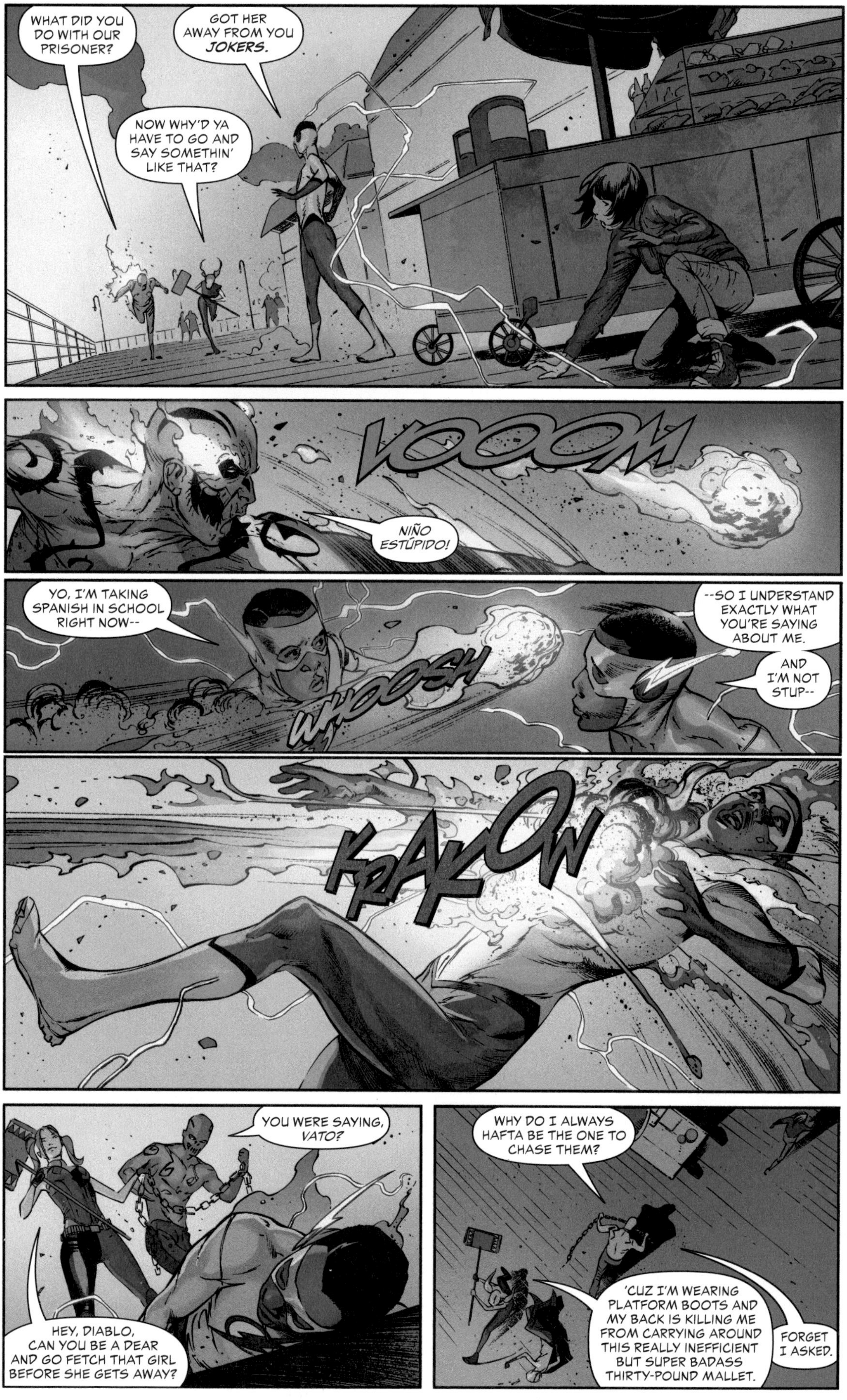
WHAT DID YOU DO WITH OUR PRISONER?
GOT HER AWAY FROM YOU *JOKERS.*
NOW WHY'D YA HAVE TO GO AND SAY SOMETHIN' LIKE THAT?
VOOOOM
NIÑO ESTÚPIDO!
YO, I'M TAKING SPANISH IN SCHOOL RIGHT NOW--
WHOOOSH
--SO I UNDERSTAND EXACTLY WHAT YOU'RE SAYING ABOUT ME.
AND I'M NOT STUP--
KRAKOW
YOU WERE SAYING, *VATO?*
HEY, DIABLO, CAN YOU BE A DEAR AND GO FETCH THAT GIRL BEFORE SHE GETS AWAY?
WHY DO I ALWAYS HAFTA BE THE ONE TO CHASE THEM?
'CUZ I'M WEARING PLATFORM BOOTS AND MY BACK IS KILLING ME FROM CARRYING AROUND THIS REALLY INEFFICIENT BUT SUPER BADASS THIRTY-POUND MALLET.
FORGET I ASKED.

LISTEN UP, POLITICALLY CORRECT FLASH.

I GOT A JOB TO DO, NO QUESTIONS ASKED. SO UNLESS YOU WANNA SPANKING, LEAVE MISS HARLEY TO HER BUSINESS!

≷Cough≷ I KNOW ALL ABOUT THE SUICIDE SQUAD.

SO, THIS IS ALL PRETTY PERSONAL TO ME.

DON'T KNOW WHAT YOU'RE TALKING ABOUT, KID. MAYBE ALL THAT RUNNING AROUND HAS RATTLED YOUR BRAIN.

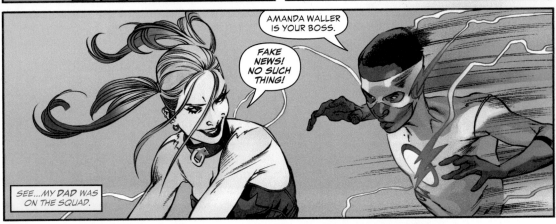

AMANDA WALLER IS YOUR BOSS.

FAKE NEWS! NO SUCH THING!

SEE...MY DAD WAS ON THE SQUAD.

STAND STILL SO I CAN STAB YA!

YOU HAVE AN IMPLANT IN YOUR NECK--

--THAT WILL BLOW YOUR HEAD OFF--

--IF YOU DON'T OBEY.

I PLEAD THE FIFTH, SIXTH, SEVENTH AND EIGHTH.

AND DIED BECAUSE OF THEM.

YOU FASTER THAN A SPEEDING BULLET?

OH WAIT, THAT'S THE OTHER GUY!

HEY, STOP HORSING AROUND, QUINN. WE GOT A PROBLEM!

*Uh-oh,* THAT DOESN'T LOOK GOOD.

WHAT THE HELL DID YOU DO TO HER? SHE LOOKS LIKE SHE'S GONNA--!

KRAKOOM

VAROOOSH

KRAKOW

VOOSH
VOOSH
VOOSH

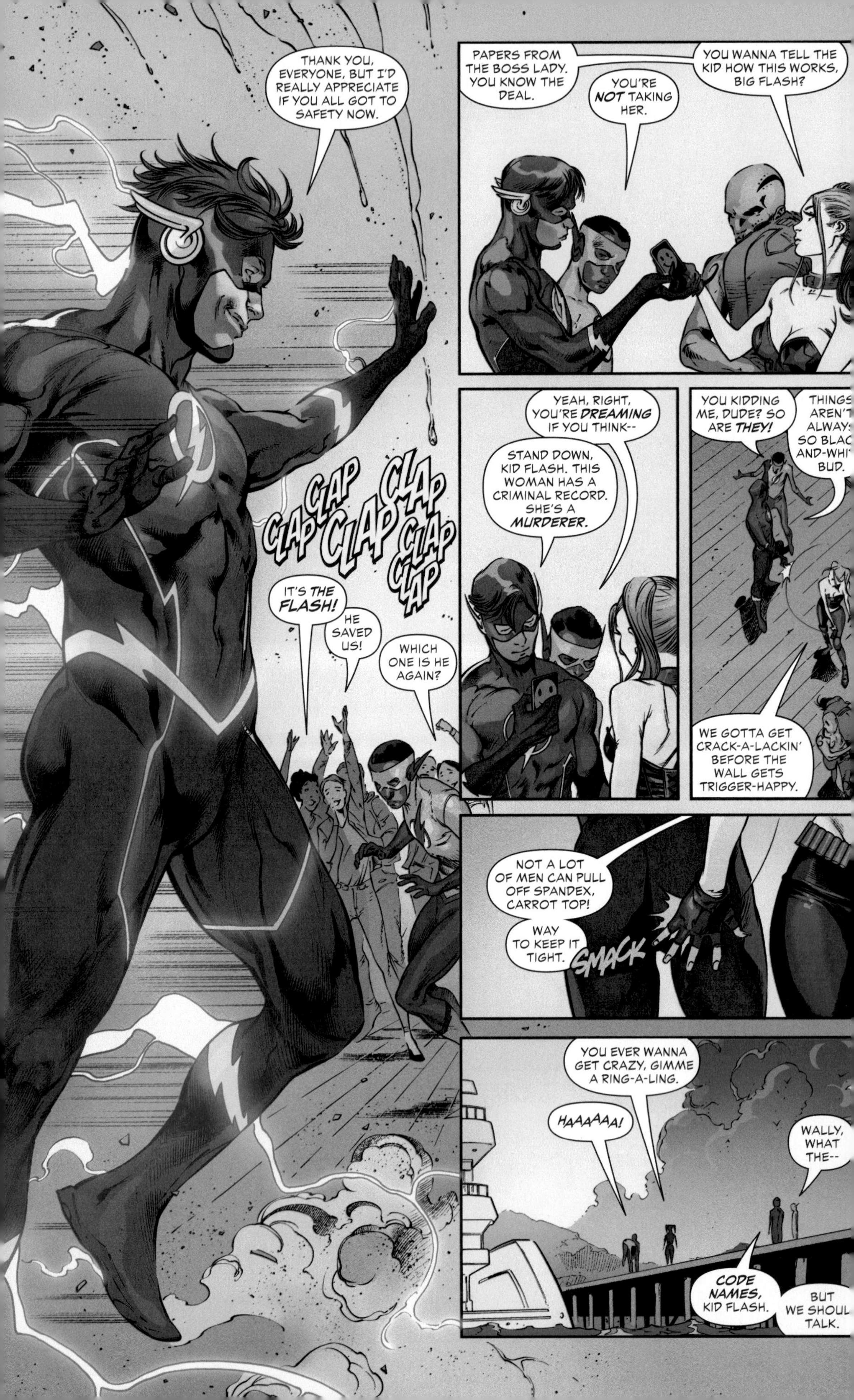
THANK YOU, EVERYONE, BUT I'D REALLY APPRECIATE IF YOU ALL GOT TO SAFETY NOW.
CLAP CLAP CLAP CLAP CLAP CLAP CLAP
IT'S THE FLASH!
HE SAVED US!
WHICH ONE IS HE AGAIN?
PAPERS FROM THE BOSS LADY. YOU KNOW THE DEAL.
YOU'RE NOT TAKING HER.
YOU WANNA TELL THE KID HOW THIS WORKS, BIG FLASH?
YEAH, RIGHT, YOU'RE DREAMING IF YOU THINK--
STAND DOWN, KID FLASH. THIS WOMAN HAS A CRIMINAL RECORD. SHE'S A MURDERER.
YOU KIDDING ME, DUDE? SO ARE THEY!
WE GOTTA GET CRACK-A-LACKIN' BEFORE THE WALL GETS TRIGGER-HAPPY.
NOT A LOT OF MEN CAN PULL OFF SPANDEX, CARROT TOP!
WAY TO KEEP IT TIGHT.
SMACK
YOU EVER WANNA GET CRAZY, GIMME A RING-A-LING.
HAAAAAA!
WALLY, WHAT THE--
CODE NAMES, KID FLASH.

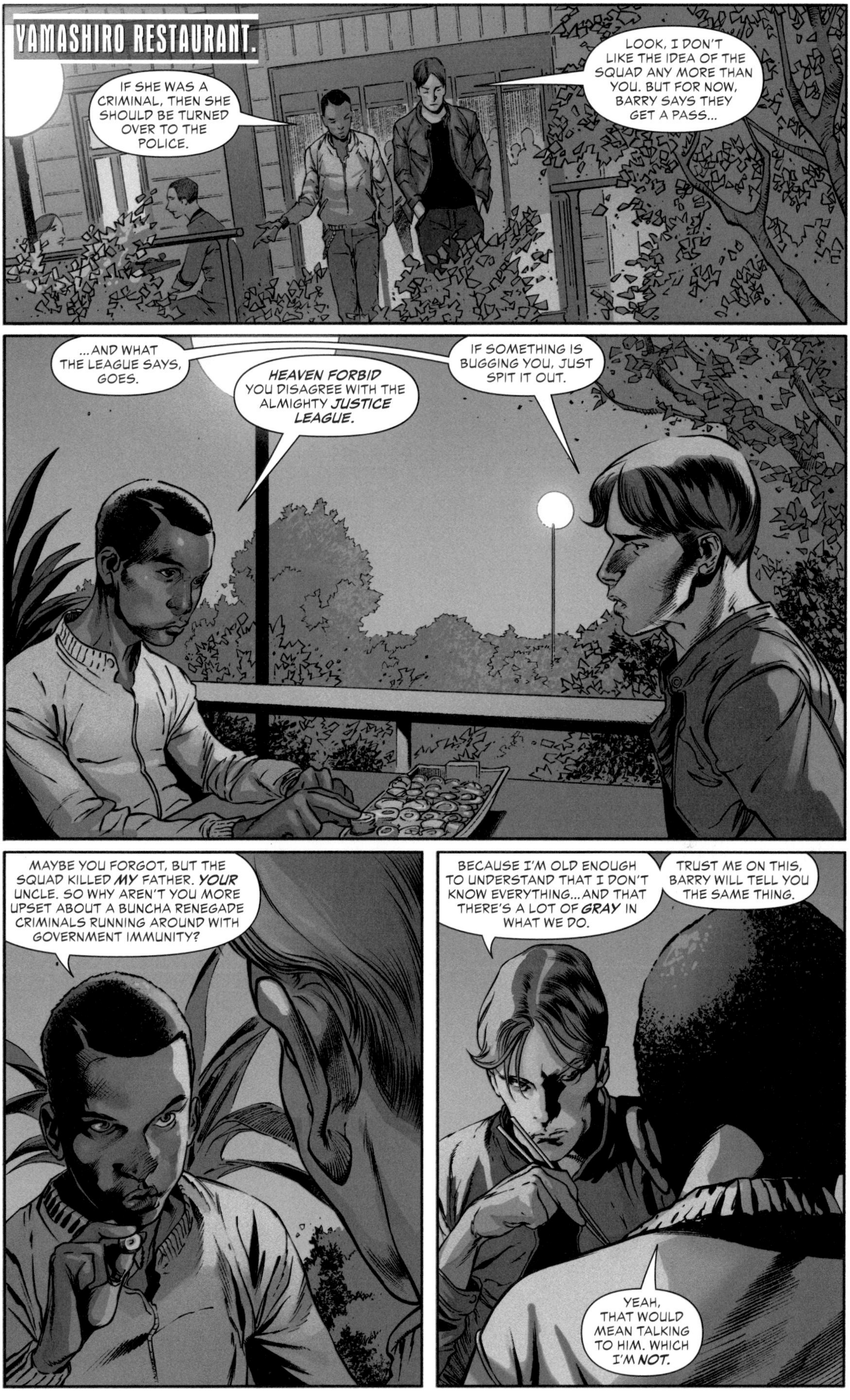
YAMASHIRO RESTAURANT.
IF SHE WAS A CRIMINAL, THEN SHE SHOULD BE TURNED OVER TO THE POLICE.
LOOK, I DON'T LIKE THE IDEA OF THE SQUAD ANY MORE THAN YOU. BUT FOR NOW, BARRY SAYS THEY GET A PASS...
...AND WHAT THE LEAGUE SAYS, GOES.
HEAVEN FORBID YOU DISAGREE WITH THE ALMIGHTY JUSTICE LEAGUE.
IF SOMETHING IS BUGGING YOU, JUST SPIT IT OUT.
MAYBE YOU FORGOT, BUT THE SQUAD KILLED MY FATHER. YOUR UNCLE. SO WHY AREN'T YOU MORE UPSET ABOUT A BUNCHA RENEGADE CRIMINALS RUNNING AROUND WITH GOVERNMENT IMMUNITY?
BECAUSE I'M OLD ENOUGH TO UNDERSTAND THAT I DON'T KNOW EVERYTHING...AND THAT THERE'S A LOT OF GRAY IN WHAT WE DO.
TRUST ME ON THIS, BARRY WILL TELL YOU THE SAME THING.
YEAH, THAT WOULD MEAN TALKING TO HIM. WHICH I'M NOT.

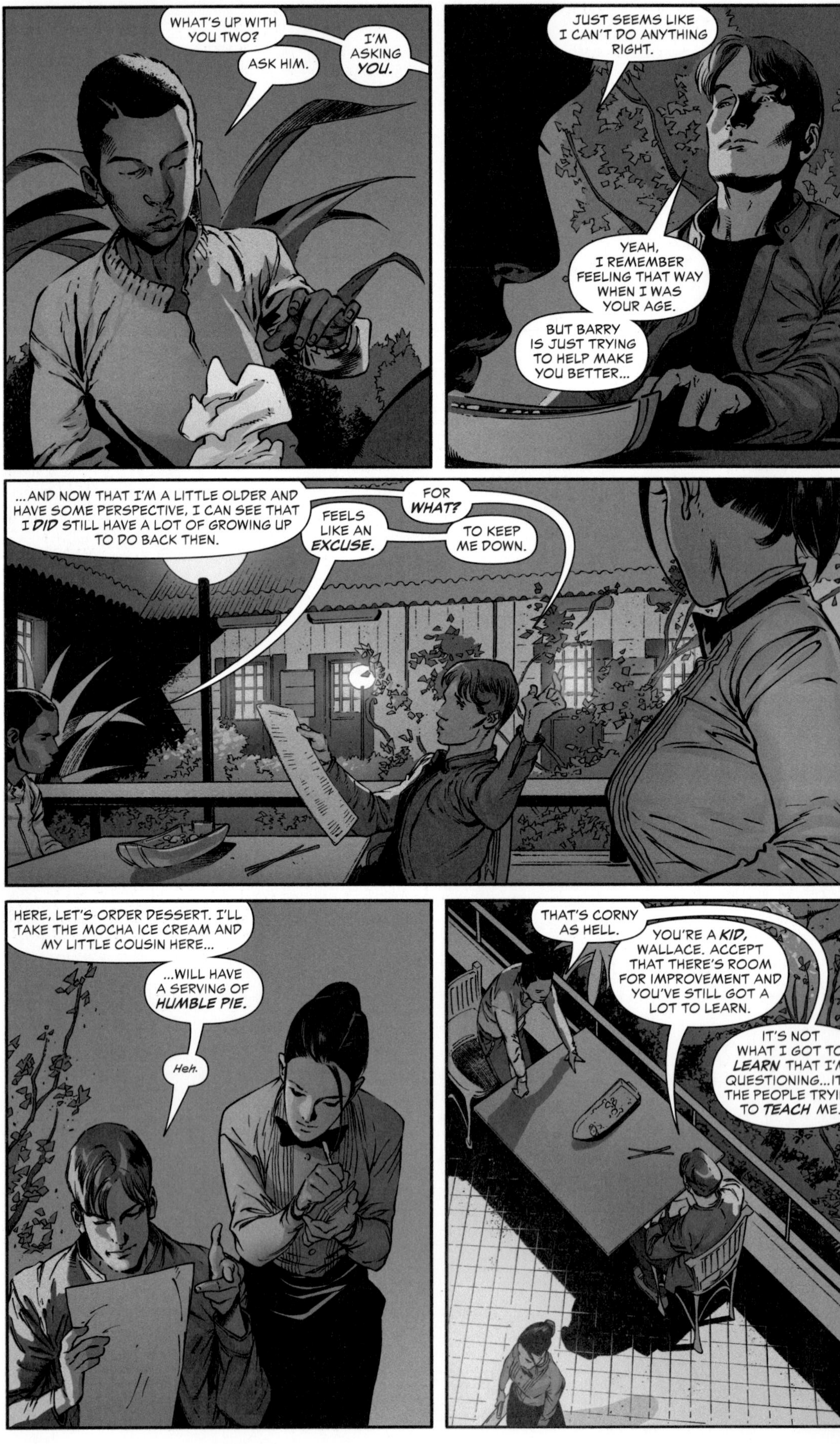

WHAT'S UP WITH YOU TWO?
ASK HIM.
I'M ASKING *YOU.*
JUST SEEMS LIKE I CAN'T DO ANYTHING RIGHT.
YEAH, I REMEMBER FEELING THAT WAY WHEN I WAS YOUR AGE.
BUT BARRY IS JUST TRYING TO HELP MAKE YOU BETTER...
...AND NOW THAT I'M A LITTLE OLDER AND HAVE SOME PERSPECTIVE, I CAN SEE THAT I *DID* STILL HAVE A LOT OF GROWING UP TO DO BACK THEN.
FEELS LIKE AN *EXCUSE.*
FOR *WHAT?*
TO KEEP ME DOWN.
HERE, LET'S ORDER DESSERT. I'LL TAKE THE MOCHA ICE CREAM AND MY LITTLE COUSIN HERE...
...WILL HAVE A SERVING OF *HUMBLE PIE.*
*Heh.*
THAT'S CORNY AS HELL.
YOU'RE A *KID,* WALLACE. ACCEPT THAT THERE'S ROOM FOR IMPROVEMENT AND YOU'VE STILL GOT A LOT TO LEARN.
IT'S NOT WHAT I GOT TO *LEARN* THAT I'M QUESTIONING...IT'S THE PEOPLE TRYING TO *TEACH* ME.

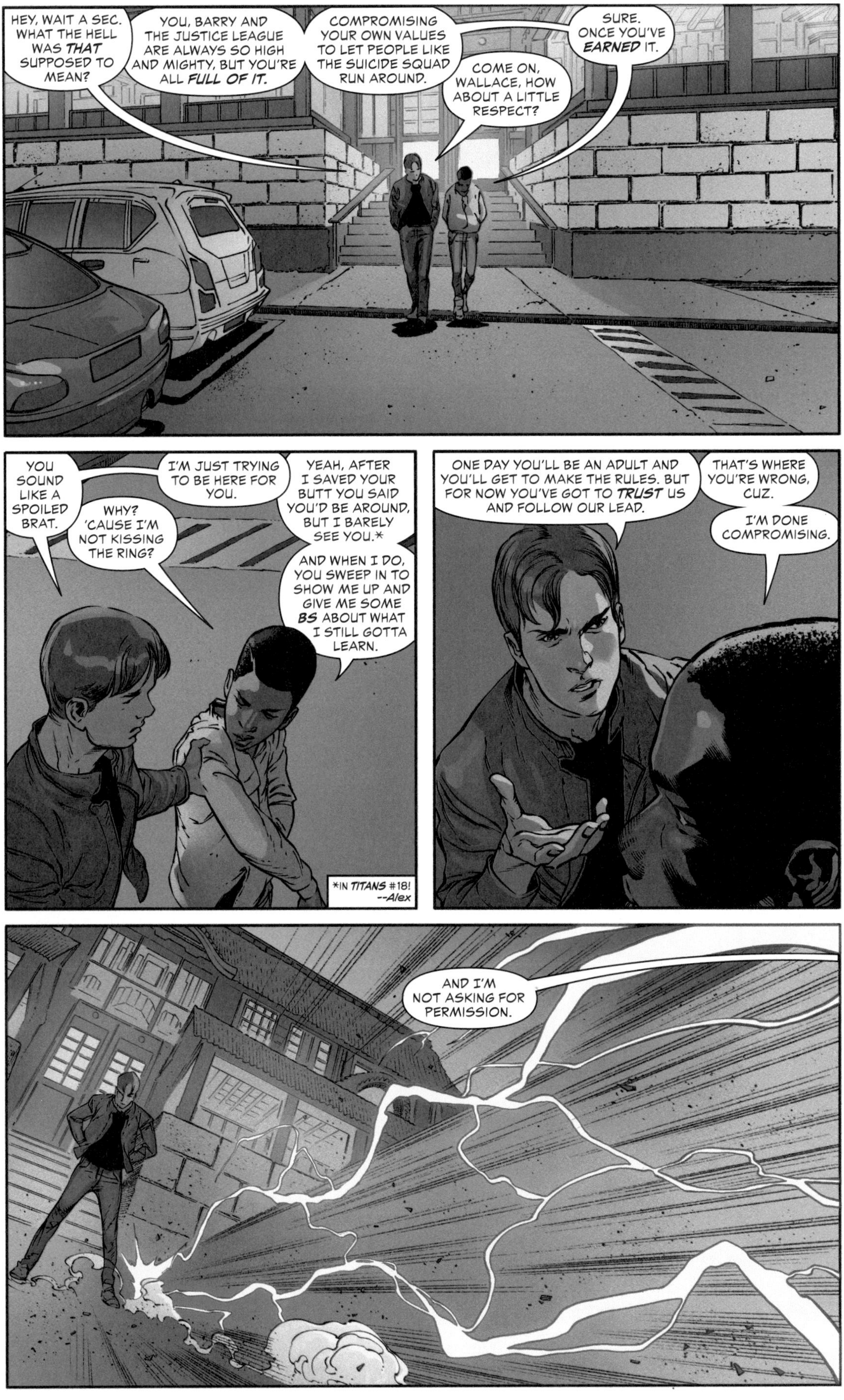

HEY, WAIT A SEC. WHAT THE HELL WAS *THAT* SUPPOSED TO MEAN?
YOU, BARRY AND THE JUSTICE LEAGUE ARE ALWAYS SO HIGH AND MIGHTY, BUT YOU'RE ALL *FULL OF IT.*
COMPROMISING YOUR OWN VALUES TO LET PEOPLE LIKE THE SUICIDE SQUAD RUN AROUND.
SURE. ONCE YOU'VE *EARNED* IT.
COME ON, WALLACE, HOW ABOUT A LITTLE RESPECT?
YOU SOUND LIKE A SPOILED BRAT.
WHY? 'CAUSE I'M NOT KISSING THE RING?
I'M JUST TRYING TO BE HERE FOR YOU.
YEAH, AFTER I SAVED YOUR BUTT YOU SAID YOU'D BE AROUND, BUT I BARELY SEE YOU.*
AND WHEN I DO, YOU SWEEP IN TO SHOW ME UP AND GIVE ME SOME *BS* ABOUT WHAT I STILL GOTTA LEARN.
*IN *TITANS* #18! --*Alex*
ONE DAY YOU'LL BE AN ADULT AND YOU'LL GET TO MAKE THE RULES. BUT FOR NOW YOU'VE GOT TO *TRUST* US AND FOLLOW OUR LEAD.
THAT'S WHERE YOU'RE WRONG, CUZ.
I'M DONE COMPROMISING.
AND I'M NOT ASKING FOR PERMISSION.

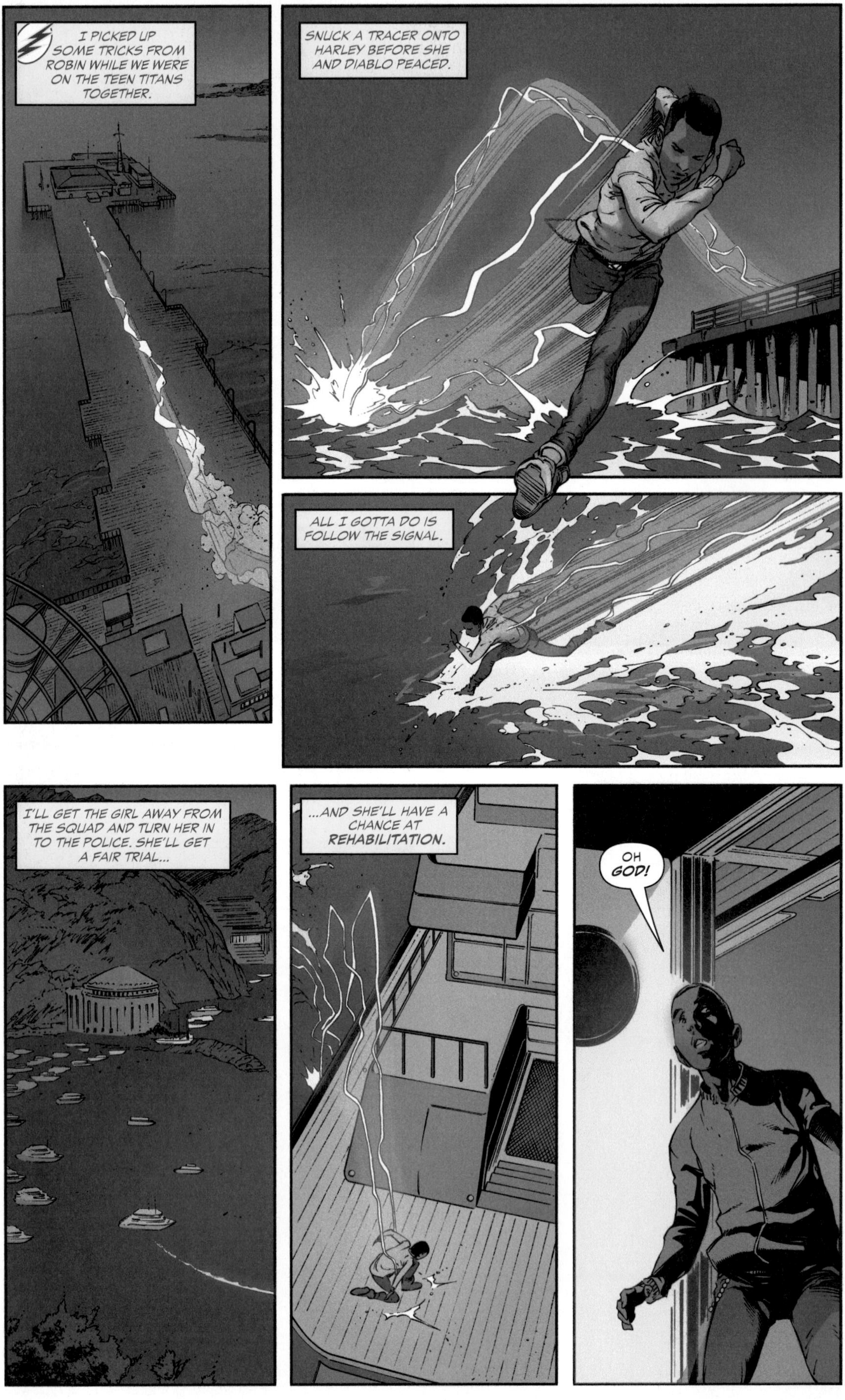
I PICKED UP SOME TRICKS FROM ROBIN WHILE WE WERE ON THE TEEN TITANS TOGETHER.
SNUCK A TRACER ONTO HARLEY BEFORE SHE AND DIABLO PEACED.
ALL I GOTTA DO IS FOLLOW THE SIGNAL.
I'LL GET THE GIRL AWAY FROM THE SQUAD AND TURN HER IN TO THE POLICE. SHE'LL GET A FAIR TRIAL...
...AND SHE'LL HAVE A CHANCE AT REHABILITATION.
OH GOD!

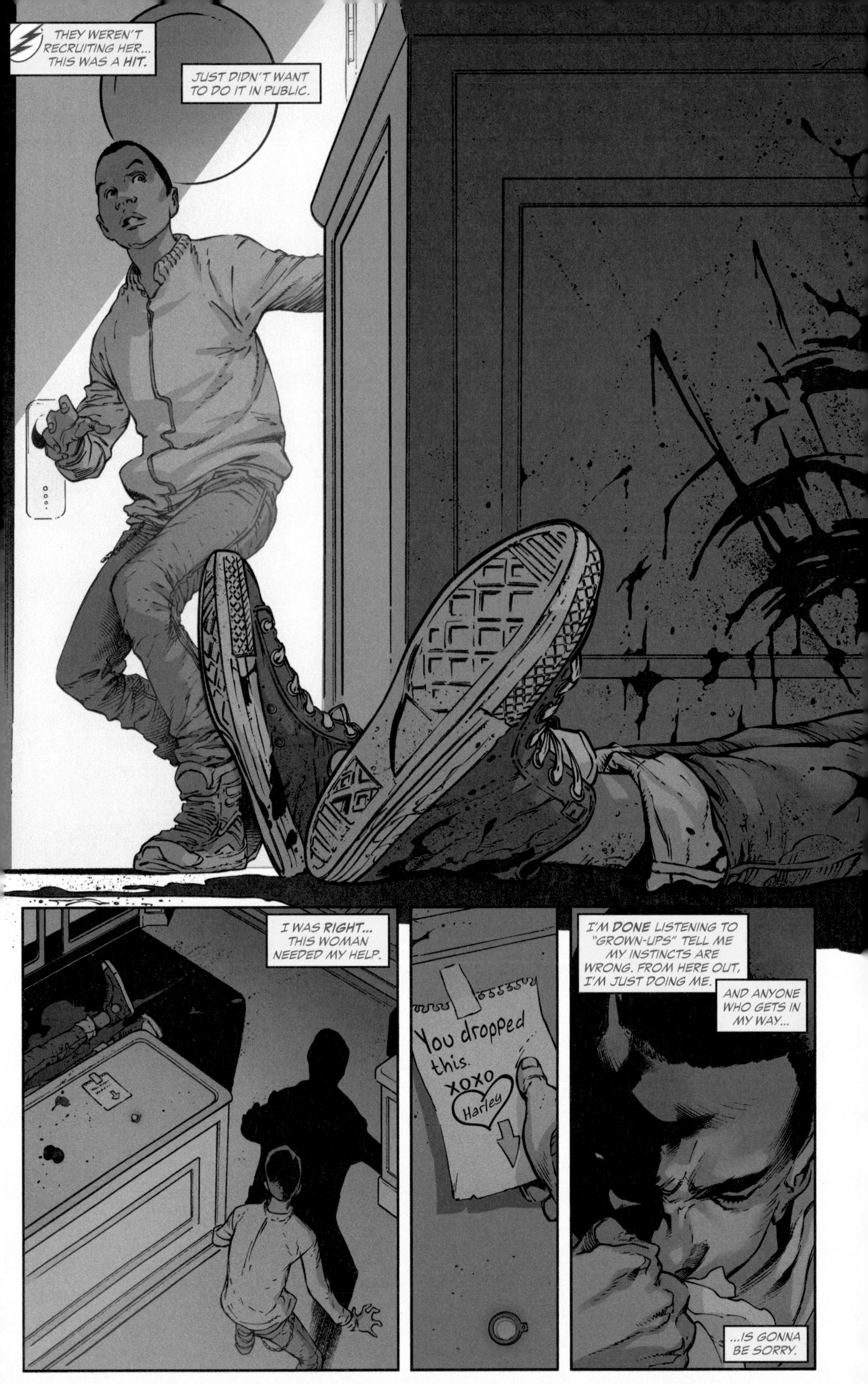
THEY WEREN'T RECRUITING HER... THIS WAS A HIT.
JUST DIDN'T WANT TO DO IT IN PUBLIC.
I WAS RIGHT... THIS WOMAN NEEDED MY HELP.
You dropped this. xoxo Harley
I'M DONE LISTENING TO "GROWN-UPS" TELL ME MY INSTINCTS ARE WRONG. FROM HERE OUT, I'M JUST DOING ME.
AND ANYONE WHO GETS IN MY WAY...
...IS GONNA BE SORRY.

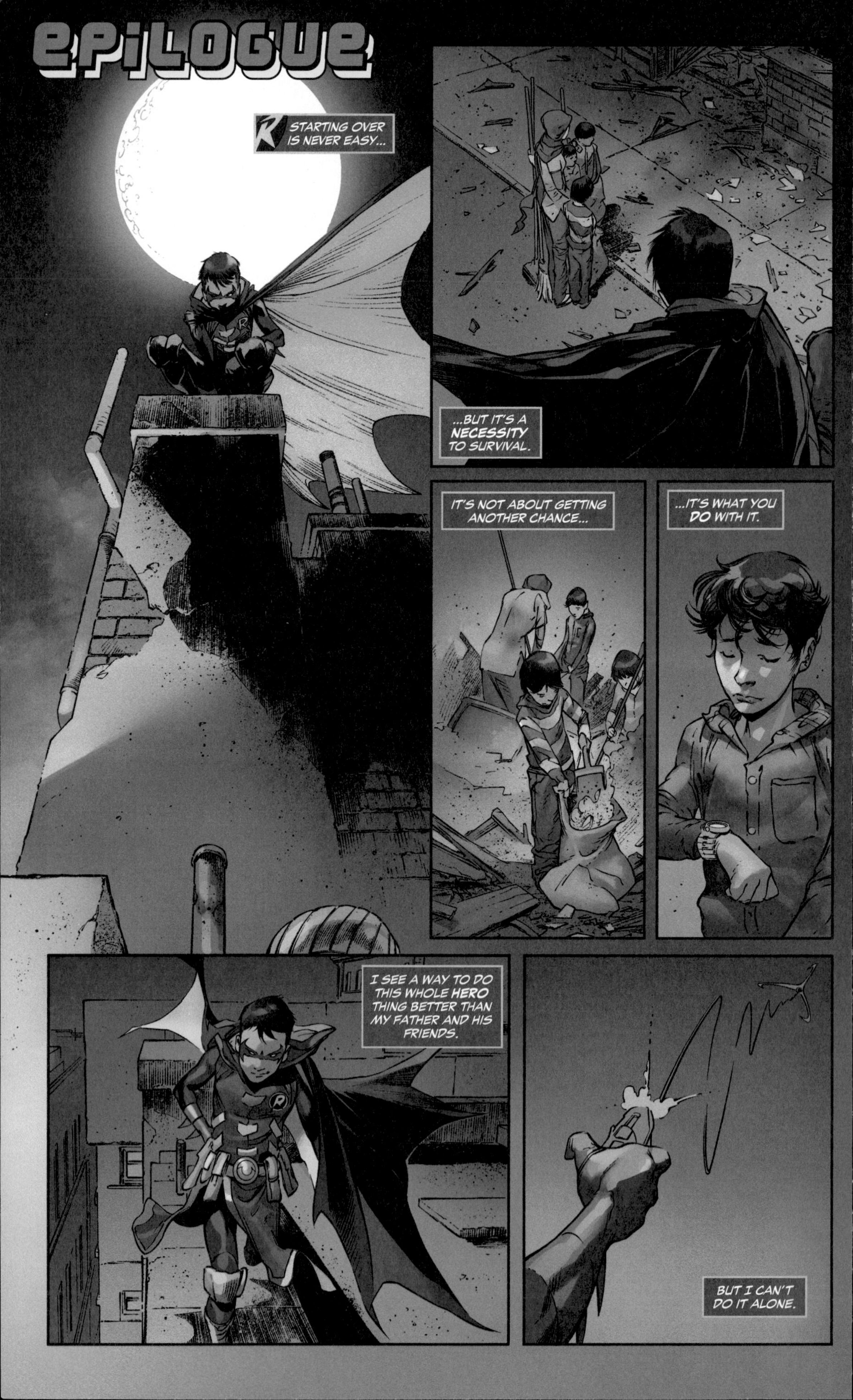
EPILOGUE
STARTING OVER IS NEVER EASY...
...BUT IT'S A NECESSITY TO SURVIVAL.
IT'S NOT ABOUT GETTING ANOTHER CHANCE...
...IT'S WHAT YOU DO WITH IT.
I SEE A WAY TO DO THIS WHOLE HERO THING BETTER THAN MY FATHER AND HIS FRIENDS.
BUT I CAN'T DO IT ALONE.

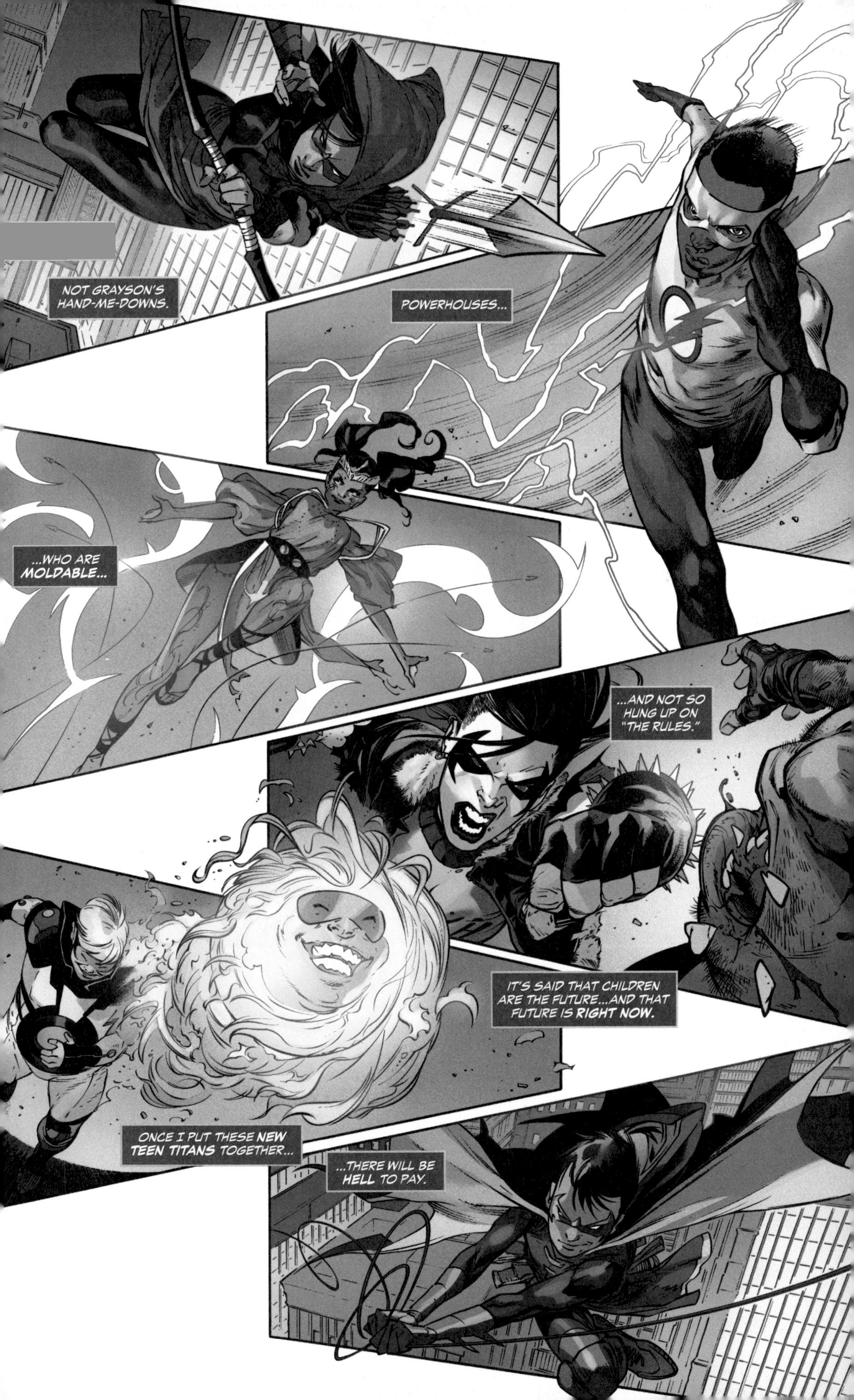
NOT GRAYSON'S HAND-ME-DOWNS.
POWERHOUSES...
...WHO ARE MOLDABLE...
...AND NOT SO HUNG UP ON "THE RULES."
IT'S SAID THAT CHILDREN ARE THE FUTURE...AND THAT FUTURE IS RIGHT NOW.
ONCE I PUT THESE NEW TEEN TITANS TOGETHER...
...THERE WILL BE HELL TO PAY.

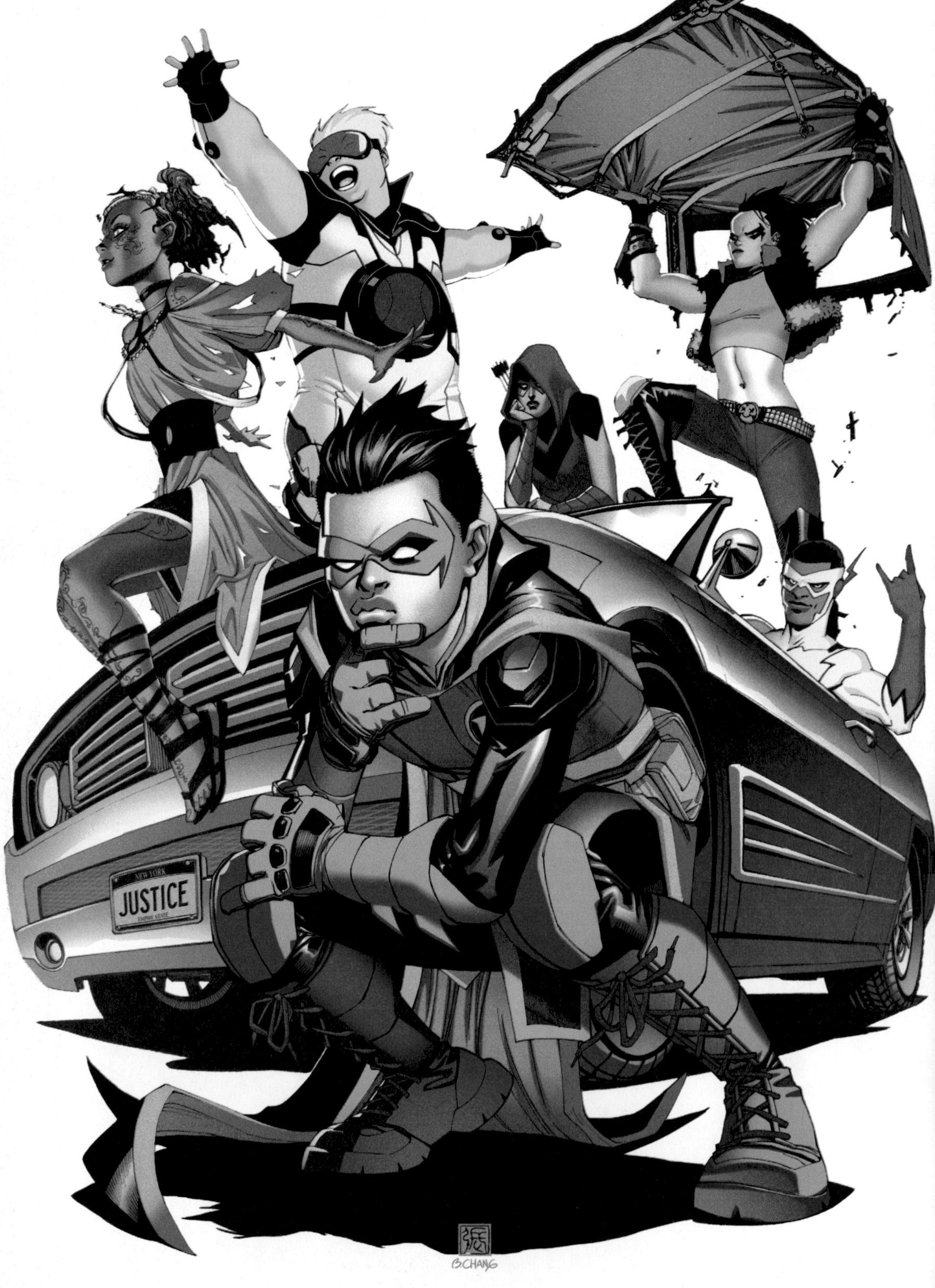
NEW YORK
JUSTICE
EMPIRE STATE
B.CHANG

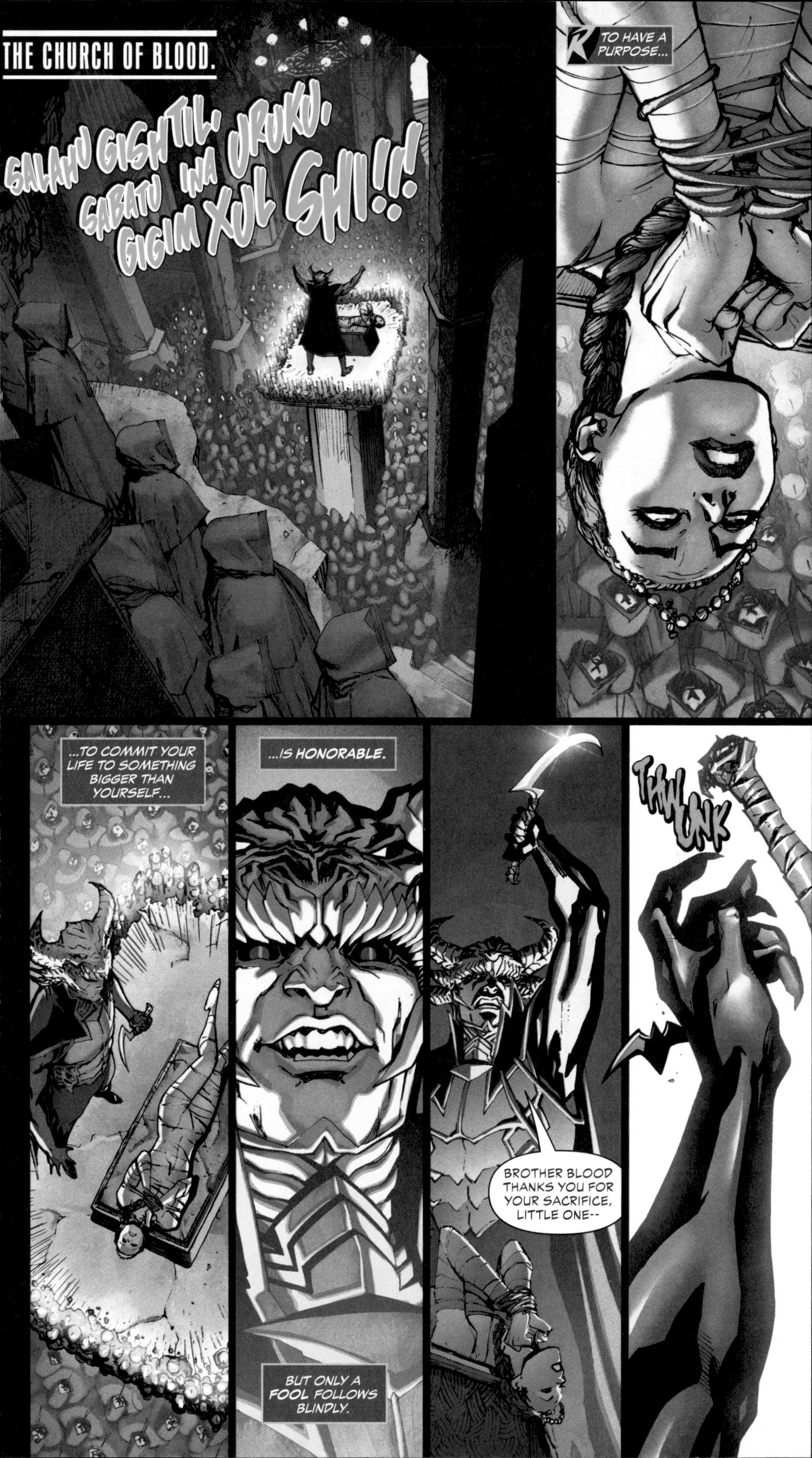

THE CHURCH OF BLOOD.
SALAHU GISHTIL, SABATU INA URUKU, GIGIM XUL SHI!!!
TO HAVE A PURPOSE...
...TO COMMIT YOUR LIFE TO SOMETHING BIGGER THAN YOURSELF...
...IS HONORABLE.
BUT ONLY A FOOL FOLLOWS BLINDLY.
BROTHER BLOOD THANKS YOU FOR YOUR SACRIFICE, LITTLE ONE--
THWUNK

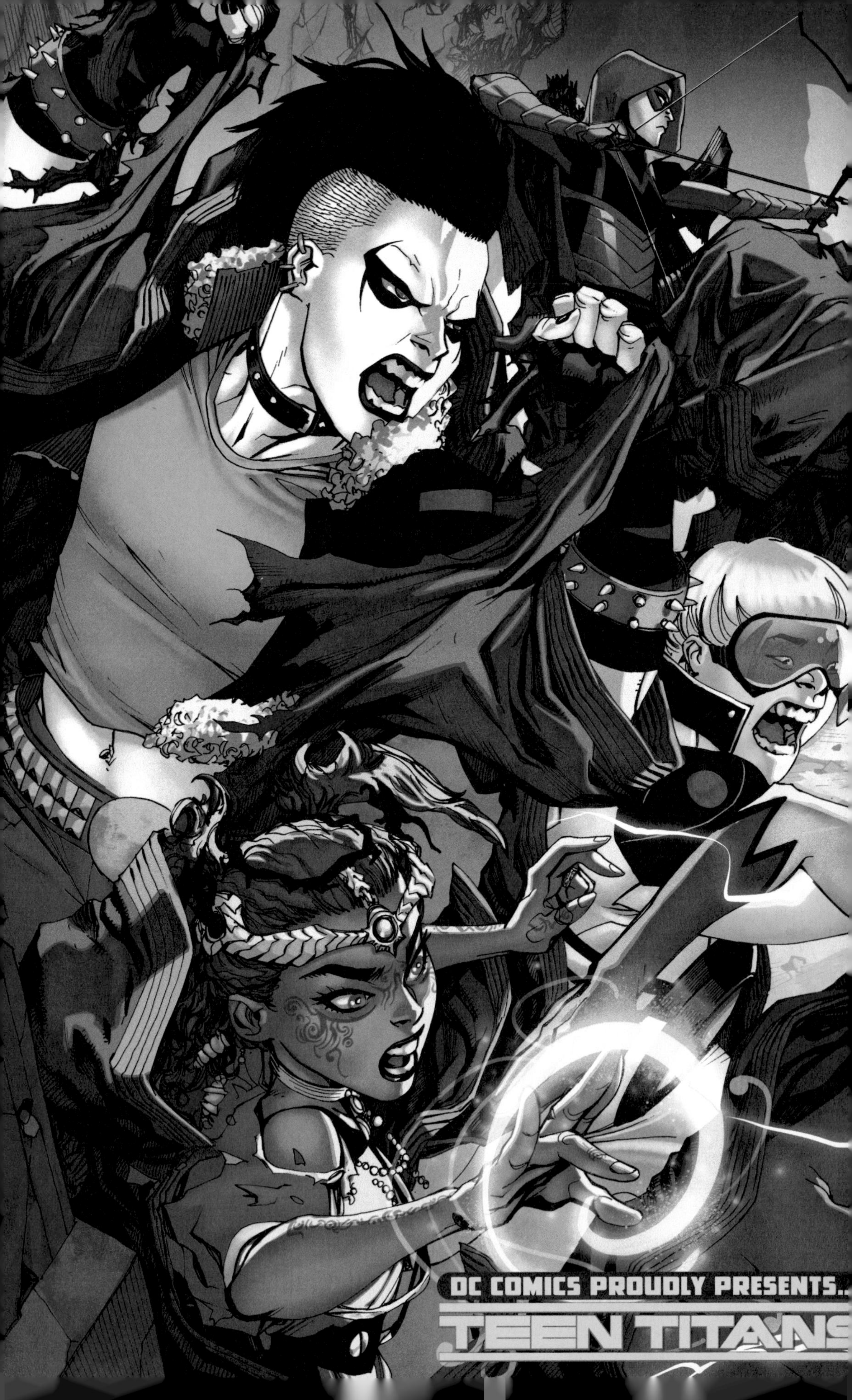
DC COMICS PROUDLY PRESENTS...
TEEN TITANS

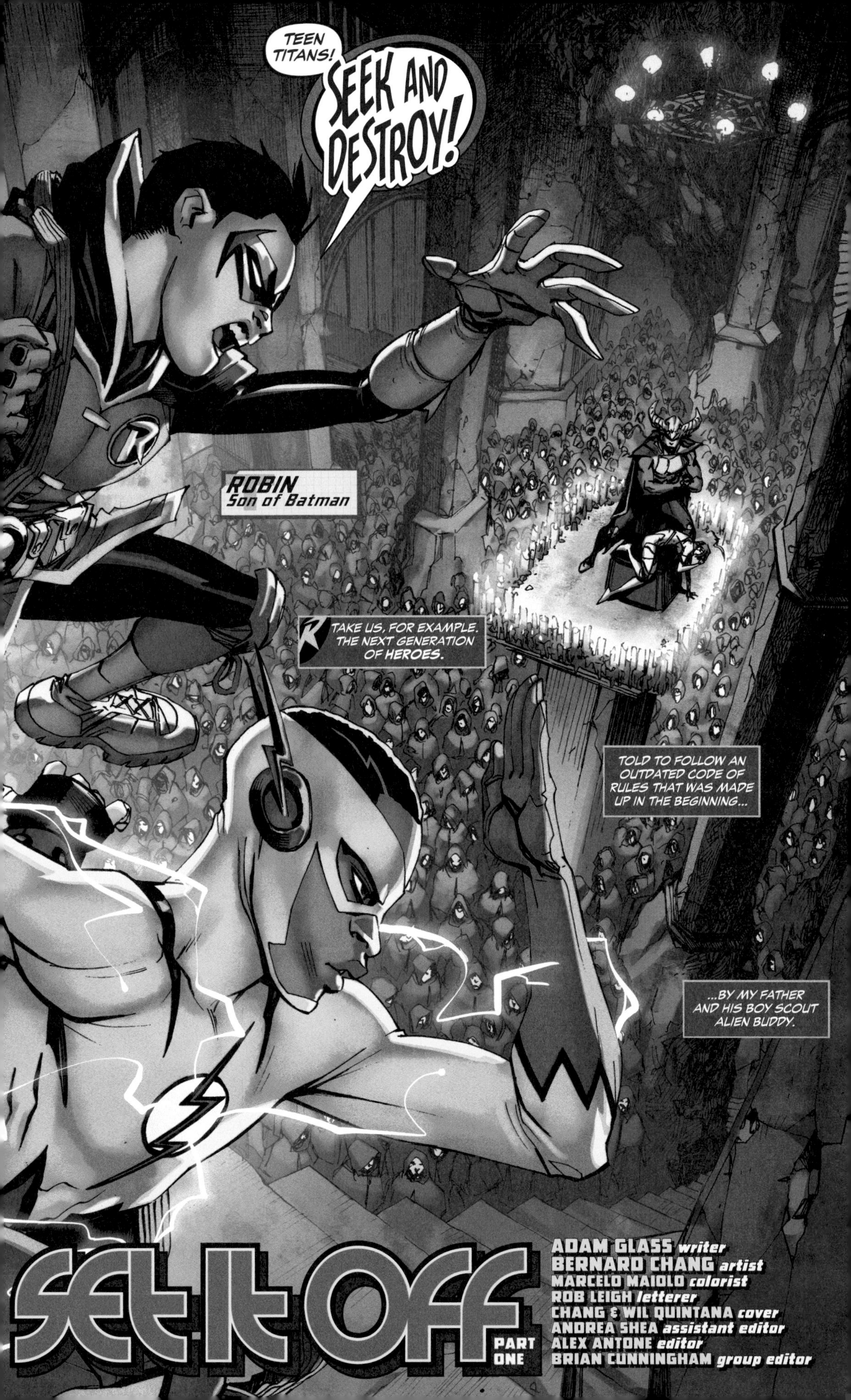
TEEN TITANS!
SEEK AND DESTROY!
ROBIN
Son of Batman
TAKE US, FOR EXAMPLE. THE NEXT GENERATION OF HEROES.
TOLD TO FOLLOW AN OUTDATED CODE OF RULES THAT WAS MADE UP IN THE BEGINNING...
...BY MY FATHER AND HIS BOY SCOUT ALIEN BUDDY.
SET IT OFF
PART ONE
ADAM GLASS writer
BERNARD CHANG artist
MARCELO MAIOLO colorist
ROB LEIGH letterer
CHANG & WIL QUINTANA cover
ANDREA SHEA assistant editor
ALEX ANTONE editor
BRIAN CUNNINGHAM group editor

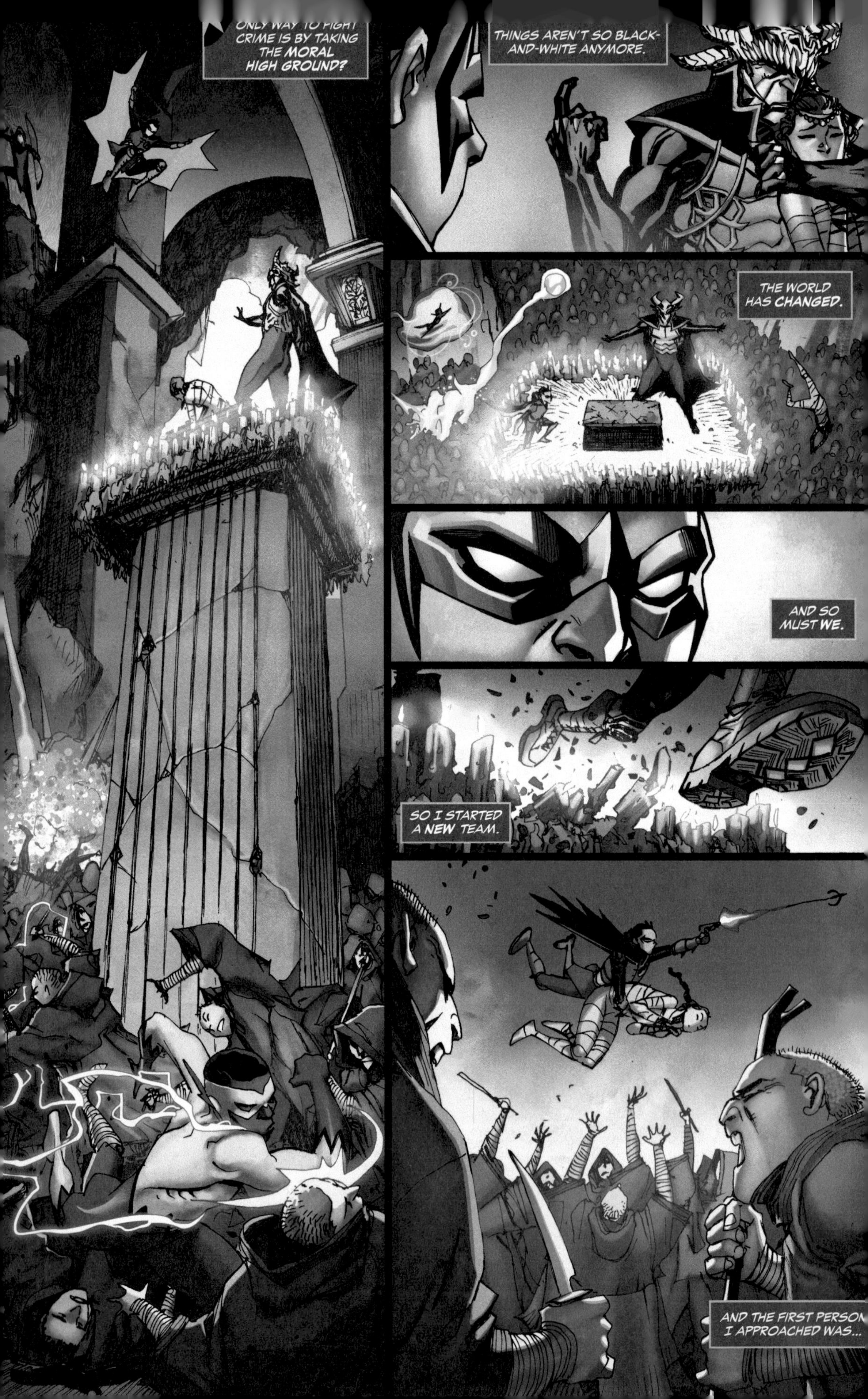
ONLY WAY TO FIGHT CRIME IS BY TAKING THE MORAL HIGH GROUND?
THINGS AREN'T SO BLACK-AND-WHITE ANYMORE.
THE WORLD HAS CHANGED.
AND SO MUST WE.
SO I STARTED A NEW TEAM.
AND THE FIRST PERSON I APPROACHED WAS...

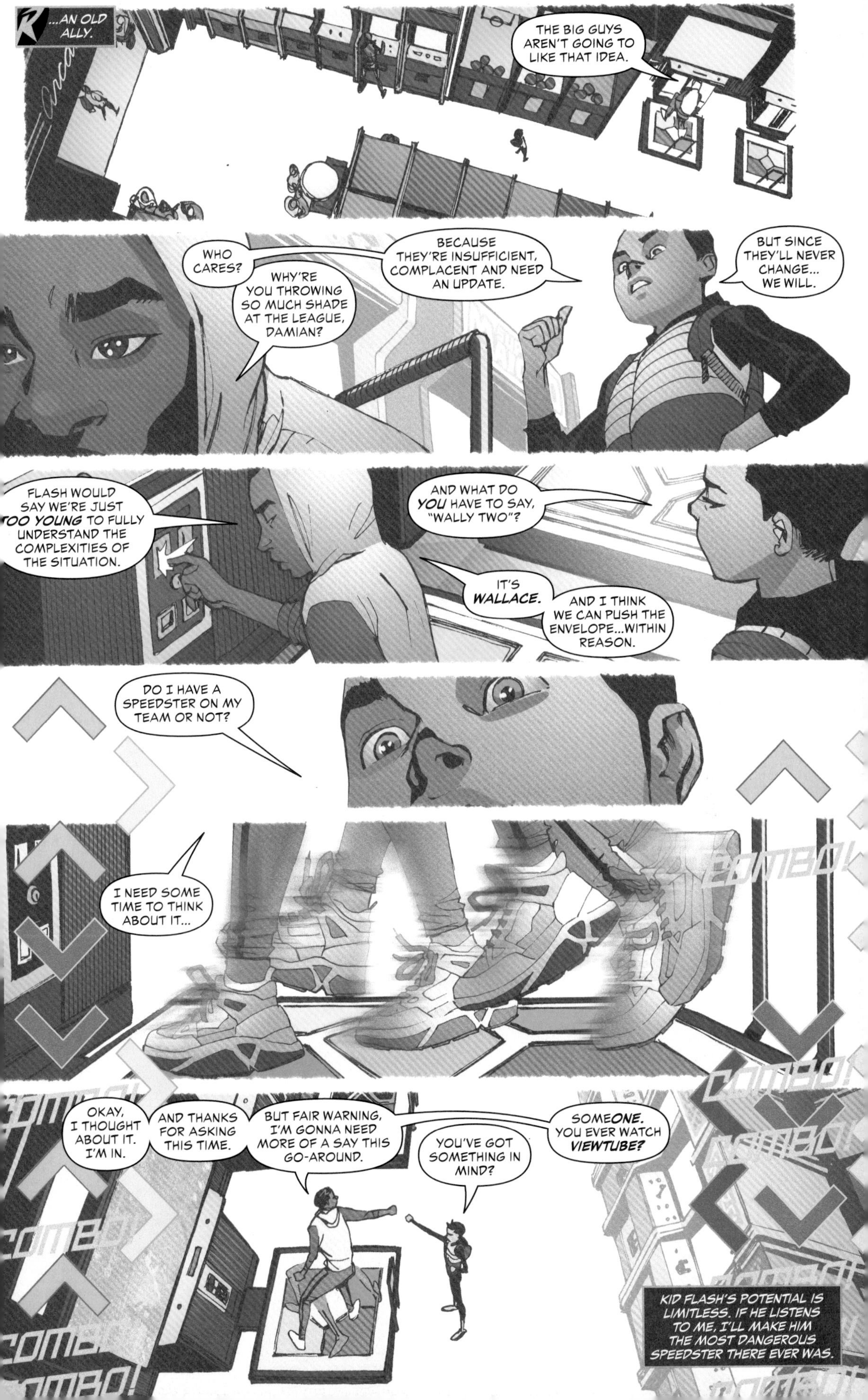
...AN OLD ALLY.
THE BIG GUYS AREN'T GOING TO LIKE THAT IDEA.
WHO CARES?
WHY'RE YOU THROWING SO MUCH SHADE AT THE LEAGUE, DAMIAN?
BECAUSE THEY'RE INSUFFICIENT, COMPLACENT AND NEED AN UPDATE.
BUT SINCE THEY'LL NEVER CHANGE... WE WILL.
FLASH WOULD SAY WE'RE JUST TOO YOUNG TO FULLY UNDERSTAND THE COMPLEXITIES OF THE SITUATION.
AND WHAT DO YOU HAVE TO SAY, "WALLY TWO"?
IT'S WALLACE.
AND I THINK WE CAN PUSH THE ENVELOPE...WITHIN REASON.
DO I HAVE A SPEEDSTER ON MY TEAM OR NOT?
I NEED SOME TIME TO THINK ABOUT IT...
COMBO!
OKAY, I THOUGHT ABOUT IT. I'M IN.
AND THANKS FOR ASKING THIS TIME.
BUT FAIR WARNING, I'M GONNA NEED MORE OF A SAY THIS GO-AROUND.
YOU'VE GOT SOMETHING IN MIND?
SOMEONE. YOU EVER WATCH VIEWTUBE?
KID FLASH'S POTENTIAL IS LIMITLESS. IF HE LISTENS TO ME, I'LL MAKE HIM THE MOST DANGEROUS SPEEDSTER THERE EVER WAS.

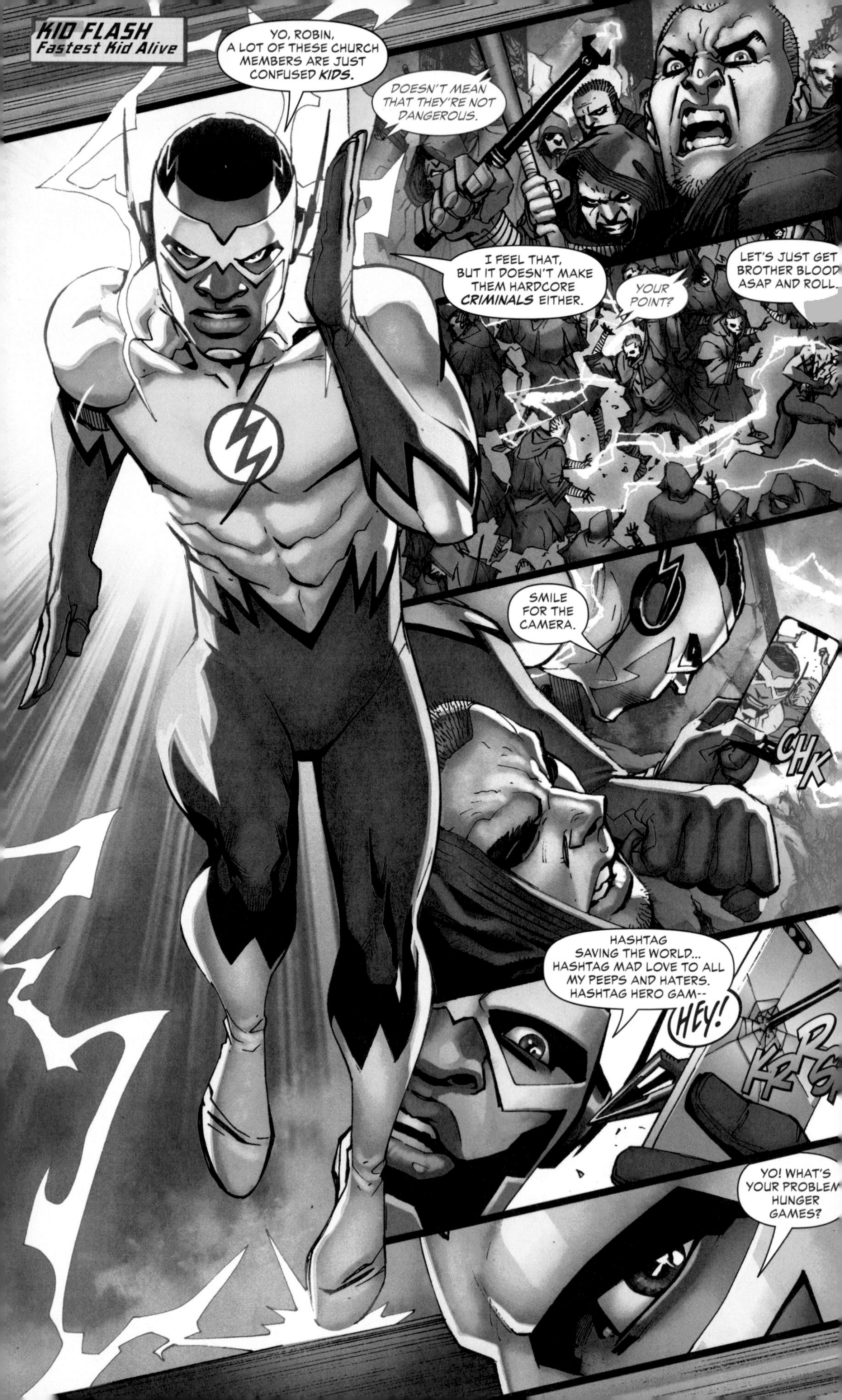

KID FLASH
Fastest Kid Alive
YO, ROBIN, A LOT OF THESE CHURCH MEMBERS ARE JUST CONFUSED KIDS.
DOESN'T MEAN THAT THEY'RE NOT DANGEROUS.
I FEEL THAT, BUT IT DOESN'T MAKE THEM HARDCORE CRIMINALS EITHER.
YOUR POINT?
LET'S JUST GET BROTHER BLOOD ASAP AND ROLL.
SMILE FOR THE CAMERA.
CHK
HASHTAG SAVING THE WORLD... HASHTAG MAD LOVE TO ALL MY PEEPS AND HATERS. HASHTAG HERO GAM--
HEY!
YO! WHAT'S YOUR PROBLEM HUNGER GAMES?

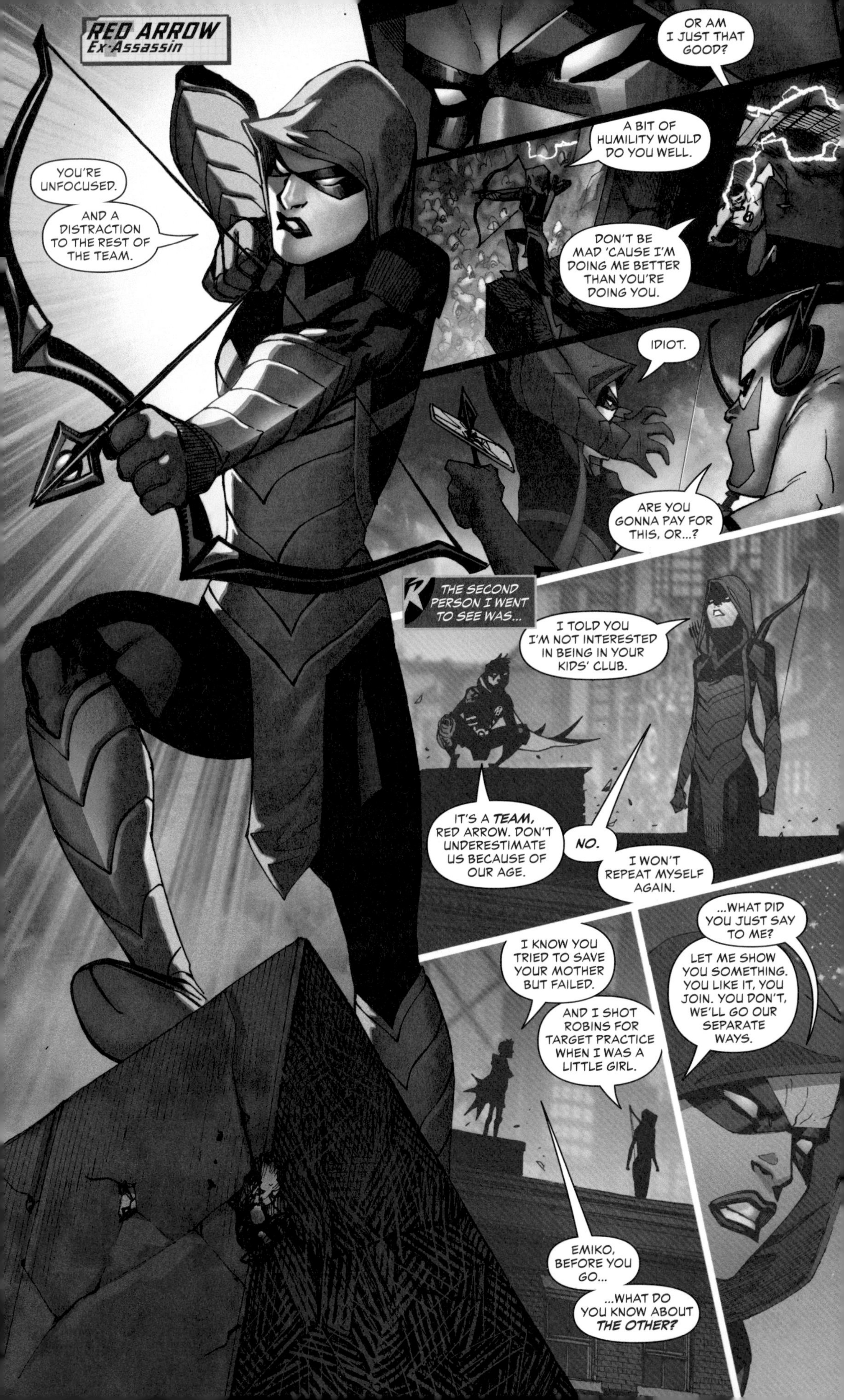
RED ARROW Ex-Assassin
YOU'RE UNFOCUSED.
AND A DISTRACTION TO THE REST OF THE TEAM.
OR AM I JUST THAT GOOD?
A BIT OF HUMILITY WOULD DO YOU WELL.
DON'T BE MAD 'CAUSE I'M DOING ME BETTER THAN YOU'RE DOING YOU.
IDIOT.
ARE YOU GONNA PAY FOR THIS, OR...?
THE SECOND PERSON I WENT TO SEE WAS...
I TOLD YOU I'M NOT INTERESTED IN BEING IN YOUR KIDS' CLUB.
IT'S A TEAM, RED ARROW. DON'T UNDERESTIMATE US BECAUSE OF OUR AGE.
NO.
I WON'T REPEAT MYSELF AGAIN.
I KNOW YOU TRIED TO SAVE YOUR MOTHER BUT FAILED.
AND I SHOT ROBINS FOR TARGET PRACTICE WHEN I WAS A LITTLE GIRL.
...WHAT DID YOU JUST SAY TO ME?
LET ME SHOW YOU SOMETHING. YOU LIKE IT, YOU JOIN. YOU DON'T, WE'LL GO OUR SEPARATE WAYS.
EMIKO, BEFORE YOU GO...
...WHAT DO YOU KNOW ABOUT THE OTHER?

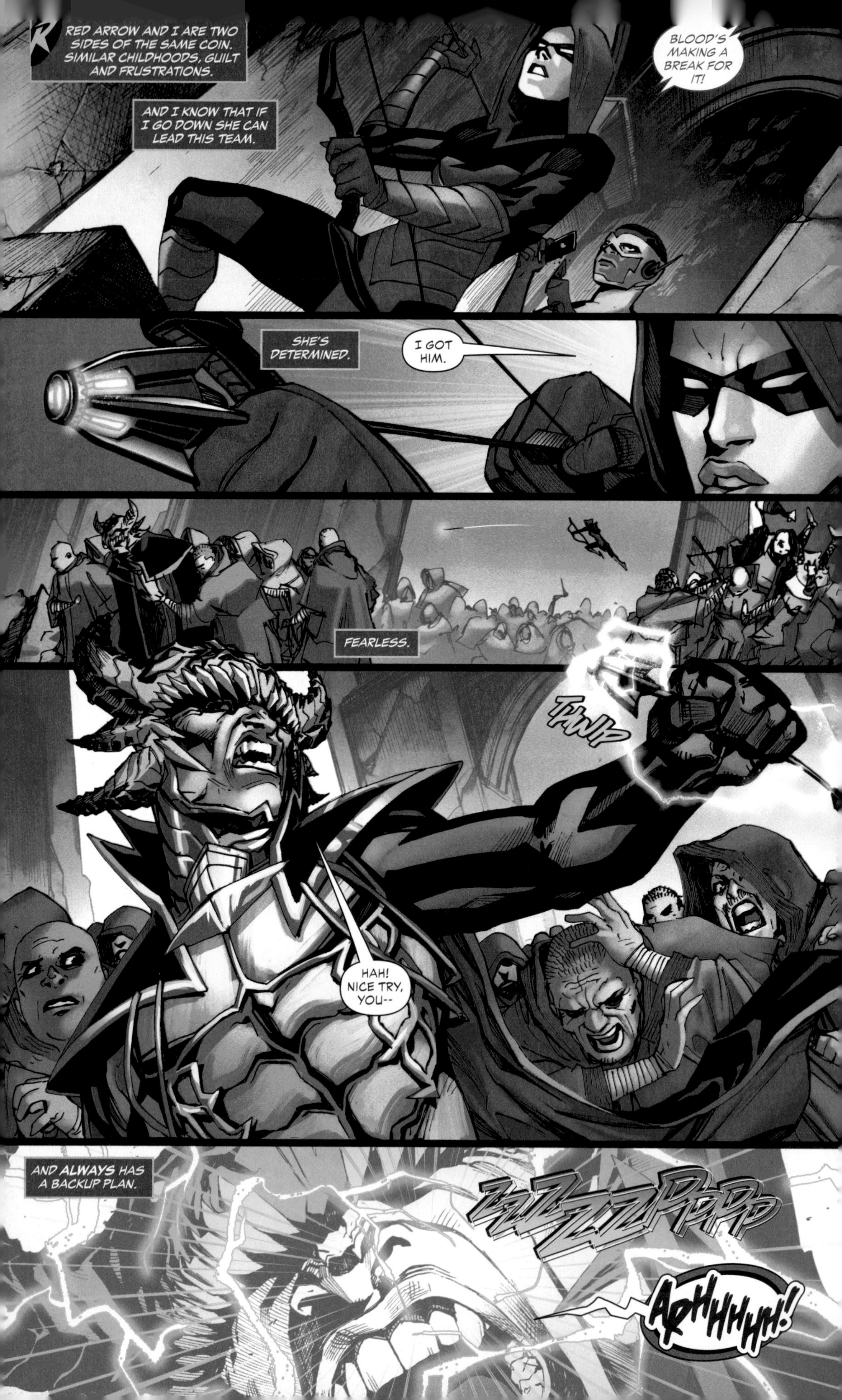
RED ARROW AND I ARE TWO SIDES OF THE SAME COIN. SIMILAR CHILDHOODS, GUILT AND FRUSTRATIONS.
AND I KNOW THAT IF I GO DOWN SHE CAN LEAD THIS TEAM.
BLOOD'S MAKING A BREAK FOR IT!
SHE'S DETERMINED.
I GOT HIM.
FEARLESS.
THWIP
HAH! NICE TRY, YOU--
AND ALWAYS HAS A BACKUP PLAN.
ZZZZZZZPPPP
AAHHHHH!

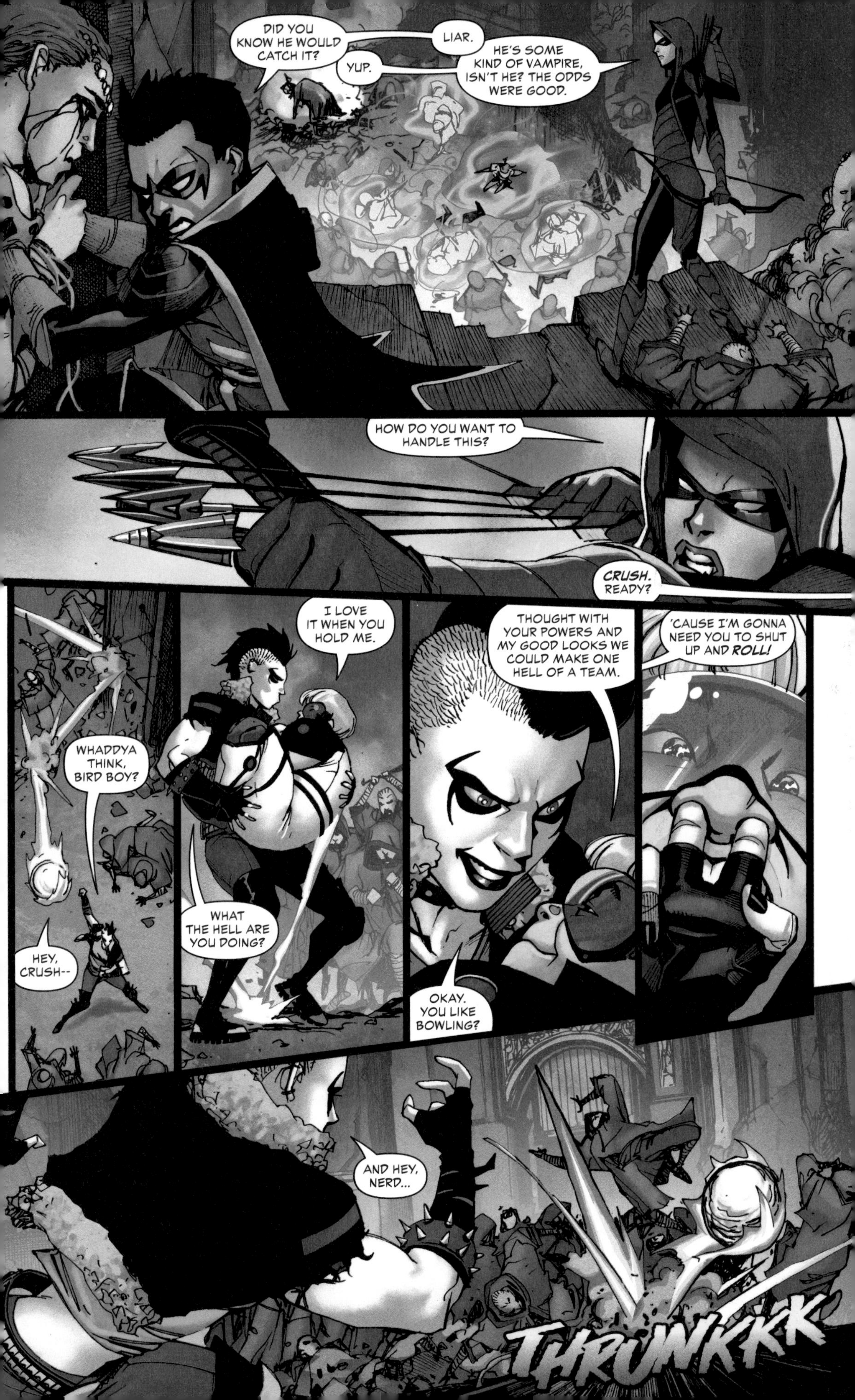
DID YOU KNOW HE WOULD CATCH IT?
LIAR.
YUP.
HE'S SOME KIND OF VAMPIRE, ISN'T HE? THE ODDS WERE GOOD.
HOW DO YOU WANT TO HANDLE THIS?
CRUSH. READY?
WHADDYA THINK, BIRD BOY?
HEY, CRUSH--
I LOVE IT WHEN YOU HOLD ME.
WHAT THE HELL ARE YOU DOING?
THOUGHT WITH YOUR POWERS AND MY GOOD LOOKS WE COULD MAKE ONE HELL OF A TEAM.
OKAY. YOU LIKE BOWLING?
'CAUSE I'M GONNA NEED YOU TO SHUT UP AND ROLL!
AND HEY, NERD...
THRUNKKK

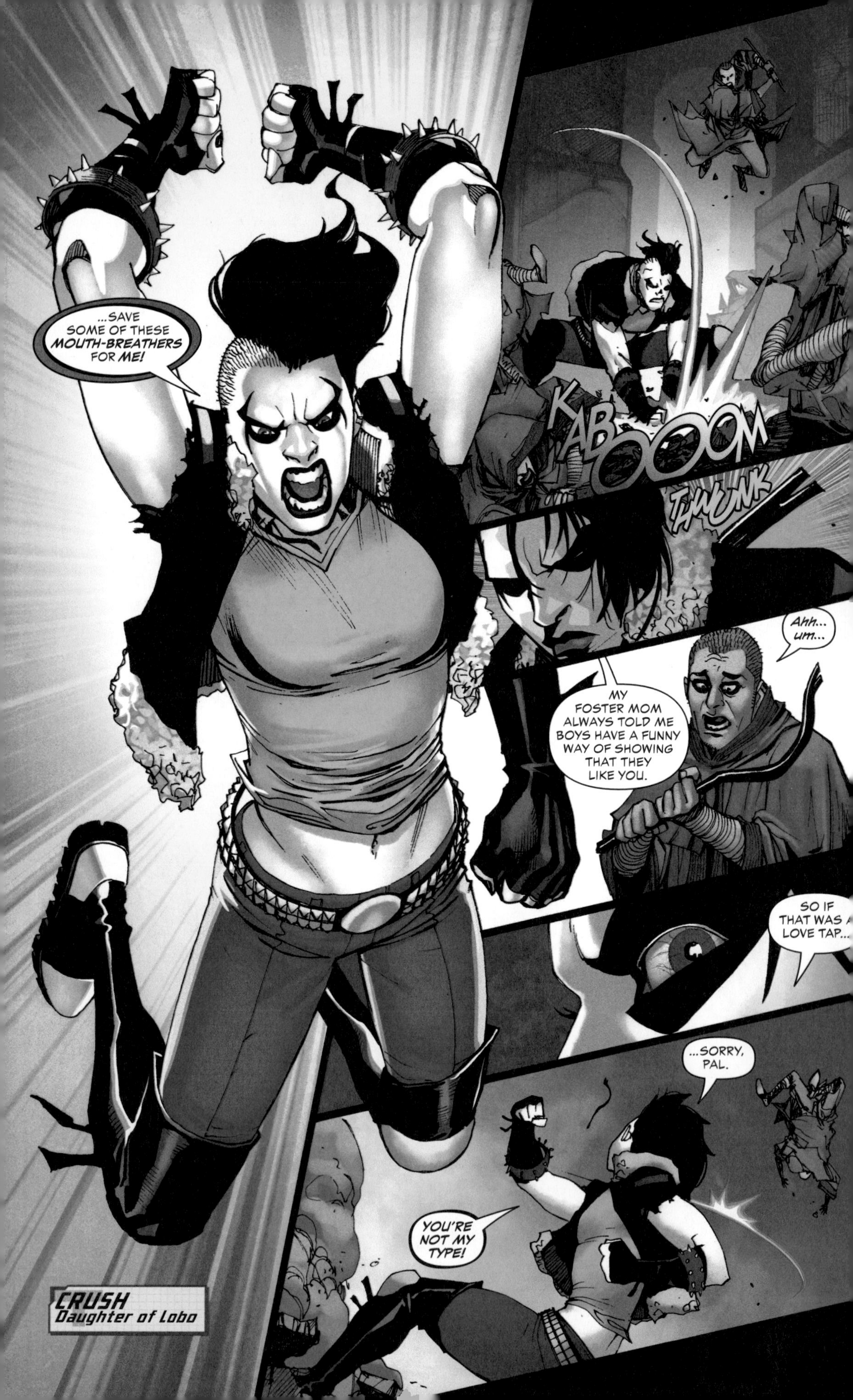
...SAVE SOME OF THESE MOUTH-BREATHERS FOR ME!
KABOOOOM
THWUNK
Ahh... um...
MY FOSTER MOM ALWAYS TOLD ME BOYS HAVE A FUNNY WAY OF SHOWING THAT THEY LIKE YOU.
SO IF THAT WAS A LOVE TAP...
...SORRY, PAL.
YOU'RE NOT MY TYPE!
CRUSH
Daughter of Lobo

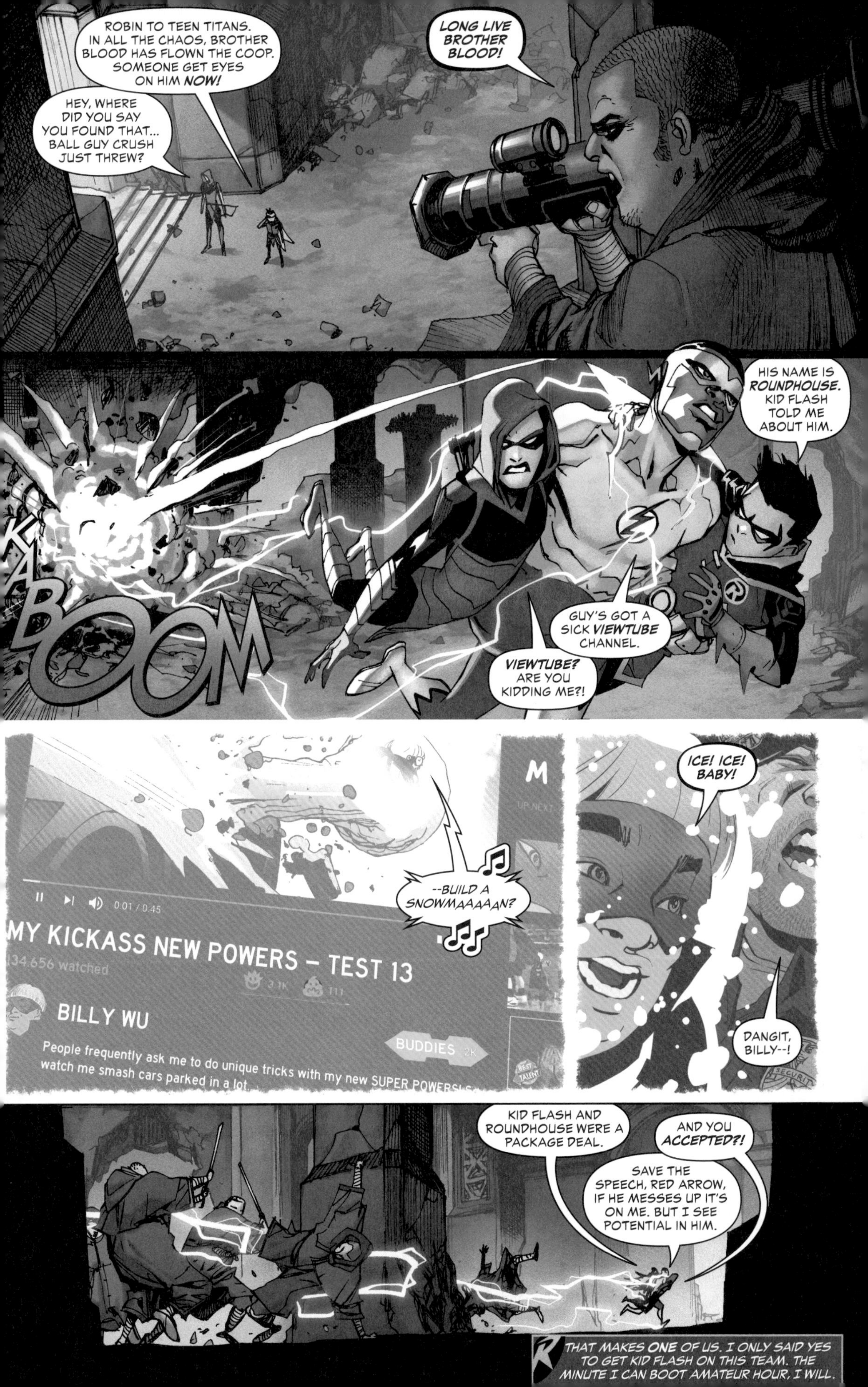
ROBIN TO TEEN TITANS. IN ALL THE CHAOS, BROTHER BLOOD HAS FLOWN THE COOP. SOMEONE GET EYES ON HIM NOW!
LONG LIVE BROTHER BLOOD!
HEY, WHERE DID YOU SAY YOU FOUND THAT... BALL GUY CRUSH JUST THREW?
KABOOOM
HIS NAME IS ROUNDHOUSE. KID FLASH TOLD ME ABOUT HIM.
GUY'S GOT A SICK VIEWTUBE CHANNEL.
VIEWTUBE? ARE YOU KIDDING ME?!
--BUILD A SNOWMAAAAAN?
0:01 / 0:45
MY KICKASS NEW POWERS – TEST 13
134,656 watched
3.1K
111
BILLY WU
BUDDIES 2K
People frequently ask me to do unique tricks with my new SUPER POWERS!
watch me smash cars parked in a lot.
ICE! ICE! BABY!
DANGIT, BILLY--!
KID FLASH AND ROUNDHOUSE WERE A PACKAGE DEAL.
AND YOU ACCEPTED?!
SAVE THE SPEECH, RED ARROW, IF HE MESSES UP IT'S ON ME. BUT I SEE POTENTIAL IN HIM.
THAT MAKES ONE OF US. I ONLY SAID YES TO GET KID FLASH ON THIS TEAM. THE MINUTE I CAN BOOT AMATEUR HOUR, I WILL.

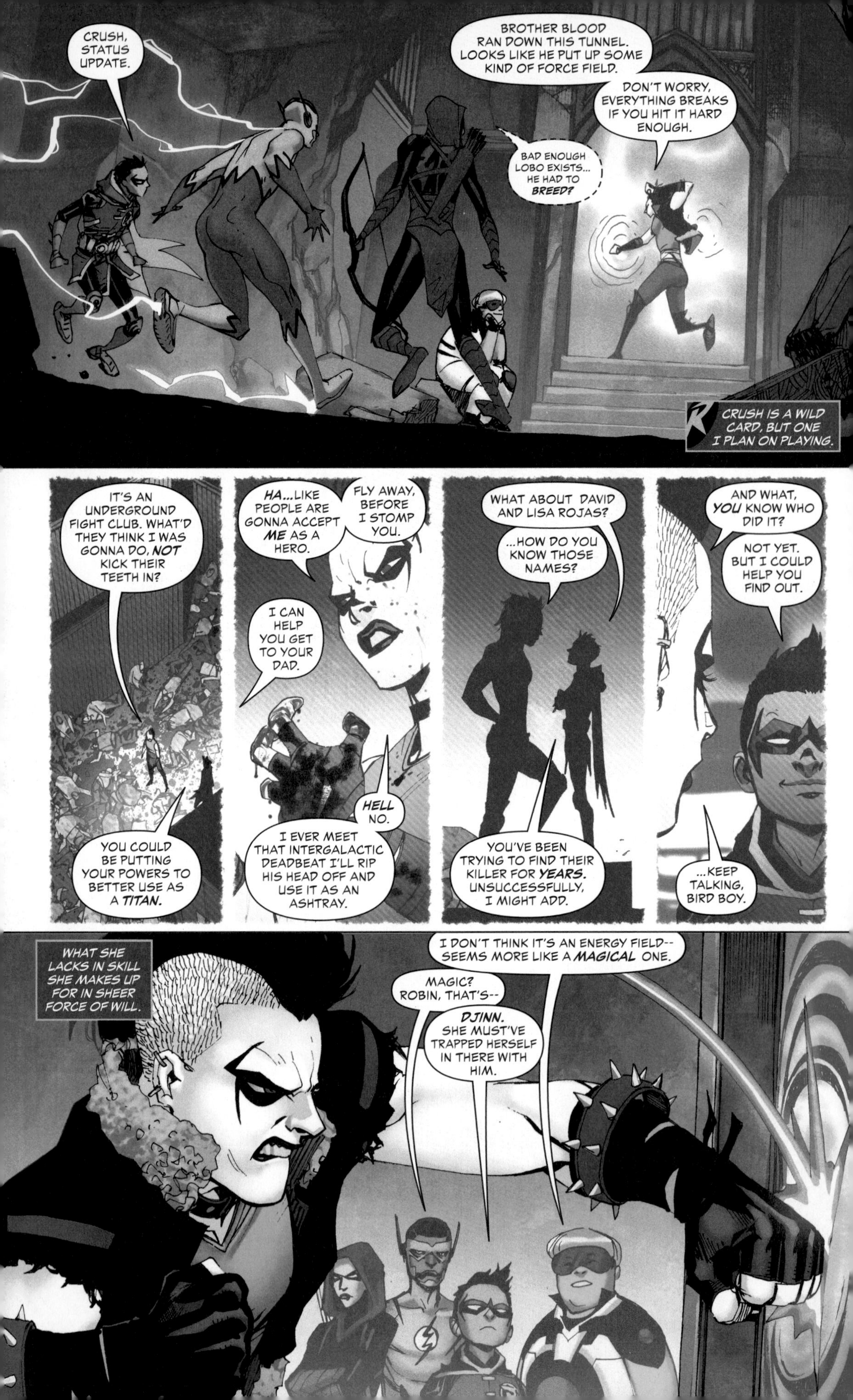
CRUSH, STATUS UPDATE.
BROTHER BLOOD RAN DOWN THIS TUNNEL. LOOKS LIKE HE PUT UP SOME KIND OF FORCE FIELD.
DON'T WORRY, EVERYTHING BREAKS IF YOU HIT IT HARD ENOUGH.
BAD ENOUGH LOBO EXISTS... HE HAD TO BREED?
CRUSH IS A WILD CARD, BUT ONE I PLAN ON PLAYING.
IT'S AN UNDERGROUND FIGHT CLUB. WHAT'D THEY THINK I WAS GONNA DO, NOT KICK THEIR TEETH IN?
YOU COULD BE PUTTING YOUR POWERS TO BETTER USE AS A TITAN.
HA...LIKE PEOPLE ARE GONNA ACCEPT ME AS A HERO.
FLY AWAY, BEFORE I STOMP YOU.
I CAN HELP YOU GET TO YOUR DAD.
HELL NO.
I EVER MEET THAT INTERGALACTIC DEADBEAT I'LL RIP HIS HEAD OFF AND USE IT AS AN ASHTRAY.
WHAT ABOUT DAVID AND LISA ROJAS?
...HOW DO YOU KNOW THOSE NAMES?
YOU'VE BEEN TRYING TO FIND THEIR KILLER FOR YEARS. UNSUCCESSFULLY, I MIGHT ADD.
AND WHAT, YOU KNOW WHO DID IT?
NOT YET. BUT I COULD HELP YOU FIND OUT.
...KEEP TALKING, BIRD BOY.
WHAT SHE LACKS IN SKILL SHE MAKES UP FOR IN SHEER FORCE OF WILL.
I DON'T THINK IT'S AN ENERGY FIELD-- SEEMS MORE LIKE A MAGICAL ONE.
MAGIC? ROBIN, THAT'S--
DJINN. SHE MUST'VE TRAPPED HERSELF IN THERE WITH HIM.

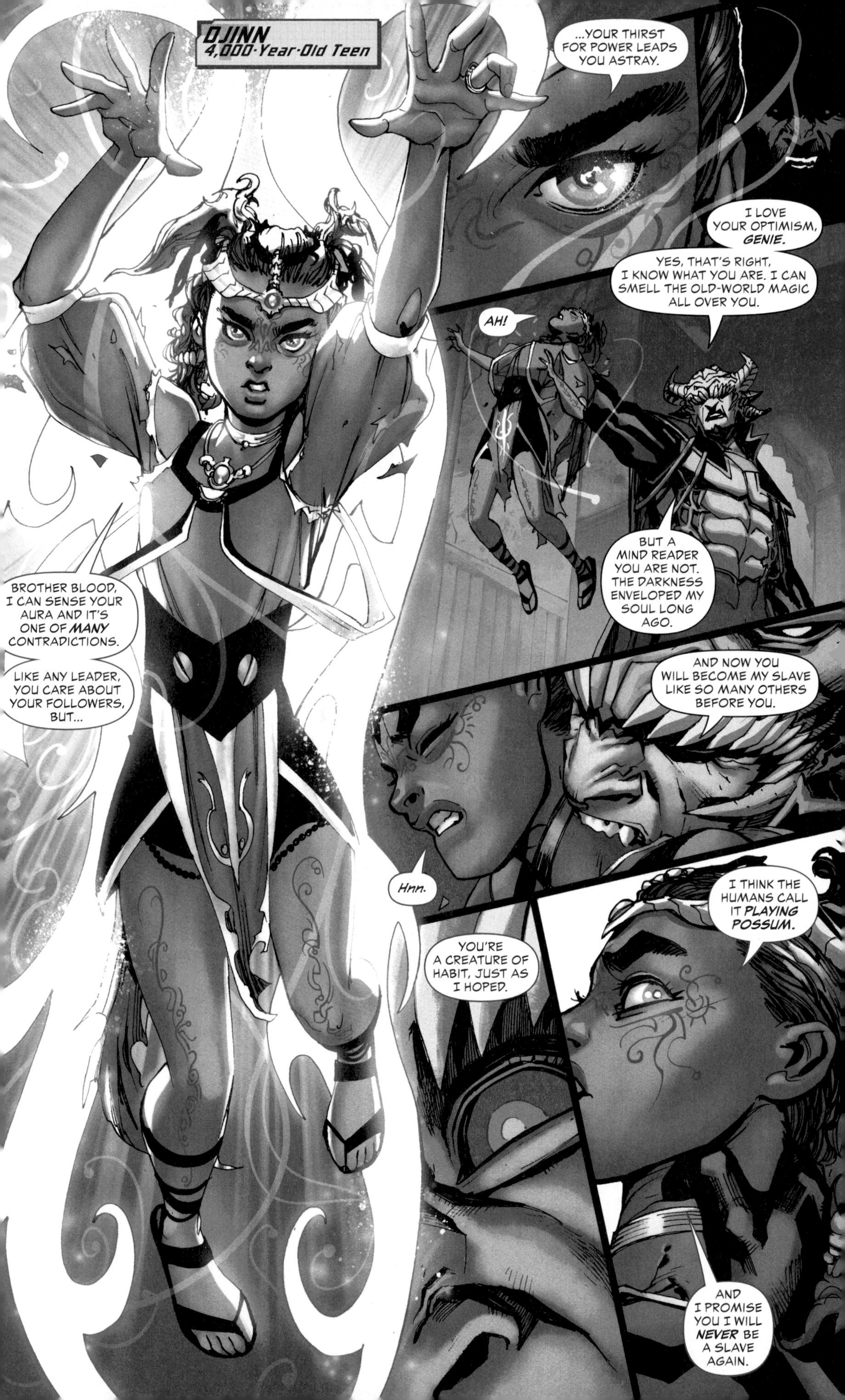
DJINN
4,000-Year-Old Teen
BROTHER BLOOD, I CAN SENSE YOUR AURA AND IT'S ONE OF MANY CONTRADICTIONS.
LIKE ANY LEADER, YOU CARE ABOUT YOUR FOLLOWERS, BUT...
...YOUR THIRST FOR POWER LEADS YOU ASTRAY.
I LOVE YOUR OPTIMISM, GENIE.
YES, THAT'S RIGHT, I KNOW WHAT YOU ARE. I CAN SMELL THE OLD-WORLD MAGIC ALL OVER YOU.
AH!
BUT A MIND READER YOU ARE NOT. THE DARKNESS ENVELOPED MY SOUL LONG AGO.
AND NOW YOU WILL BECOME MY SLAVE LIKE SO MANY OTHERS BEFORE YOU.
Hnn.
YOU'RE A CREATURE OF HABIT, JUST AS I HOPED.
I THINK THE HUMANS CALL IT PLAYING POSSUM.
AND I PROMISE YOU I WILL NEVER BE A SLAVE AGAIN.

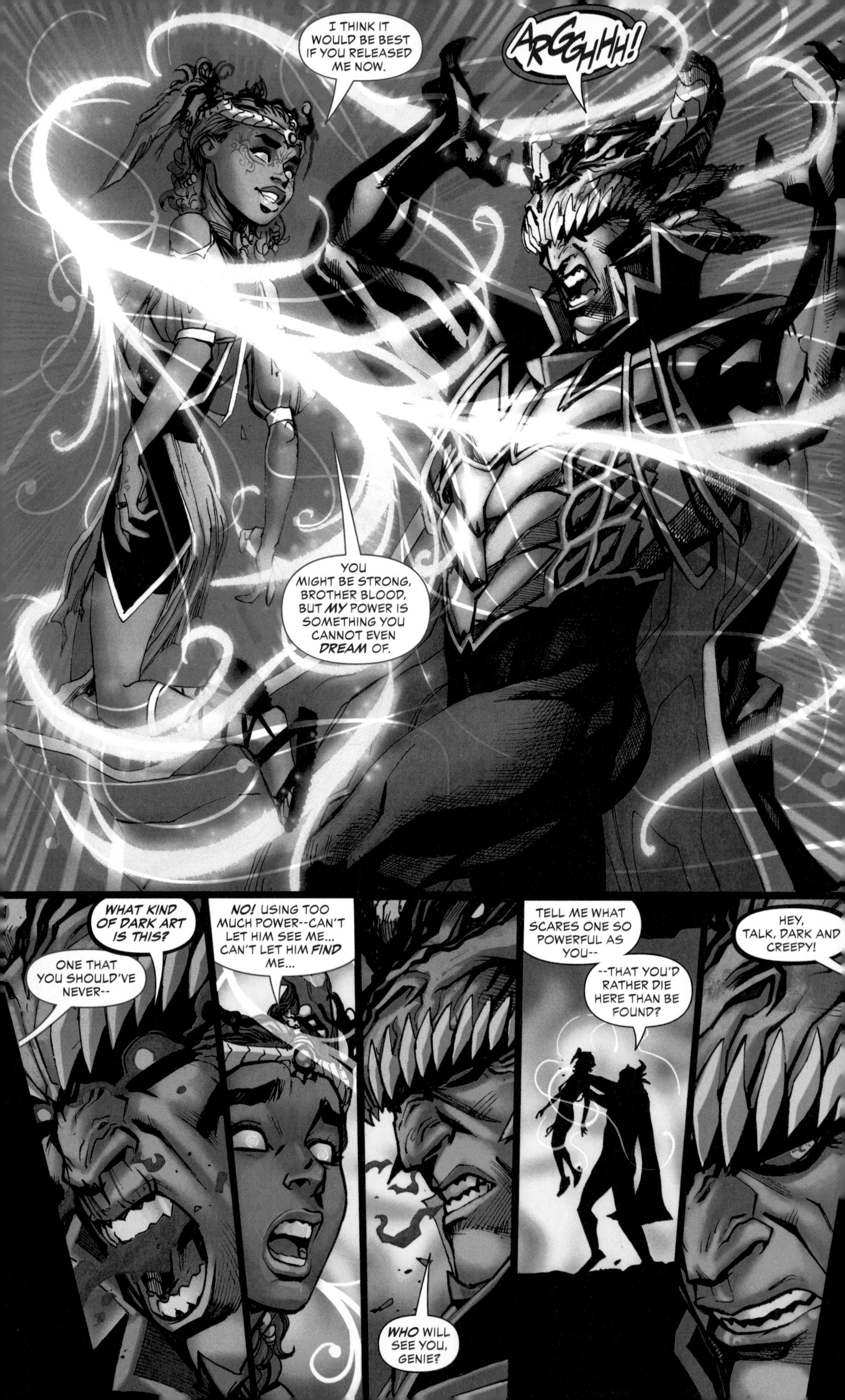
I THINK IT WOULD BE BEST IF YOU RELEASED ME NOW.
ARGGHHH!
YOU MIGHT BE STRONG, BROTHER BLOOD, BUT MY POWER IS SOMETHING YOU CANNOT EVEN DREAM OF.
WHAT KIND OF DARK ART IS THIS?
ONE THAT YOU SHOULD'VE NEVER--
NO! USING TOO MUCH POWER--CAN'T LET HIM SEE ME... CAN'T LET HIM FIND ME...
WHO WILL SEE YOU, GENIE?
TELL ME WHAT SCARES ONE SO POWERFUL AS YOU--
--THAT YOU'D RATHER DIE HERE THAN BE FOUND?
HEY, TALK, DARK AND CREEPY!

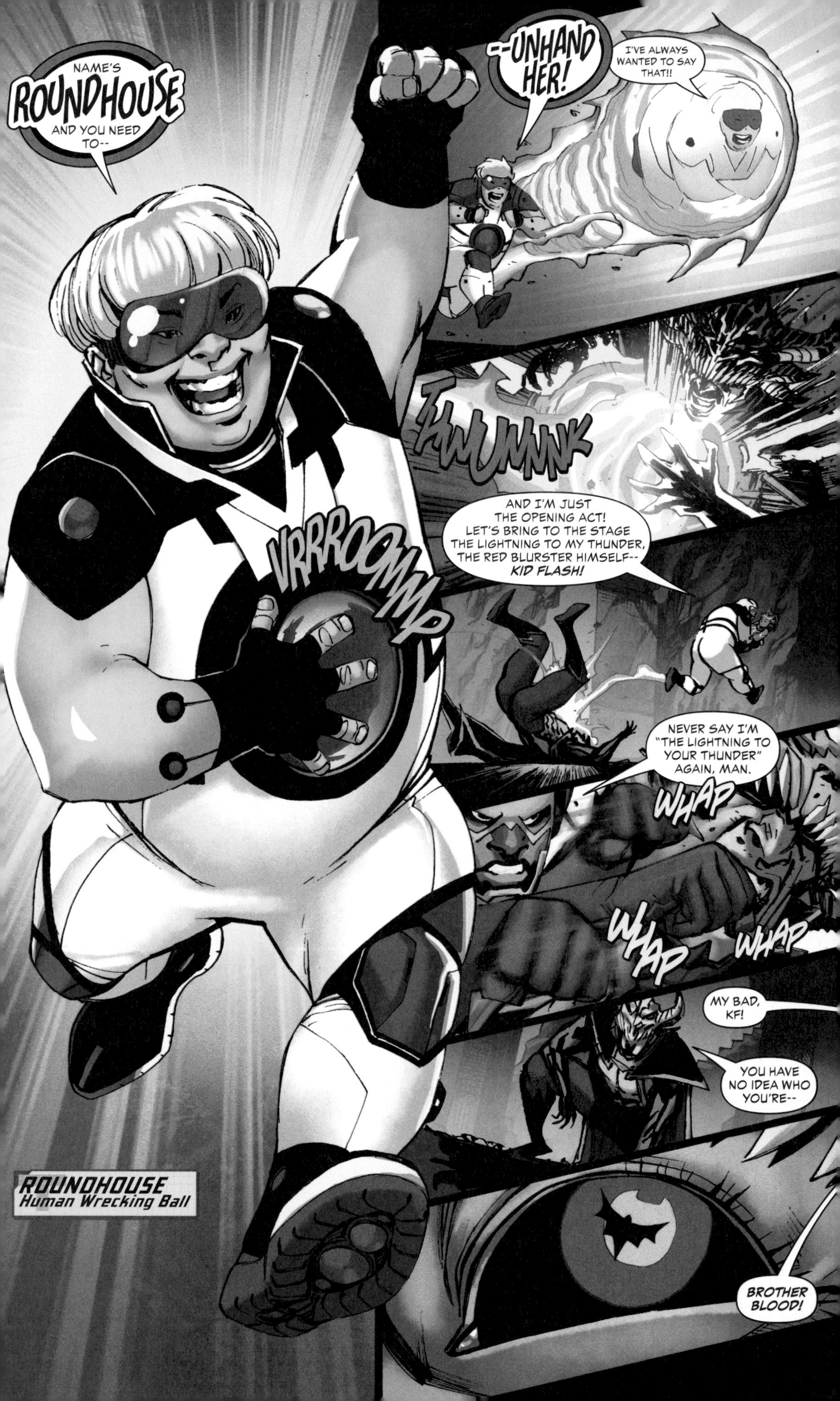

NAME'S ROUNDHOUSE AND YOU NEED TO--
--UNHAND HER!
I'VE ALWAYS WANTED TO SAY THAT!!
THWUNNNK
VRRROOMMP
AND I'M JUST THE OPENING ACT! LET'S BRING TO THE STAGE THE LIGHTNING TO MY THUNDER, THE RED BLURSTER HIMSELF-- KID FLASH!
NEVER SAY I'M "THE LIGHTNING TO YOUR THUNDER" AGAIN, MAN.
WHAP
WHAP
WHAP
MY BAD, KF!
YOU HAVE NO IDEA WHO YOU'RE--
BROTHER BLOOD!
ROUNDHOUSE
Human Wrecking Ball

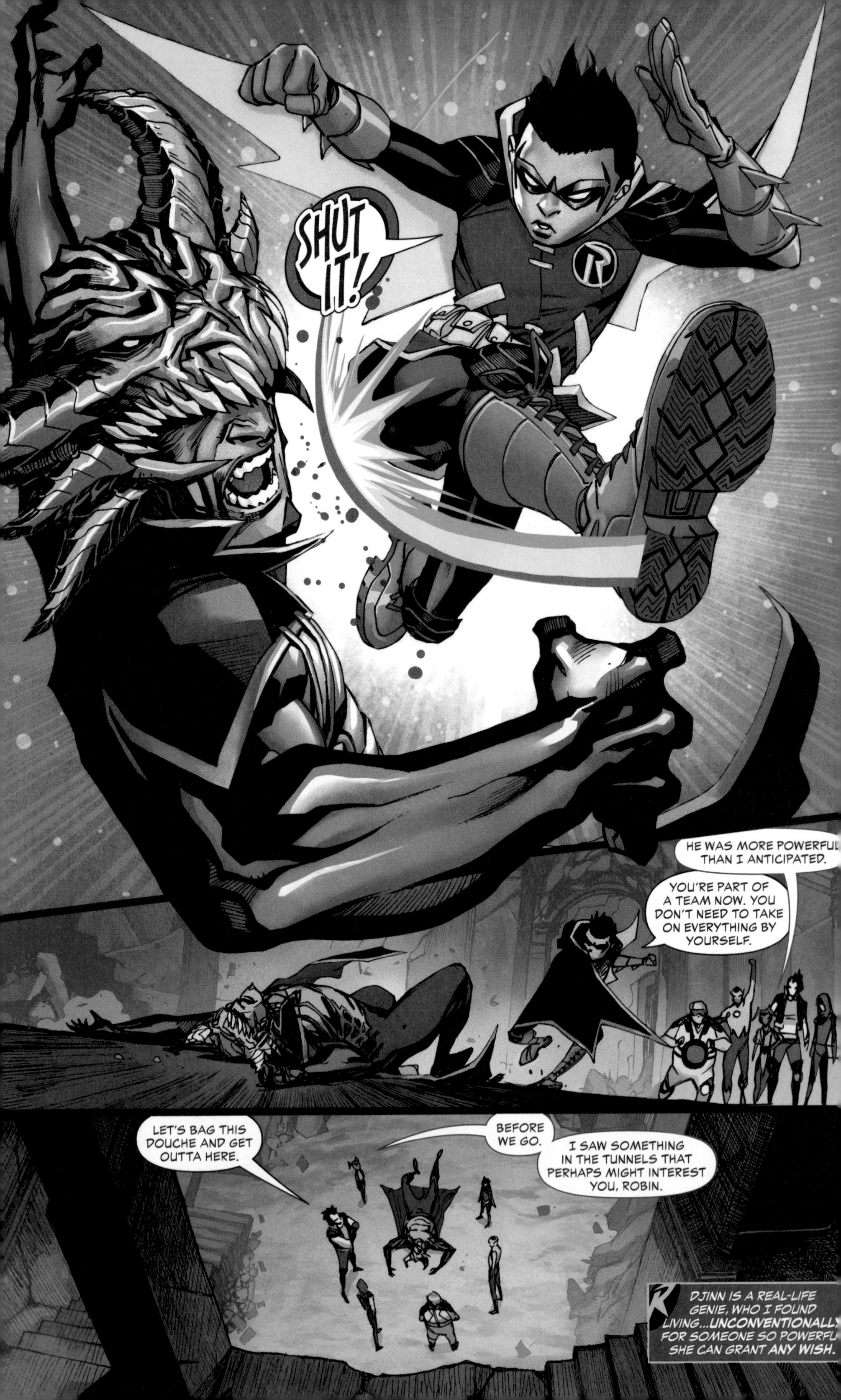
SHUT IT!
HE WAS MORE POWERFUL THAN I ANTICIPATED.
YOU'RE PART OF A TEAM NOW. YOU DON'T NEED TO TAKE ON EVERYTHING BY YOURSELF.
LET'S BAG THIS DOUCHE AND GET OUTTA HERE.
BEFORE WE GO.
I SAW SOMETHING IN THE TUNNELS THAT PERHAPS MIGHT INTEREST YOU, ROBIN.
DJINN IS A REAL-LIFE GENIE, WHO I FOUND LIVING...UNCONVENTIONALLY FOR SOMEONE SO POWERFUL SHE CAN GRANT ANY WISH.

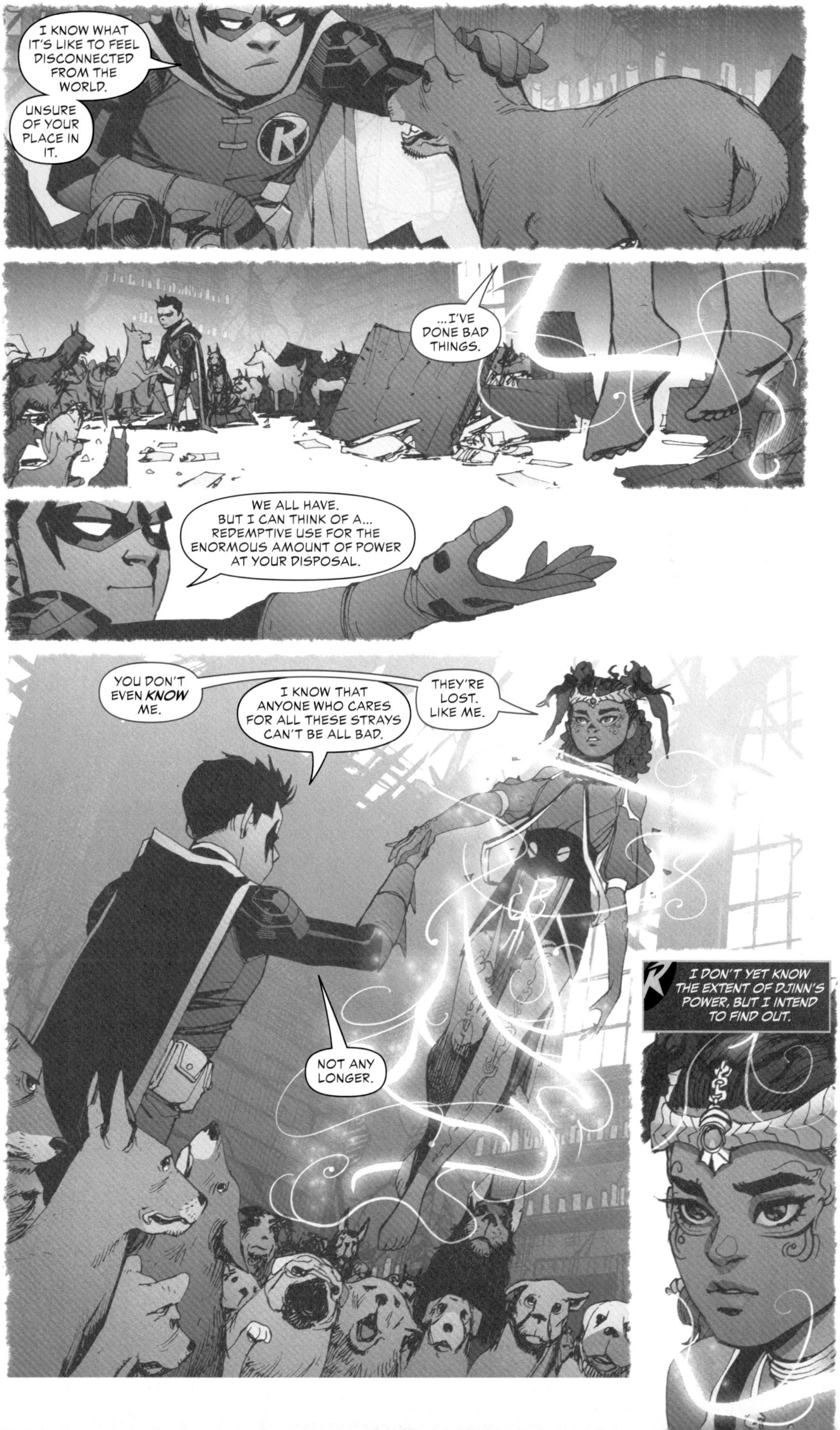
I KNOW WHAT IT'S LIKE TO FEEL DISCONNECTED FROM THE WORLD.
UNSURE OF YOUR PLACE IN IT.
...I'VE DONE BAD THINGS.
WE ALL HAVE. BUT I CAN THINK OF A... REDEMPTIVE USE FOR THE ENORMOUS AMOUNT OF POWER AT YOUR DISPOSAL.
THEY'RE LOST. LIKE ME.
YOU DON'T EVEN *KNOW* ME.
I KNOW THAT ANYONE WHO CARES FOR ALL THESE STRAYS CAN'T BE ALL BAD.
NOT ANY LONGER.
I DON'T YET KNOW THE EXTENT OF DJINN'S POWER, BUT I INTEND TO FIND OUT.

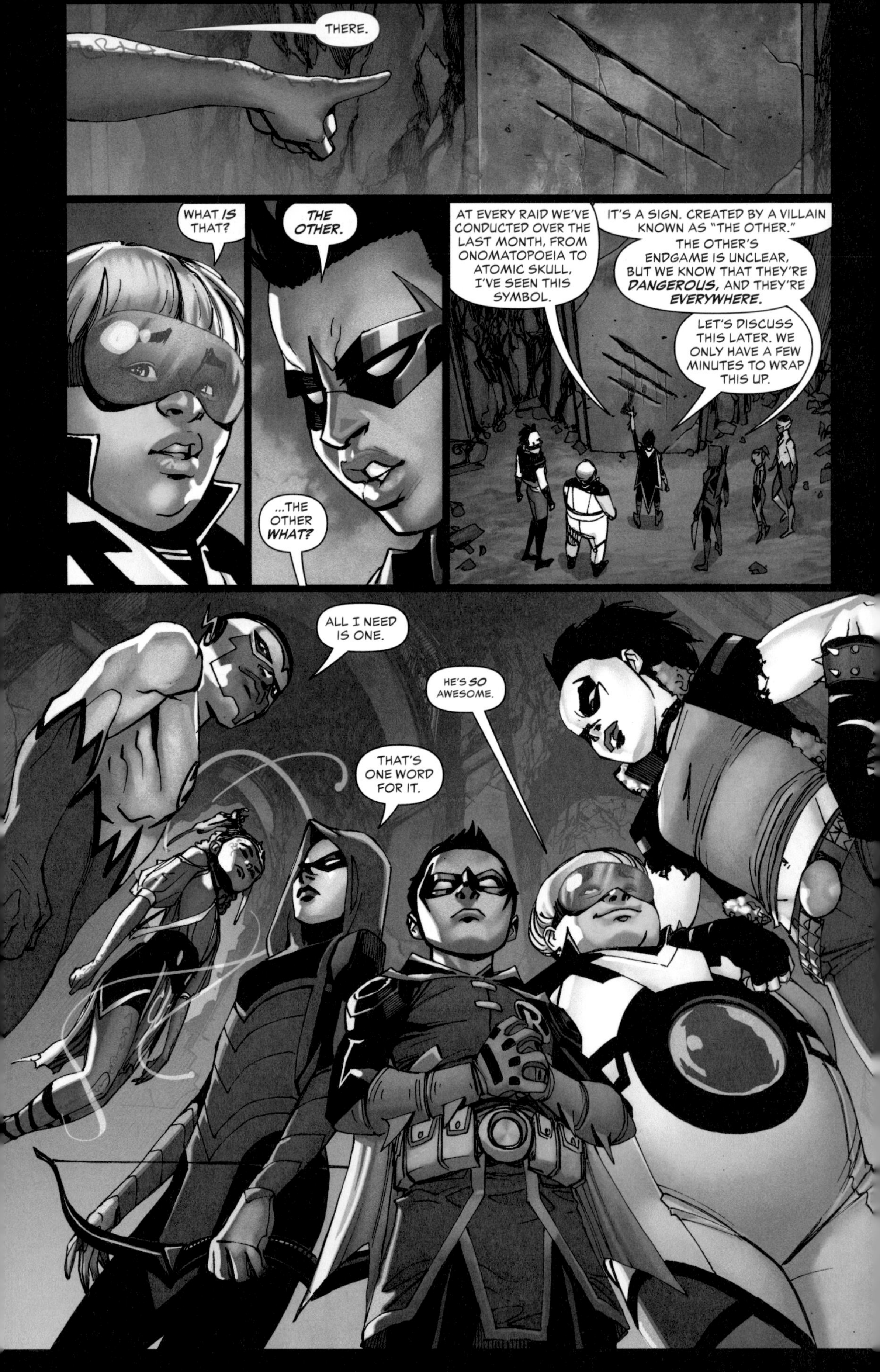

THERE.
WHAT *IS* THAT?
*THE OTHER.*
...THE OTHER *WHAT?*
AT EVERY RAID WE'VE CONDUCTED OVER THE LAST MONTH, FROM ONOMATOPOEIA TO ATOMIC SKULL, I'VE SEEN THIS SYMBOL.
IT'S A SIGN. CREATED BY A VILLAIN KNOWN AS "THE OTHER."
THE OTHER'S ENDGAME IS UNCLEAR, BUT WE KNOW THAT THEY'RE *DANGEROUS,* AND THEY'RE *EVERYWHERE.*
LET'S DISCUSS THIS LATER. WE ONLY HAVE A FEW MINUTES TO WRAP THIS UP.
ALL I NEED IS ONE.
HE'S *SO* AWESOME.
THAT'S ONE WORD FOR IT.

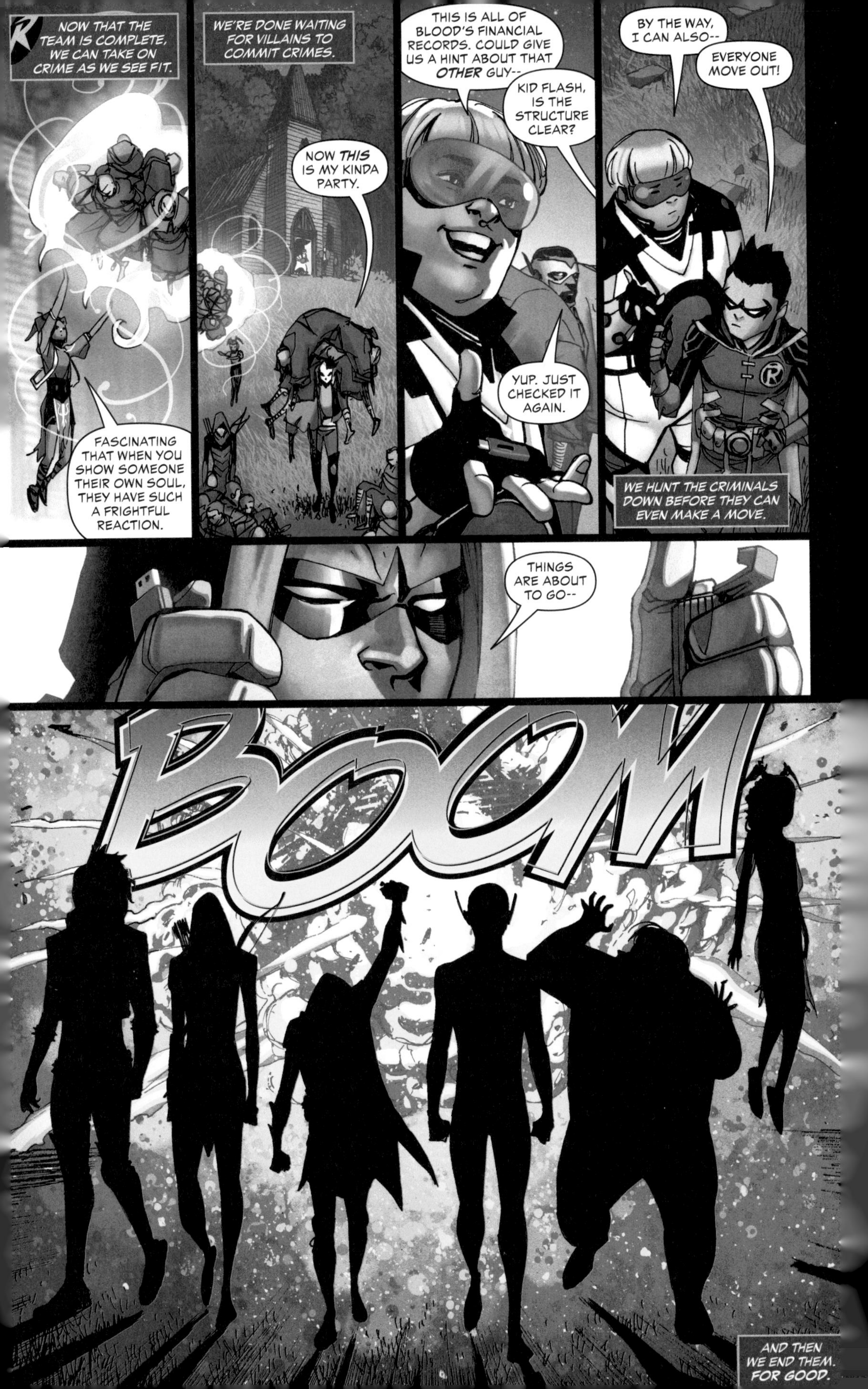
NOW THAT THE TEAM IS COMPLETE, WE CAN TAKE ON CRIME AS WE SEE FIT.
FASCINATING THAT WHEN YOU SHOW SOMEONE THEIR OWN SOUL, THEY HAVE SUCH A FRIGHTFUL REACTION.
WE'RE DONE WAITING FOR VILLAINS TO COMMIT CRIMES.
NOW THIS IS MY KINDA PARTY.
THIS IS ALL OF BLOOD'S FINANCIAL RECORDS. COULD GIVE US A HINT ABOUT THAT OTHER GUY--
KID FLASH, IS THE STRUCTURE CLEAR?
YUP. JUST CHECKED IT AGAIN.
BY THE WAY, I CAN ALSO--
EVERYONE MOVE OUT!
WE HUNT THE CRIMINALS DOWN BEFORE THEY CAN EVEN MAKE A MOVE.
THINGS ARE ABOUT TO GO--
BOOM
AND THEN WE END THEM. FOR GOOD.

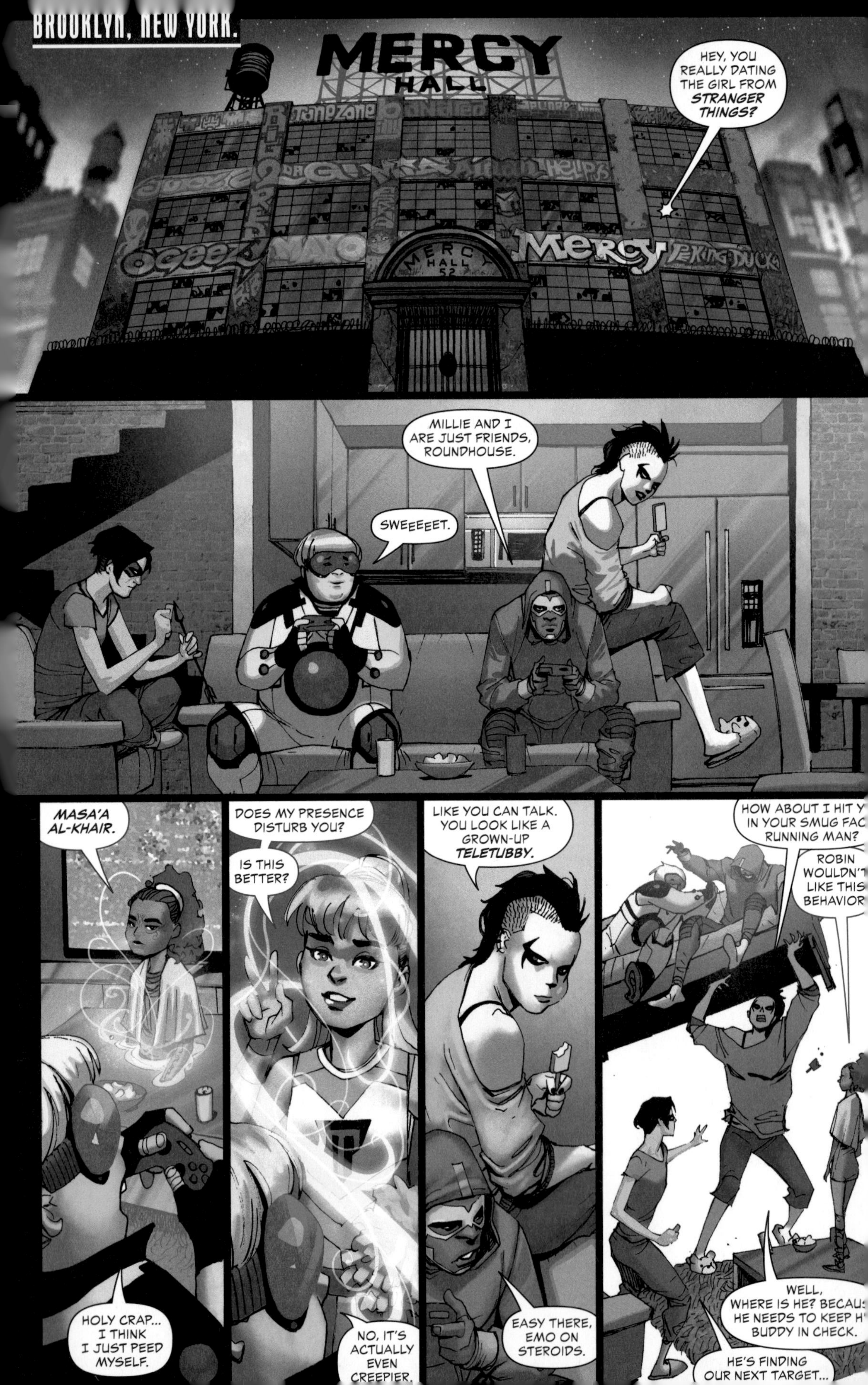
BROOKLYN, NEW YORK.
MERCY HALL
HEY, YOU REALLY DATING THE GIRL FROM STRANGER THINGS?
MILLIE AND I ARE JUST FRIENDS, ROUNDHOUSE.
SWEEEEEET.
MASA'A AL-KHAIR.
HOLY CRAP... I THINK I JUST PEED MYSELF.
DOES MY PRESENCE DISTURB YOU?
IS THIS BETTER?
NO, IT'S ACTUALLY EVEN CREEPIER.
LIKE YOU CAN TALK. YOU LOOK LIKE A GROWN-UP TELETUBBY.
EASY THERE, EMO ON STEROIDS.
HOW ABOUT I HIT Y IN YOUR SMUG FAC RUNNING MAN?
ROBIN WOULDN'T LIKE THIS BEHAVIOR
WELL, WHERE IS HE? BECAU HE NEEDS TO KEEP H BUDDY IN CHECK.
HE'S FINDING OUR NEXT TARGET...

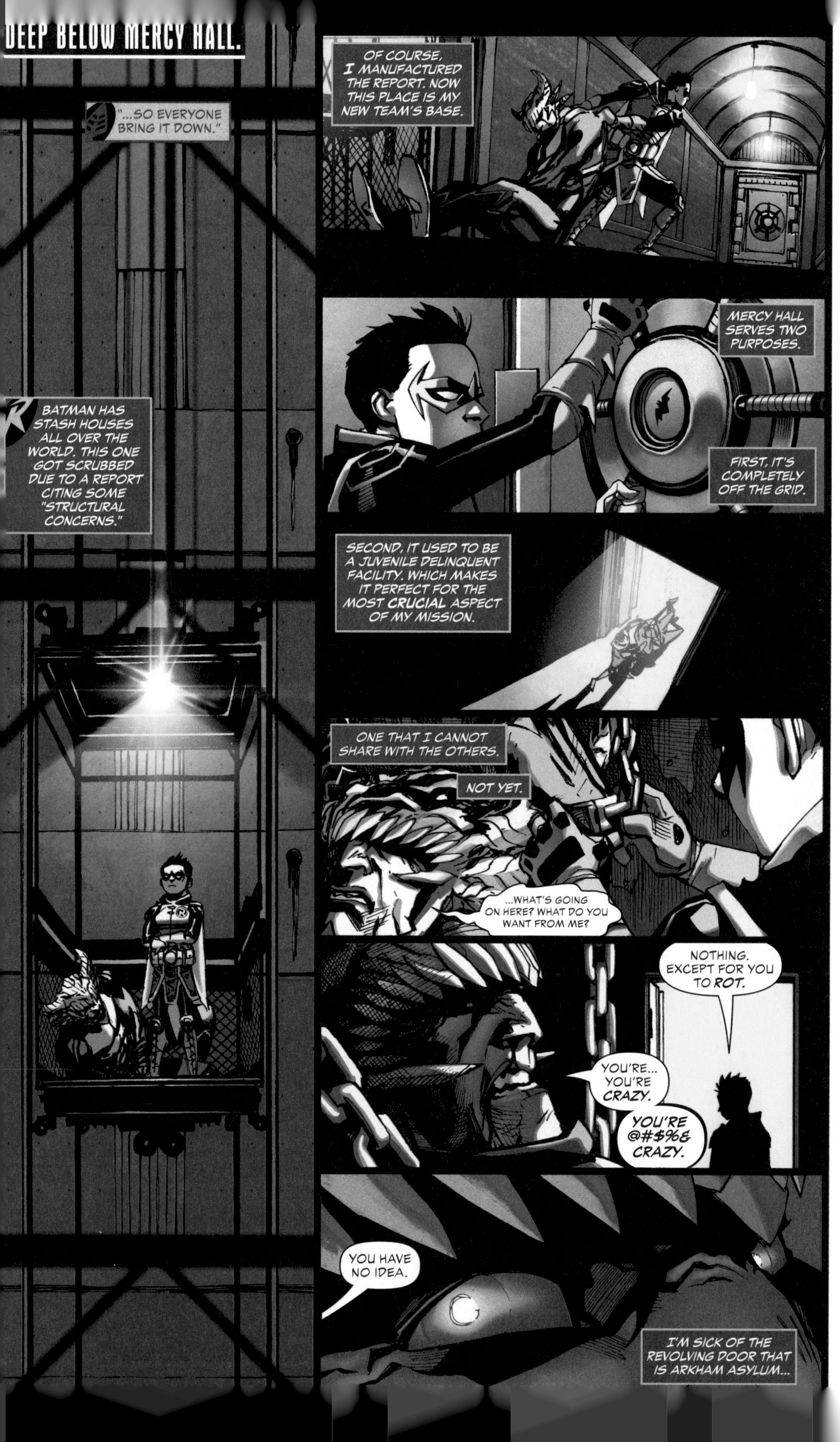
DEEP BELOW MERCY HALL.
"...SO EVERYONE BRING IT DOWN."
BATMAN HAS STASH HOUSES ALL OVER THE WORLD. THIS ONE GOT SCRUBBED DUE TO A REPORT CITING SOME "STRUCTURAL CONCERNS."
OF COURSE, I MANUFACTURED THE REPORT. NOW THIS PLACE IS MY NEW TEAM'S BASE.
MERCY HALL SERVES TWO PURPOSES.
FIRST, IT'S COMPLETELY OFF THE GRID.
SECOND, IT USED TO BE A JUVENILE DELINQUENT FACILITY. WHICH MAKES IT PERFECT FOR THE MOST CRUCIAL ASPECT OF MY MISSION.
ONE THAT I CANNOT SHARE WITH THE OTHERS.
NOT YET.
...WHAT'S GOING ON HERE? WHAT DO YOU WANT FROM ME?
NOTHING. EXCEPT FOR YOU TO ROT.
YOU'RE... YOU'RE CRAZY.
YOU'RE @#$%& CRAZY.
YOU HAVE NO IDEA.
I'M SICK OF THE REVOLVING DOOR THAT IS ARKHAM ASYLUM...

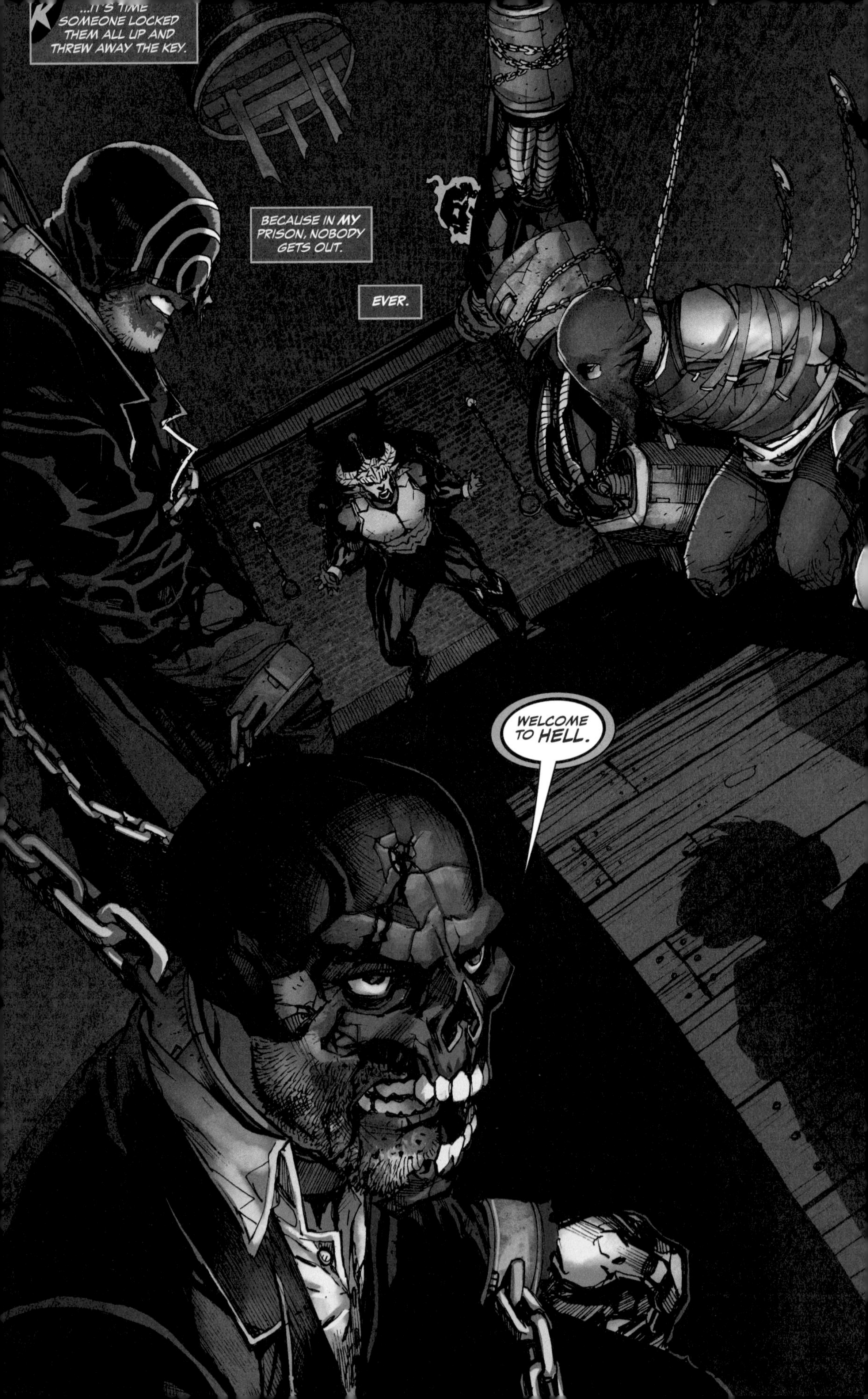
...IT'S TIME SOMEONE LOCKED THEM ALL UP AND THREW AWAY THE KEY.
BECAUSE IN MY PRISON, NOBODY GETS OUT.
EVER.
WELCOME TO HELL.

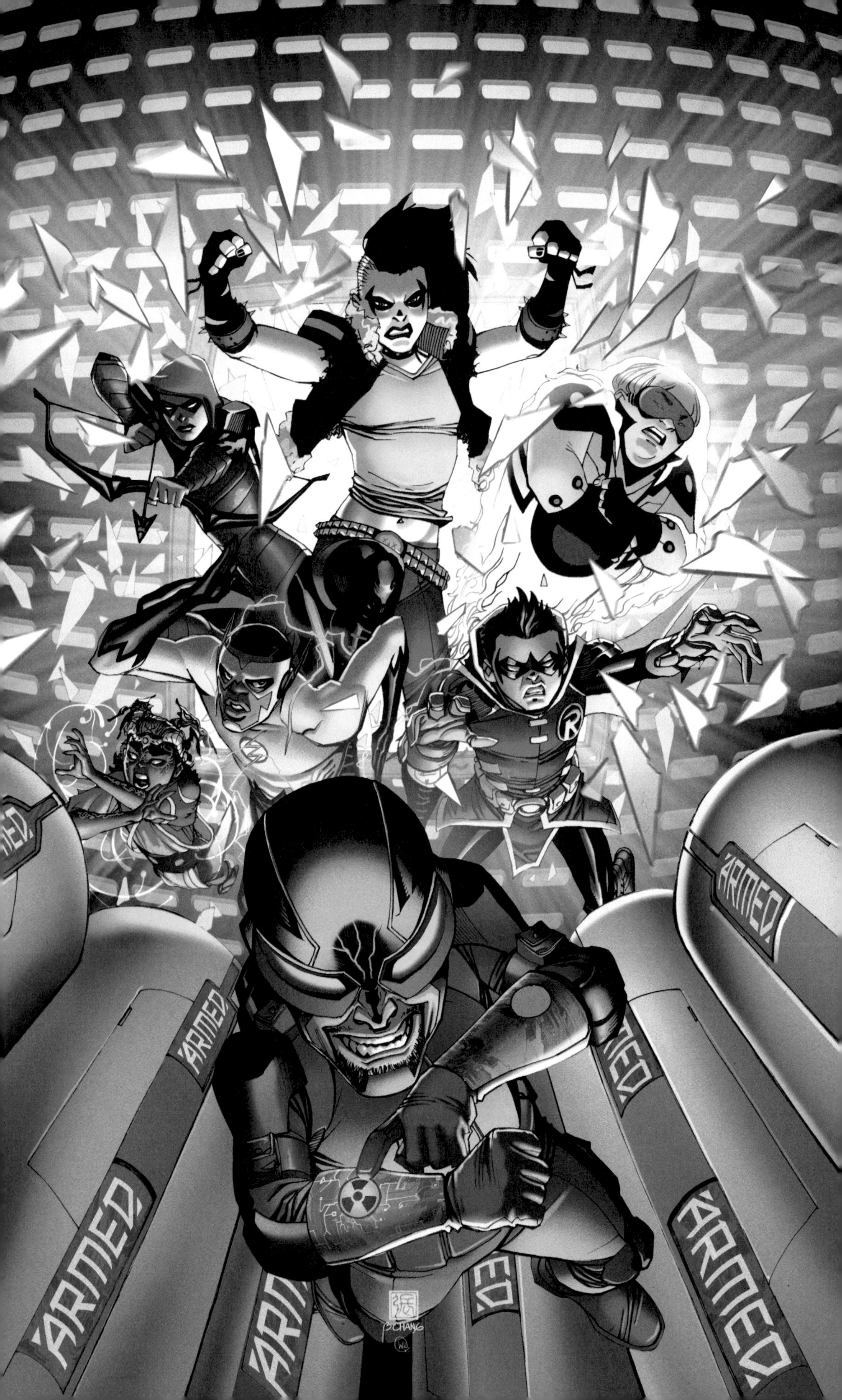
ARMED.
ARMED.
ARMED.
ARMED.
ARMED.

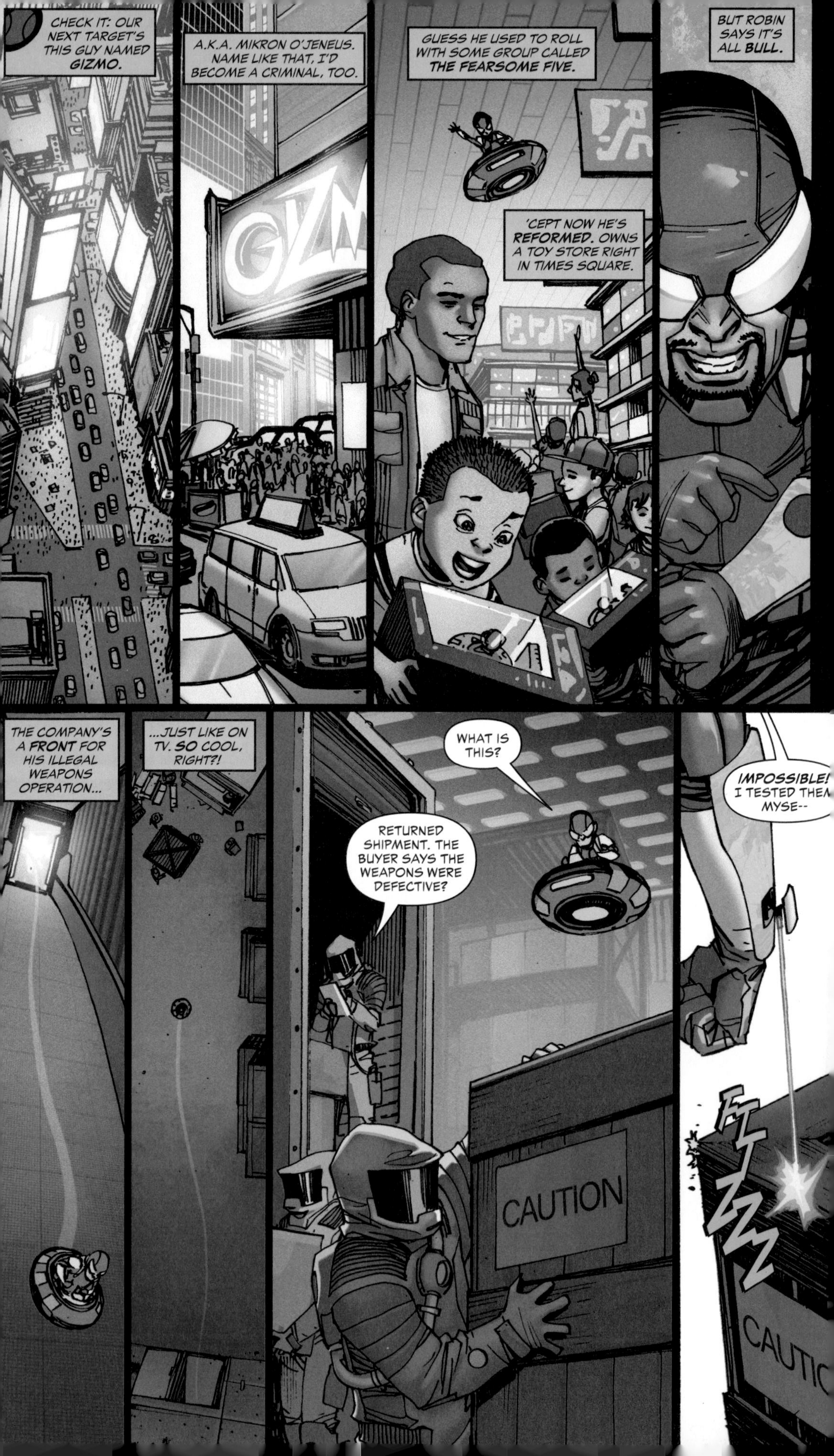

CHECK IT: OUR NEXT TARGET'S THIS GUY NAMED GIZMO.
A.K.A. MIKRON O'JENEUS. NAME LIKE THAT, I'D BECOME A CRIMINAL, TOO.
GIZM
GUESS HE USED TO ROLL WITH SOME GROUP CALLED THE FEARSOME FIVE.
'CEPT NOW HE'S REFORMED. OWNS A TOY STORE RIGHT IN TIMES SQUARE.
BUT ROBIN SAYS IT'S ALL BULL.
THE COMPANY'S A FRONT FOR HIS ILLEGAL WEAPONS OPERATION...
...JUST LIKE ON TV. SO COOL, RIGHT?!
WHAT IS THIS?
RETURNED SHIPMENT. THE BUYER SAYS THE WEAPONS WERE DEFECTIVE?
CAUTION
IMPOSSIBLE! I TESTED THEM MYSE--
FZZZ
CAUTI

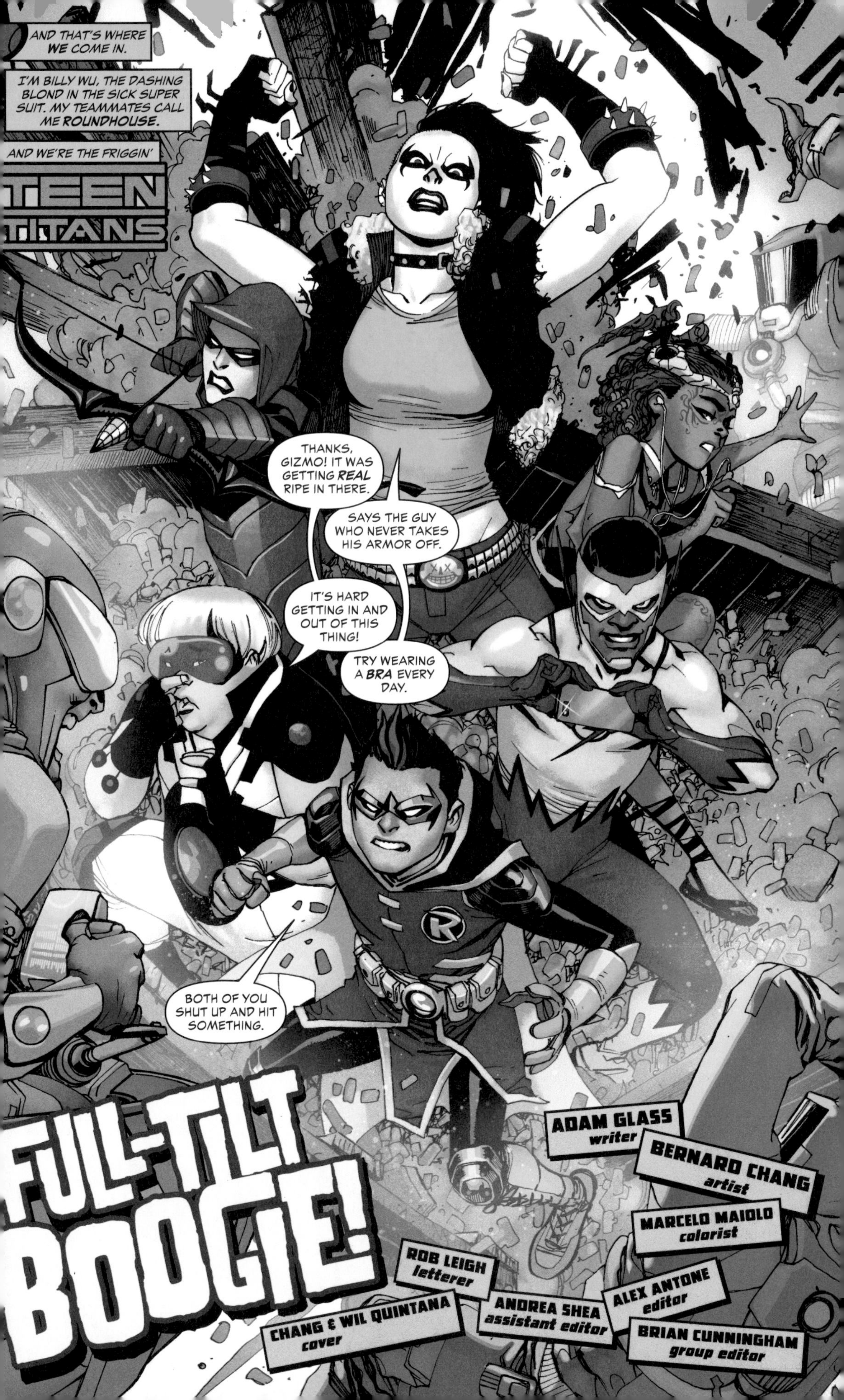
AND THAT'S WHERE WE COME IN.
I'M BILLY WU, THE DASHING BLOND IN THE SICK SUPER SUIT. MY TEAMMATES CALL ME ROUNDHOUSE.
AND WE'RE THE FRIGGIN'
TEEN TITANS
THANKS, GIZMO! IT WAS GETTING REAL RIPE IN THERE.
SAYS THE GUY WHO NEVER TAKES HIS ARMOR OFF.
IT'S HARD GETTING IN AND OUT OF THIS THING!
TRY WEARING A BRA EVERY DAY.
BOTH OF YOU SHUT UP AND HIT SOMETHING.
FULL-TILT BOOGIE!
ADAM GLASS writer
BERNARD CHANG artist
MARCELO MAIOLO colorist
ROB LEIGH letterer
CHANG & WIL QUINTANA cover
ANDREA SHEA assistant editor
ALEX ANTONE editor
BRIAN CUNNINGHAM group editor

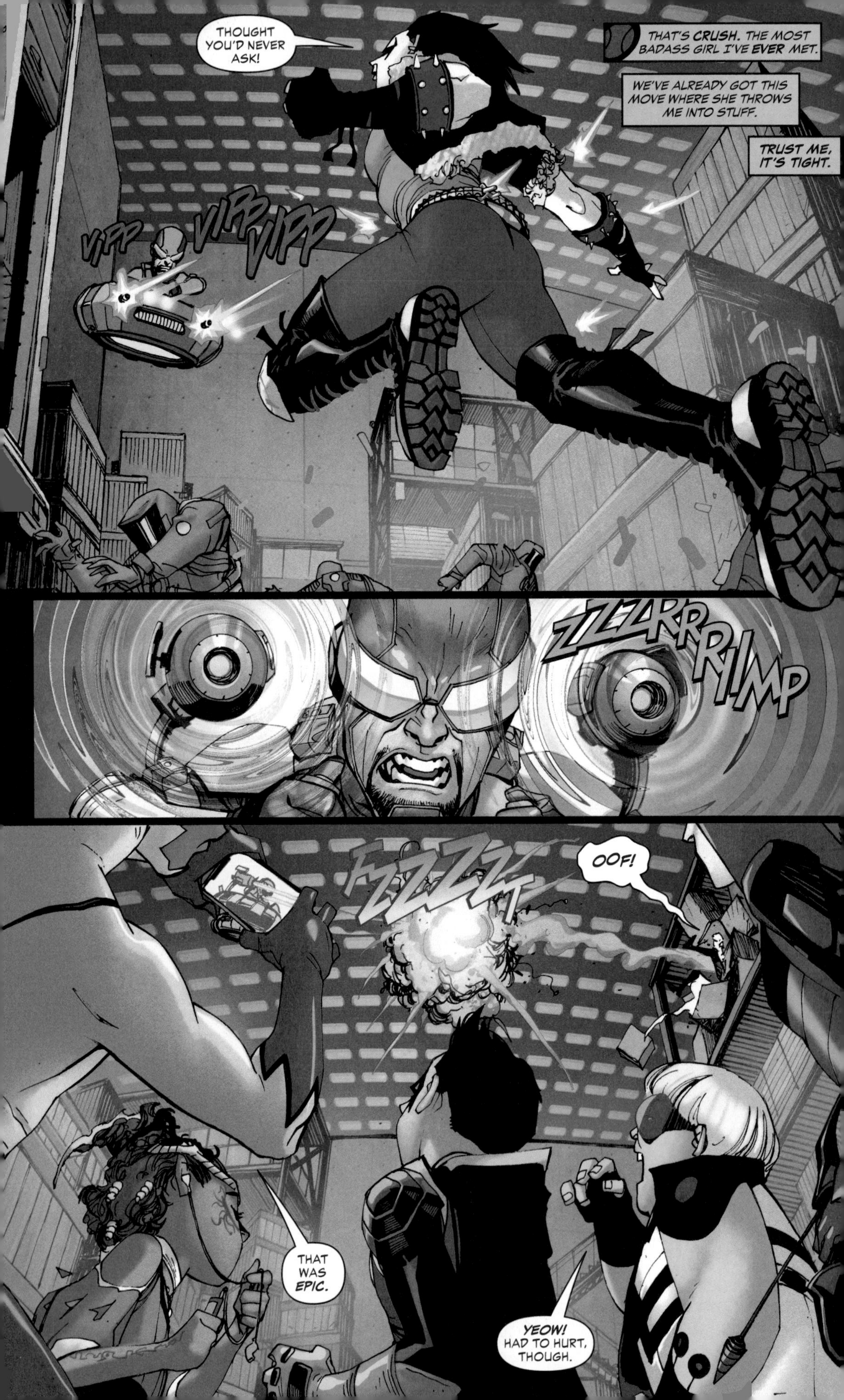
THOUGHT YOU'D NEVER ASK!
THAT'S CRUSH. THE MOST BADASS GIRL I'VE EVER MET.
WE'VE ALREADY GOT THIS MOVE WHERE SHE THROWS ME INTO STUFF.
TRUST ME, IT'S TIGHT.
VIPP VIPP VIPP
ZZZZRRRIMP
FZZZZT
OOF!
THAT WAS EPIC.
YEOW! HAD TO HURT, THOUGH.

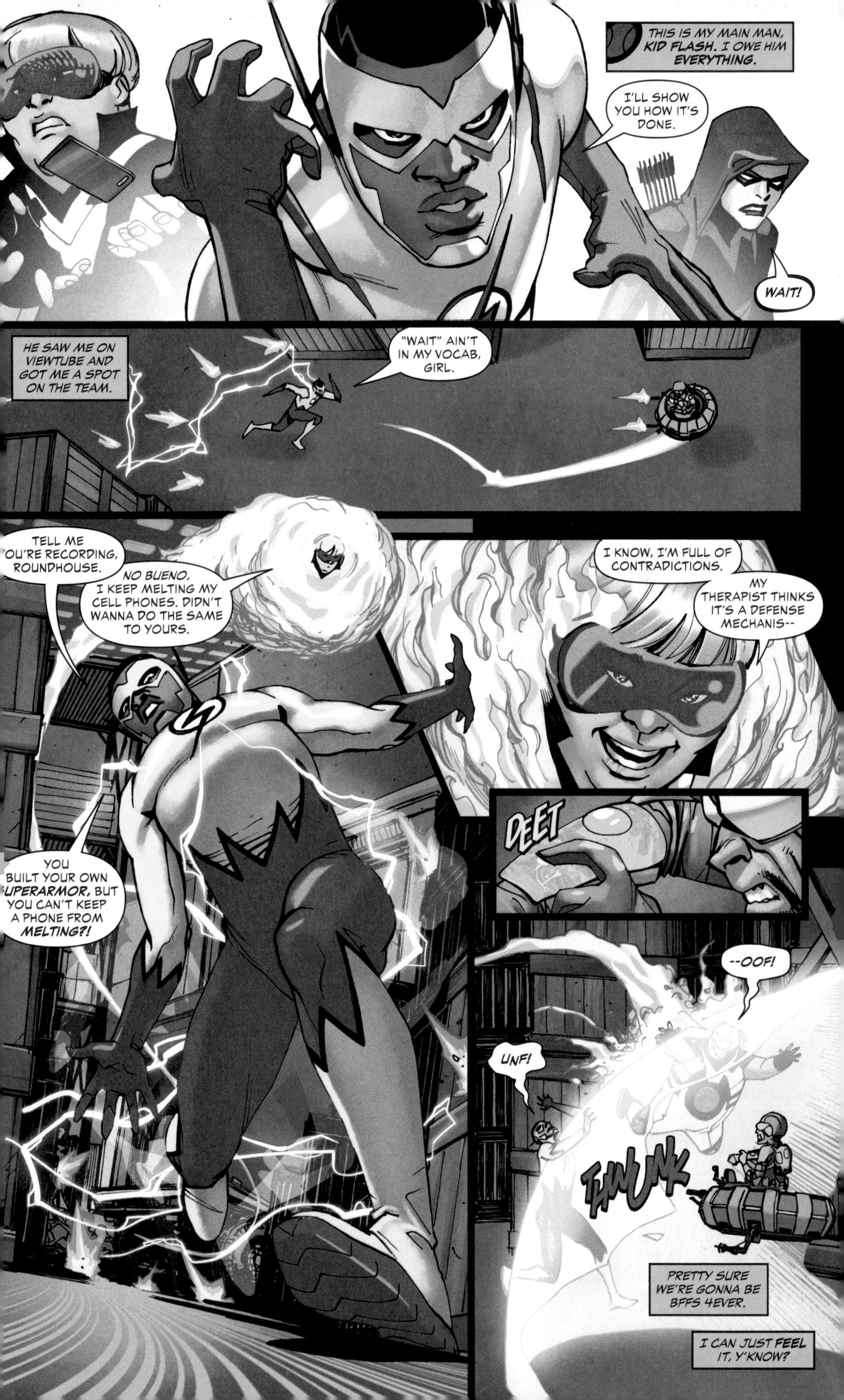
THIS IS MY MAIN MAN, KID FLASH. I OWE HIM EVERYTHING.
I'LL SHOW YOU HOW IT'S DONE.
WAIT!
HE SAW ME ON VIEWTUBE AND GOT ME A SPOT ON THE TEAM.
"WAIT" AIN'T IN MY VOCAB, GIRL.
TELL ME YOU'RE RECORDING, ROUNDHOUSE.
NO BUENO, I KEEP MELTING MY CELL PHONES. DIDN'T WANNA DO THE SAME TO YOURS.
YOU BUILT YOUR OWN SUPERARMOR, BUT YOU CAN'T KEEP A PHONE FROM MELTING?!
I KNOW, I'M FULL OF CONTRADICTIONS.
MY THERAPIST THINKS IT'S A DEFENSE MECHANIS--
DEET
--OOF!
UNF!
THWUNK
PRETTY SURE WE'RE GONNA BE BFFS 4EVER.
I CAN JUST FEEL IT, Y'KNOW?

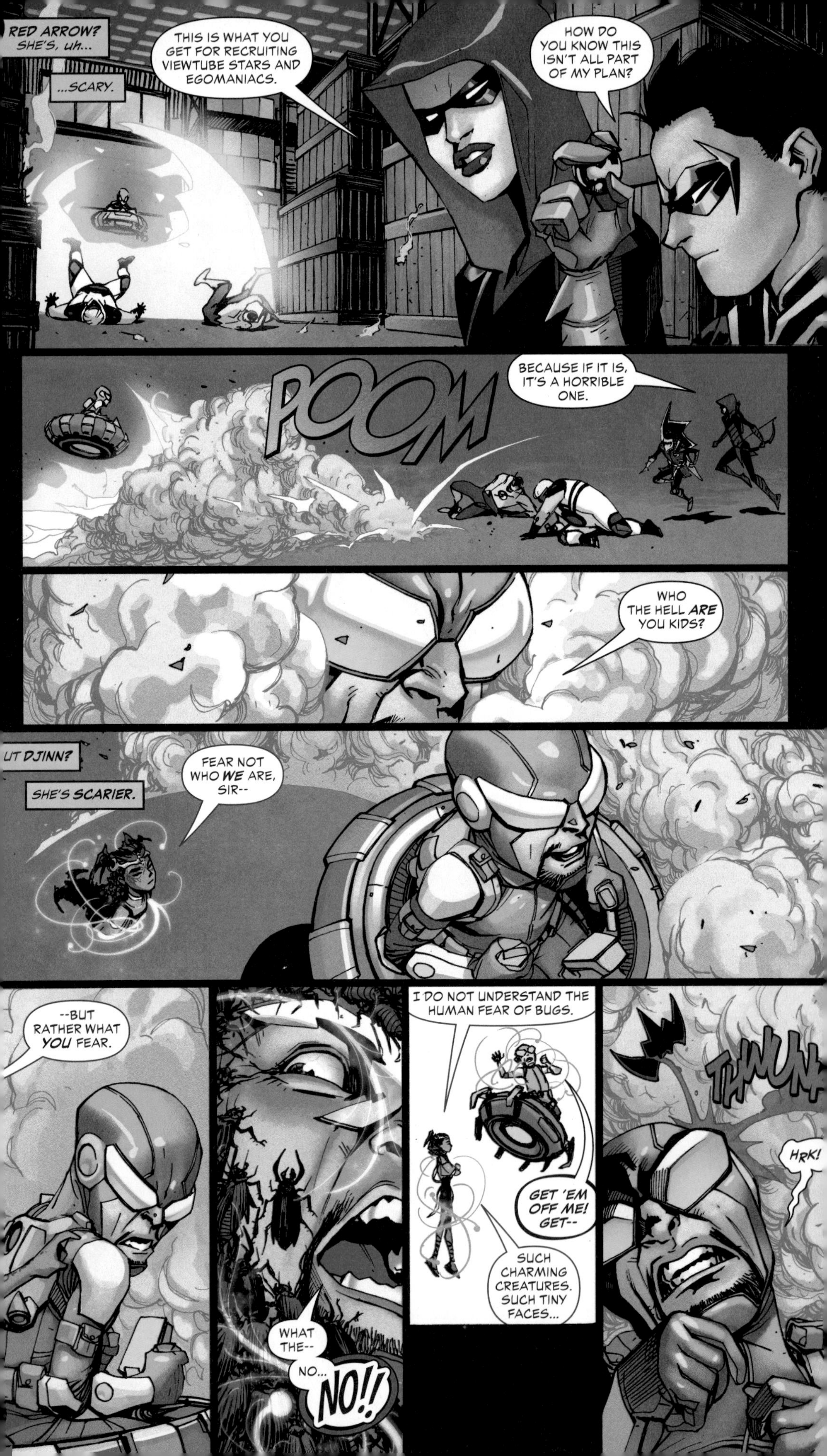
RED ARROW? SHE'S, uh...
...SCARY.
THIS IS WHAT YOU GET FOR RECRUITING VIEWTUBE STARS AND EGOMANIACS.
HOW DO YOU KNOW THIS ISN'T ALL PART OF MY PLAN?
POOM
BECAUSE IF IT IS, IT'S A HORRIBLE ONE.
WHO THE HELL ARE YOU KIDS?
UT DJINN?
SHE'S SCARIER.
FEAR NOT WHO WE ARE, SIR--
--BUT RATHER WHAT YOU FEAR.
WHAT THE--
NO...
NO!!
I DO NOT UNDERSTAND THE HUMAN FEAR OF BUGS.
GET 'EM OFF ME! GET--
SUCH CHARMING CREATURES. SUCH TINY FACES...
THWUNK
HRK!

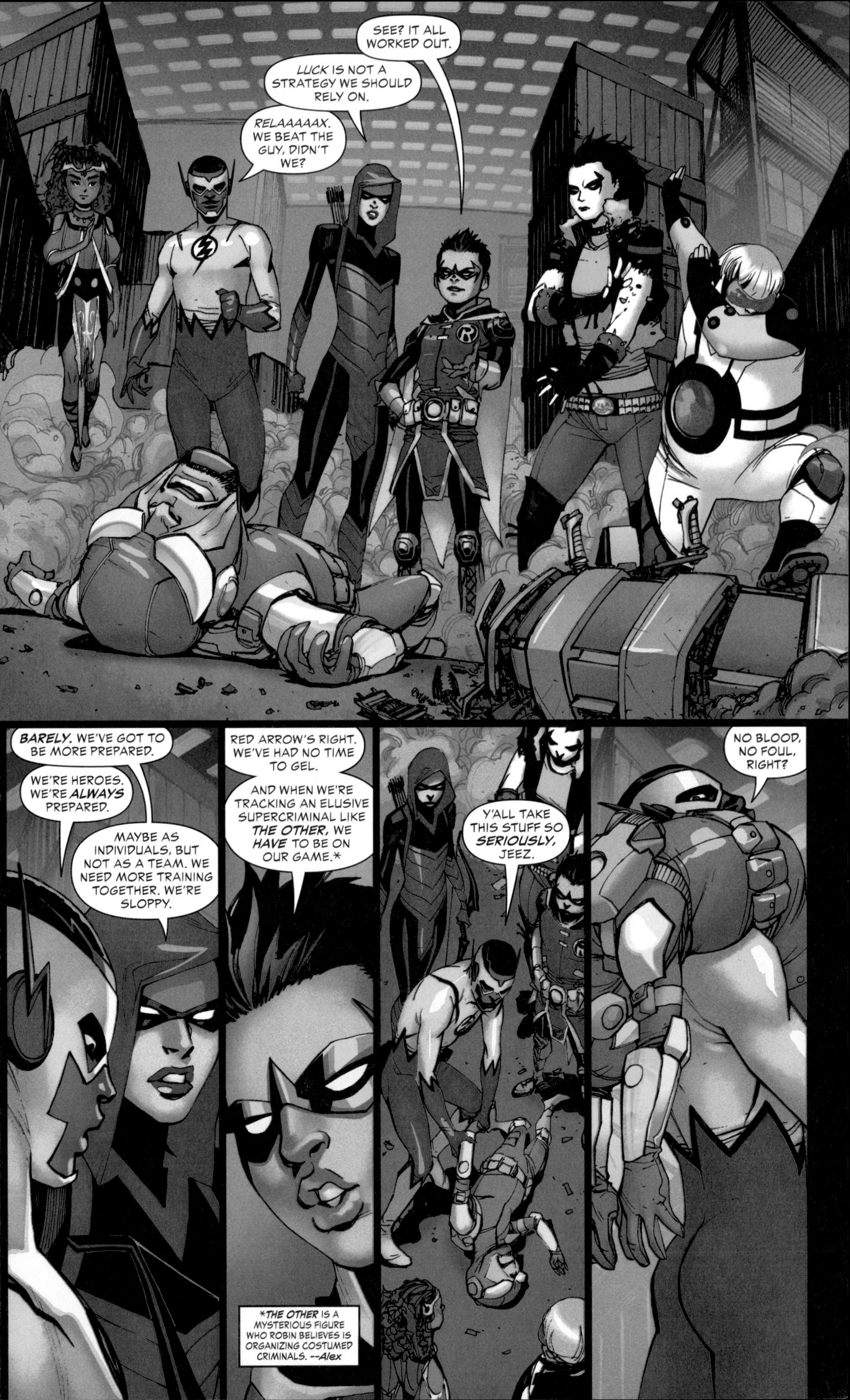

RELAAAAAX. WE BEAT THE GUY, DIDN'T WE?
LUCK IS NOT A STRATEGY WE SHOULD RELY ON.
SEE? IT ALL WORKED OUT.
BARELY. WE'VE GOT TO BE MORE PREPARED.
WE'RE HEROES. WE'RE ALWAYS PREPARED.
MAYBE AS INDIVIDUALS, BUT NOT AS A TEAM. WE NEED MORE TRAINING TOGETHER. WE'RE SLOPPY.
RED ARROW'S RIGHT. WE'VE HAD NO TIME TO GEL.
AND WHEN WE'RE TRACKING AN ELUSIVE SUPERCRIMINAL LIKE THE OTHER, WE HAVE TO BE ON OUR GAME.*
*THE OTHER IS A MYSTERIOUS FIGURE WHO ROBIN BELIEVES IS ORGANIZING COSTUMED CRIMINALS. --Alex
Y'ALL TAKE THIS STUFF SO SERIOUSLY, JEEZ.
NO BLOOD, NO FOUL, RIGHT?

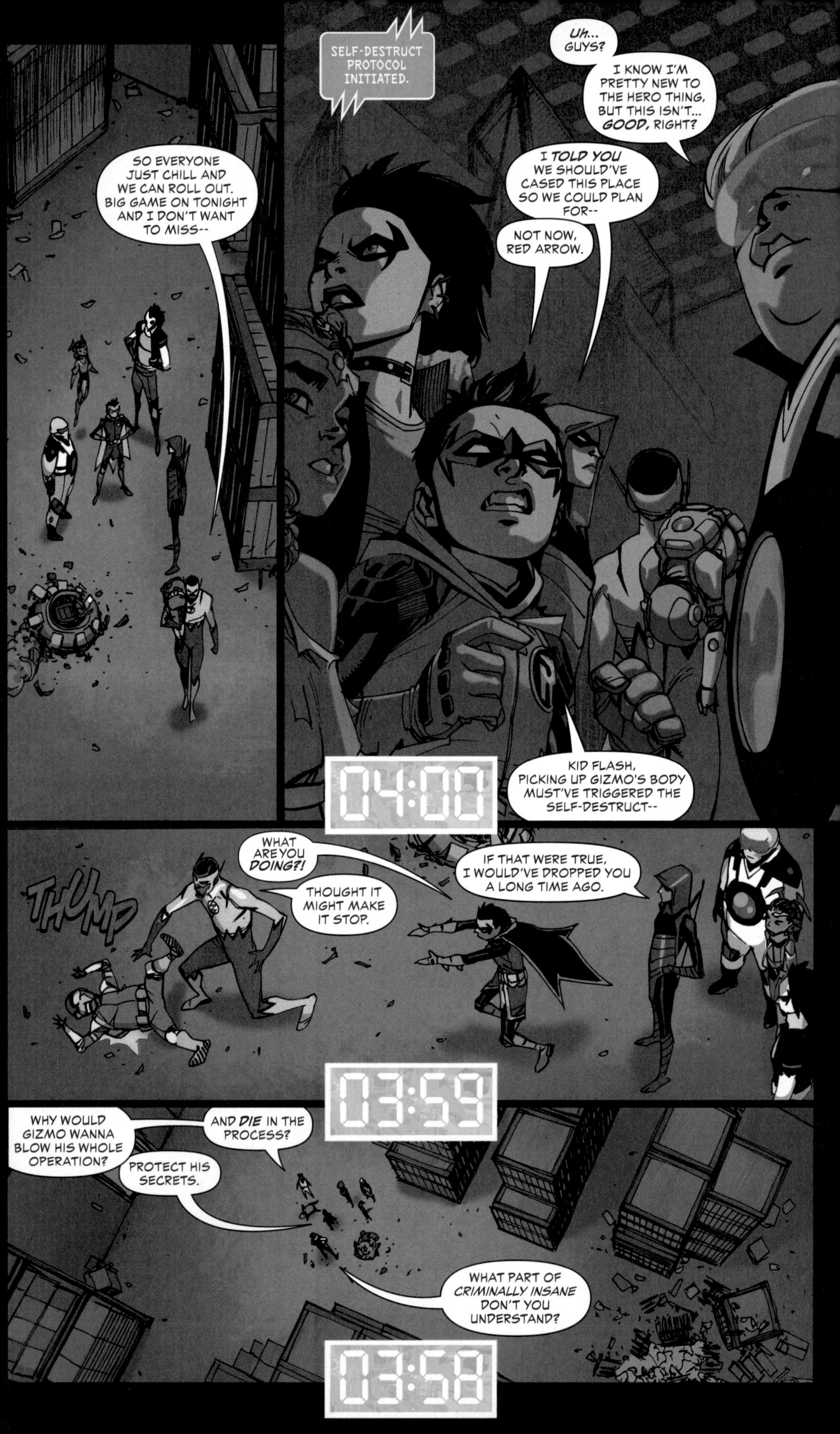

SO EVERYONE JUST CHILL AND WE CAN ROLL OUT. BIG GAME ON TONIGHT AND I DON'T WANT TO MISS--
SELF-DESTRUCT PROTOCOL INITIATED.
Uh... GUYS?
I KNOW I'M PRETTY NEW TO THE HERO THING, BUT THIS ISN'T... GOOD, RIGHT?
I TOLD YOU WE SHOULD'VE CASED THIS PLACE SO WE COULD PLAN FOR--
NOT NOW, RED ARROW.
KID FLASH, PICKING UP GIZMO'S BODY MUST'VE TRIGGERED THE SELF-DESTRUCT--
04:00
THUMP
WHAT ARE YOU DOING?!
THOUGHT IT MIGHT MAKE IT STOP.
IF THAT WERE TRUE, I WOULD'VE DROPPED YOU A LONG TIME AGO.
03:59
WHY WOULD GIZMO WANNA BLOW HIS WHOLE OPERATION?
AND DIE IN THE PROCESS?
PROTECT HIS SECRETS.
WHAT PART OF CRIMINALLY INSANE DON'T YOU UNDERSTAND?
03:58

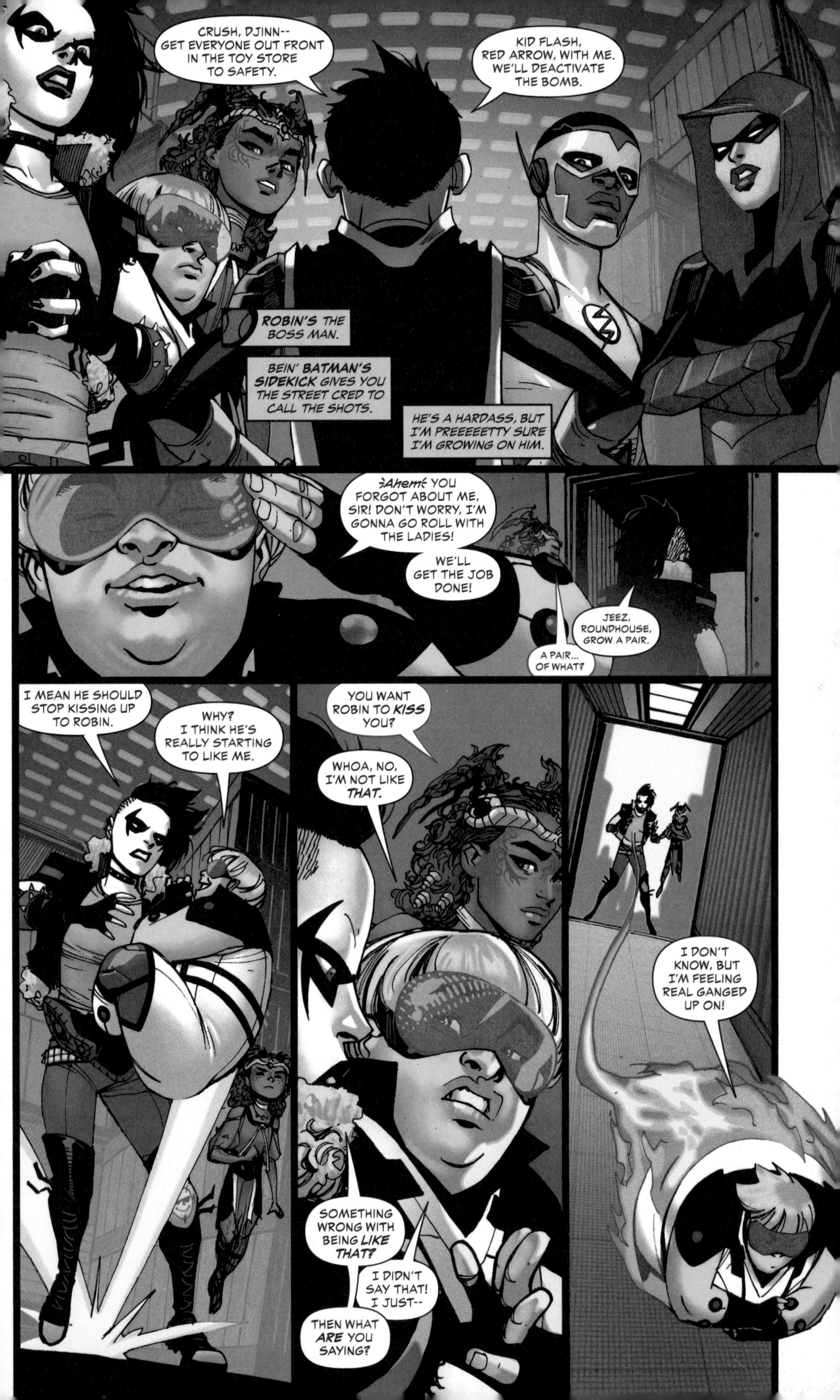
CRUSH, DJINN-- GET EVERYONE OUT FRONT IN THE TOY STORE TO SAFETY.
KID FLASH, RED ARROW, WITH ME. WE'LL DEACTIVATE THE BOMB.
*ROBIN'S* THE BOSS MAN.
BEIN' *BATMAN'S SIDEKICK* GIVES YOU THE STREET CRED TO CALL THE SHOTS.
HE'S A HARDASS, BUT I'M PREEEEETTY SURE I'M GROWING ON HIM.
*Ahem* YOU FORGOT ABOUT ME, SIR! DON'T WORRY, I'M GONNA GO ROLL WITH THE LADIES!
WE'LL GET THE JOB DONE!
JEEZ, ROUNDHOUSE, GROW A PAIR.
A PAIR... OF WHAT?
I MEAN HE SHOULD STOP KISSING UP TO ROBIN.
WHY? I THINK HE'S REALLY STARTING TO LIKE ME.
YOU WANT ROBIN TO *KISS* YOU?
WHOA, NO, I'M NOT LIKE *THAT.*
SOMETHING WRONG WITH BEING *LIKE THAT?*
I DIDN'T SAY THAT! I JUST--
THEN WHAT *ARE* YOU SAYING?
I DON'T KNOW, BUT I'M FEELING REAL GANGED UP ON!

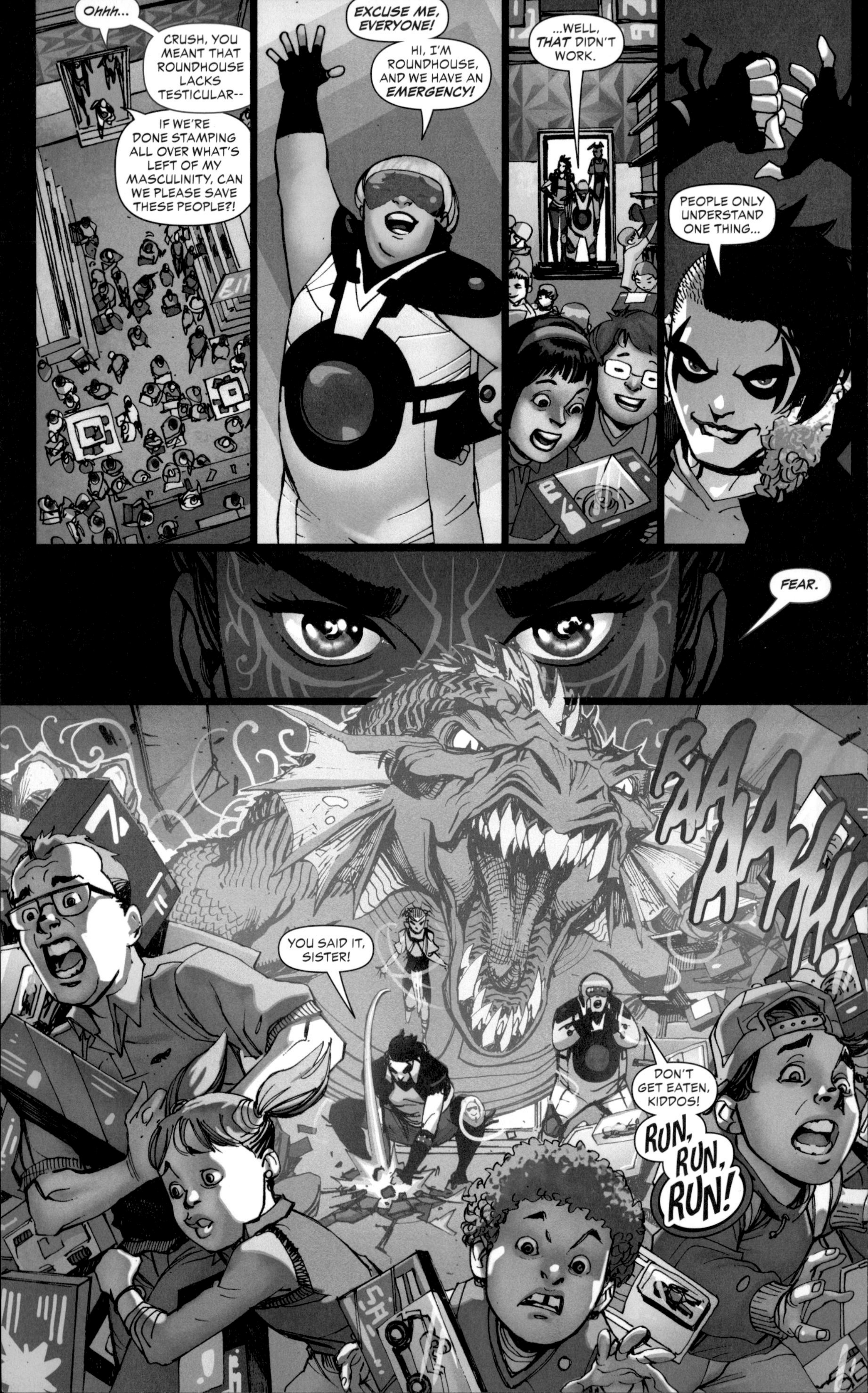
Ohhh...
CRUSH, YOU MEANT THAT ROUNDHOUSE LACKS TESTICULAR--
IF WE'RE DONE STAMPING ALL OVER WHAT'S LEFT OF MY MASCULINITY, CAN WE PLEASE SAVE THESE PEOPLE?!
EXCUSE ME, EVERYONE!
HI, I'M ROUNDHOUSE, AND WE HAVE AN EMERGENCY!
...WELL, THAT DIDN'T WORK.
PEOPLE ONLY UNDERSTAND ONE THING...
FEAR.
RAAAHH!
YOU SAID IT, SISTER!
DON'T GET EATEN, KIDDOS!
RUN, RUN, RUN!

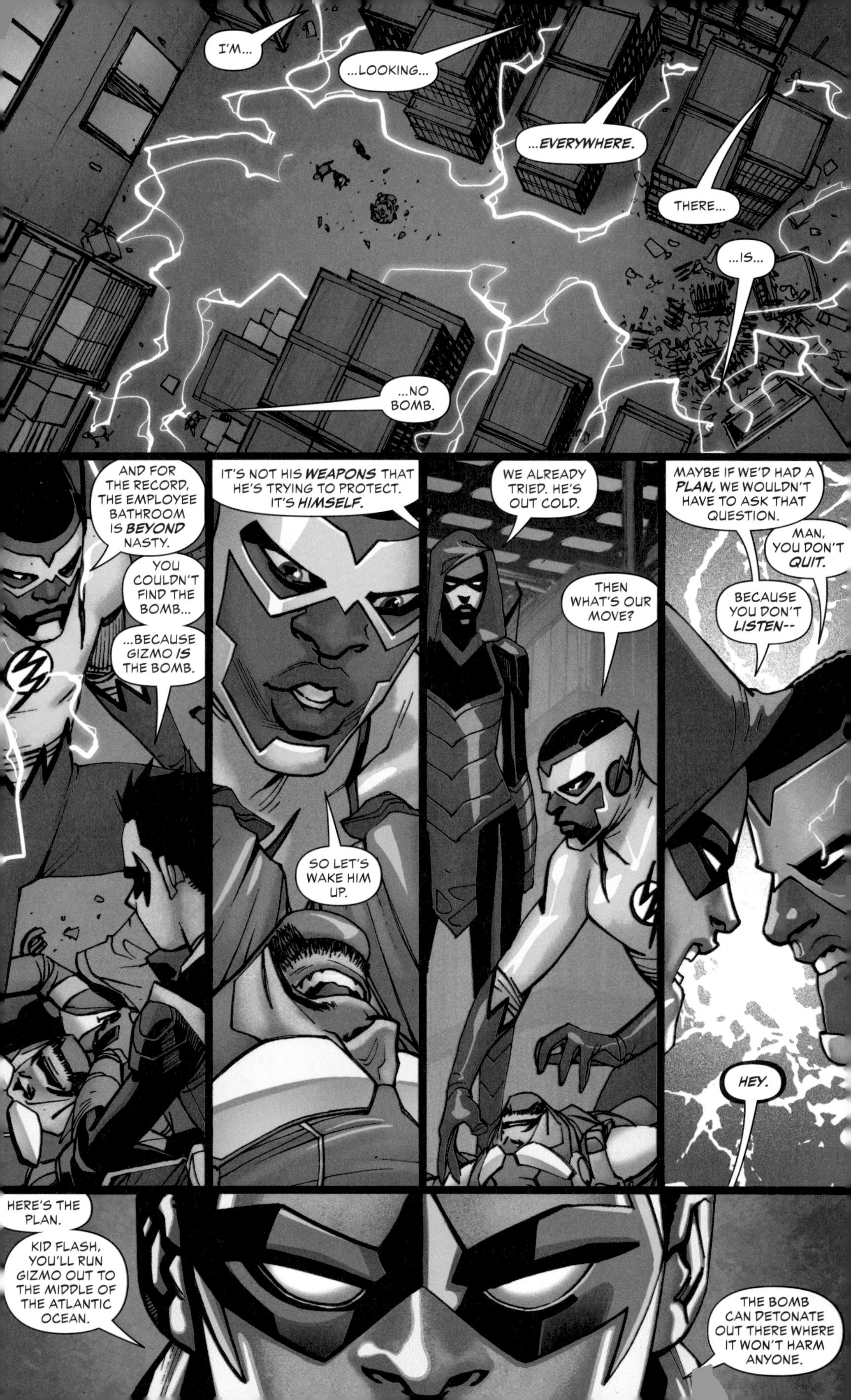
I'M...
...LOOKING...
...EVERYWHERE.
THERE...
...IS...
...NO BOMB.
AND FOR THE RECORD, THE EMPLOYEE BATHROOM IS BEYOND NASTY.
YOU COULDN'T FIND THE BOMB...
...BECAUSE GIZMO IS THE BOMB.
IT'S NOT HIS WEAPONS THAT HE'S TRYING TO PROTECT. IT'S HIMSELF.
SO LET'S WAKE HIM UP.
WE ALREADY TRIED. HE'S OUT COLD.
THEN WHAT'S OUR MOVE?
MAYBE IF WE'D HAD A PLAN, WE WOULDN'T HAVE TO ASK THAT QUESTION.
MAN, YOU DON'T QUIT.
BECAUSE YOU DON'T LISTEN--
HEY.
HERE'S THE PLAN.
KID FLASH, YOU'LL RUN GIZMO OUT TO THE MIDDLE OF THE ATLANTIC OCEAN.
THE BOMB CAN DETONATE OUT THERE WHERE IT WON'T HARM ANYONE.

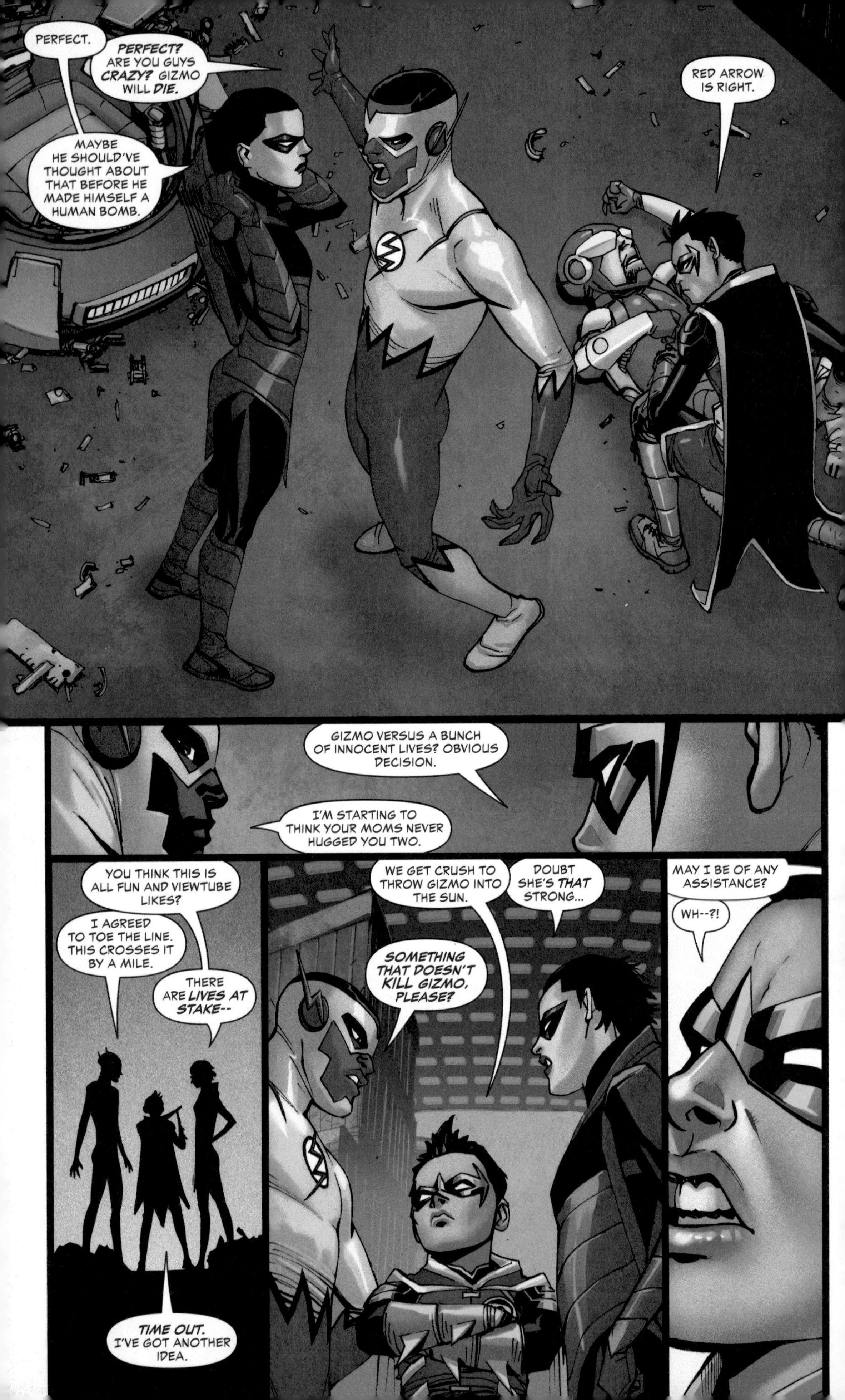
PERFECT.
PERFECT? ARE YOU GUYS CRAZY? GIZMO WILL DIE.
MAYBE HE SHOULD'VE THOUGHT ABOUT THAT BEFORE HE MADE HIMSELF A HUMAN BOMB.
RED ARROW IS RIGHT.
GIZMO VERSUS A BUNCH OF INNOCENT LIVES? OBVIOUS DECISION.
I'M STARTING TO THINK YOUR MOMS NEVER HUGGED YOU TWO.
YOU THINK THIS IS ALL FUN AND VIEWTUBE LIKES?
I AGREED TO TOE THE LINE. THIS CROSSES IT BY A MILE.
THERE ARE LIVES AT STAKE--
TIME OUT. I'VE GOT ANOTHER IDEA.
WE GET CRUSH TO THROW GIZMO INTO THE SUN.
DOUBT SHE'S THAT STRONG...
SOMETHING THAT DOESN'T KILL GIZMO, PLEASE?
MAY I BE OF ANY ASSISTANCE?
WH--?!

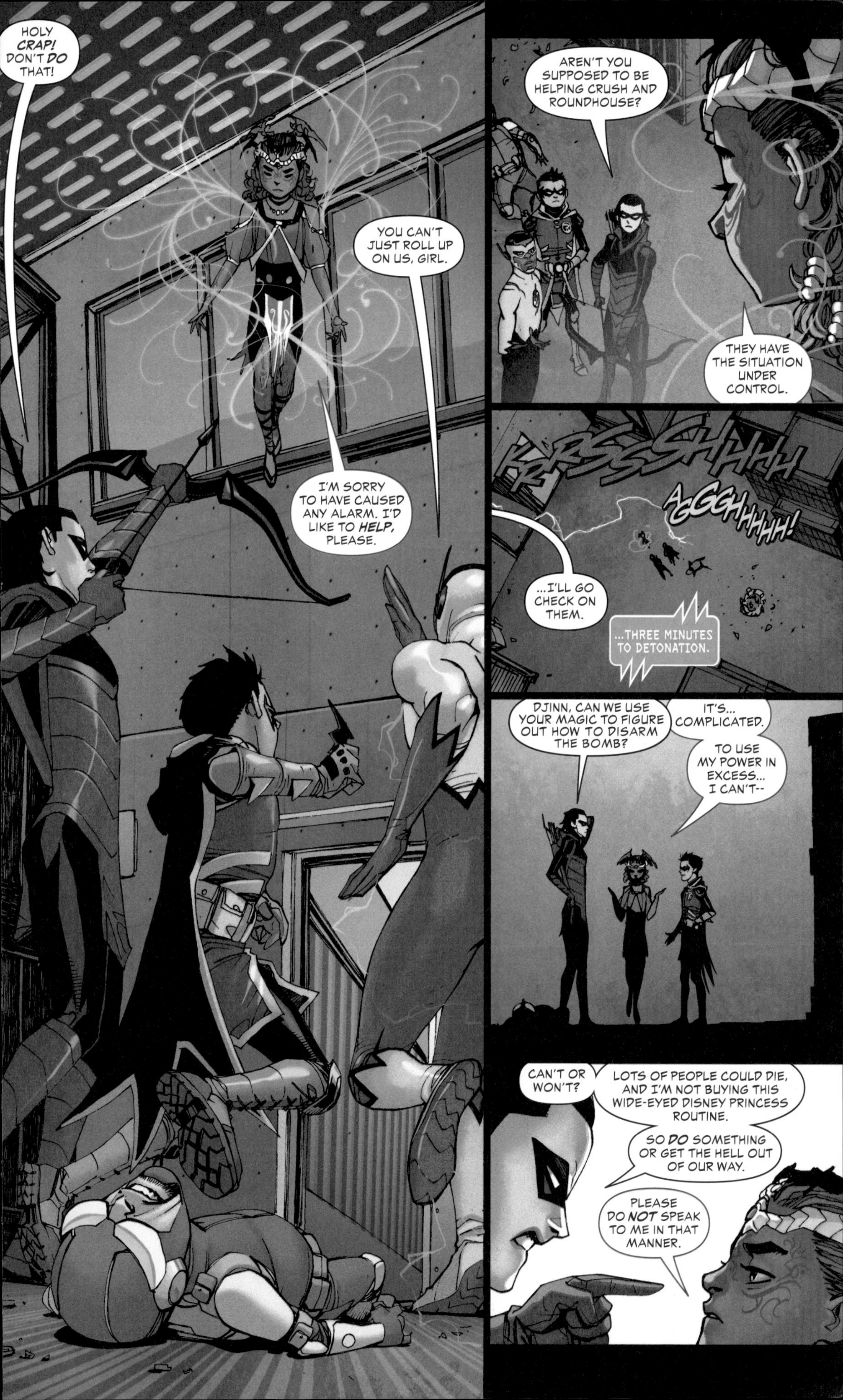
HOLY CRAP! DON'T DO THAT!
YOU CAN'T JUST ROLL UP ON US, GIRL.
I'M SORRY TO HAVE CAUSED ANY ALARM. I'D LIKE TO HELP, PLEASE.
AREN'T YOU SUPPOSED TO BE HELPING CRUSH AND ROUNDHOUSE?
THEY HAVE THE SITUATION UNDER CONTROL.
KRRSSSSHHHH
AGGGHHHHH!
...I'LL GO CHECK ON THEM.
...THREE MINUTES TO DETONATION.
DJINN, CAN WE USE YOUR MAGIC TO FIGURE OUT HOW TO DISARM THE BOMB?
IT'S... COMPLICATED.
TO USE MY POWER IN EXCESS... I CAN'T--
CAN'T OR WON'T?
LOTS OF PEOPLE COULD DIE, AND I'M NOT BUYING THIS WIDE-EYED DISNEY PRINCESS ROUTINE.
SO DO SOMETHING OR GET THE HELL OUT OF OUR WAY.
PLEASE DO NOT SPEAK TO ME IN THAT MANNER.

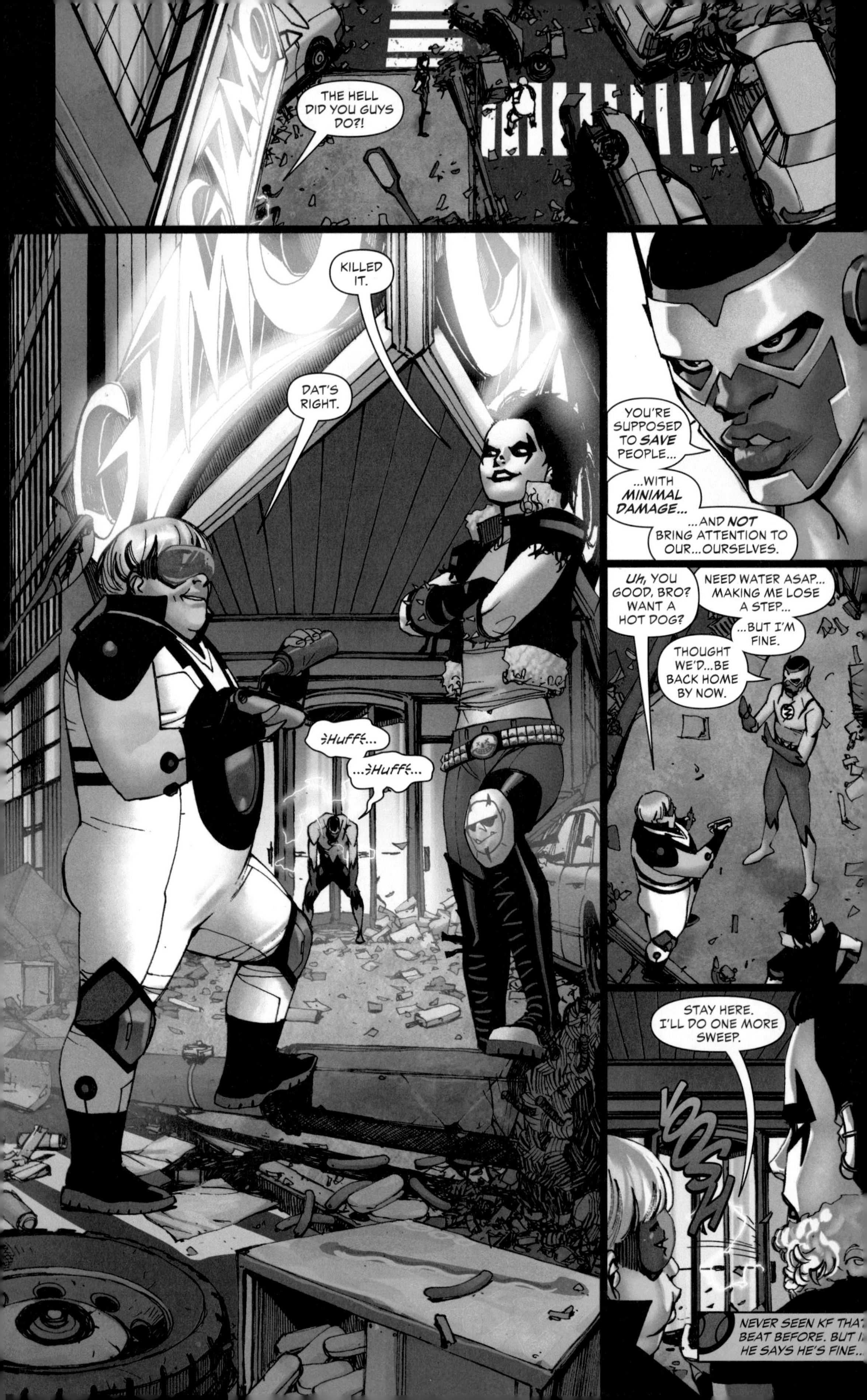
THE HELL DID YOU GUYS DO?!
KILLED IT.
DAT'S RIGHT.
Huff...
...Huff...
YOU'RE SUPPOSED TO SAVE PEOPLE...
...WITH MINIMAL DAMAGE...
...AND NOT BRING ATTENTION TO OUR...OURSELVES.
Uh, YOU GOOD, BRO? WANT A HOT DOG?
NEED WATER ASAP... MAKING ME LOSE A STEP...
...BUT I'M FINE.
THOUGHT WE'D...BE BACK HOME BY NOW.
STAY HERE. I'LL DO ONE MORE SWEEP.
VOOM
NEVER SEEN KF THA BEAT BEFORE. BUT I HE SAYS HE'S FINE...

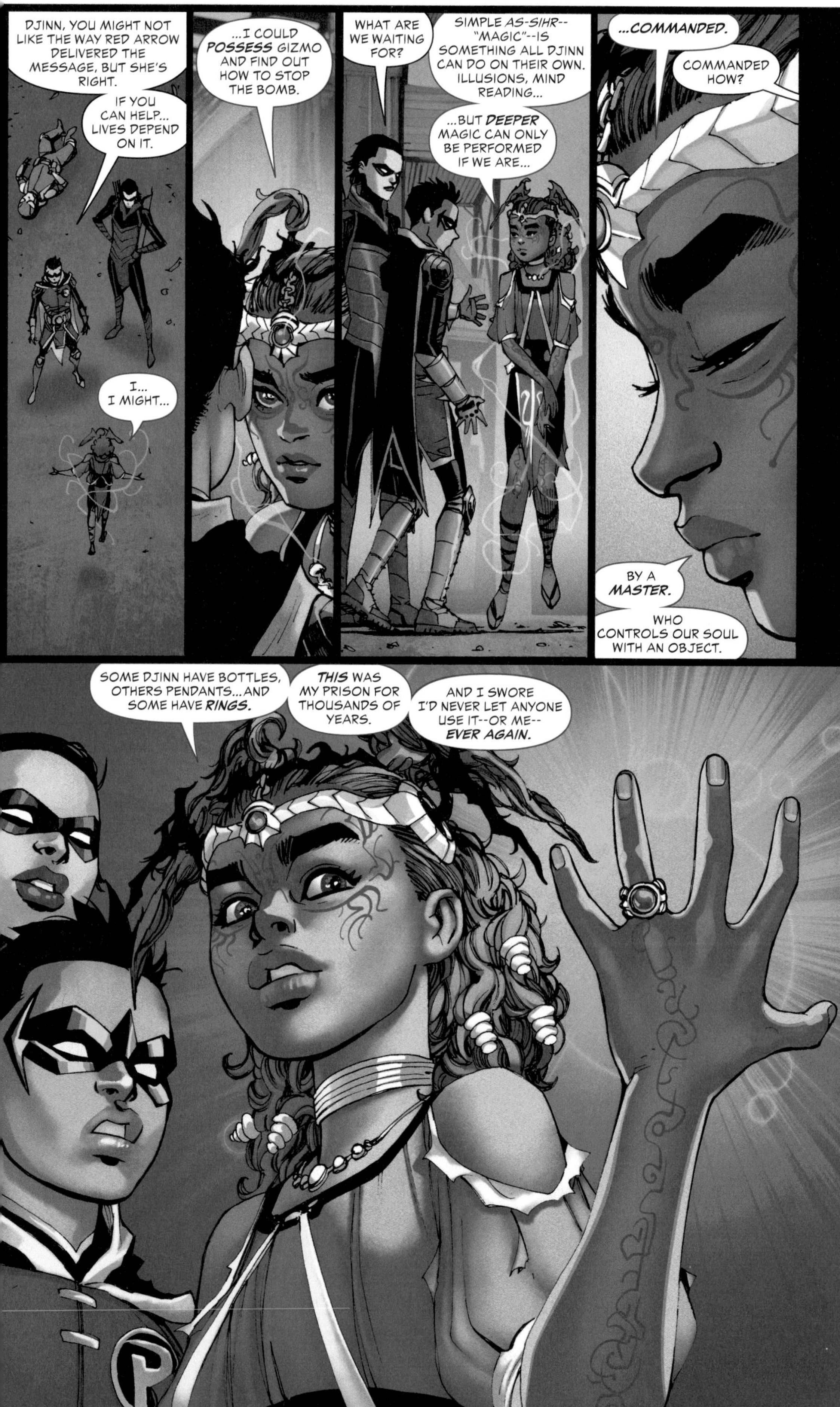
DJINN, YOU MIGHT NOT LIKE THE WAY RED ARROW DELIVERED THE MESSAGE, BUT SHE'S RIGHT.
IF YOU CAN HELP... LIVES DEPEND ON IT.
I... I MIGHT...
...I COULD POSSESS GIZMO AND FIND OUT HOW TO STOP THE BOMB.
WHAT ARE WE WAITING FOR?
SIMPLE AS-SIHR-- "MAGIC"--IS SOMETHING ALL DJINN CAN DO ON THEIR OWN. ILLUSIONS, MIND READING...
...BUT DEEPER MAGIC CAN ONLY BE PERFORMED IF WE ARE...
...COMMANDED.
COMMANDED HOW?
BY A MASTER.
WHO CONTROLS OUR SOUL WITH AN OBJECT.
SOME DJINN HAVE BOTTLES, OTHERS PENDANTS...AND SOME HAVE RINGS.
THIS WAS MY PRISON FOR THOUSANDS OF YEARS.
AND I SWORE I'D NEVER LET ANYONE USE IT--OR ME-- EVER AGAIN.

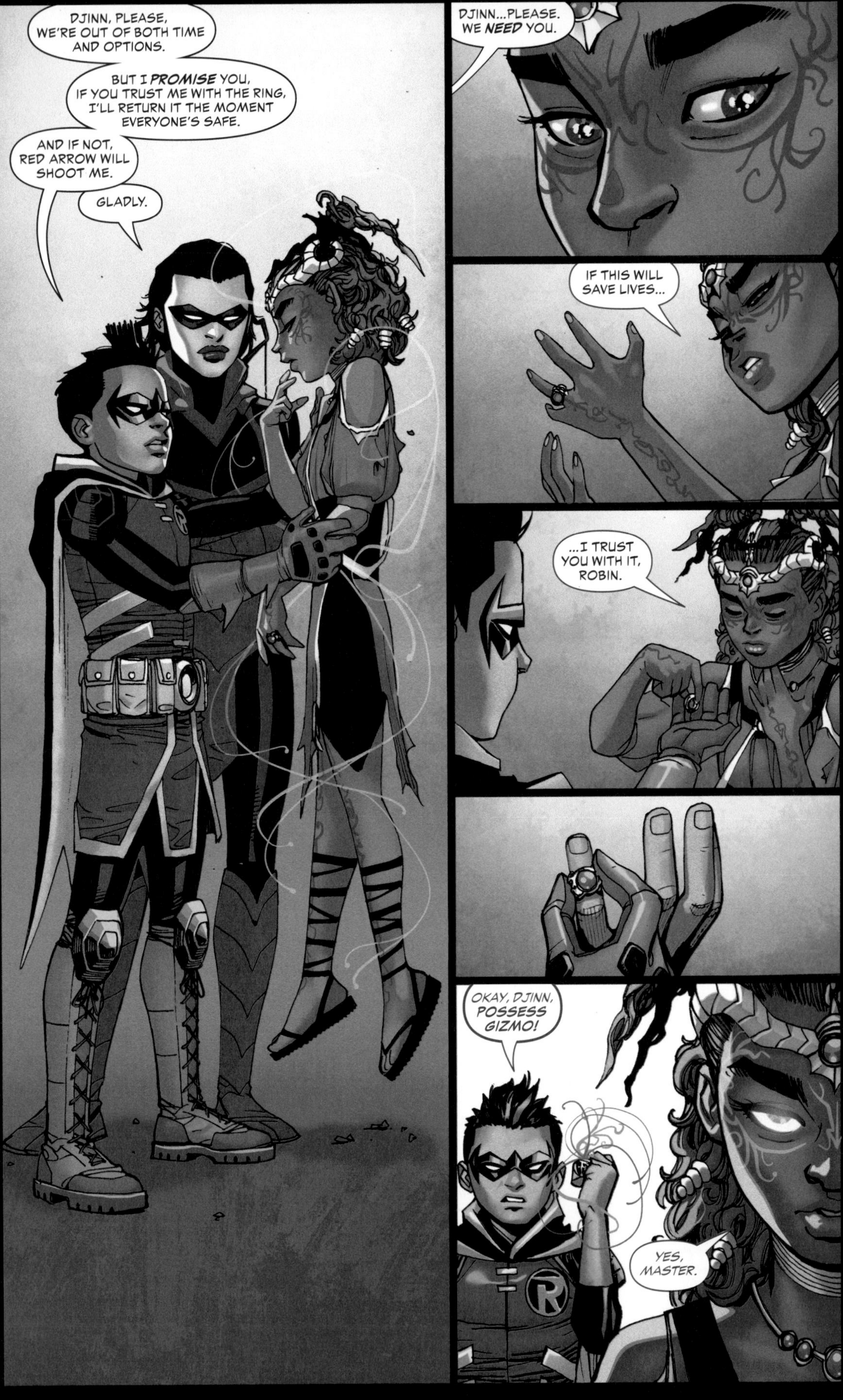
DJINN, PLEASE, WE'RE OUT OF BOTH TIME AND OPTIONS.
BUT I PROMISE YOU, IF YOU TRUST ME WITH THE RING, I'LL RETURN IT THE MOMENT EVERYONE'S SAFE.
AND IF NOT, RED ARROW WILL SHOOT ME.
GLADLY.
DJINN...PLEASE. WE NEED YOU.
IF THIS WILL SAVE LIVES...
...I TRUST YOU WITH IT, ROBIN.
OKAY, DJINN, POSSESS GIZMO!
YES, MASTER.

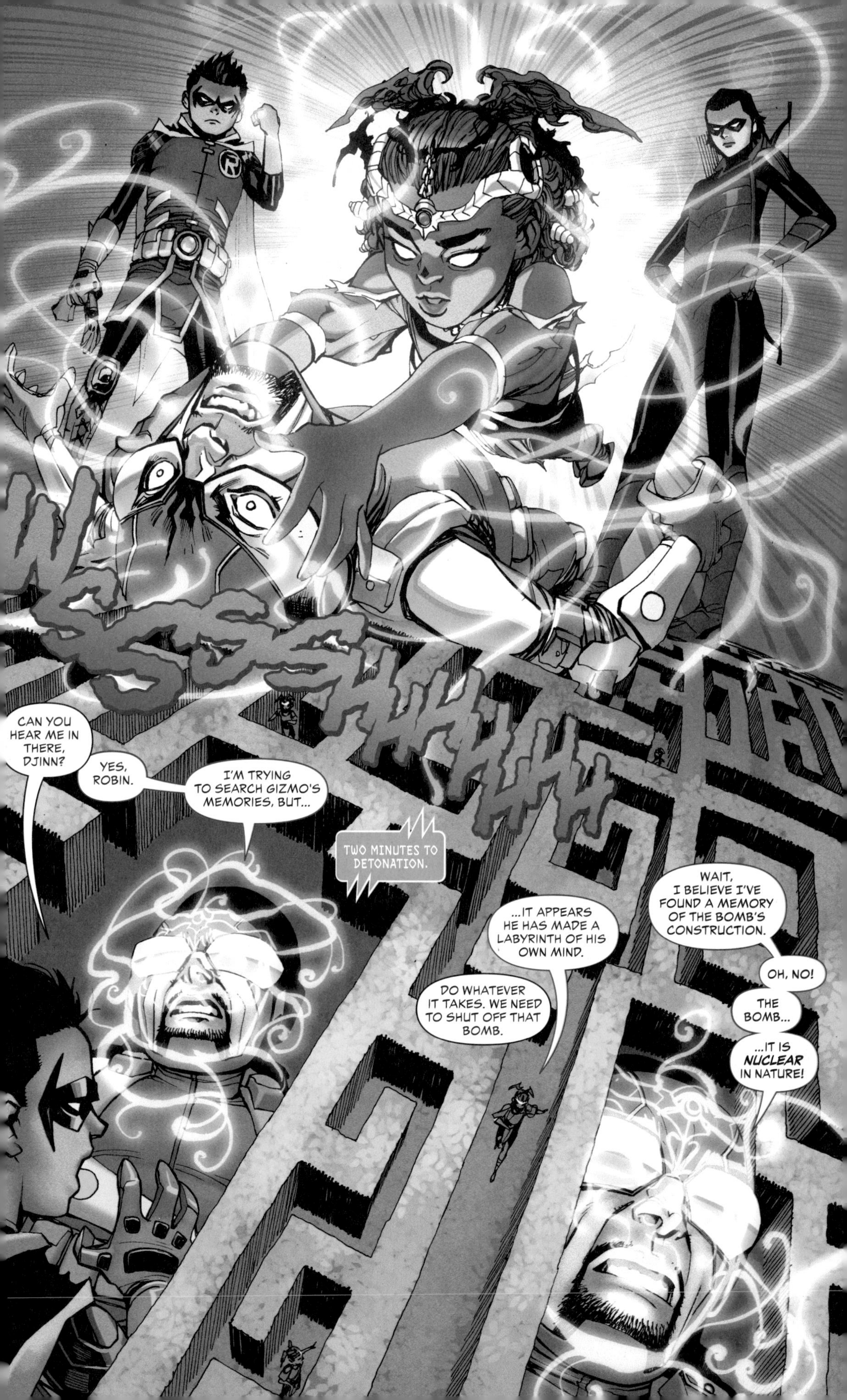
WSSSHHHHH
CAN YOU HEAR ME IN THERE, DJINN?
YES, ROBIN.
I'M TRYING TO SEARCH GIZMO'S MEMORIES, BUT...
TWO MINUTES TO DETONATION.
...IT APPEARS HE HAS MADE A LABYRINTH OF HIS OWN MIND.
DO WHATEVER IT TAKES. WE NEED TO SHUT OFF THAT BOMB.
WAIT, I BELIEVE I'VE FOUND A MEMORY OF THE BOMB'S CONSTRUCTION.
OH, NO!
THE BOMB...
...IT IS **NUCLEAR** IN NATURE!

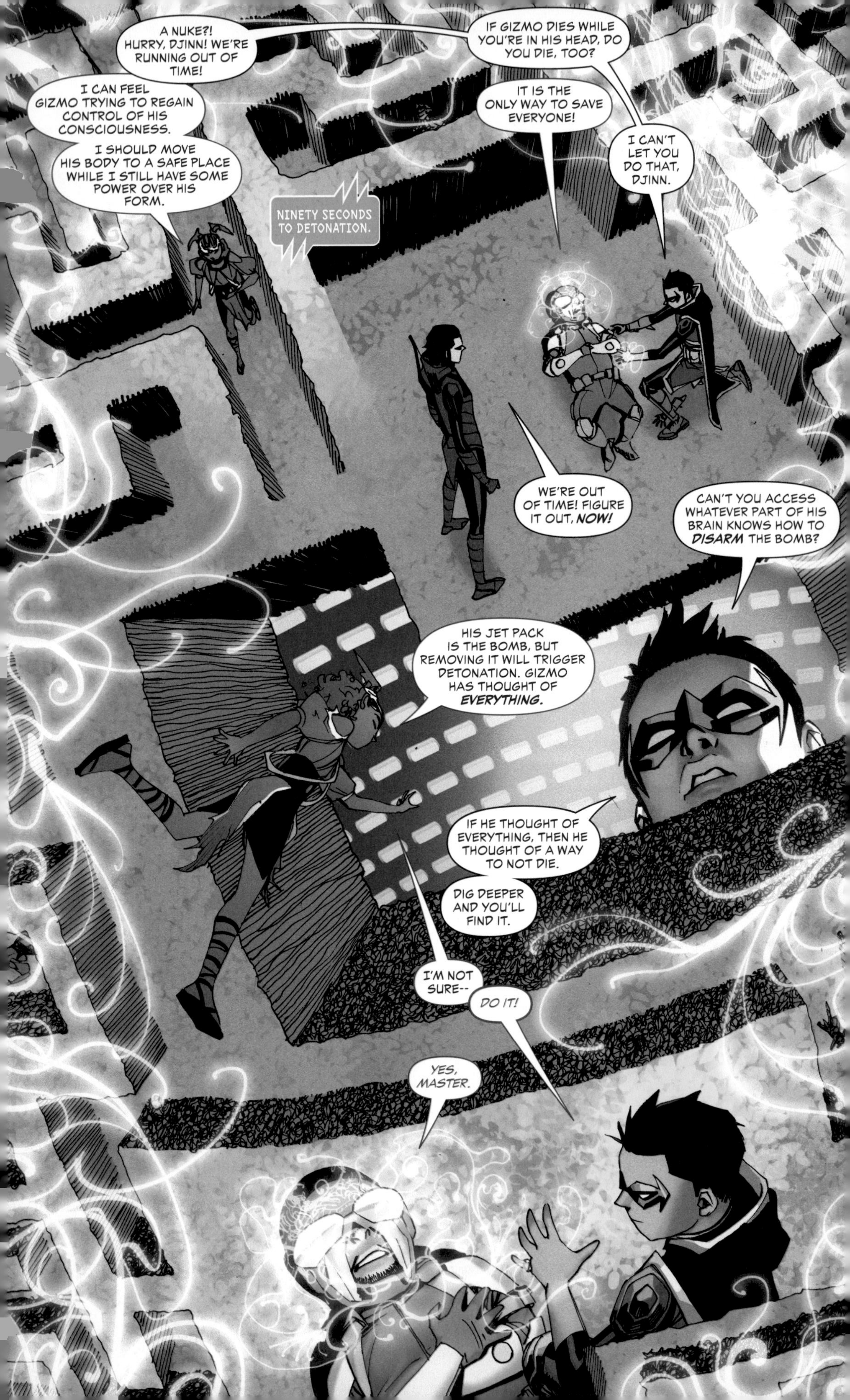
A NUKE?! HURRY, DJINN! WE'RE RUNNING OUT OF TIME!
IF GIZMO DIES WHILE YOU'RE IN HIS HEAD, DO YOU DIE, TOO?
I CAN FEEL GIZMO TRYING TO REGAIN CONTROL OF HIS CONSCIOUSNESS.
I SHOULD MOVE HIS BODY TO A SAFE PLACE WHILE I STILL HAVE SOME POWER OVER HIS FORM.
IT IS THE ONLY WAY TO SAVE EVERYONE!
I CAN'T LET YOU DO THAT, DJINN.
NINETY SECONDS TO DETONATION.
WE'RE OUT OF TIME! FIGURE IT OUT, NOW!
CAN'T YOU ACCESS WHATEVER PART OF HIS BRAIN KNOWS HOW TO DISARM THE BOMB?
HIS JET PACK IS THE BOMB, BUT REMOVING IT WILL TRIGGER DETONATION. GIZMO HAS THOUGHT OF EVERYTHING.
IF HE THOUGHT OF EVERYTHING, THEN HE THOUGHT OF A WAY TO NOT DIE.
DIG DEEPER AND YOU'LL FIND IT.
I'M NOT SURE--
DO IT!
YES, MASTER.

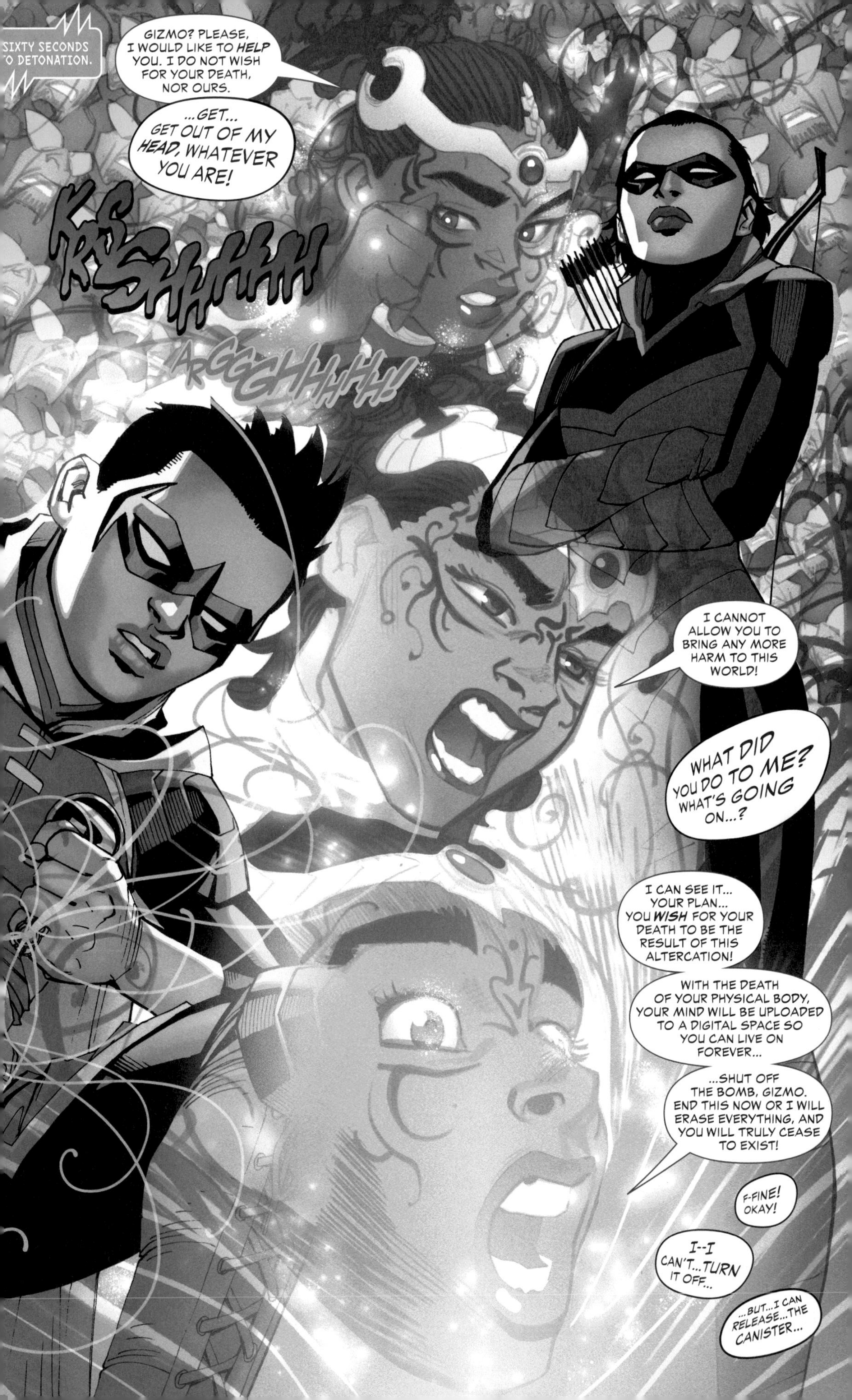
SIXTY SECONDS TO DETONATION.
GIZMO? PLEASE, I WOULD LIKE TO HELP YOU. I DO NOT WISH FOR YOUR DEATH, NOR OURS.
...GET... GET OUT OF MY HEAD, WHATEVER YOU ARE!
KRSSHHHHH
ARGGGHHHHH!
I CANNOT ALLOW YOU TO BRING ANY MORE HARM TO THIS WORLD!
WHAT DID YOU DO TO ME? WHAT'S GOING ON...?
I CAN SEE IT... YOUR PLAN... YOU WISH FOR YOUR DEATH TO BE THE RESULT OF THIS ALTERCATION!
WITH THE DEATH OF YOUR PHYSICAL BODY, YOUR MIND WILL BE UPLOADED TO A DIGITAL SPACE SO YOU CAN LIVE ON FOREVER...
...SHUT OFF THE BOMB, GIZMO. END THIS NOW OR I WILL ERASE EVERYTHING, AND YOU WILL TRULY CEASE TO EXIST!
F-FINE! OKAY!
I--I CAN'T...TURN IT OFF...
...BUT...I CAN RELEASE...THE CANISTER...

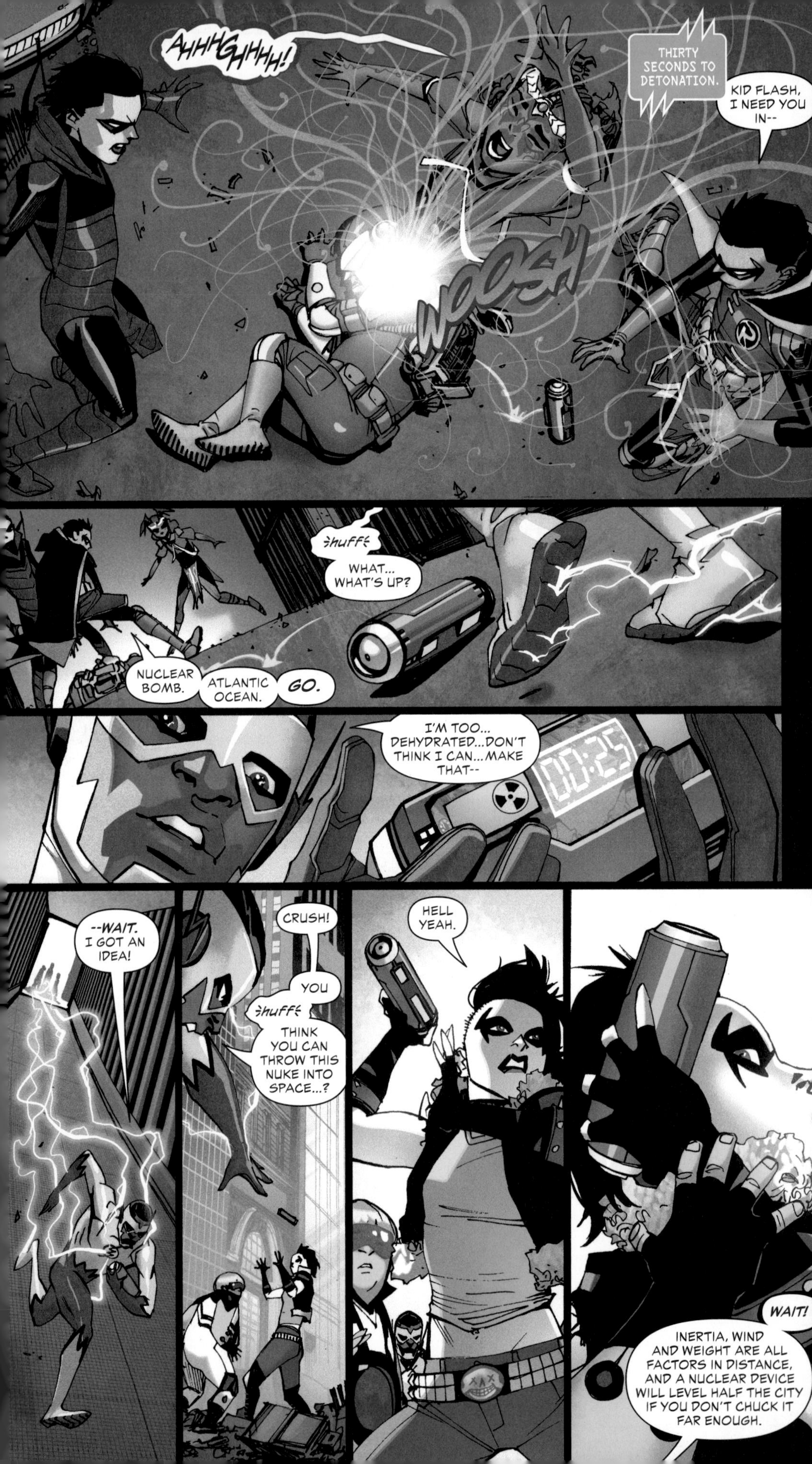
AHHHGHHHH!
THIRTY SECONDS TO DETONATION.
KID FLASH, I NEED YOU IN--
WOOSH
huff
WHAT... WHAT'S UP?
NUCLEAR BOMB.
ATLANTIC OCEAN.
GO.
I'M TOO... DEHYDRATED...DON'T THINK I CAN...MAKE THAT--
00:25
--WAIT. I GOT AN IDEA!
CRUSH!
YOU
huff
THINK YOU CAN THROW THIS NUKE INTO SPACE...?
HELL YEAH.
WAIT!
INERTIA, WIND AND WEIGHT ARE ALL FACTORS IN DISTANCE, AND A NUCLEAR DEVICE WILL LEVEL HALF THE CITY IF YOU DON'T CHUCK IT FAR ENOUGH.

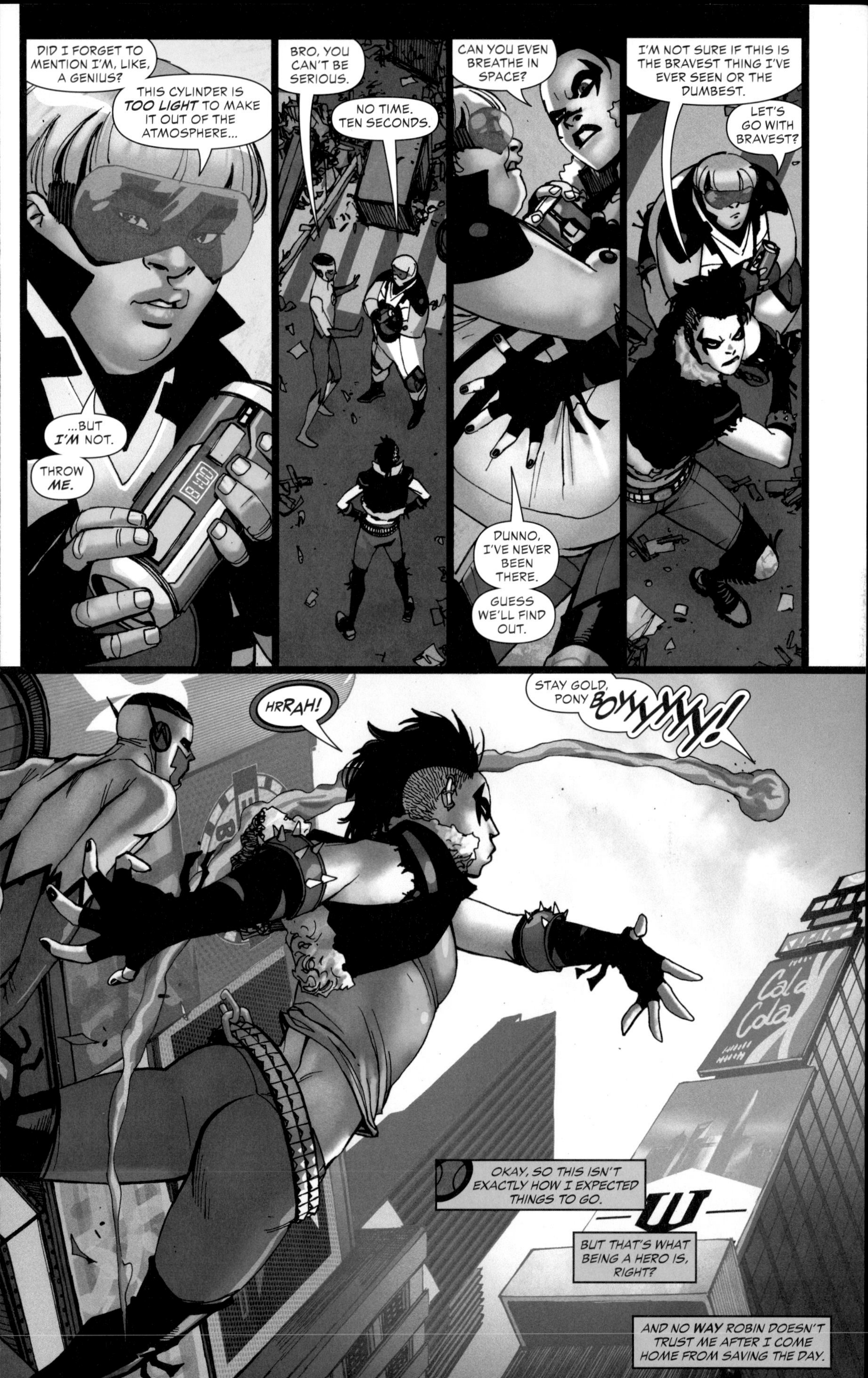

DID I FORGET TO MENTION I'M, LIKE, A GENIUS?
THIS CYLINDER IS TOO LIGHT TO MAKE IT OUT OF THE ATMOSPHERE...
...BUT I'M NOT.
THROW ME.
BRO, YOU CAN'T BE SERIOUS.
NO TIME. TEN SECONDS.
CAN YOU EVEN BREATHE IN SPACE?
DUNNO, I'VE NEVER BEEN THERE.
GUESS WE'LL FIND OUT.
I'M NOT SURE IF THIS IS THE BRAVEST THING I'VE EVER SEEN OR THE DUMBEST.
LET'S GO WITH BRAVEST?
HRRAH!
STAY GOLD, PONY BOYYYYYY!
Cola Cola
OKAY, SO THIS ISN'T EXACTLY HOW I EXPECTED THINGS TO GO.
BUT THAT'S WHAT BEING A HERO IS, RIGHT?
AND NO WAY ROBIN DOESN'T TRUST ME AFTER I COME HOME FROM SAVING THE DAY.

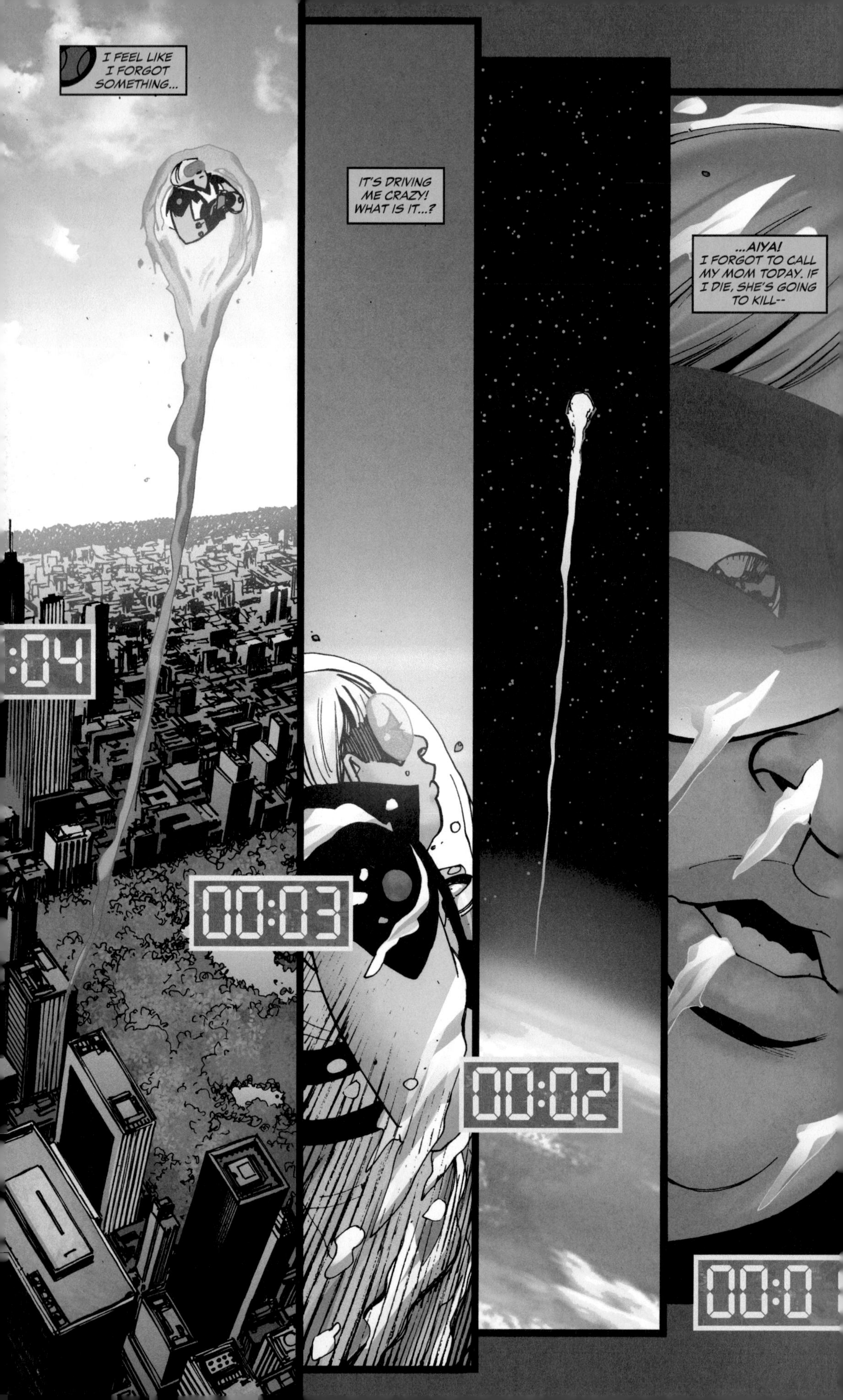
I FEEL LIKE I FORGOT SOMETHING...
:04
IT'S DRIVING ME CRAZY! WHAT IS IT...?
00:03
00:02
...AIYA! I FORGOT TO CALL MY MOM TODAY. IF I DIE, SHE'S GOING TO KILL--
00:0

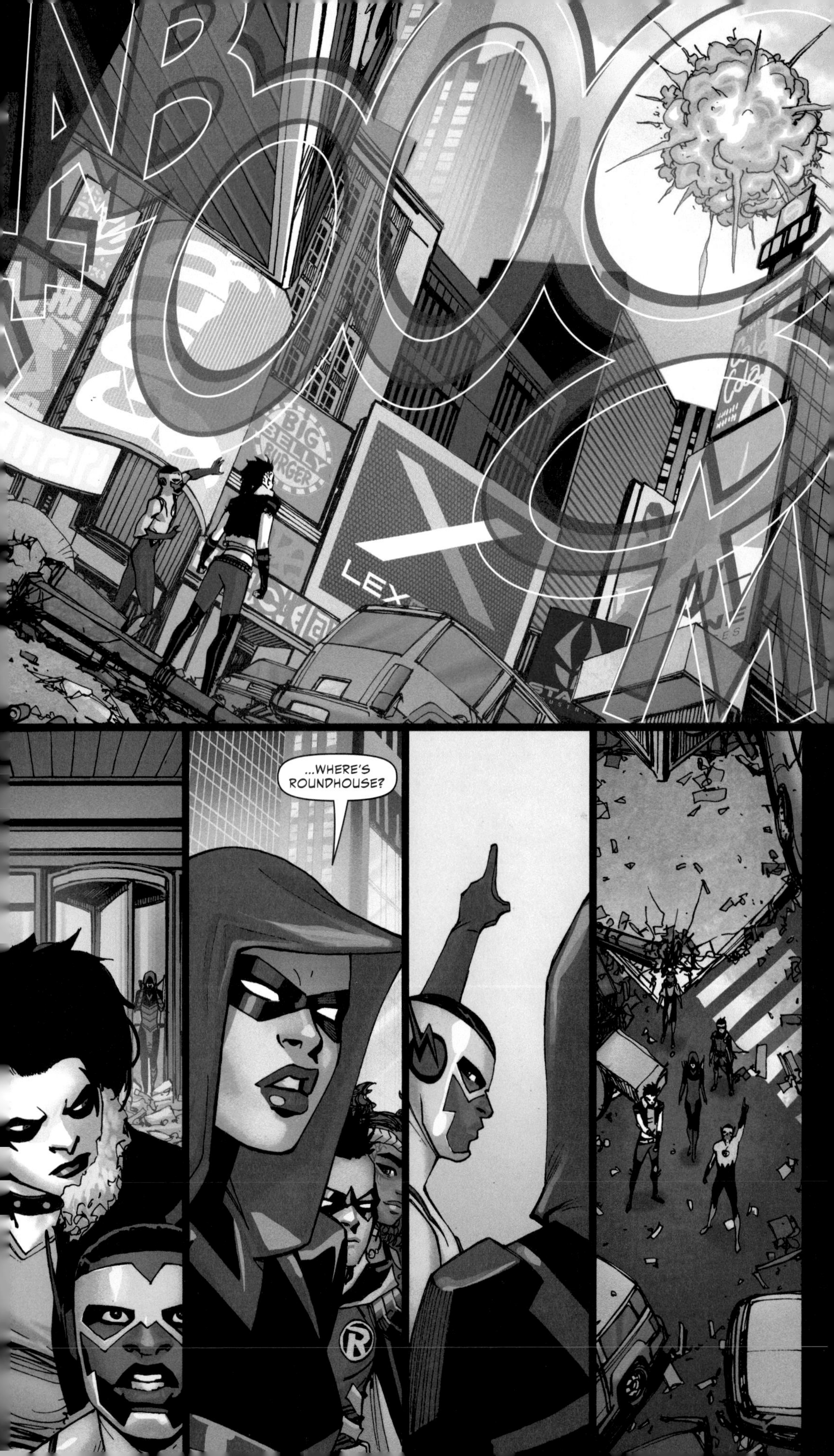
BIG BELLY BURGER
LEX
...WHERE'S ROUNDHOUSE?

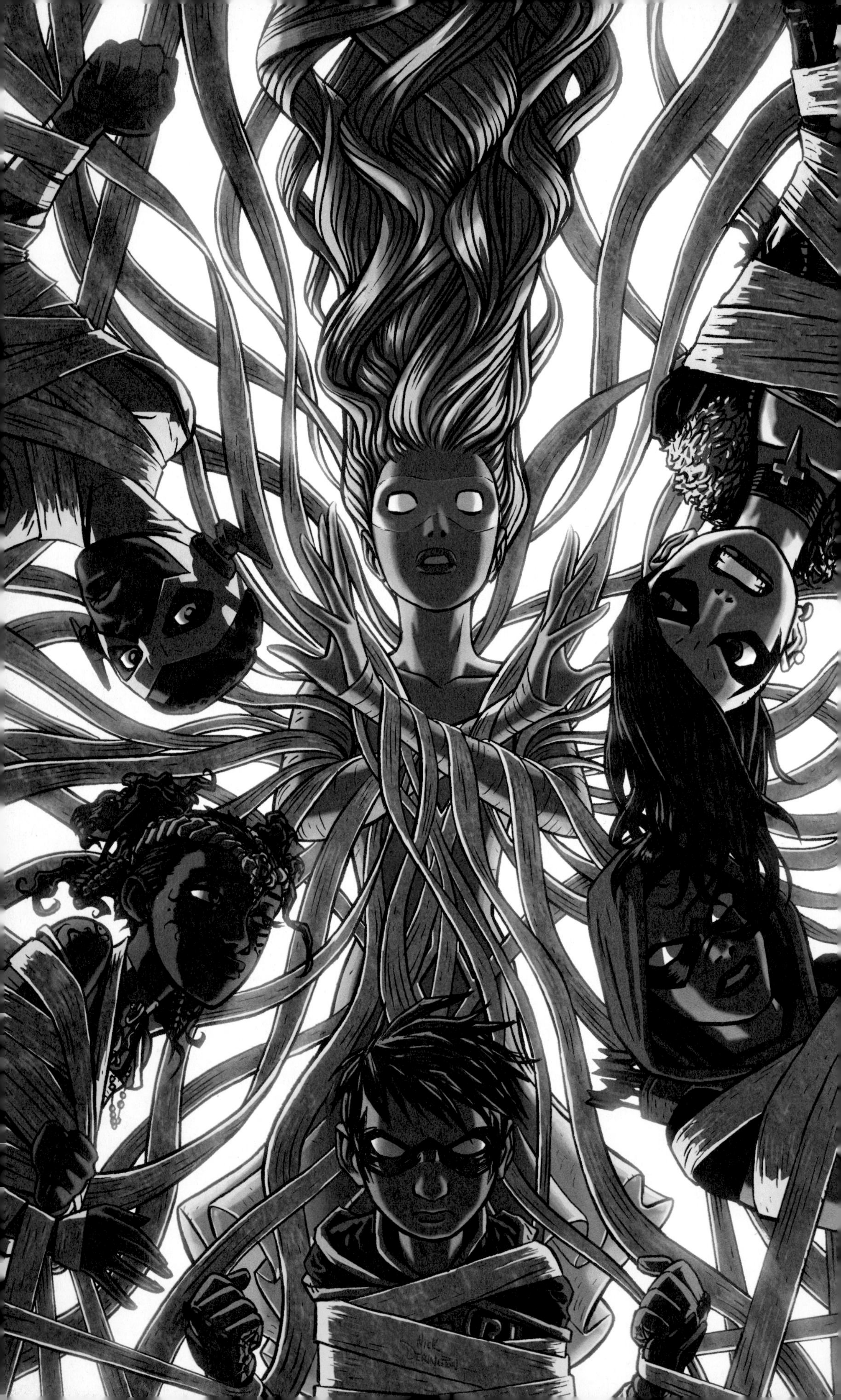

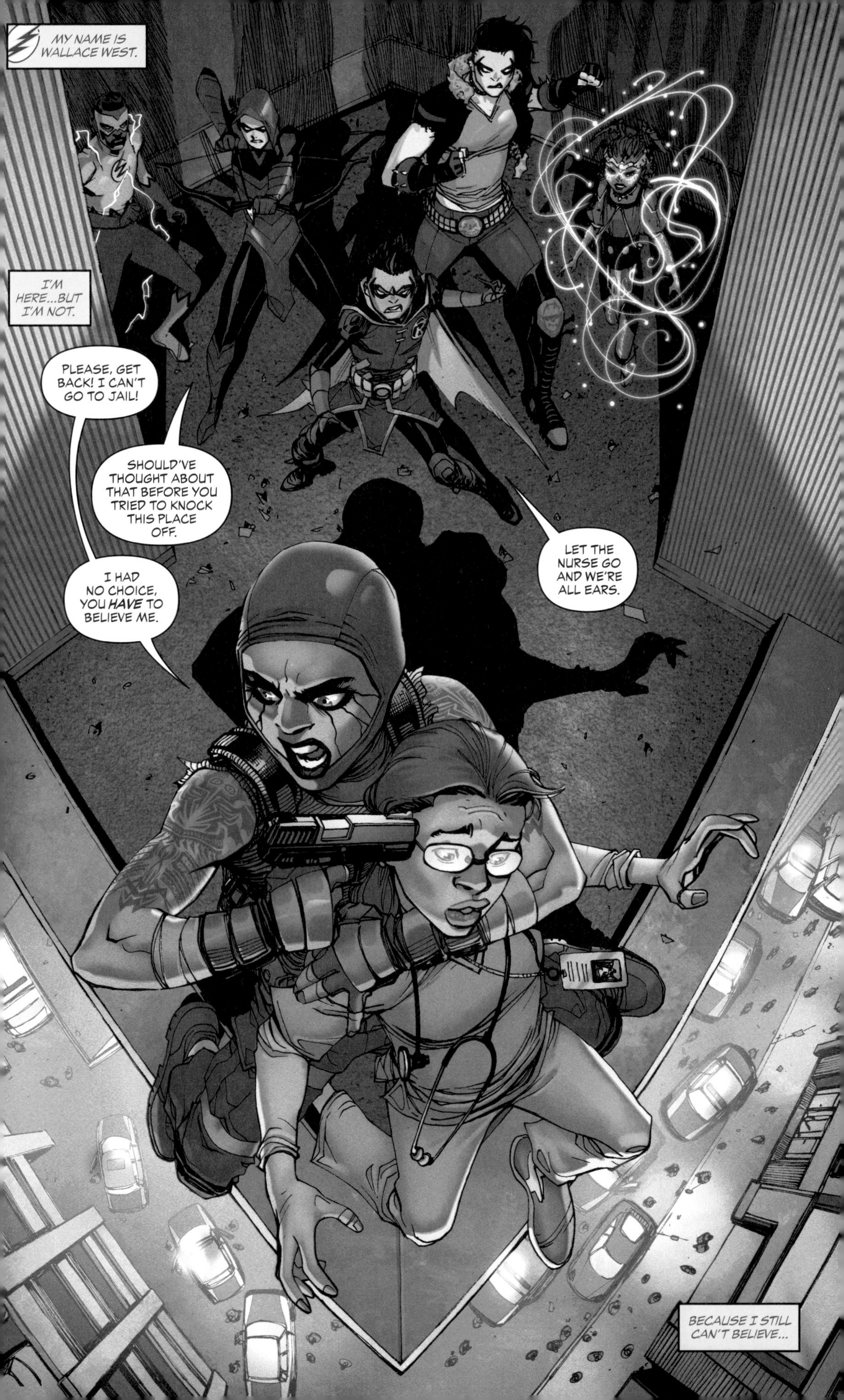
MY NAME IS WALLACE WEST.
I'M HERE...BUT I'M NOT.
PLEASE, GET BACK! I CAN'T GO TO JAIL!
SHOULD'VE THOUGHT ABOUT THAT BEFORE YOU TRIED TO KNOCK THIS PLACE OFF.
I HAD NO CHOICE, YOU *HAVE* TO BELIEVE ME.
LET THE NURSE GO AND WE'RE ALL EARS.
BECAUSE I STILL CAN'T BELIEVE...

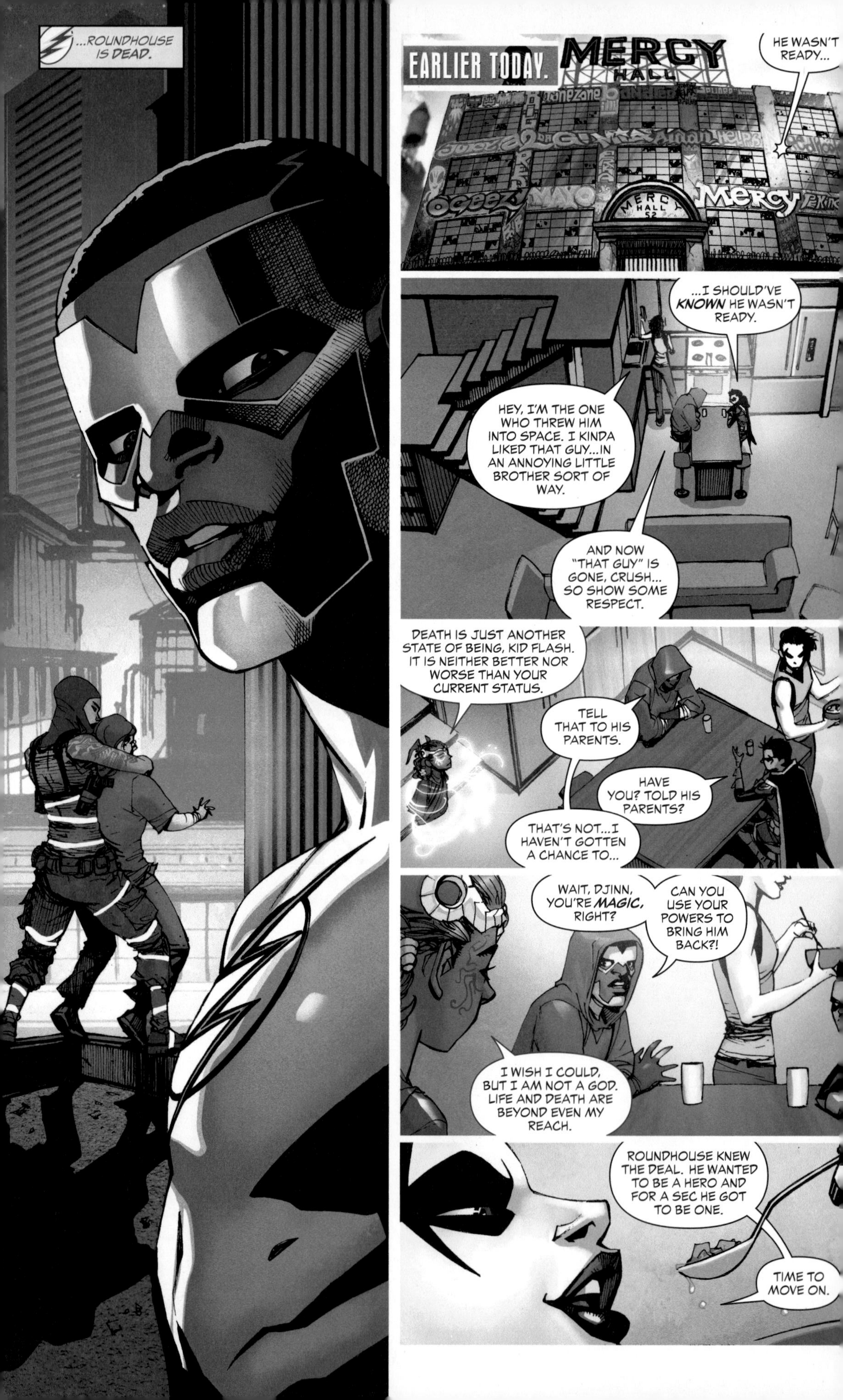
...ROUNDHOUSE IS DEAD.
EARLIER TODAY.
MERCY HALL
HE WASN'T READY...
...I SHOULD'VE KNOWN HE WASN'T READY.
HEY, I'M THE ONE WHO THREW HIM INTO SPACE. I KINDA LIKED THAT GUY...IN AN ANNOYING LITTLE BROTHER SORT OF WAY.
AND NOW "THAT GUY" IS GONE, CRUSH... SO SHOW SOME RESPECT.
DEATH IS JUST ANOTHER STATE OF BEING, KID FLASH. IT IS NEITHER BETTER NOR WORSE THAN YOUR CURRENT STATUS.
TELL THAT TO HIS PARENTS.
HAVE YOU? TOLD HIS PARENTS?
THAT'S NOT...I HAVEN'T GOTTEN A CHANCE TO...
WAIT, DJINN, YOU'RE MAGIC, RIGHT?
CAN YOU USE YOUR POWERS TO BRING HIM BACK?!
I WISH I COULD, BUT I AM NOT A GOD. LIFE AND DEATH ARE BEYOND EVEN MY REACH.
ROUNDHOUSE KNEW THE DEAL. HE WANTED TO BE A HERO AND FOR A SEC HE GOT TO BE ONE.
TIME TO MOVE ON.

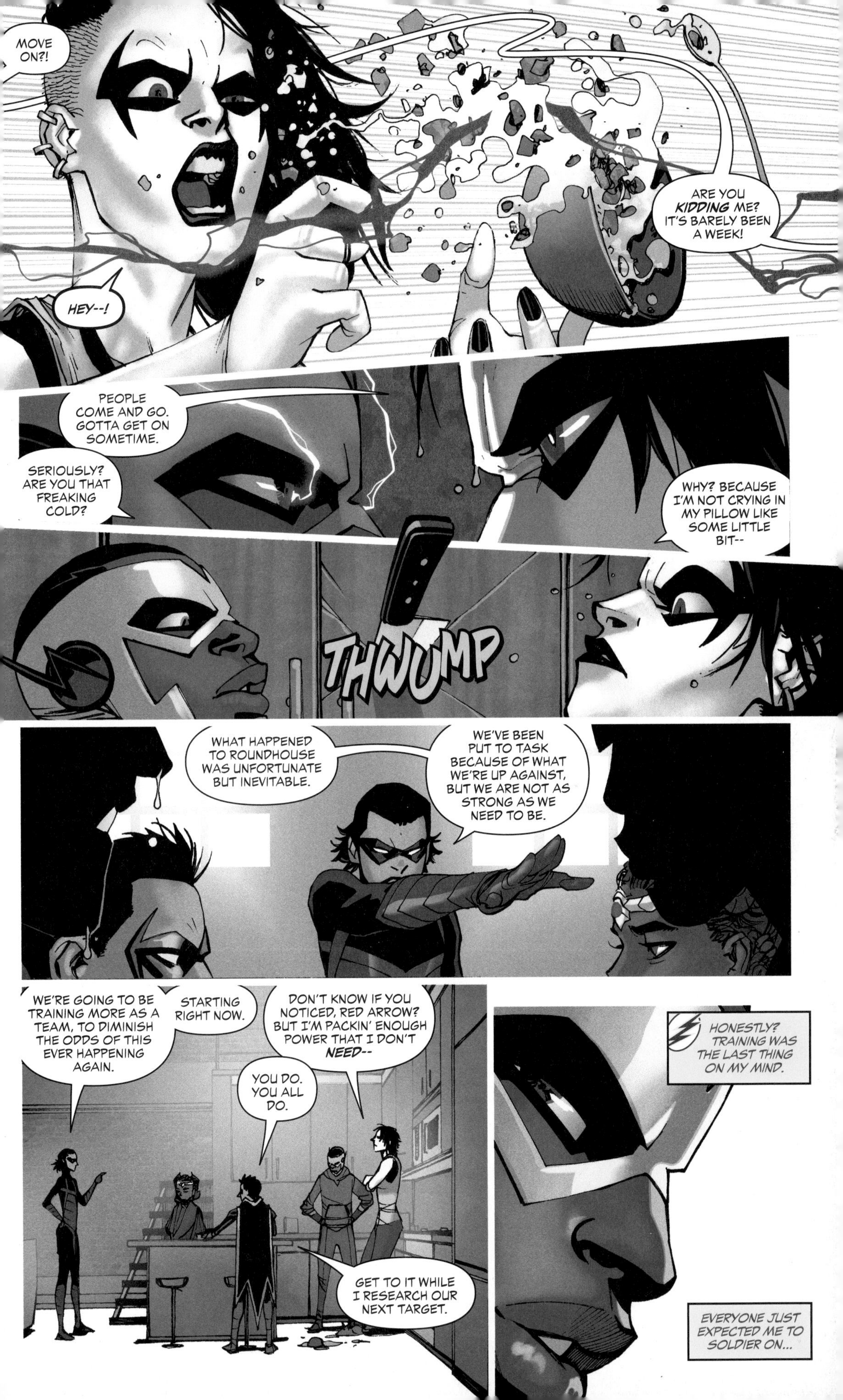
MOVE ON?!
ARE YOU *KIDDING* ME? IT'S BARELY BEEN A WEEK!
HEY--!
PEOPLE COME AND GO. GOTTA GET ON SOMETIME.
SERIOUSLY? ARE YOU THAT FREAKING COLD?
WHY? BECAUSE I'M NOT CRYING IN MY PILLOW LIKE SOME LITTLE BIT--
THWUMP
WHAT HAPPENED TO ROUNDHOUSE WAS UNFORTUNATE BUT INEVITABLE.
WE'VE BEEN PUT TO TASK BECAUSE OF WHAT WE'RE UP AGAINST, BUT WE ARE NOT AS STRONG AS WE NEED TO BE.
WE'RE GOING TO BE TRAINING MORE AS A TEAM, TO DIMINISH THE ODDS OF THIS EVER HAPPENING AGAIN.
STARTING RIGHT NOW.
DON'T KNOW IF YOU NOTICED, RED ARROW? BUT I'M PACKIN' ENOUGH POWER THAT I DON'T *NEED*--
YOU DO. YOU ALL DO.
GET TO IT WHILE I RESEARCH OUR NEXT TARGET.
HONESTLY? TRAINING WAS THE LAST THING ON MY MIND.
EVERYONE JUST EXPECTED ME TO SOLDIER ON...

MERCY HALL COURTYARD.

...WHEN I'D BARELY EVEN HAD TIME TO PROCESS.

BUT TRY TELLING DRILL SERGEANT ARROW SOMETHING LIKE THAT, SEE HOW IT GOES FOR YOU.

# TEEN TITANS
# BRING IT ON

**ADAM GLASS**
Writer

**BERNARD CHANG**
Artist

**MARCELO MAIOLO**
Colors

**DERON BENNETT**
Letters

**NICK DERINGTON**
Cover

**ANDREA SHEA**
Assistant Editor

**ALEX ANTONE**
Editor

**BRIAN CUNNINGHAM**
Group Editor

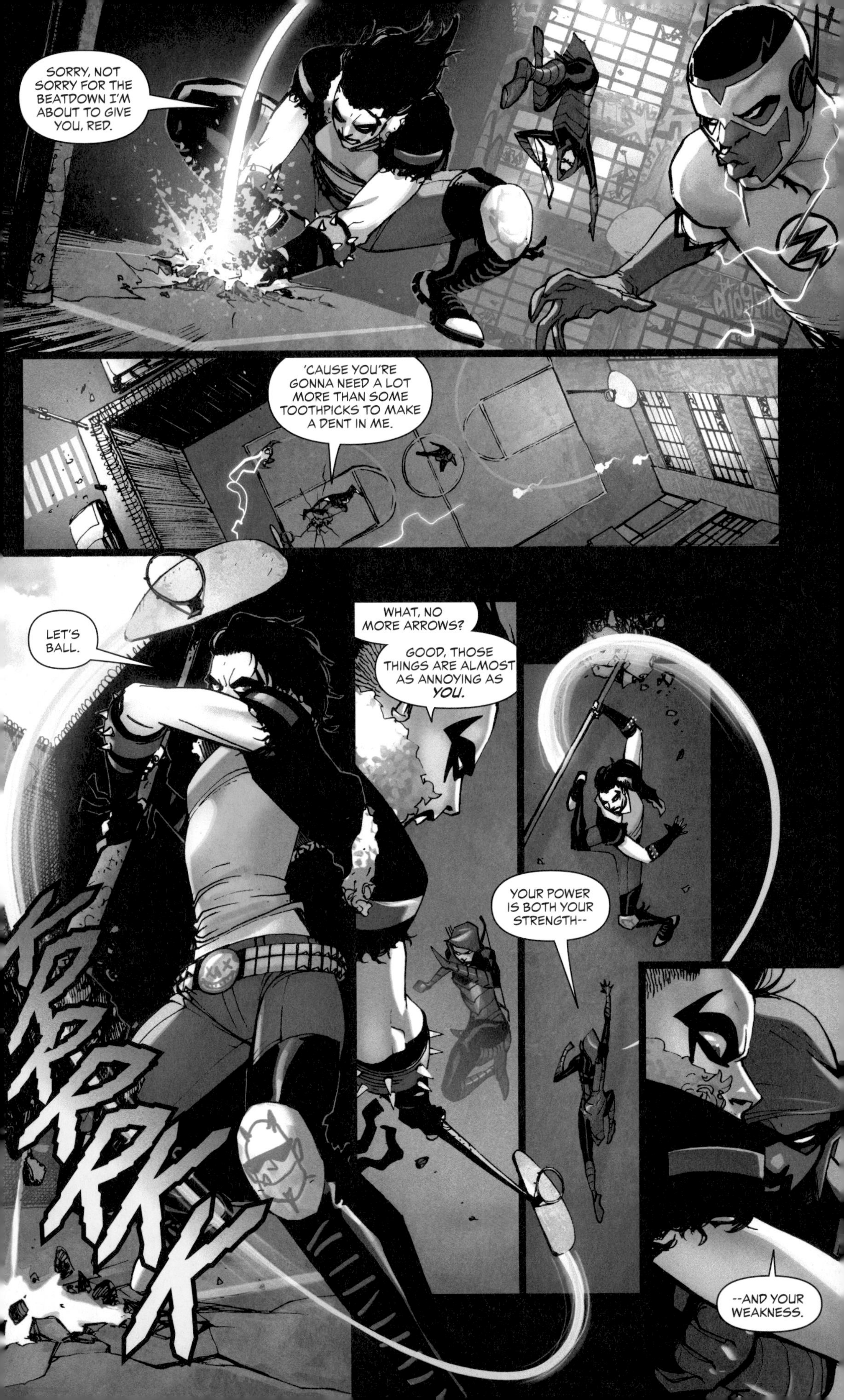
SORRY, NOT SORRY FOR THE BEATDOWN I'M ABOUT TO GIVE YOU, RED.
'CAUSE YOU'RE GONNA NEED A LOT MORE THAN SOME TOOTHPICKS TO MAKE A DENT IN ME.
LET'S BALL.
KRRKK
WHAT, NO MORE ARROWS?
GOOD, THOSE THINGS ARE ALMOST AS ANNOYING AS *YOU.*
YOUR POWER IS BOTH YOUR STRENGTH--
--AND YOUR WEAKNESS.

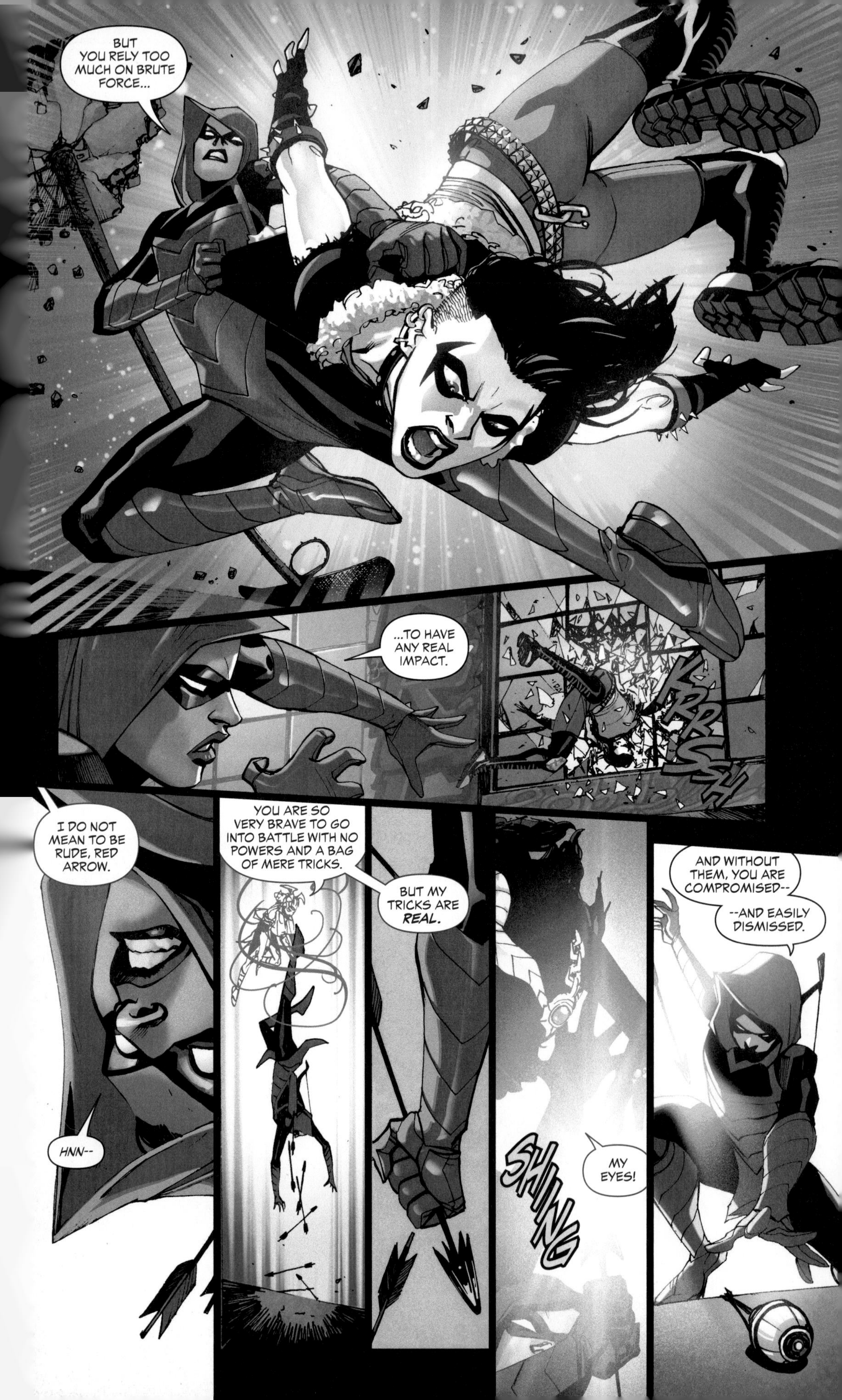
BUT YOU RELY TOO MUCH ON BRUTE FORCE...
...TO HAVE ANY REAL IMPACT.
KRRSSH
I DO NOT MEAN TO BE RUDE, RED ARROW.
HNN--
YOU ARE SO VERY BRAVE TO GO INTO BATTLE WITH NO POWERS AND A BAG OF MERE TRICKS.
BUT MY TRICKS ARE *REAL.*
SHING
MY EYES!
AND WITHOUT THEM, YOU ARE COMPROMISED--
--AND EASILY DISMISSED.

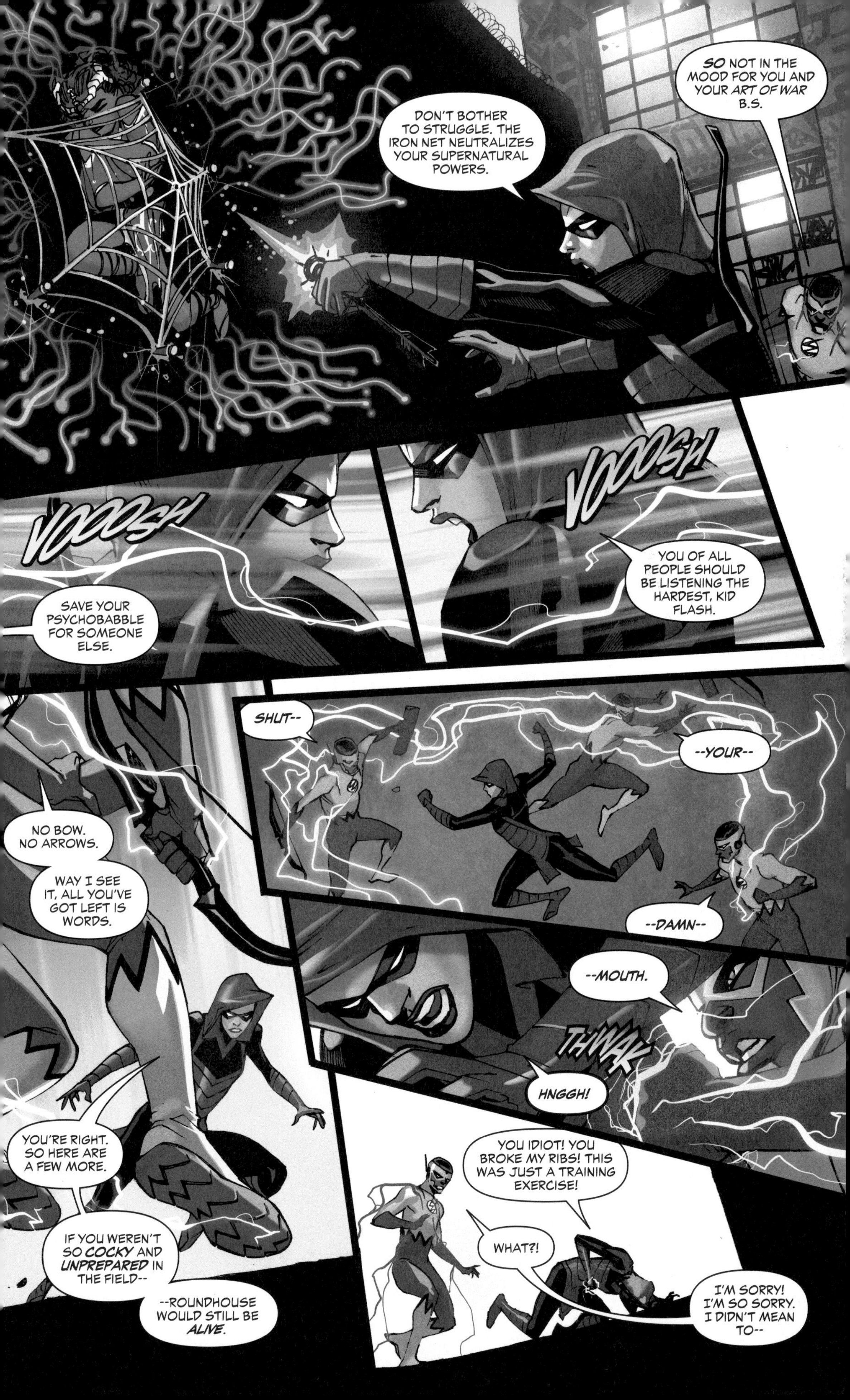
DON'T BOTHER TO STRUGGLE. THE IRON NET NEUTRALIZES YOUR SUPERNATURAL POWERS.
SO NOT IN THE MOOD FOR YOU AND YOUR ART OF WAR B.S.
VOOOSH
SAVE YOUR PSYCHOBABBLE FOR SOMEONE ELSE.
VOOOSH
YOU OF ALL PEOPLE SHOULD BE LISTENING THE HARDEST, KID FLASH.
NO BOW. NO ARROWS.
WAY I SEE IT, ALL YOU'VE GOT LEFT IS WORDS.
YOU'RE RIGHT. SO HERE ARE A FEW MORE.
IF YOU WEREN'T SO COCKY AND UNPREPARED IN THE FIELD--
--ROUNDHOUSE WOULD STILL BE ALIVE.
SHUT--
--YOUR--
--DAMN--
--MOUTH.
THWAK
HNGGH!
YOU IDIOT! YOU BROKE MY RIBS! THIS WAS JUST A TRAINING EXERCISE!
WHAT?!
I'M SORRY! I'M SO SORRY. I DIDN'T MEAN TO--

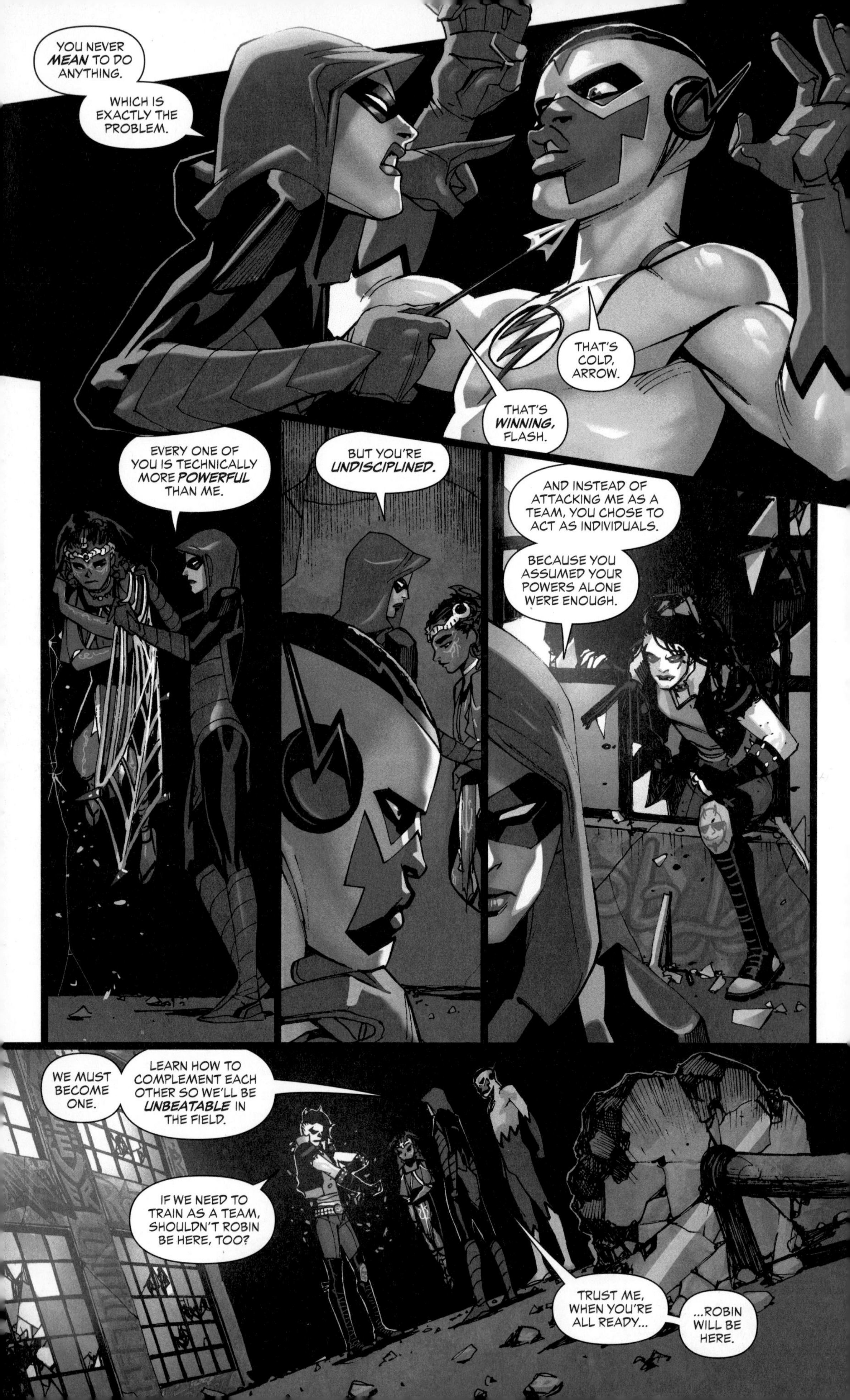
YOU NEVER MEAN TO DO ANYTHING.
WHICH IS EXACTLY THE PROBLEM.
THAT'S COLD, ARROW.
THAT'S WINNING, FLASH.
EVERY ONE OF YOU IS TECHNICALLY MORE POWERFUL THAN ME.
BUT YOU'RE UNDISCIPLINED.
AND INSTEAD OF ATTACKING ME AS A TEAM, YOU CHOSE TO ACT AS INDIVIDUALS.
BECAUSE YOU ASSUMED YOUR POWERS ALONE WERE ENOUGH.
WE MUST BECOME ONE.
LEARN HOW TO COMPLEMENT EACH OTHER SO WE'LL BE UNBEATABLE IN THE FIELD.
IF WE NEED TO TRAIN AS A TEAM, SHOULDN'T ROBIN BE HERE, TOO?
TRUST ME, WHEN YOU'RE ALL READY...
...ROBIN WILL BE HERE.

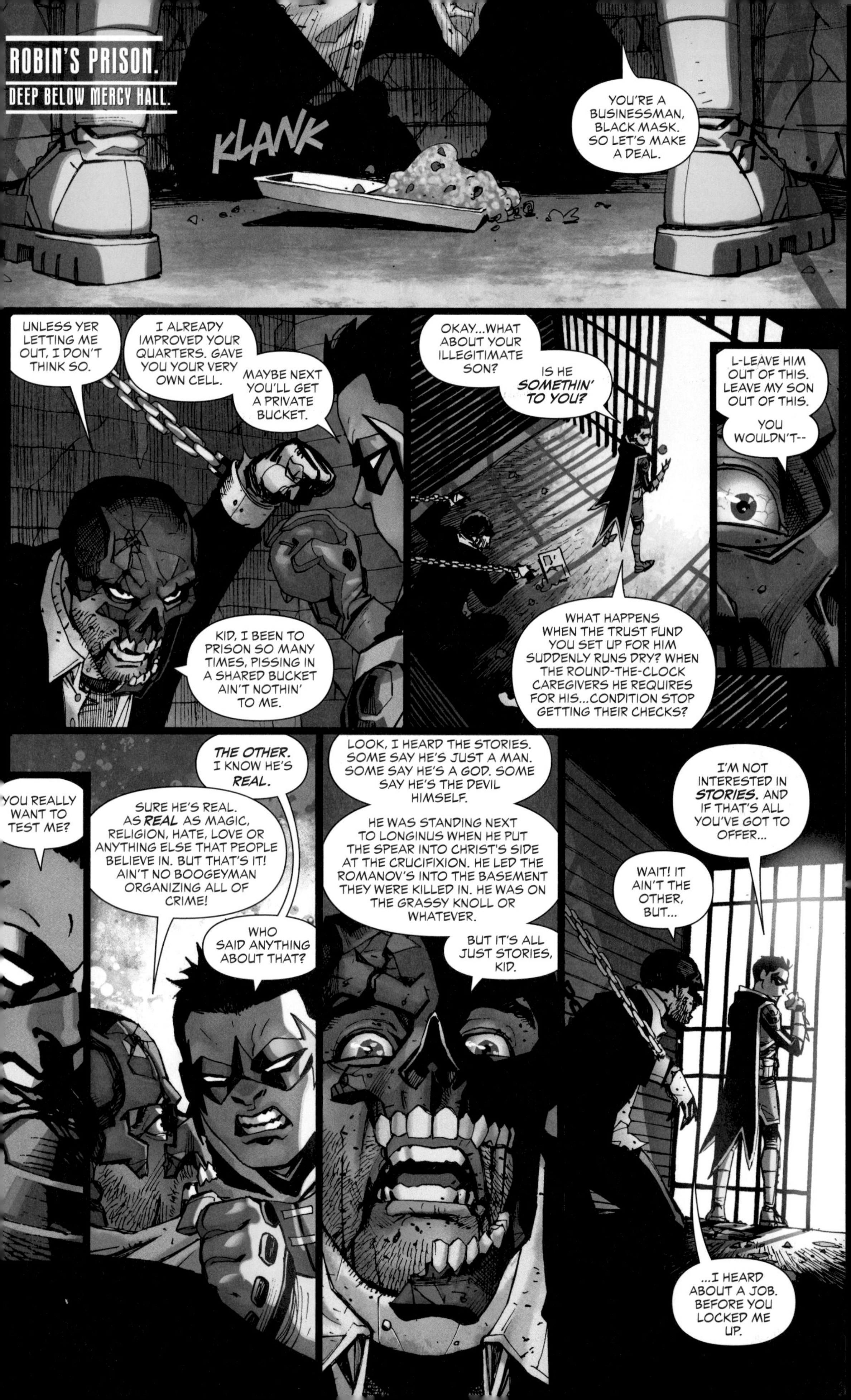
ROBIN'S PRISON.
DEEP BELOW MERCY HALL.
KLANK
YOU'RE A BUSINESSMAN, BLACK MASK. SO LET'S MAKE A DEAL.
UNLESS YER LETTING ME OUT, I DON'T THINK SO.
I ALREADY IMPROVED YOUR QUARTERS. GAVE YOU YOUR VERY OWN CELL.
MAYBE NEXT YOU'LL GET A PRIVATE BUCKET.
KID, I BEEN TO PRISON SO MANY TIMES, PISSING IN A SHARED BUCKET AIN'T NOTHIN' TO ME.
OKAY...WHAT ABOUT YOUR ILLEGITIMATE SON?
IS HE SOMETHIN' TO YOU?
WHAT HAPPENS WHEN THE TRUST FUND YOU SET UP FOR HIM SUDDENLY RUNS DRY? WHEN THE ROUND-THE-CLOCK CAREGIVERS HE REQUIRES FOR HIS...CONDITION STOP GETTING THEIR CHECKS?
L-LEAVE HIM OUT OF THIS. LEAVE MY SON OUT OF THIS.
YOU WOULDN'T--
YOU REALLY WANT TO TEST ME?
THE OTHER. I KNOW HE'S REAL.
SURE HE'S REAL. AS REAL AS MAGIC, RELIGION, HATE, LOVE OR ANYTHING ELSE THAT PEOPLE BELIEVE IN. BUT THAT'S IT! AIN'T NO BOOGEYMAN ORGANIZING ALL OF CRIME!
WHO SAID ANYTHING ABOUT THAT?
LOOK, I HEARD THE STORIES. SOME SAY HE'S JUST A MAN. SOME SAY HE'S A GOD. SOME SAY HE'S THE DEVIL HIMSELF.
HE WAS STANDING NEXT TO LONGINUS WHEN HE PUT THE SPEAR INTO CHRIST'S SIDE AT THE CRUCIFIXION. HE LED THE ROMANOV'S INTO THE BASEMENT THEY WERE KILLED IN. HE WAS ON THE GRASSY KNOLL OR WHATEVER.
BUT IT'S ALL JUST STORIES, KID.
I'M NOT INTERESTED IN STORIES. AND IF THAT'S ALL YOU'VE GOT TO OFFER...
WAIT! IT AIN'T THE OTHER, BUT...
...I HEARD ABOUT A JOB. BEFORE YOU LOCKED ME UP.

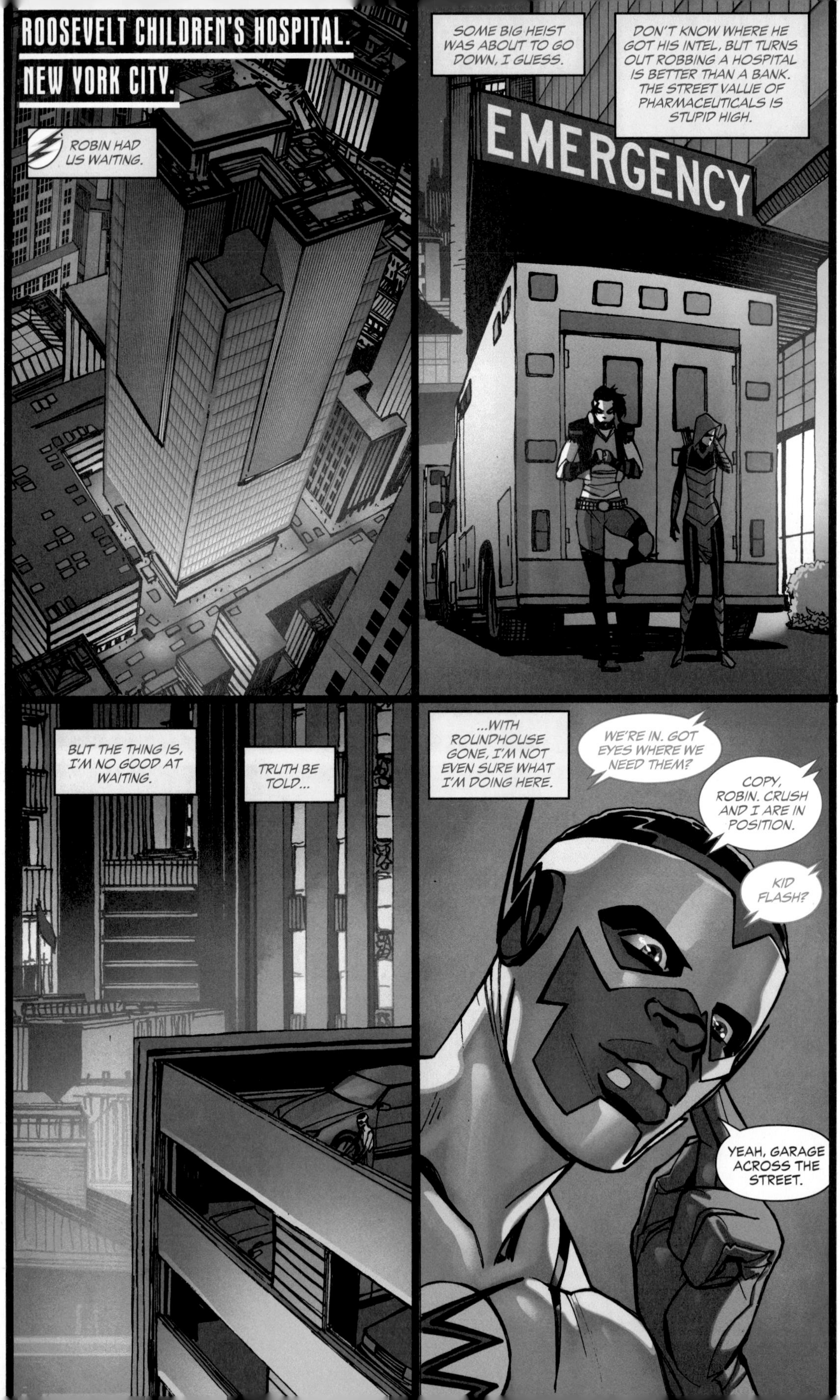
ROOSEVELT CHILDREN'S HOSPITAL.
NEW YORK CITY.
ROBIN HAD US WAITING.
SOME BIG HEIST WAS ABOUT TO GO DOWN, I GUESS.
DON'T KNOW WHERE HE GOT HIS INTEL, BUT TURNS OUT ROBBING A HOSPITAL IS BETTER THAN A BANK. THE STREET VALUE OF PHARMACEUTICALS IS STUPID HIGH.
EMERGENCY
BUT THE THING IS, I'M NO GOOD AT WAITING.
TRUTH BE TOLD...
...WITH ROUNDHOUSE GONE, I'M NOT EVEN SURE WHAT I'M DOING HERE.
WE'RE IN. GOT EYES WHERE WE NEED THEM?
COPY, ROBIN. CRUSH AND I ARE IN POSITION.
KID FLASH?
YEAH, GARAGE ACROSS THE STREET.

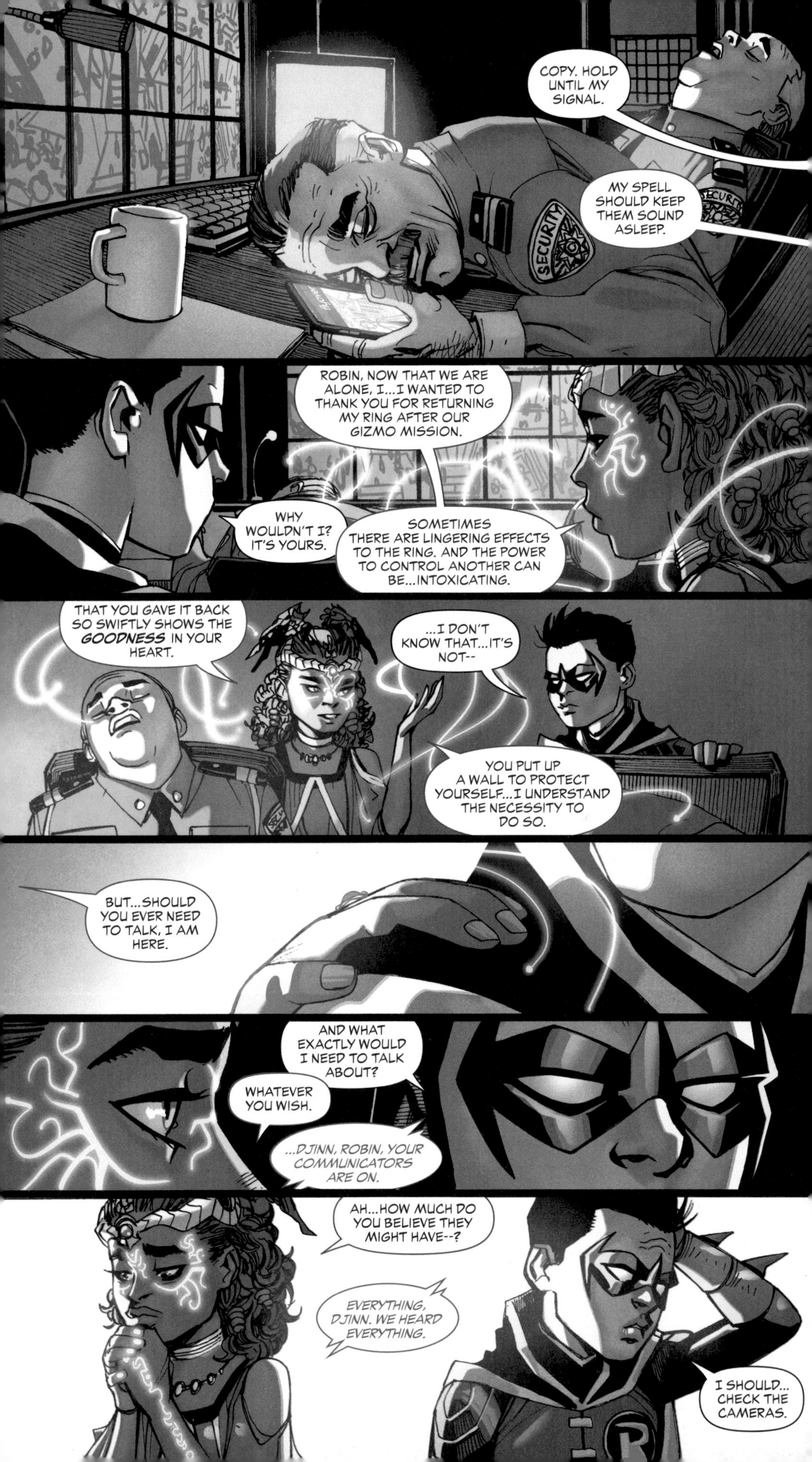
COPY. HOLD UNTIL MY SIGNAL.
MY SPELL SHOULD KEEP THEM SOUND ASLEEP.
SECURITY
ROBIN, NOW THAT WE ARE ALONE, I...I WANTED TO THANK YOU FOR RETURNING MY RING AFTER OUR GIZMO MISSION.
WHY WOULDN'T I? IT'S YOURS.
SOMETIMES THERE ARE LINGERING EFFECTS TO THE RING. AND THE POWER TO CONTROL ANOTHER CAN BE...INTOXICATING.
THAT YOU GAVE IT BACK SO SWIFTLY SHOWS THE ***GOODNESS*** IN YOUR HEART.
...I DON'T KNOW THAT...IT'S NOT--
YOU PUT UP A WALL TO PROTECT YOURSELF...I UNDERSTAND THE NECESSITY TO DO SO.
BUT...SHOULD YOU EVER NEED TO TALK, I AM HERE.
AND WHAT EXACTLY WOULD I NEED TO TALK ABOUT?
WHATEVER YOU WISH.
*...DJINN, ROBIN, YOUR COMMUNICATORS ARE ON.*
AH...HOW MUCH DO YOU BELIEVE THEY MIGHT HAVE--?
*EVERYTHING, DJINN. WE HEARD EVERYTHING.*
I SHOULD... CHECK THE CAMERAS.

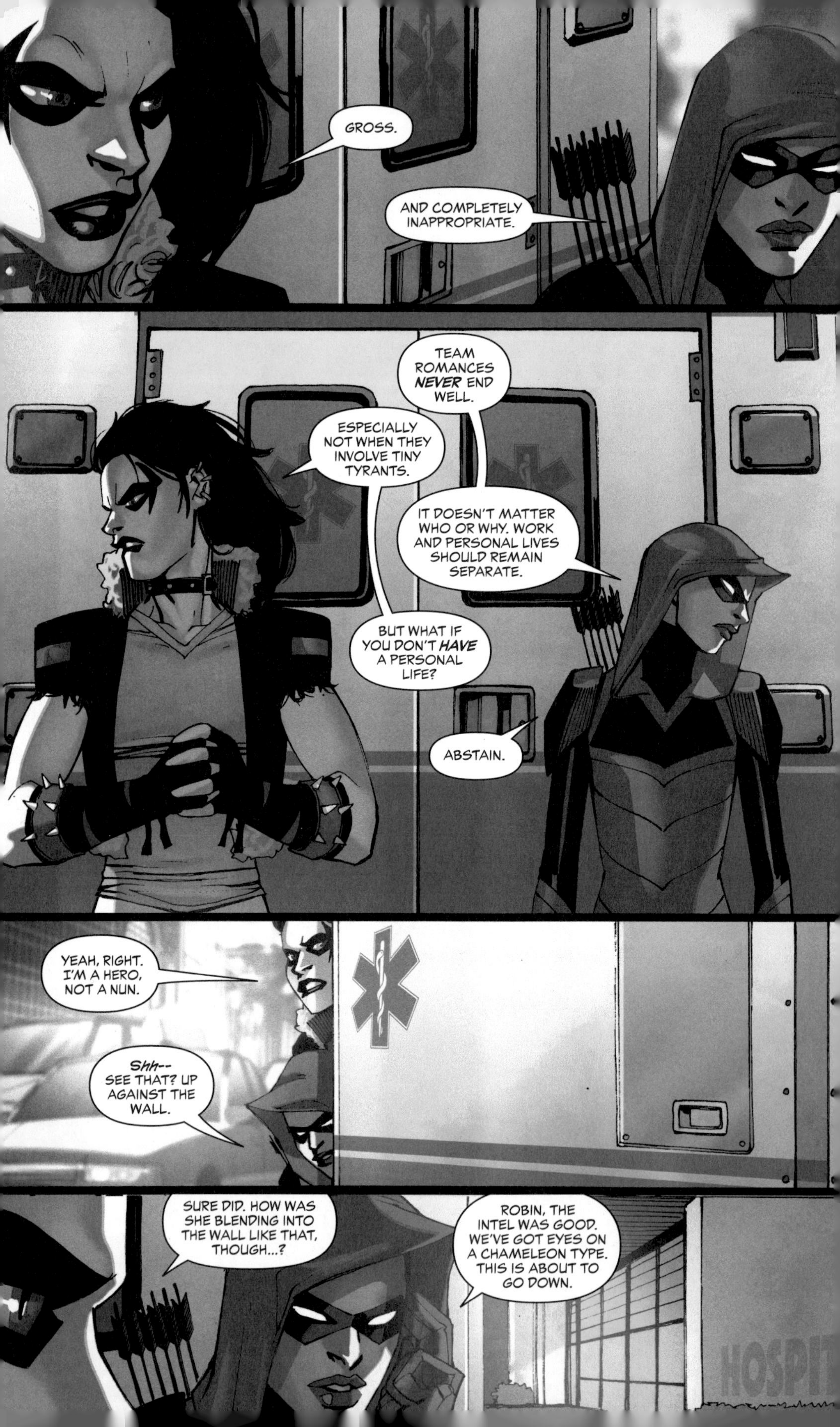
GROSS.
AND COMPLETELY INAPPROPRIATE.
TEAM ROMANCES *NEVER* END WELL.
ESPECIALLY NOT WHEN THEY INVOLVE TINY TYRANTS.
IT DOESN'T MATTER WHO OR WHY. WORK AND PERSONAL LIVES SHOULD REMAIN SEPARATE.
BUT WHAT IF YOU DON'T *HAVE* A PERSONAL LIFE?
ABSTAIN.
YEAH, RIGHT. I'M A HERO, NOT A NUN.
*Shh--* SEE THAT? UP AGAINST THE WALL.
SURE DID. HOW WAS SHE BLENDING INTO THE WALL LIKE THAT, THOUGH...?
ROBIN, THE INTEL WAS GOOD. WE'VE GOT EYES ON A CHAMELEON TYPE. THIS IS ABOUT TO GO DOWN.
HOSPIT

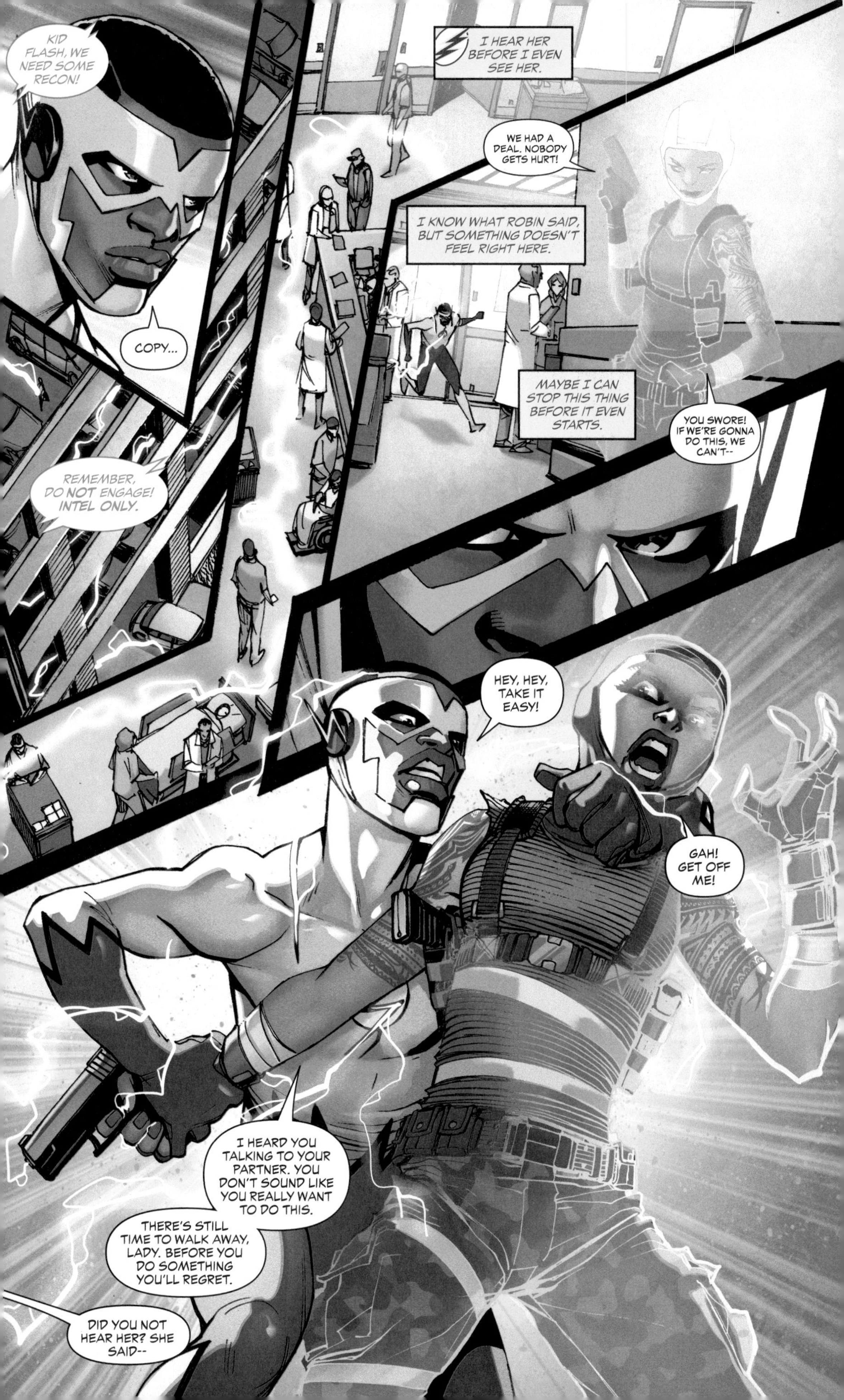
KID FLASH, WE NEED SOME RECON!
COPY...
REMEMBER, DO NOT ENGAGE! INTEL ONLY.
I HEAR HER BEFORE I EVEN SEE HER.
WE HAD A DEAL. NOBODY GETS HURT!
I KNOW WHAT ROBIN SAID, BUT SOMETHING DOESN'T FEEL RIGHT HERE.
MAYBE I CAN STOP THIS THING BEFORE IT EVEN STARTS.
YOU SWORE! IF WE'RE GONNA DO THIS, WE CAN'T--
HEY, HEY, TAKE IT EASY!
GAH! GET OFF ME!
I HEARD YOU TALKING TO YOUR PARTNER. YOU DON'T SOUND LIKE YOU REALLY WANT TO DO THIS.
THERE'S STILL TIME TO WALK AWAY, LADY. BEFORE YOU DO SOMETHING YOU'LL REGRET.
DID YOU NOT HEAR HER? SHE SAID--

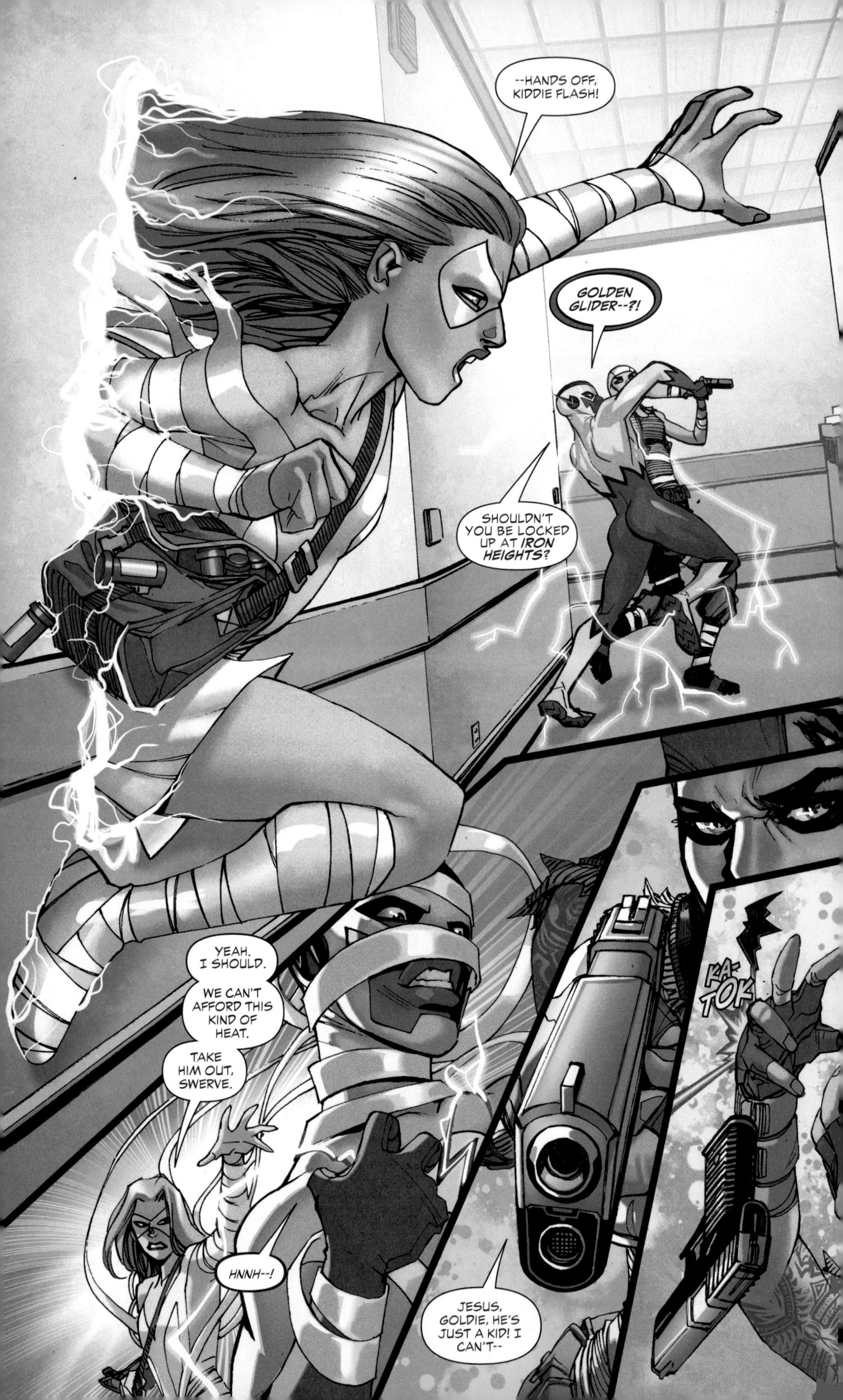
--HANDS OFF, KIDDIE FLASH!
GOLDEN GLIDER--?!
SHOULDN'T YOU BE LOCKED UP AT IRON HEIGHTS?
YEAH. I SHOULD.
WE CAN'T AFFORD THIS KIND OF HEAT.
TAKE HIM OUT, SWERVE.
HNNH--!
KA-TOK
JESUS, GOLDIE, HE'S JUST A KID! I CAN'T--

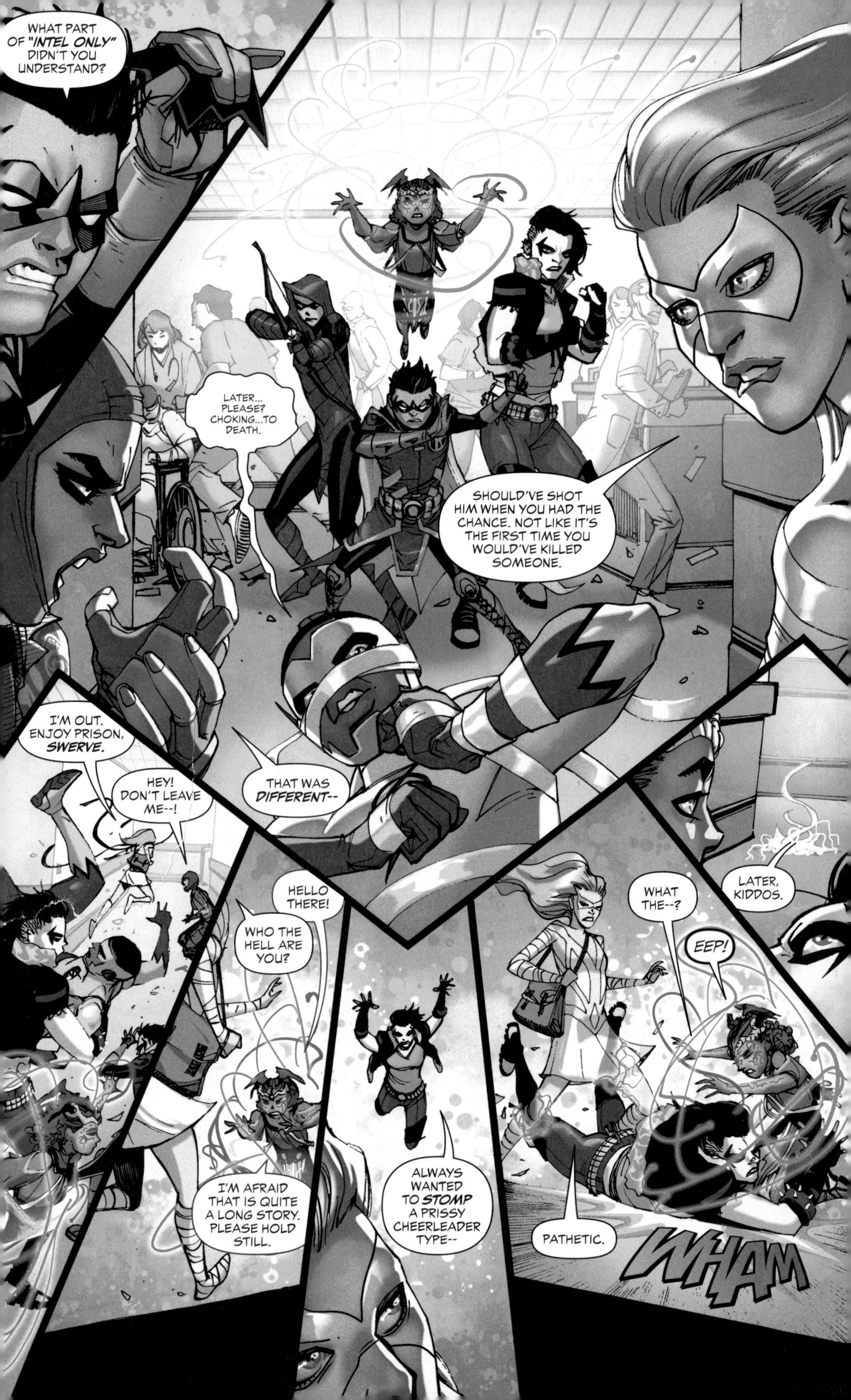
WHAT PART OF "INTEL ONLY" DIDN'T YOU UNDERSTAND?
LATER... PLEASE? CHOKING...TO DEATH.
SHOULD'VE SHOT HIM WHEN YOU HAD THE CHANCE. NOT LIKE IT'S THE FIRST TIME YOU WOULD'VE KILLED SOMEONE.
THAT WAS DIFFERENT--
I'M OUT. ENJOY PRISON, SWERVE.
HEY! DON'T LEAVE ME--!
LATER, KIDDOS.
HELLO THERE!
WHO THE HELL ARE YOU?
I'M AFRAID THAT IS QUITE A LONG STORY. PLEASE HOLD STILL.
ALWAYS WANTED TO STOMP A PRISSY CHEERLEADER TYPE--
WHAT THE--?
EEP!
PATHETIC.
WHAM

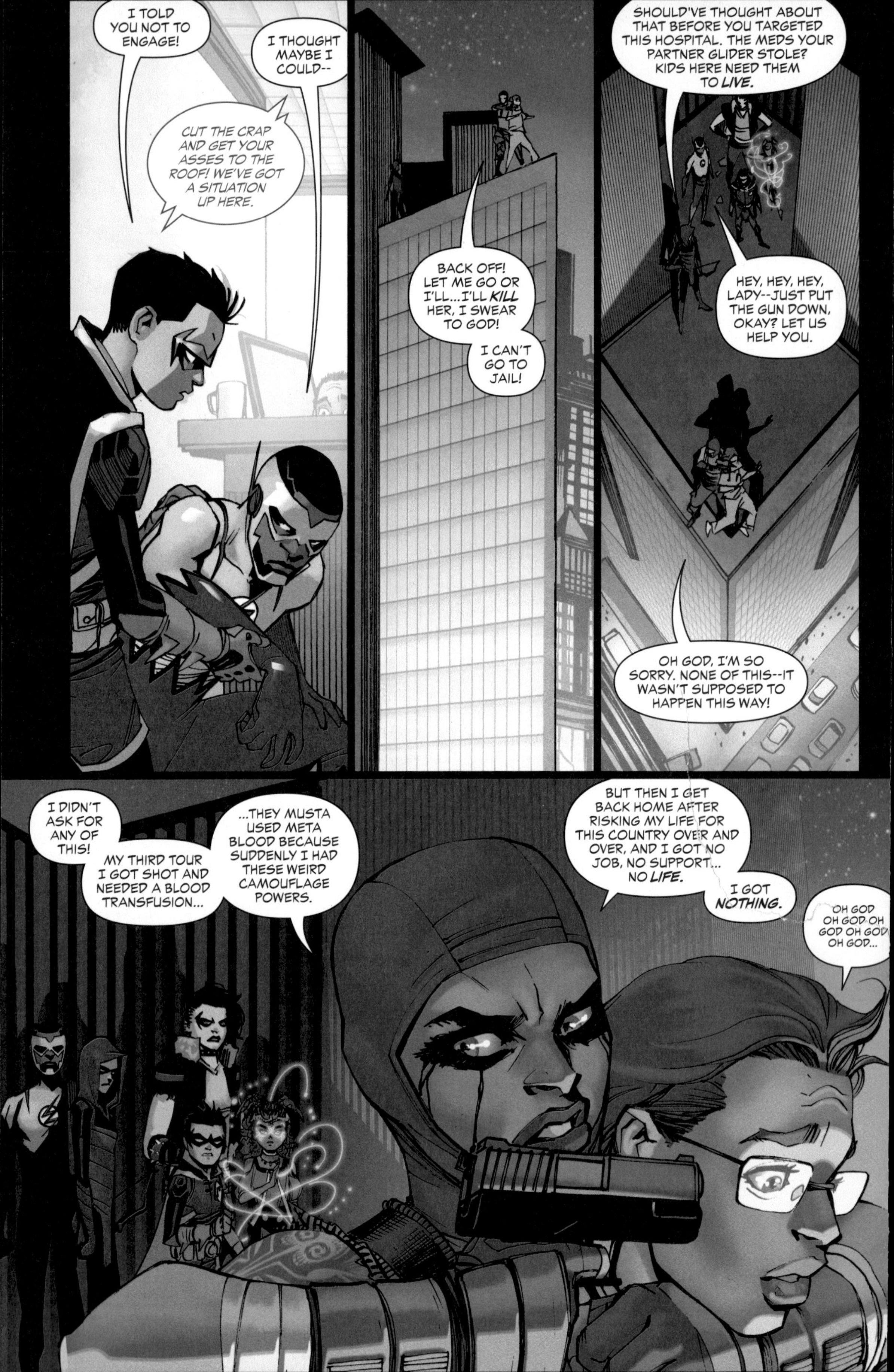
I TOLD YOU NOT TO ENGAGE!
I THOUGHT MAYBE I COULD--
CUT THE CRAP AND GET YOUR ASSES TO THE ROOF! WE'VE GOT A SITUATION UP HERE.
BACK OFF! LET ME GO OR I'LL...I'LL KILL HER, I SWEAR TO GOD!
I CAN'T GO TO JAIL!
SHOULD'VE THOUGHT ABOUT THAT BEFORE YOU TARGETED THIS HOSPITAL. THE MEDS YOUR PARTNER GLIDER STOLE? KIDS HERE NEED THEM TO LIVE.
HEY, HEY, HEY, LADY--JUST PUT THE GUN DOWN, OKAY? LET US HELP YOU.
OH GOD, I'M SO SORRY. NONE OF THIS--IT WASN'T SUPPOSED TO HAPPEN THIS WAY!
I DIDN'T ASK FOR ANY OF THIS!
MY THIRD TOUR I GOT SHOT AND NEEDED A BLOOD TRANSFUSION...
...THEY MUSTA USED META BLOOD BECAUSE SUDDENLY I HAD THESE WEIRD CAMOUFLAGE POWERS.
BUT THEN I GET BACK HOME AFTER RISKING MY LIFE FOR THIS COUNTRY OVER AND OVER, AND I GOT NO JOB, NO SUPPORT... NO LIFE.
I GOT NOTHING.
OH GOD OH GOD OH GOD OH GOD OH GOD...

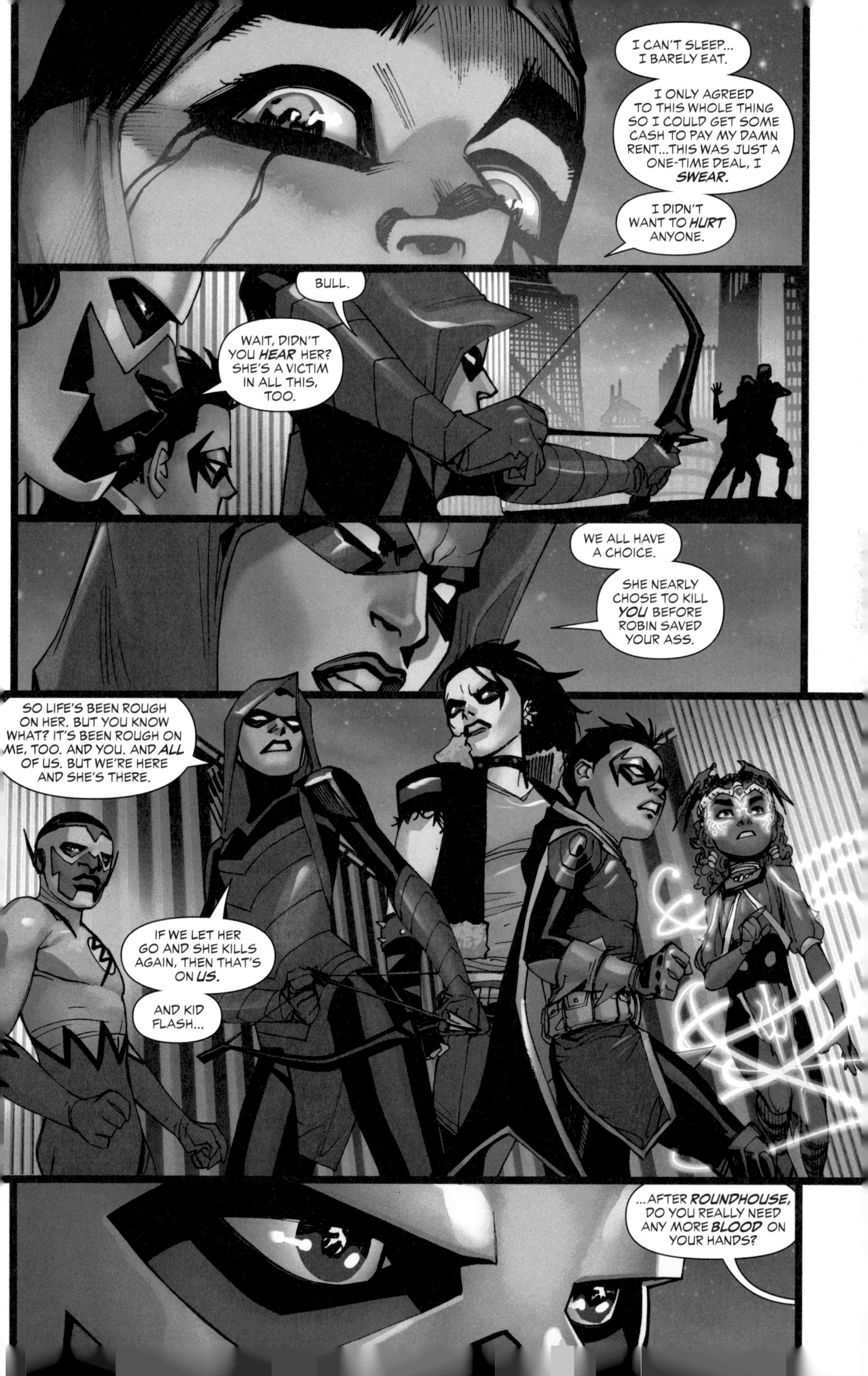
I CAN'T SLEEP... I BARELY EAT.
I ONLY AGREED TO THIS WHOLE THING SO I COULD GET SOME CASH TO PAY MY DAMN RENT...THIS WAS JUST A ONE-TIME DEAL, I SWEAR.
I DIDN'T WANT TO HURT ANYONE.
BULL.
WAIT, DIDN'T YOU HEAR HER? SHE'S A VICTIM IN ALL THIS, TOO.
WE ALL HAVE A CHOICE.
SHE NEARLY CHOSE TO KILL YOU BEFORE ROBIN SAVED YOUR ASS.
SO LIFE'S BEEN ROUGH ON HER. BUT YOU KNOW WHAT? IT'S BEEN ROUGH ON ME, TOO. AND YOU. AND ALL OF US. BUT WE'RE HERE AND SHE'S THERE.
IF WE LET HER GO AND SHE KILLS AGAIN, THEN THAT'S ON US.
AND KID FLASH...
...AFTER ROUNDHOUSE, DO YOU REALLY NEED ANY MORE BLOOD ON YOUR HANDS?

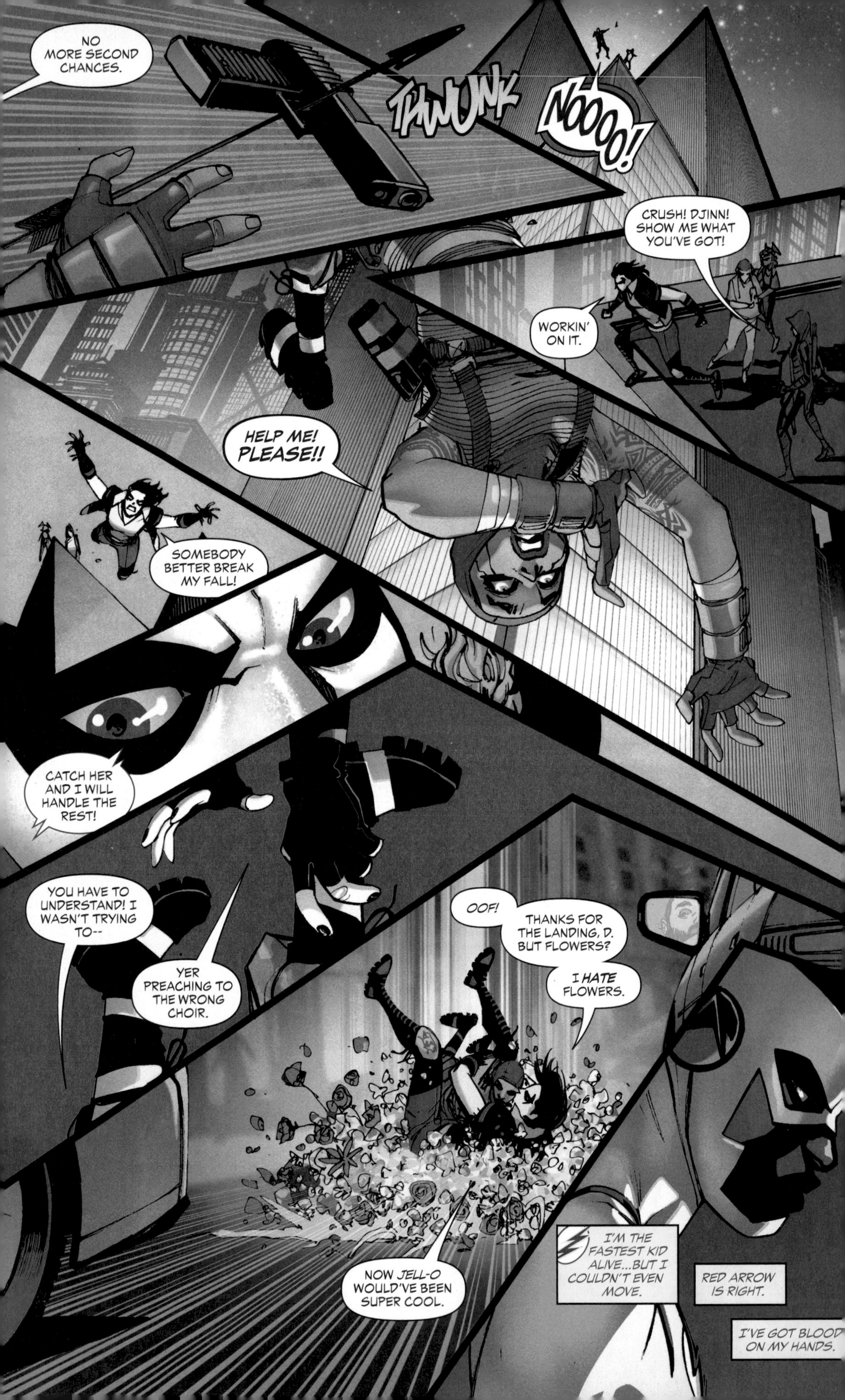
NO MORE SECOND CHANCES.
THWUNK
NOOOO!
CRUSH! DJINN! SHOW ME WHAT YOU'VE GOT!
WORKIN' ON IT.
HELP ME! PLEASE!!
SOMEBODY BETTER BREAK MY FALL!
CATCH HER AND I WILL HANDLE THE REST!
YOU HAVE TO UNDERSTAND! I WASN'T TRYING TO--
YER PREACHING TO THE WRONG CHOIR.
OOF!
THANKS FOR THE LANDING, D. BUT FLOWERS?
I HATE FLOWERS.
NOW JELL-O WOULD'VE BEEN SUPER COOL.
I'M THE FASTEST KID ALIVE...BUT I COULDN'T EVEN MOVE.
RED ARROW IS RIGHT.
I'VE GOT BLOOD ON MY HANDS.

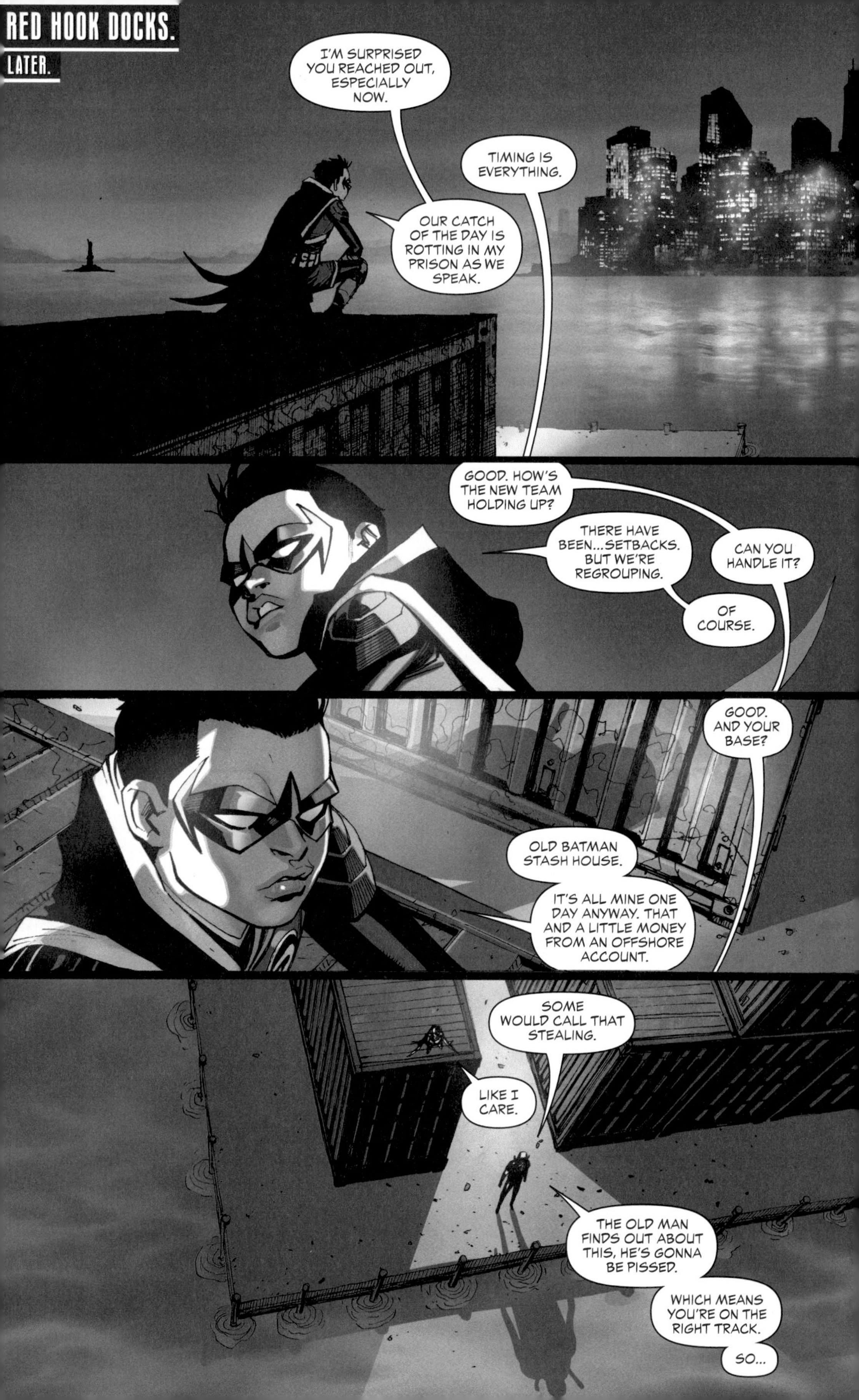
RED HOOK DOCKS.
LATER.
I'M SURPRISED YOU REACHED OUT, ESPECIALLY NOW.
TIMING IS EVERYTHING.
OUR CATCH OF THE DAY IS ROTTING IN MY PRISON AS WE SPEAK.
GOOD. HOW'S THE NEW TEAM HOLDING UP?
THERE HAVE BEEN...SETBACKS. BUT WE'RE REGROUPING.
CAN YOU HANDLE IT?
OF COURSE.
GOOD. AND YOUR BASE?
OLD BATMAN STASH HOUSE.
IT'S ALL MINE ONE DAY ANYWAY. THAT AND A LITTLE MONEY FROM AN OFFSHORE ACCOUNT.
SOME WOULD CALL THAT STEALING.
LIKE I CARE.
THE OLD MAN FINDS OUT ABOUT THIS, HE'S GONNA BE PISSED.
WHICH MEANS YOU'RE ON THE RIGHT TRACK.
SO...

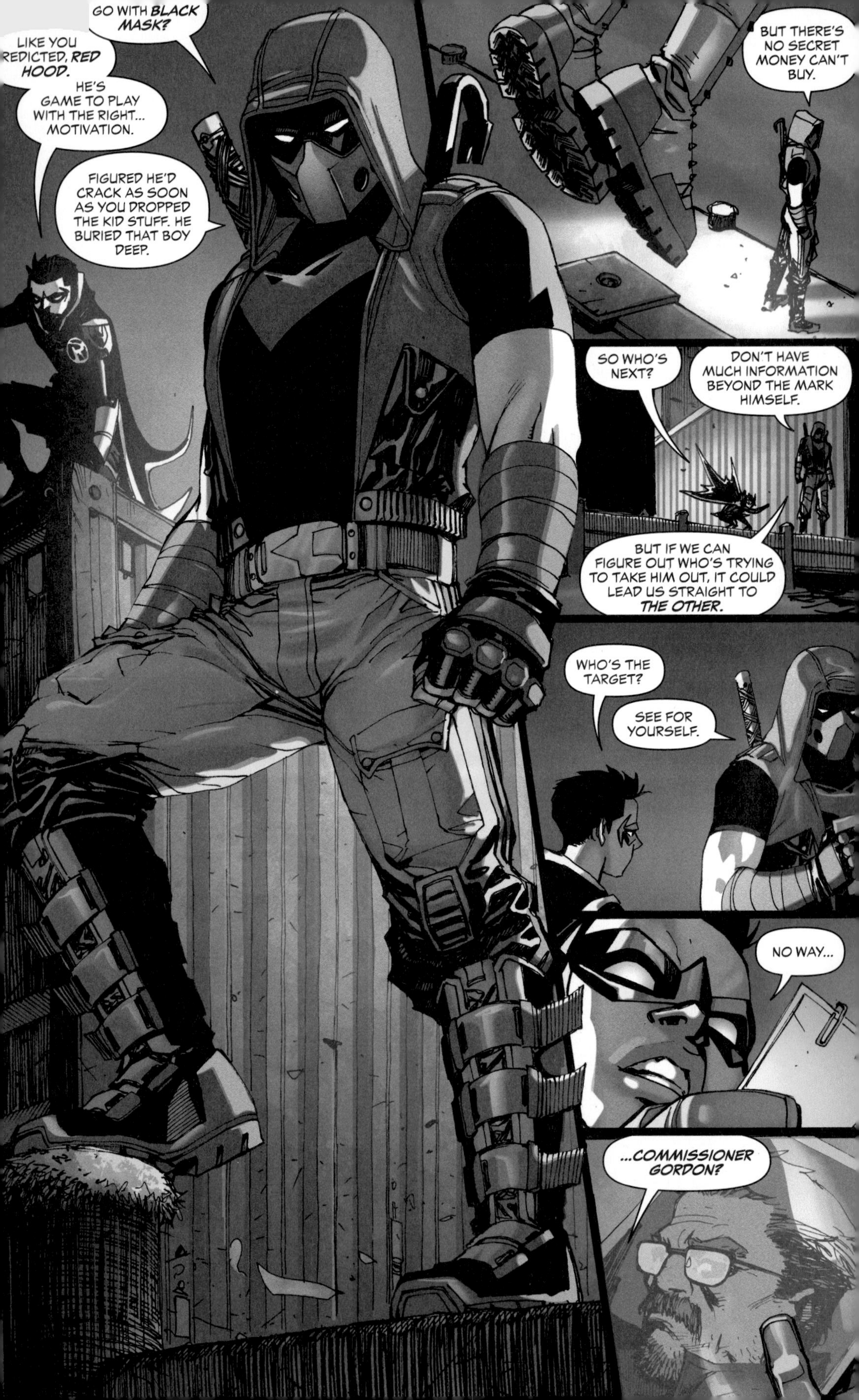
GO WITH BLACK MASK?
LIKE YOU PREDICTED, RED HOOD.
HE'S GAME TO PLAY WITH THE RIGHT... MOTIVATION.
FIGURED HE'D CRACK AS SOON AS YOU DROPPED THE KID STUFF. HE BURIED THAT BOY DEEP.
BUT THERE'S NO SECRET MONEY CAN'T BUY.
SO WHO'S NEXT?
DON'T HAVE MUCH INFORMATION BEYOND THE MARK HIMSELF.
BUT IF WE CAN FIGURE OUT WHO'S TRYING TO TAKE HIM OUT, IT COULD LEAD US STRAIGHT TO THE OTHER.
WHO'S THE TARGET?
SEE FOR YOURSELF.
NO WAY...
...COMMISSIONER GORDON?

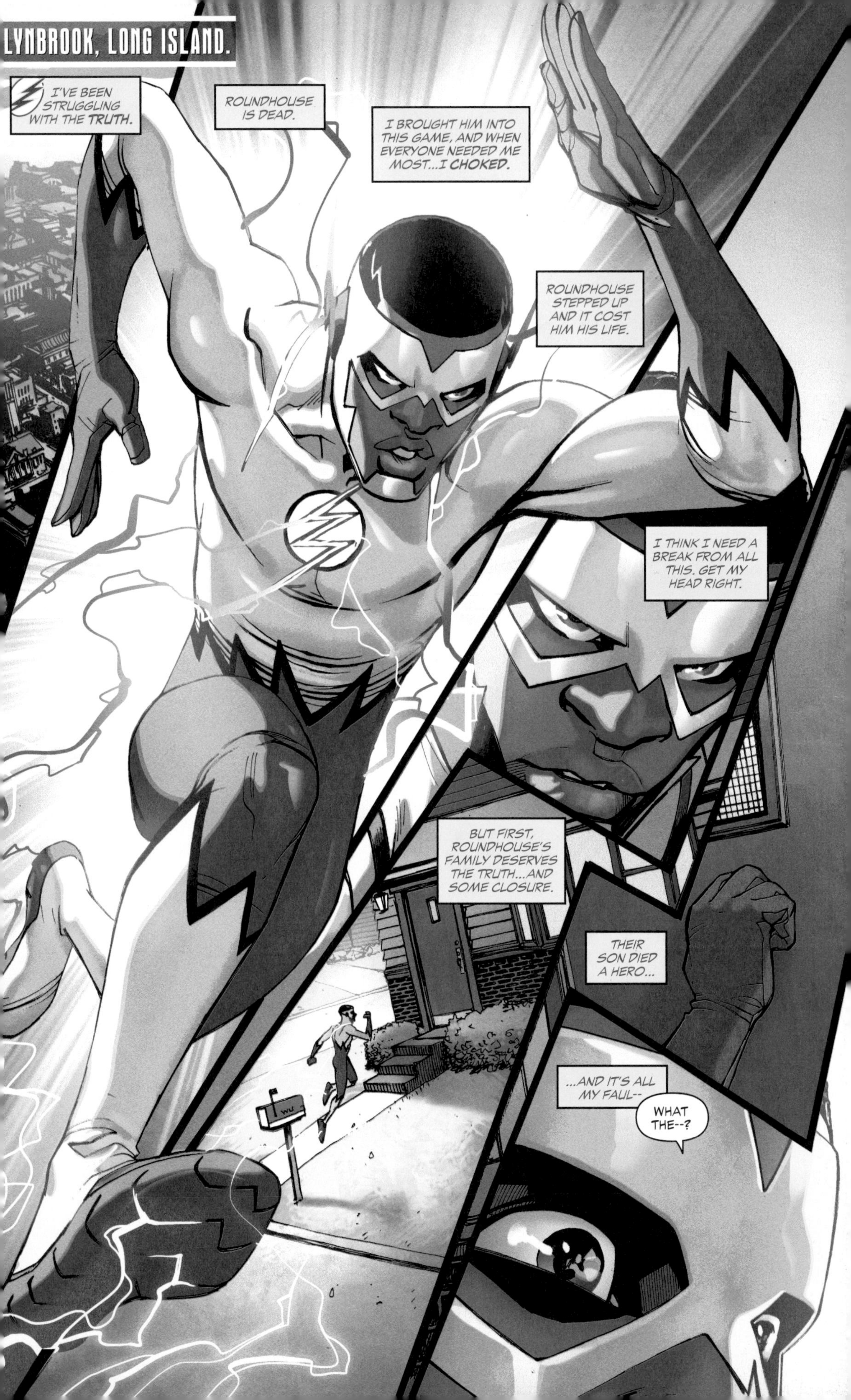
LYNBROOK, LONG ISLAND.
I'VE BEEN STRUGGLING WITH THE TRUTH.
ROUNDHOUSE IS DEAD.
I BROUGHT HIM INTO THIS GAME, AND WHEN EVERYONE NEEDED ME MOST...I CHOKED.
ROUNDHOUSE STEPPED UP AND IT COST HIM HIS LIFE.
I THINK I NEED A BREAK FROM ALL THIS. GET MY HEAD RIGHT.
BUT FIRST, ROUNDHOUSE'S FAMILY DESERVES THE TRUTH...AND SOME CLOSURE.
THEIR SON DIED A HERO...
...AND IT'S ALL MY FAUL--
WHAT THE--?

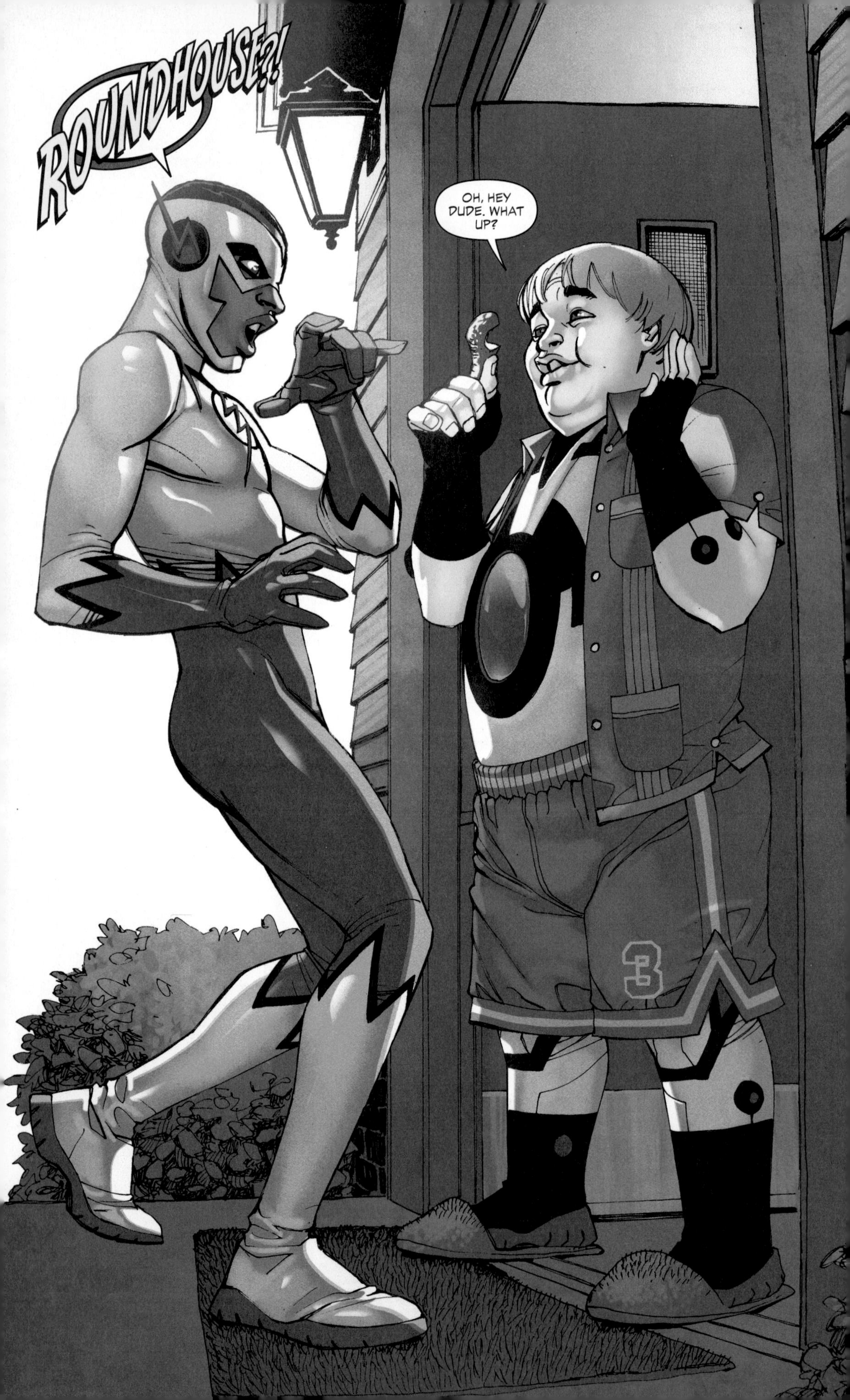
ROUNDHOUSE?!
OH, HEY DUDE. WHAT UP?

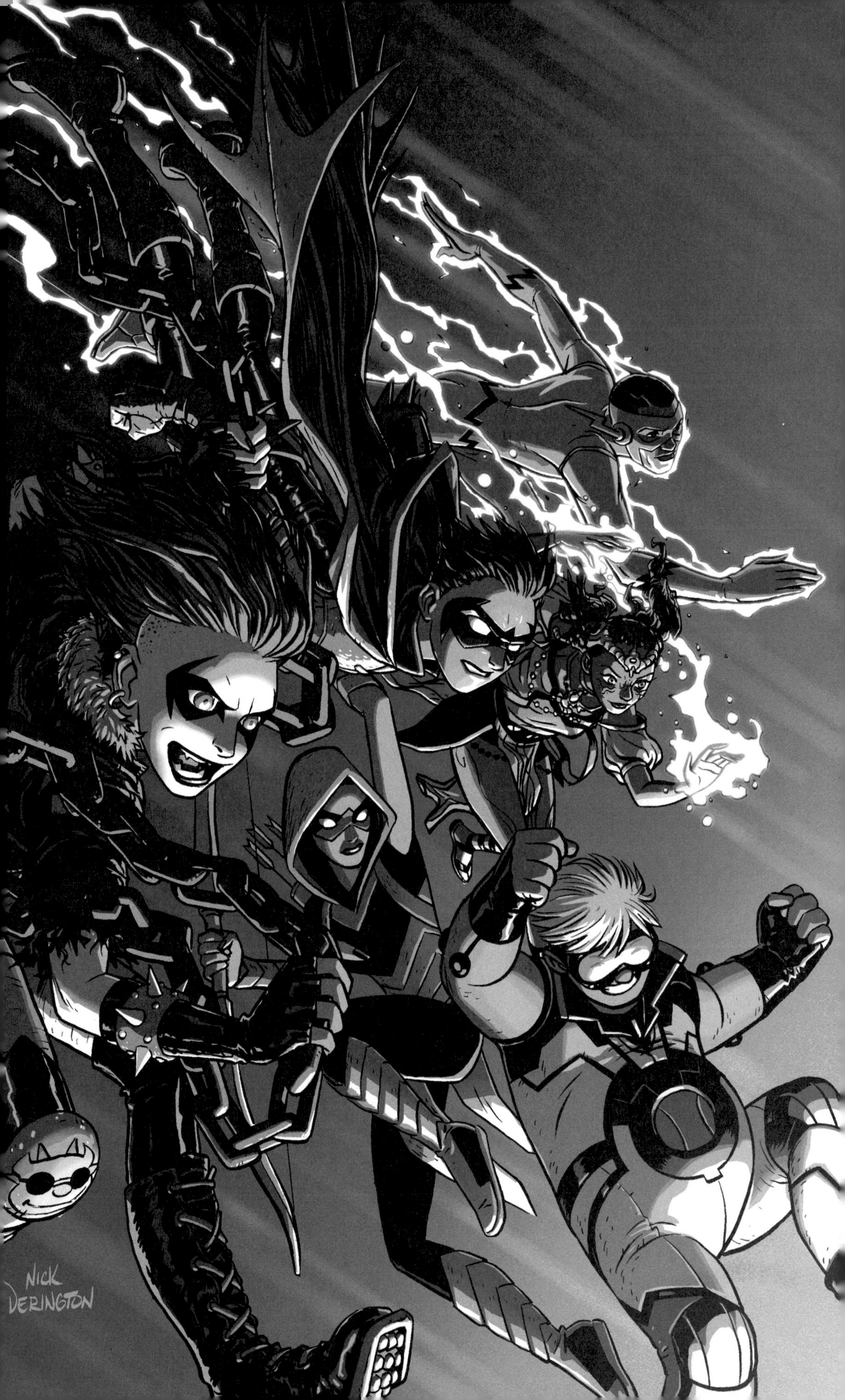
NICK DERINGTON

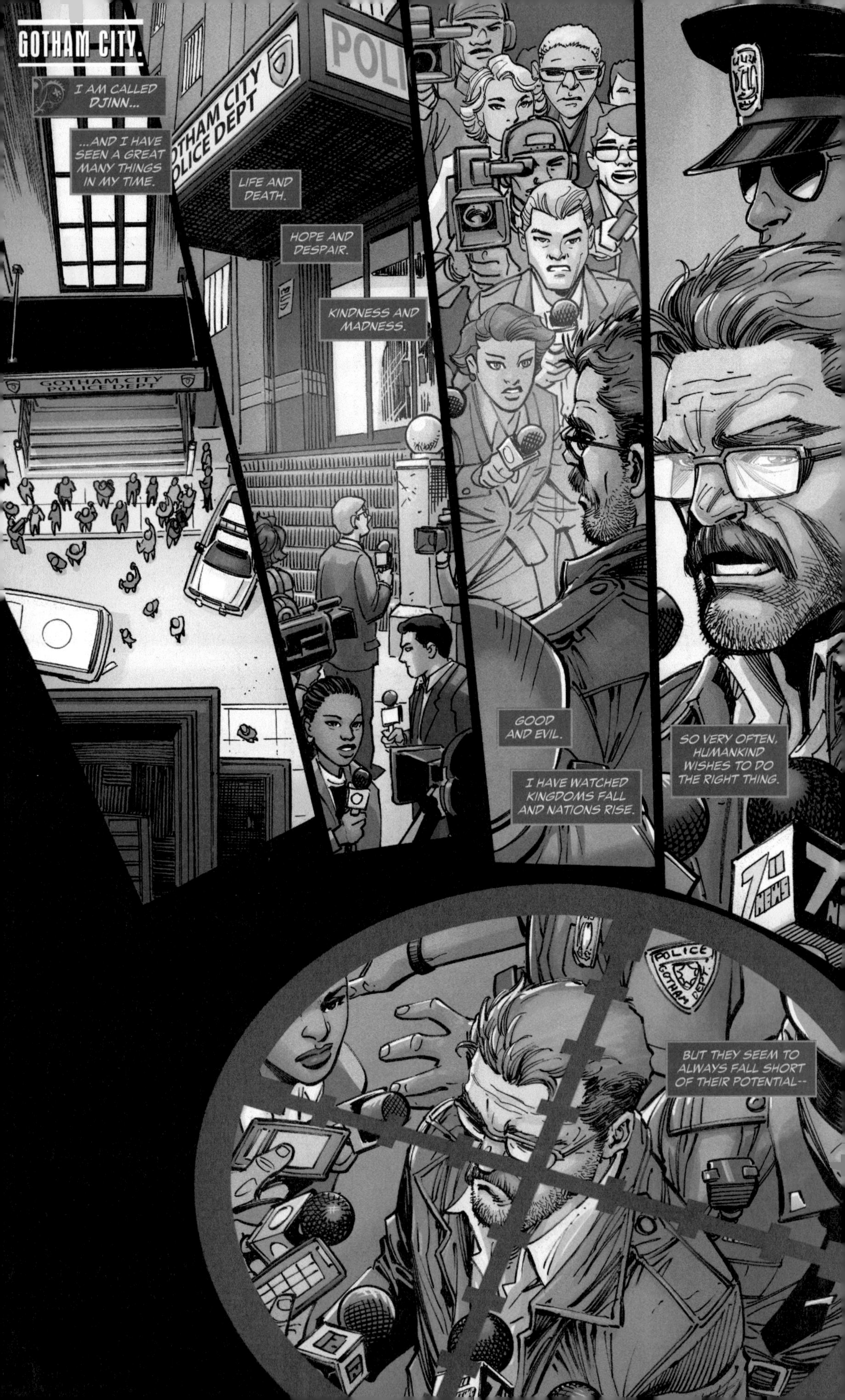
GOTHAM CITY.
I AM CALLED DJINN...
...AND I HAVE SEEN A GREAT MANY THINGS IN MY TIME.
LIFE AND DEATH.
HOPE AND DESPAIR.
KINDNESS AND MADNESS.
GOOD AND EVIL.
I HAVE WATCHED KINGDOMS FALL AND NATIONS RISE.
SO VERY OFTEN, HUMANKIND WISHES TO DO THE RIGHT THING.
BUT THEY SEEM TO ALWAYS FALL SHORT OF THEIR POTENTIAL--

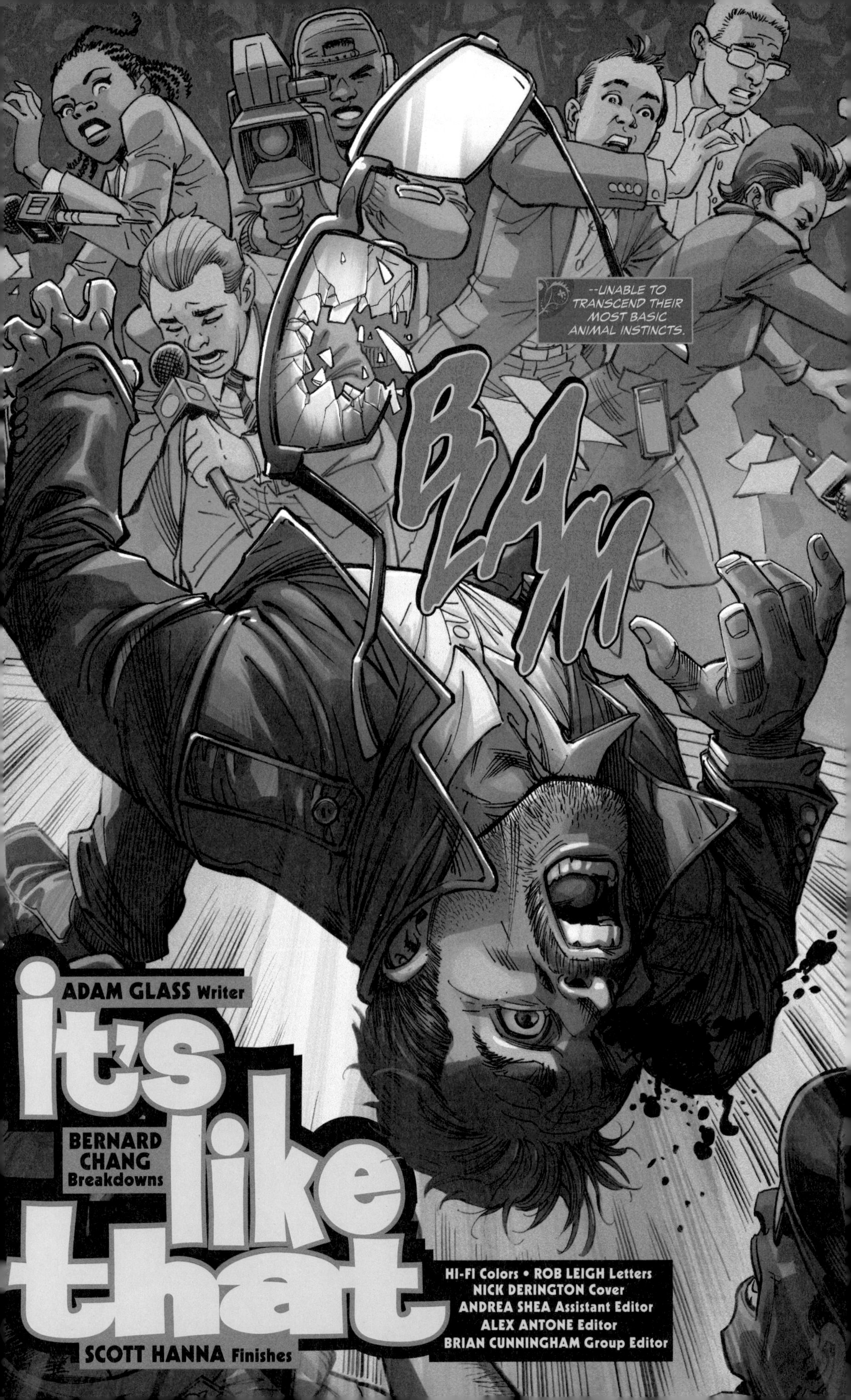
--UNABLE TO TRANSCEND THEIR MOST BASIC ANIMAL INSTINCTS.
BLAM
it's like that
ADAM GLASS Writer
BERNARD CHANG Breakdowns
SCOTT HANNA Finishes
HI-FI Colors • ROB LEIGH Letters
NICK DERINGTON Cover
ANDREA SHEA Assistant Editor
ALEX ANTONE Editor
BRIAN CUNNINGHAM Group Editor

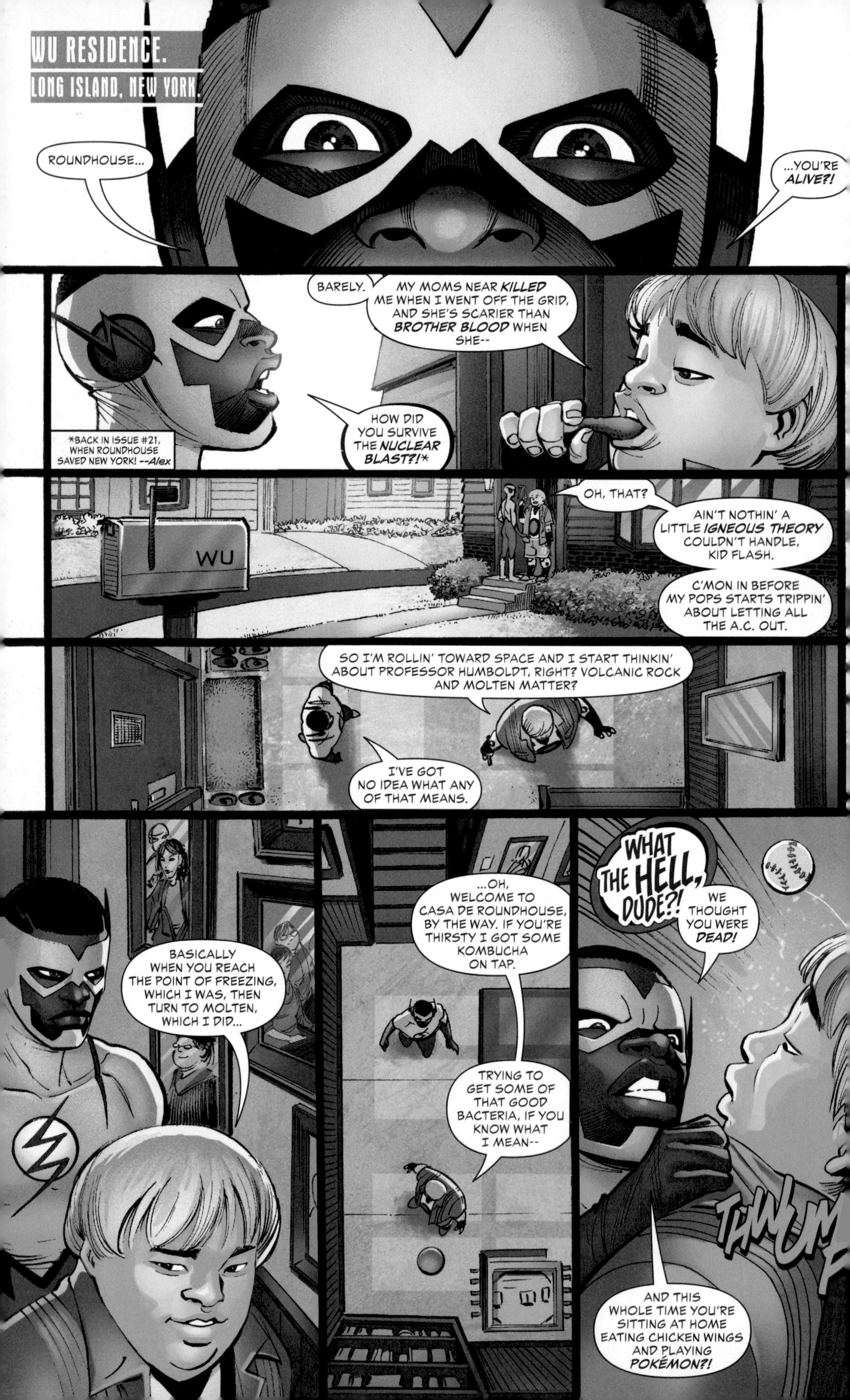
WU RESIDENCE.
LONG ISLAND, NEW YORK.
ROUNDHOUSE...
...YOU'RE ALIVE?!
BARELY.
MY MOMS NEAR KILLED ME WHEN I WENT OFF THE GRID, AND SHE'S SCARIER THAN BROTHER BLOOD WHEN SHE--
HOW DID YOU SURVIVE THE NUCLEAR BLAST?!*
*BACK IN ISSUE #21, WHEN ROUNDHOUSE SAVED NEW YORK! --Alex
WU
OH, THAT?
AIN'T NOTHIN' A LITTLE IGNEOUS THEORY COULDN'T HANDLE, KID FLASH.
C'MON IN BEFORE MY POPS STARTS TRIPPIN' ABOUT LETTING ALL THE A.C. OUT.
SO I'M ROLLIN' TOWARD SPACE AND I START THINKIN' ABOUT PROFESSOR HUMBOLDT, RIGHT? VOLCANIC ROCK AND MOLTEN MATTER?
I'VE GOT NO IDEA WHAT ANY OF THAT MEANS.
BASICALLY WHEN YOU REACH THE POINT OF FREEZING, WHICH I WAS, THEN TURN TO MOLTEN, WHICH I DID...
...OH, WELCOME TO CASA DE ROUNDHOUSE, BY THE WAY. IF YOU'RE THIRSTY I GOT SOME KOMBUCHA ON TAP.
TRYING TO GET SOME OF THAT GOOD BACTERIA, IF YOU KNOW WHAT I MEAN--
WHAT THE HELL, DUDE?!
WE THOUGHT YOU WERE DEAD!
THWUMP
AND THIS WHOLE TIME YOU'RE SITTING AT HOME EATING CHICKEN WINGS AND PLAYING POKÉMON?!

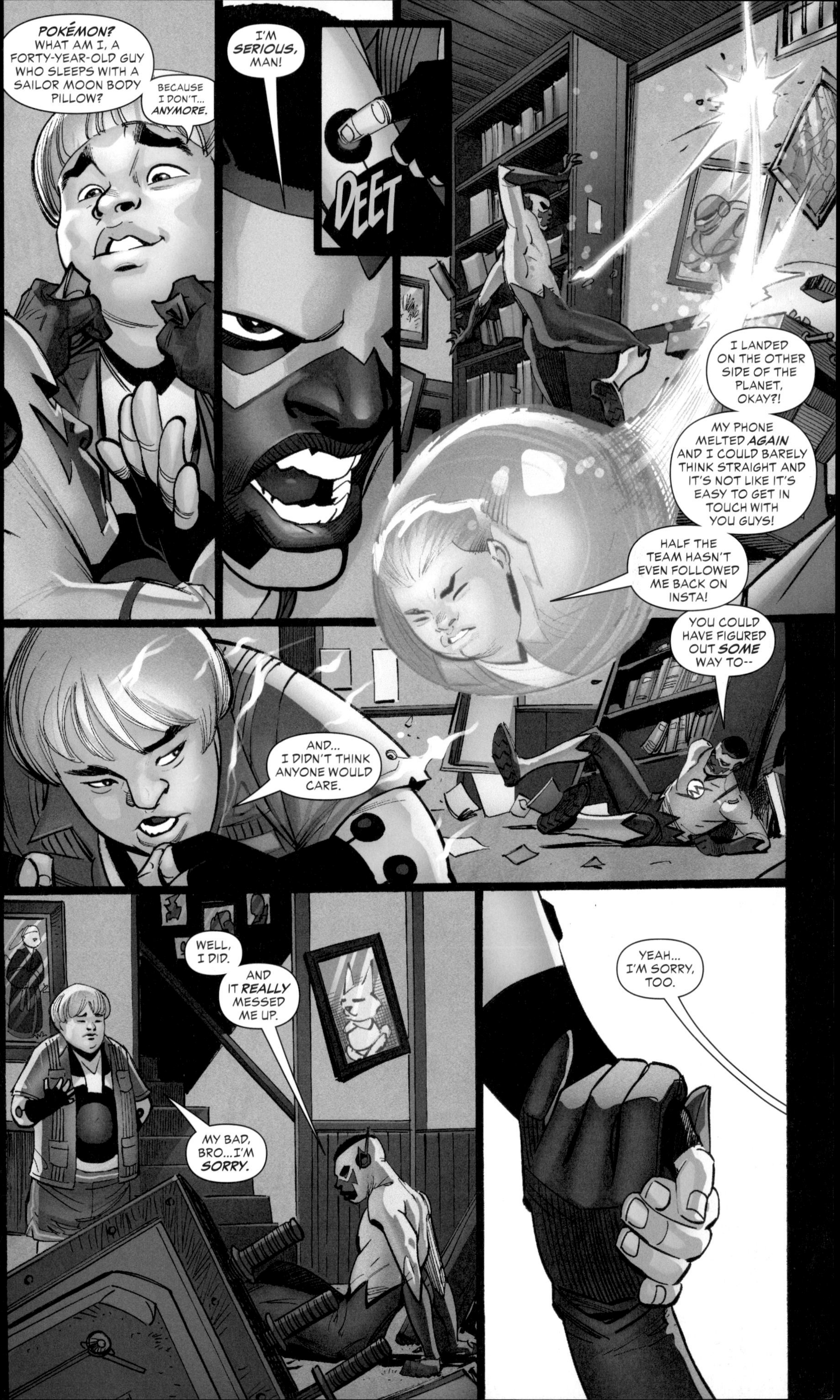
POKÉMON? WHAT AM I, A FORTY-YEAR-OLD GUY WHO SLEEPS WITH A SAILOR MOON BODY PILLOW?
BECAUSE I DON'T... ANYMORE.
I'M SERIOUS, MAN!
DEET
I LANDED ON THE OTHER SIDE OF THE PLANET, OKAY?!
MY PHONE MELTED AGAIN AND I COULD BARELY THINK STRAIGHT AND IT'S NOT LIKE IT'S EASY TO GET IN TOUCH WITH YOU GUYS!
HALF THE TEAM HASN'T EVEN FOLLOWED ME BACK ON INSTA!
YOU COULD HAVE FIGURED OUT SOME WAY TO--
AND... I DIDN'T THINK ANYONE WOULD CARE.
WELL, I DID.
AND IT REALLY MESSED ME UP.
MY BAD, BRO...I'M SORRY.
YEAH... I'M SORRY, TOO.

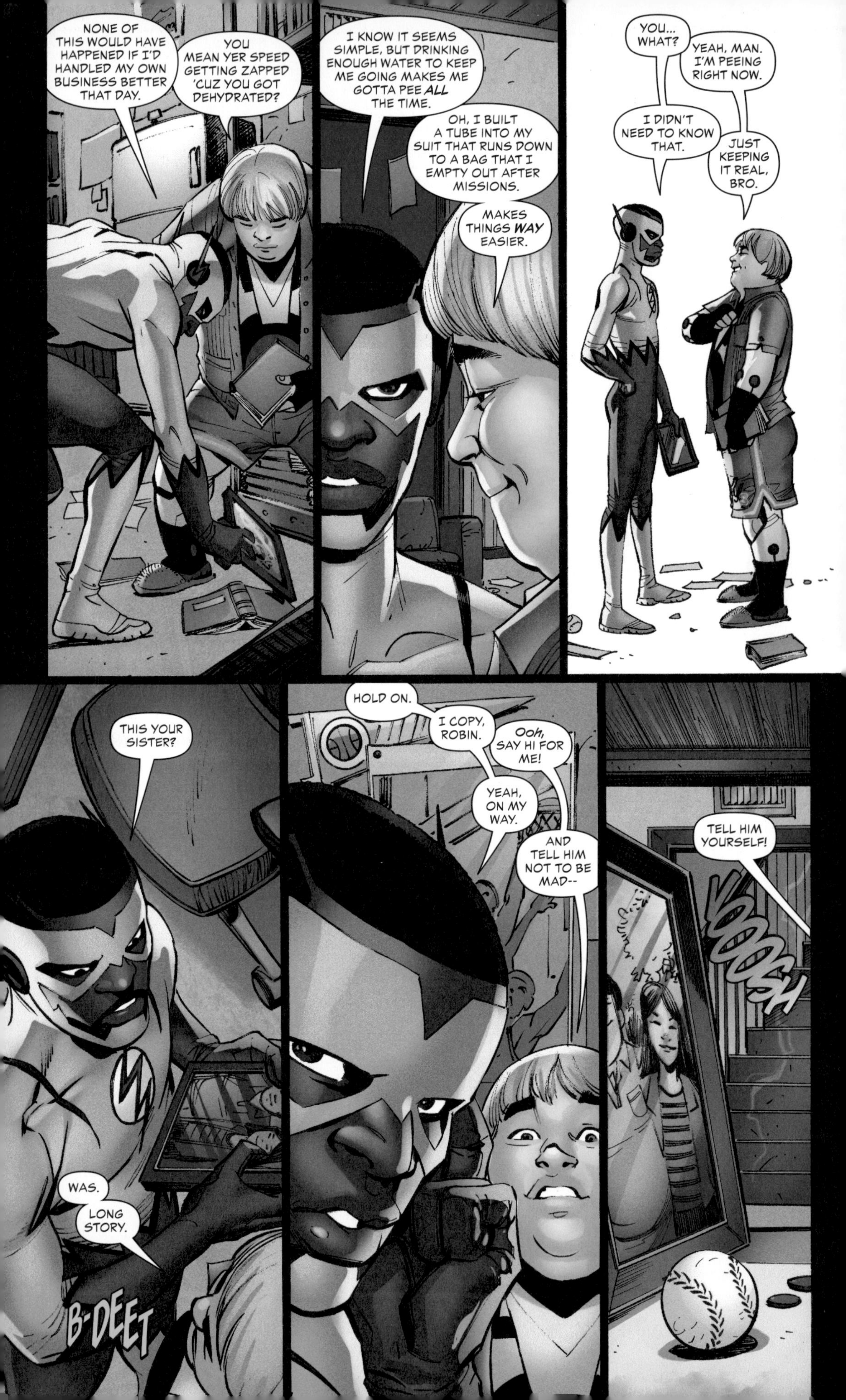
NONE OF THIS WOULD HAVE HAPPENED IF I'D HANDLED MY OWN BUSINESS BETTER THAT DAY.
YOU MEAN YER SPEED GETTING ZAPPED 'CUZ YOU GOT DEHYDRATED?
I KNOW IT SEEMS SIMPLE, BUT DRINKING ENOUGH WATER TO KEEP ME GOING MAKES ME GOTTA PEE ALL THE TIME.
OH, I BUILT A TUBE INTO MY SUIT THAT RUNS DOWN TO A BAG THAT I EMPTY OUT AFTER MISSIONS.
MAKES THINGS WAY EASIER.
YOU... WHAT?
YEAH, MAN. I'M PEEING RIGHT NOW.
I DIDN'T NEED TO KNOW THAT.
JUST KEEPING IT REAL, BRO.
THIS YOUR SISTER?
WAS.
LONG STORY.
B-DEET
HOLD ON.
I COPY, ROBIN.
Ooh, SAY HI FOR ME!
YEAH, ON MY WAY.
AND TELL HIM NOT TO BE MAD--
TELL HIM YOURSELF!
VOOOSH

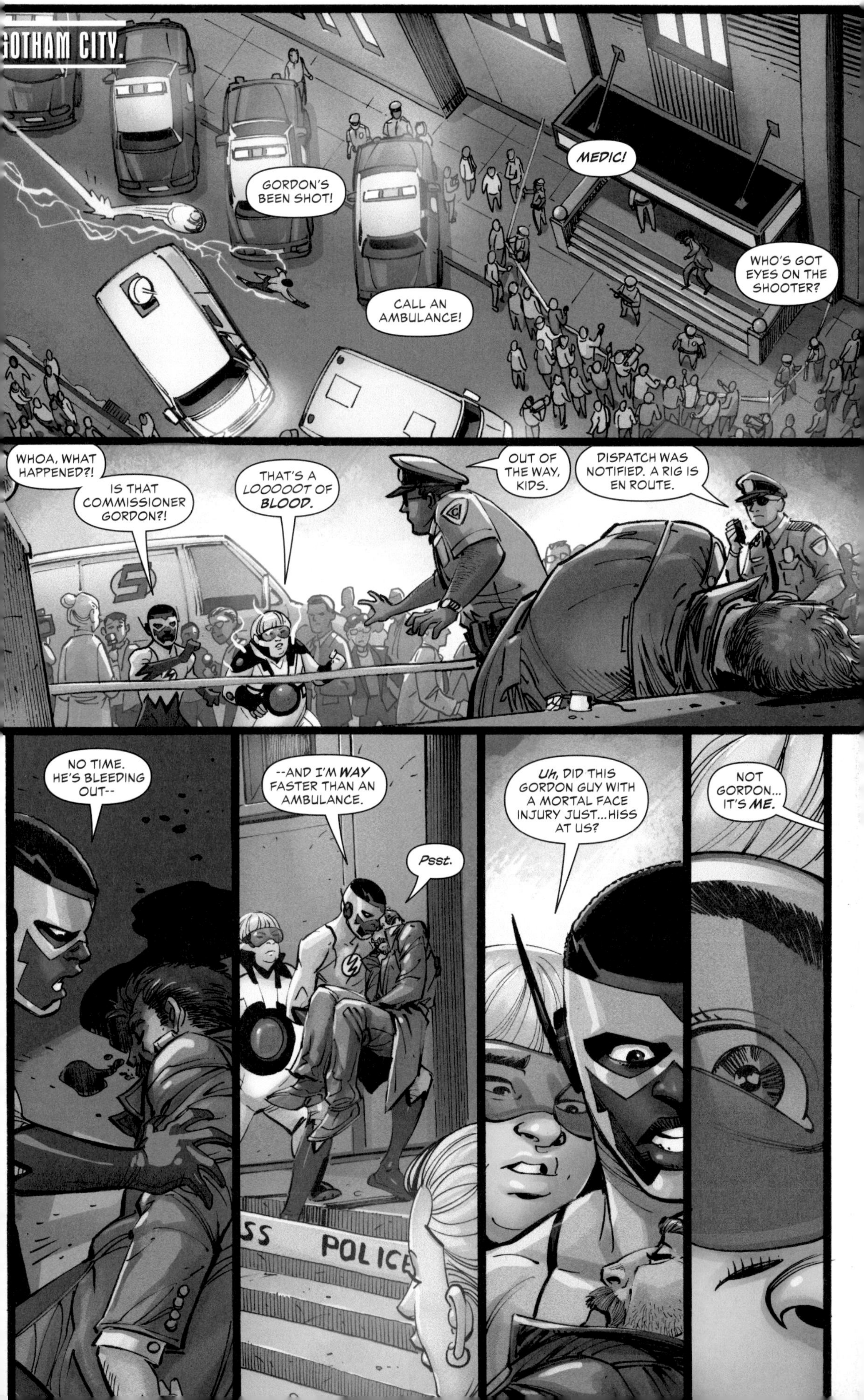
GOTHAM CITY.
GORDON'S BEEN SHOT!
MEDIC!
WHO'S GOT EYES ON THE SHOOTER?
CALL AN AMBULANCE!
WHOA, WHAT HAPPENED?!
IS THAT COMMISSIONER GORDON?!
THAT'S A LOOOOOT OF BLOOD.
OUT OF THE WAY, KIDS.
DISPATCH WAS NOTIFIED. A RIG IS EN ROUTE.
NO TIME. HE'S BLEEDING OUT--
--AND I'M WAY FASTER THAN AN AMBULANCE.
Psst.
POLICE
Uh, DID THIS GORDON GUY WITH A MORTAL FACE INJURY JUST...HISS AT US?
NOT GORDON... IT'S ME.

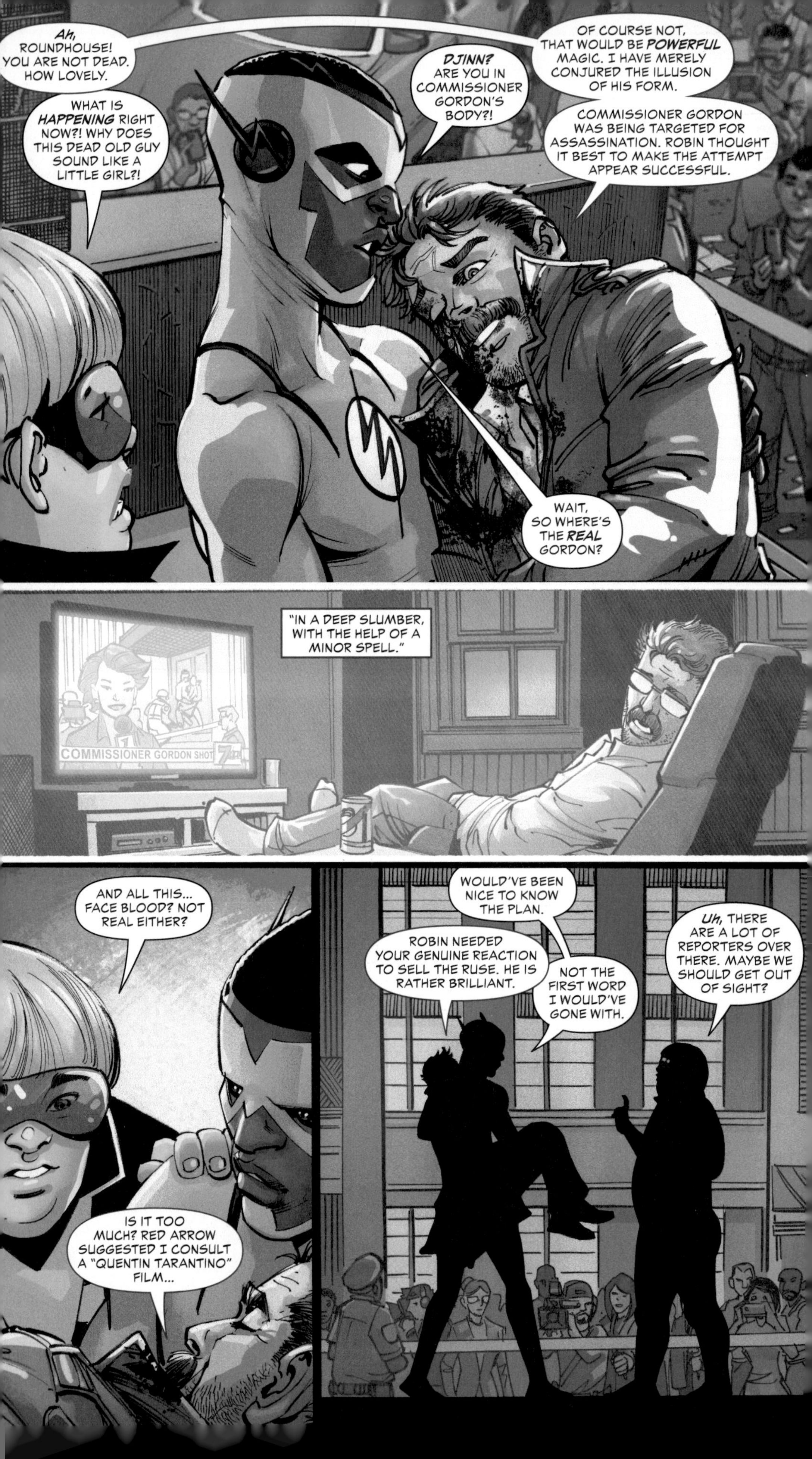
Ah, ROUNDHOUSE! YOU ARE NOT DEAD. HOW LOVELY.
WHAT IS HAPPENING RIGHT NOW?! WHY DOES THIS DEAD OLD GUY SOUND LIKE A LITTLE GIRL?!
DJINN? ARE YOU IN COMMISSIONER GORDON'S BODY?!
OF COURSE NOT, THAT WOULD BE POWERFUL MAGIC. I HAVE MERELY CONJURED THE ILLUSION OF HIS FORM.
COMMISSIONER GORDON WAS BEING TARGETED FOR ASSASSINATION. ROBIN THOUGHT IT BEST TO MAKE THE ATTEMPT APPEAR SUCCESSFUL.
WAIT, SO WHERE'S THE REAL GORDON?
"IN A DEEP SLUMBER, WITH THE HELP OF A MINOR SPELL."
COMMISSIONER GORDON SHOT
AND ALL THIS... FACE BLOOD? NOT REAL EITHER?
IS IT TOO MUCH? RED ARROW SUGGESTED I CONSULT A "QUENTIN TARANTINO" FILM...
WOULD'VE BEEN NICE TO KNOW THE PLAN.
ROBIN NEEDED YOUR GENUINE REACTION TO SELL THE RUSE. HE IS RATHER BRILLIANT.
NOT THE FIRST WORD I WOULD'VE GONE WITH.
Uh, THERE ARE A LOT OF REPORTERS OVER THERE. MAYBE WE SHOULD GET OUT OF SIGHT?

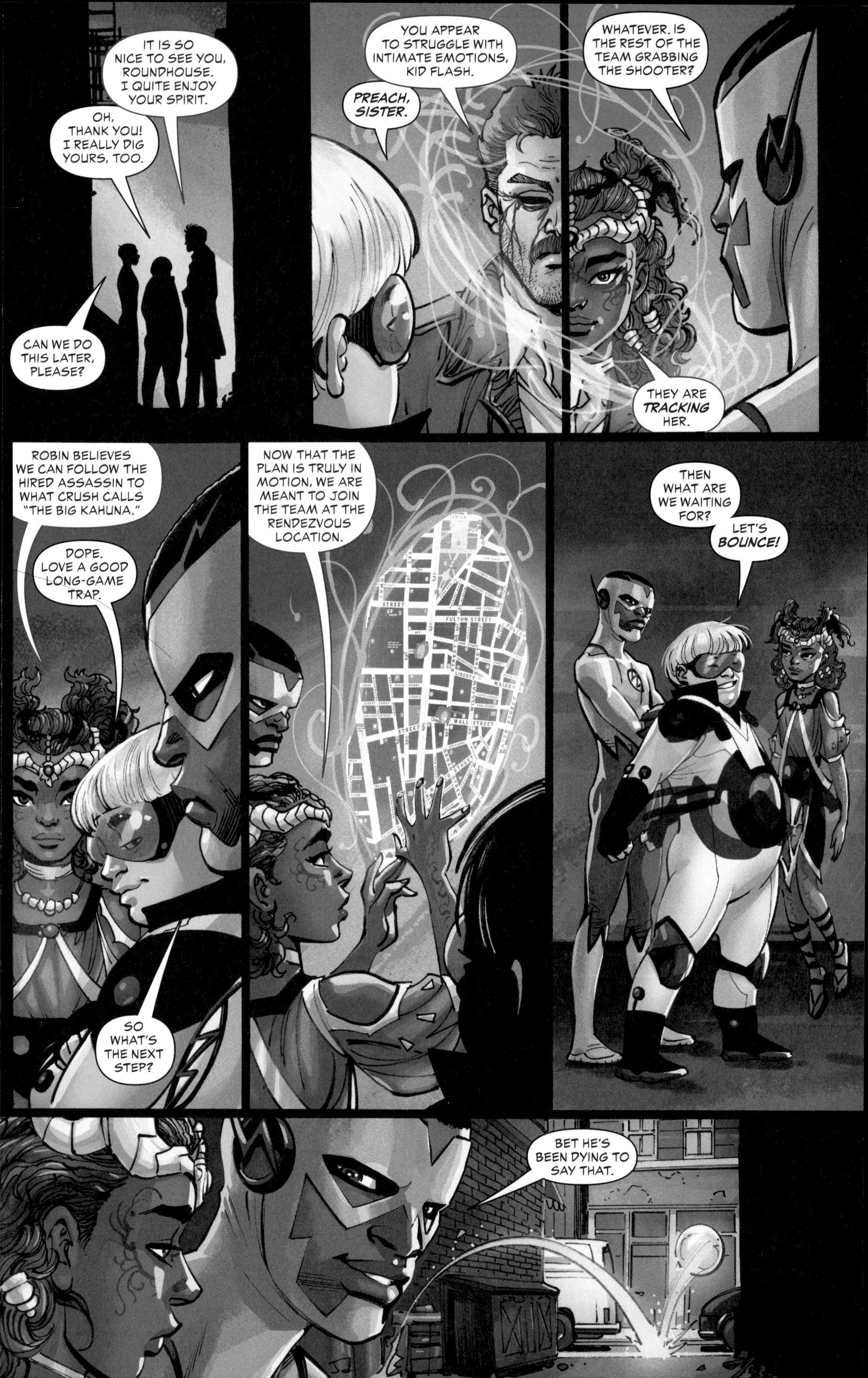
IT IS SO NICE TO SEE YOU, ROUNDHOUSE. I QUITE ENJOY YOUR SPIRIT.
OH, THANK YOU! I REALLY DIG YOURS, TOO.
CAN WE DO THIS LATER, PLEASE?
YOU APPEAR TO STRUGGLE WITH INTIMATE EMOTIONS, KID FLASH.
*PREACH, SISTER.*
WHATEVER. IS THE REST OF THE TEAM GRABBING THE SHOOTER?
THEY ARE *TRACKING* HER.
ROBIN BELIEVES WE CAN FOLLOW THE HIRED ASSASSIN TO WHAT CRUSH CALLS "THE BIG KAHUNA."
DOPE. LOVE A GOOD LONG-GAME TRAP.
SO WHAT'S THE NEXT STEP?
NOW THAT THE PLAN IS TRULY IN MOTION, WE ARE MEANT TO JOIN THE TEAM AT THE RENDEZVOUS LOCATION.
THEN WHAT ARE WE WAITING FOR?
LET'S *BOUNCE!*
BET HE'S BEEN DYING TO SAY THAT.

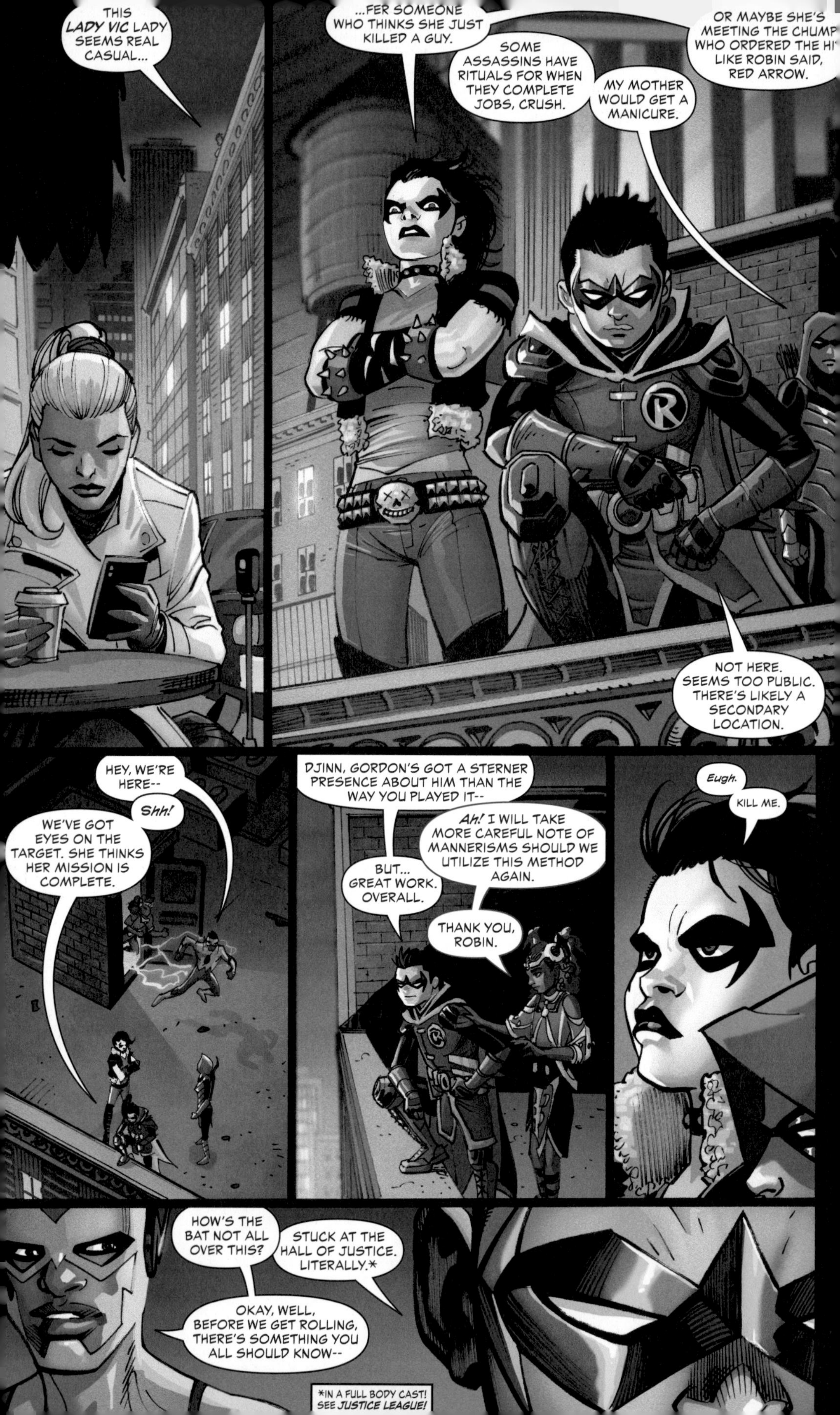
THIS LADY VIC LADY SEEMS REAL CASUAL...
...FER SOMEONE WHO THINKS SHE JUST KILLED A GUY.
SOME ASSASSINS HAVE RITUALS FOR WHEN THEY COMPLETE JOBS, CRUSH.
MY MOTHER WOULD GET A MANICURE.
OR MAYBE SHE'S MEETING THE CHUMP WHO ORDERED THE HI LIKE ROBIN SAID, RED ARROW.
NOT HERE. SEEMS TOO PUBLIC. THERE'S LIKELY A SECONDARY LOCATION.
HEY, WE'RE HERE--
Shh!
WE'VE GOT EYES ON THE TARGET. SHE THINKS HER MISSION IS COMPLETE.
DJINN, GORDON'S GOT A STERNER PRESENCE ABOUT HIM THAN THE WAY YOU PLAYED IT--
BUT... GREAT WORK. OVERALL.
Ah! I WILL TAKE MORE CAREFUL NOTE OF MANNERISMS SHOULD WE UTILIZE THIS METHOD AGAIN.
THANK YOU, ROBIN.
Eugh.
KILL ME.
HOW'S THE BAT NOT ALL OVER THIS?
STUCK AT THE HALL OF JUSTICE. LITERALLY.*
OKAY, WELL, BEFORE WE GET ROLLING, THERE'S SOMETHING YOU ALL SHOULD KNOW--
*IN A FULL BODY CAST! SEE JUSTICE LEAGUE!

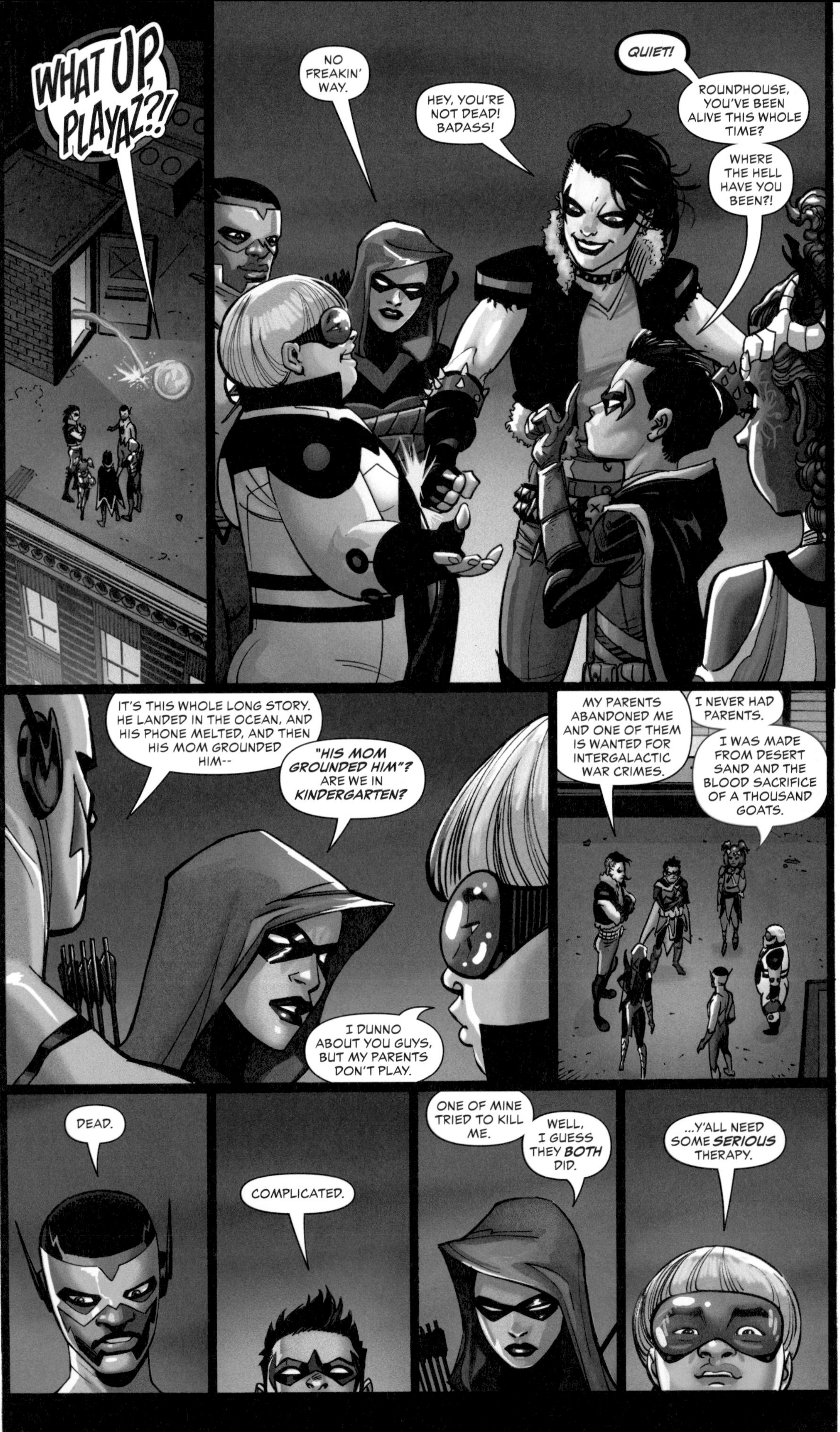
WHAT UP, PLAYAZ?!
NO FREAKIN' WAY.
HEY, YOU'RE NOT DEAD! BADASS!
QUIET!
ROUNDHOUSE, YOU'VE BEEN ALIVE THIS WHOLE TIME?
WHERE THE HELL HAVE YOU BEEN?!
IT'S THIS WHOLE LONG STORY. HE LANDED IN THE OCEAN, AND HIS PHONE MELTED, AND THEN HIS MOM GROUNDED HIM--
"HIS MOM GROUNDED HIM"? ARE WE IN KINDERGARTEN?
I DUNNO ABOUT YOU GUYS, BUT MY PARENTS DON'T PLAY.
MY PARENTS ABANDONED ME AND ONE OF THEM IS WANTED FOR INTERGALACTIC WAR CRIMES.
I NEVER HAD PARENTS.
I WAS MADE FROM DESERT SAND AND THE BLOOD SACRIFICE OF A THOUSAND GOATS.
DEAD.
COMPLICATED.
ONE OF MINE TRIED TO KILL ME.
WELL, I GUESS THEY BOTH DID.
...Y'ALL NEED SOME SERIOUS THERAPY.

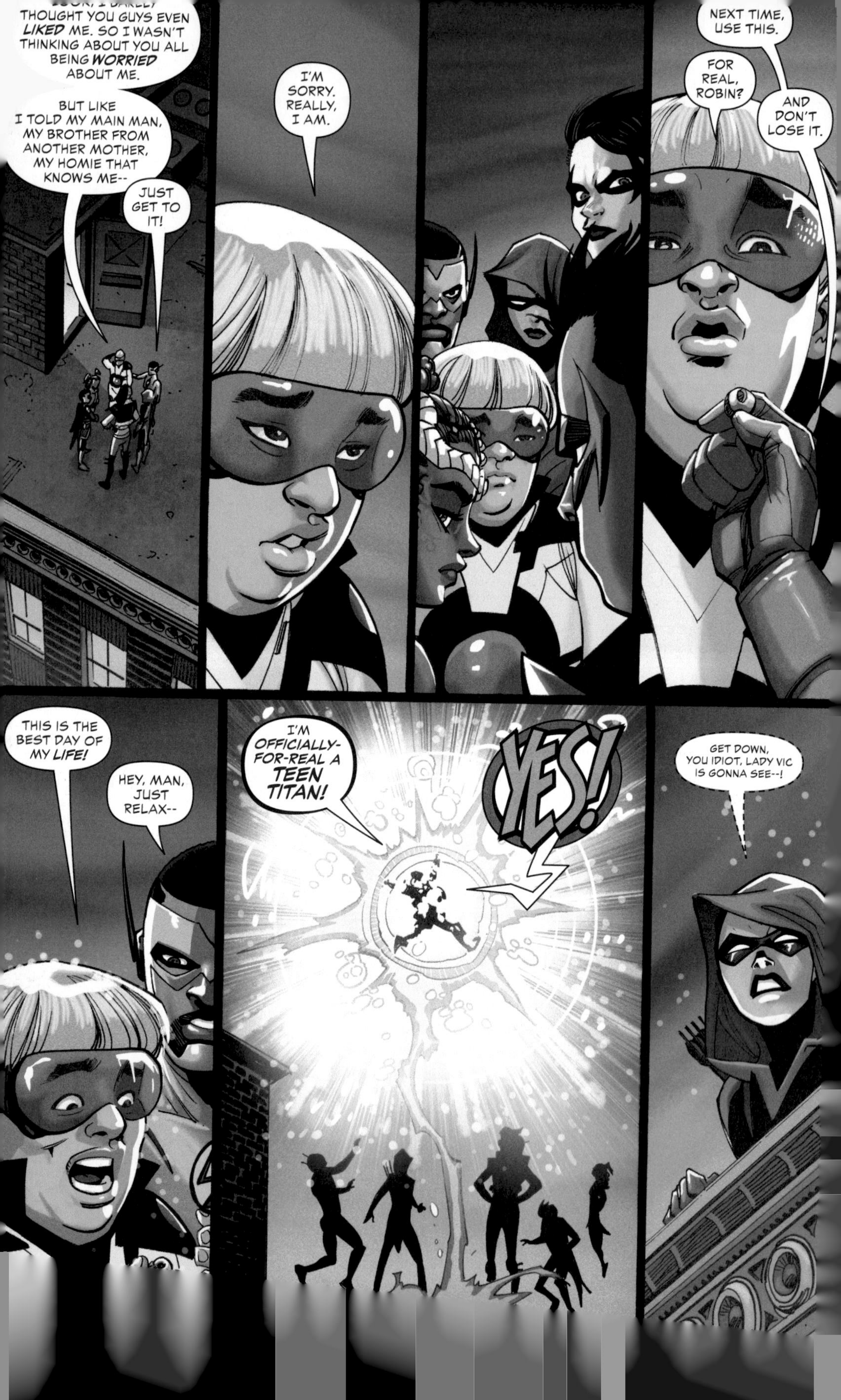
THOUGHT YOU GUYS EVEN LIKED ME. SO I WASN'T THINKING ABOUT YOU ALL BEING WORRIED ABOUT ME.
BUT LIKE I TOLD MY MAIN MAN, MY BROTHER FROM ANOTHER MOTHER, MY HOMIE THAT KNOWS ME--
JUST GET TO IT!
I'M SORRY. REALLY, I AM.
NEXT TIME, USE THIS.
FOR REAL, ROBIN?
AND DON'T LOSE IT.
THIS IS THE BEST DAY OF MY LIFE!
HEY, MAN, JUST RELAX--
I'M OFFICIALLY-FOR-REAL A TEEN TITAN!
YES!
GET DOWN, YOU IDIOT, LADY VIC IS GONNA SEE--!

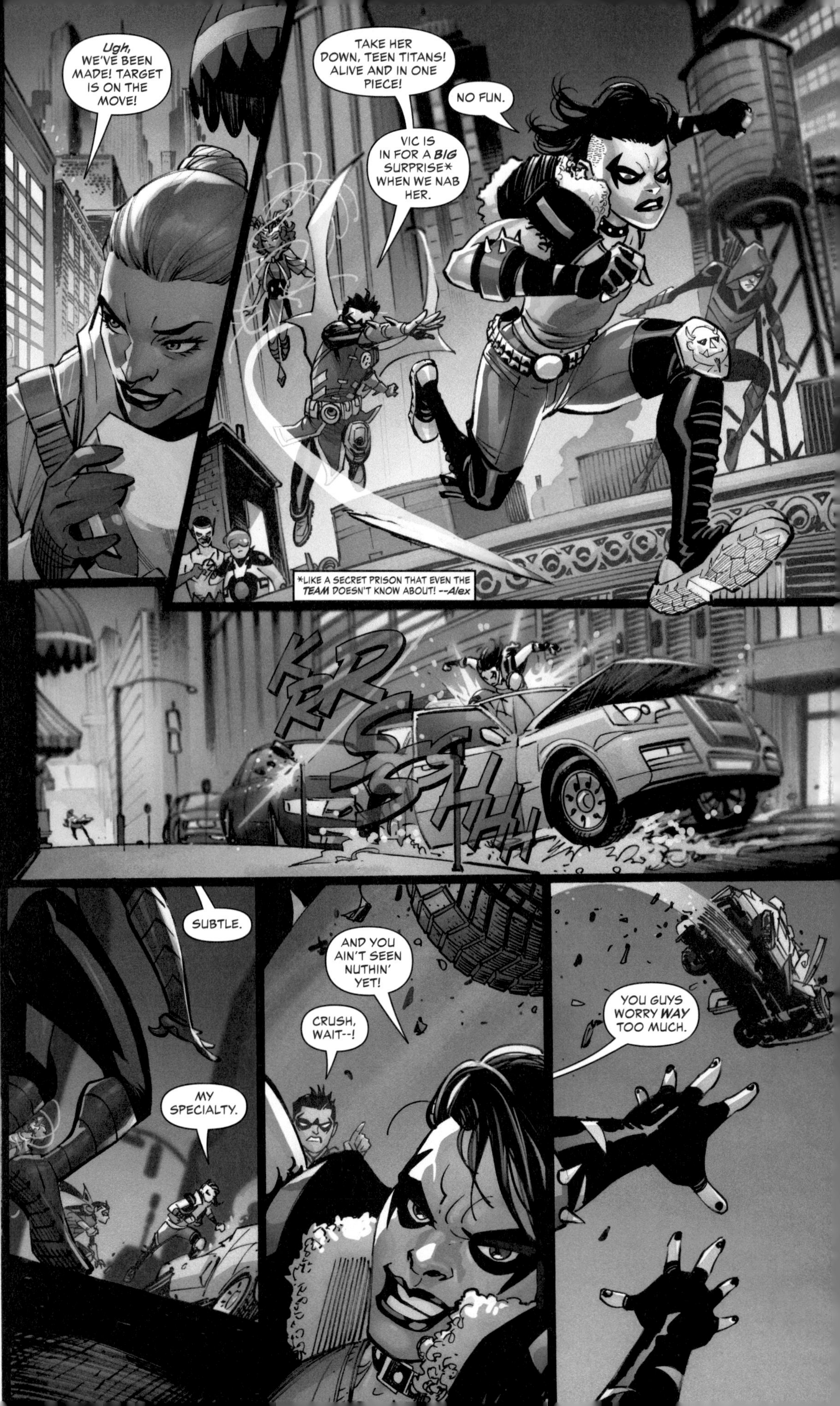
Ugh, WE'VE BEEN MADE! TARGET IS ON THE MOVE!
TAKE HER DOWN, TEEN TITANS! ALIVE AND IN ONE PIECE!
NO FUN.
VIC IS IN FOR A BIG SURPRISE* WHEN WE NAB HER.
*LIKE A SECRET PRISON THAT EVEN THE TEAM DOESN'T KNOW ABOUT! --Alex
KRRSSHH
SUBTLE.
MY SPECIALTY.
AND YOU AIN'T SEEN NUTHIN' YET!
CRUSH, WAIT--!
YOU GUYS WORRY WAY TOO MUCH.

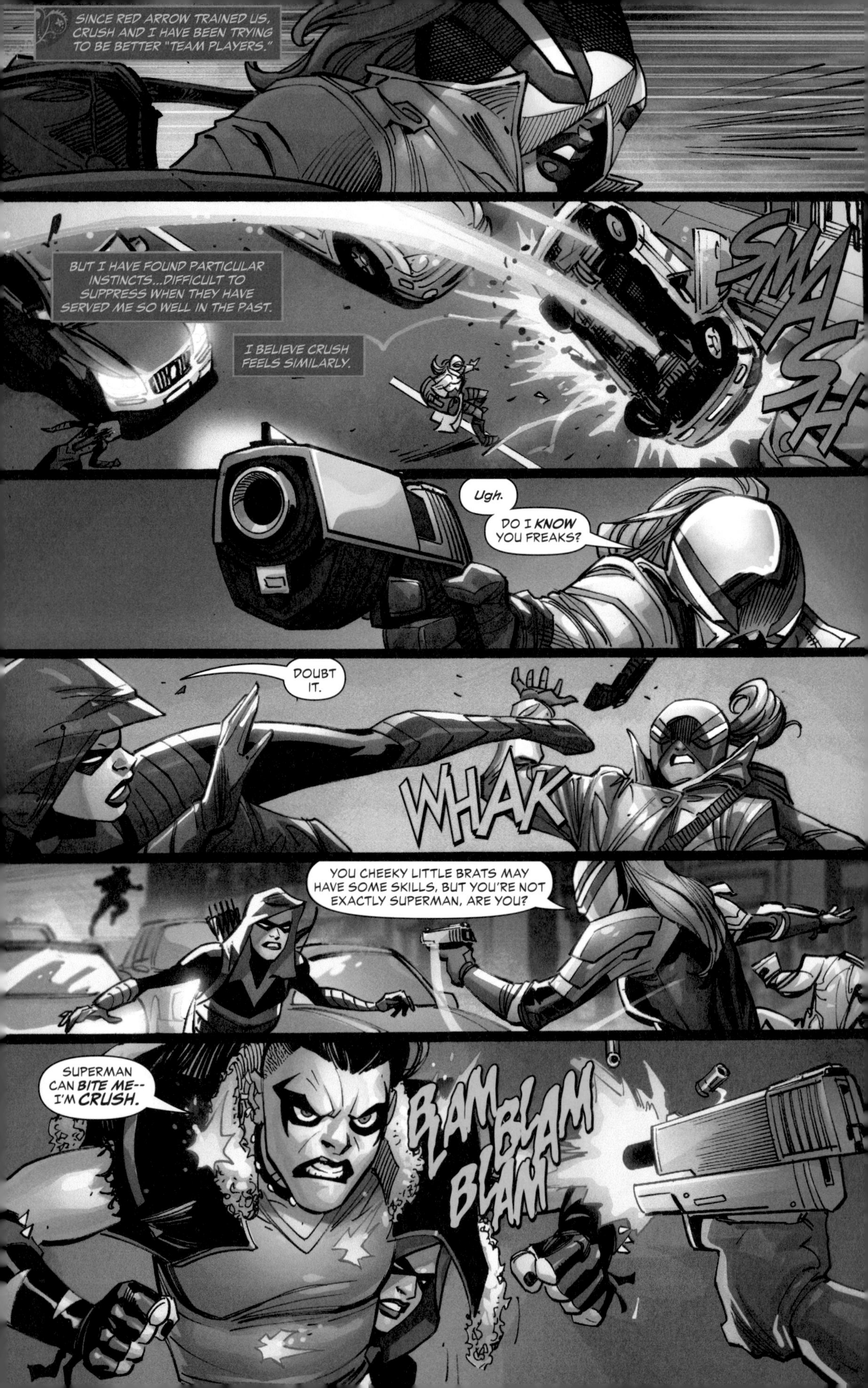
SINCE RED ARROW TRAINED US, CRUSH AND I HAVE BEEN TRYING TO BE BETTER "TEAM PLAYERS."
BUT I HAVE FOUND PARTICULAR INSTINCTS...DIFFICULT TO SUPPRESS WHEN THEY HAVE SERVED ME SO WELL IN THE PAST.
I BELIEVE CRUSH FEELS SIMILARLY.
SMASH
Ugh.
DO I KNOW YOU FREAKS?
DOUBT IT.
WHAK
YOU CHEEKY LITTLE BRATS MAY HAVE SOME SKILLS, BUT YOU'RE NOT EXACTLY SUPERMAN, ARE YOU?
SUPERMAN CAN BITE ME-- I'M CRUSH.
BLAM BLAM BLAM

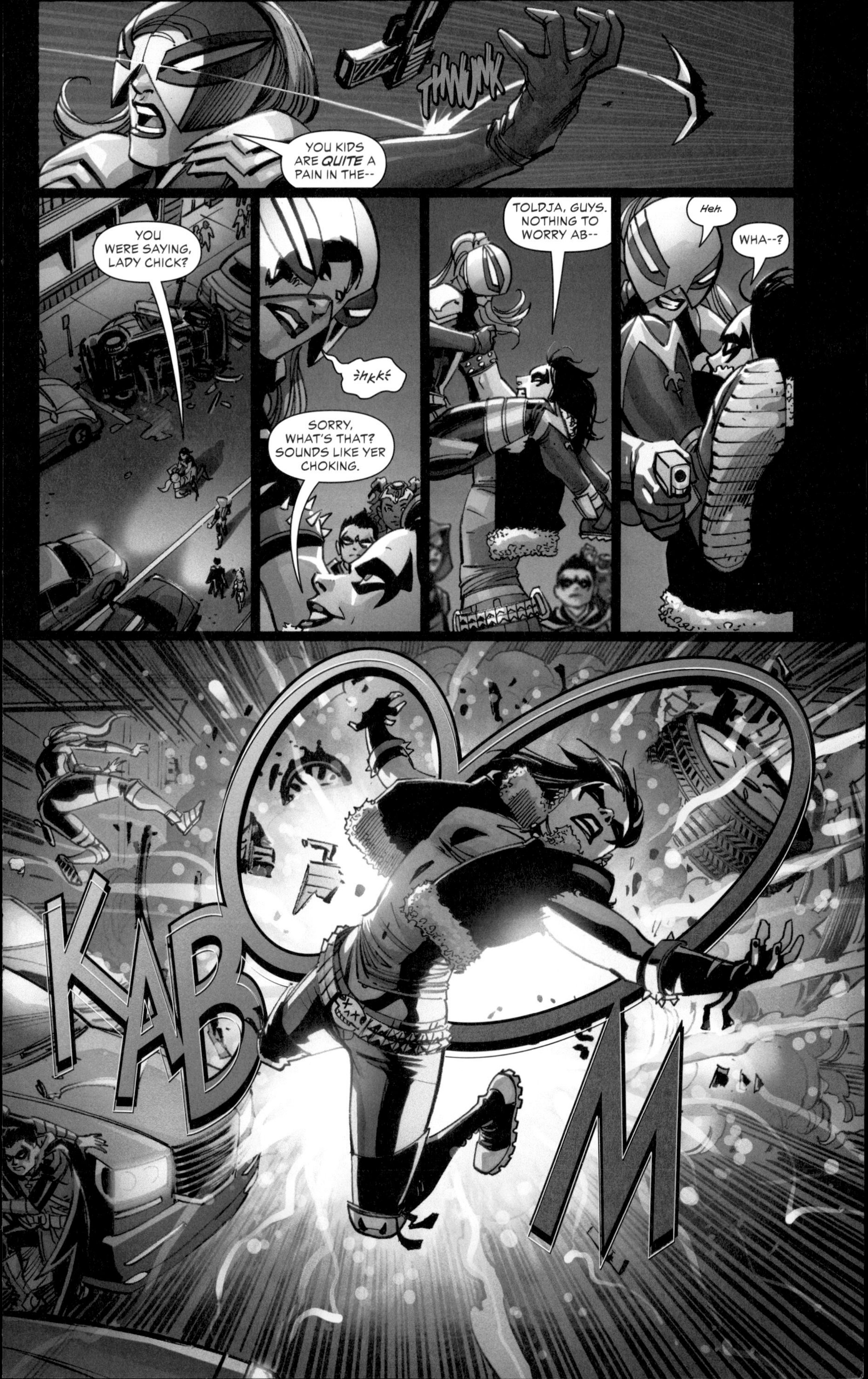
THWUNK
YOU KIDS ARE QUITE A PAIN IN THE--
YOU WERE SAYING, LADY CHICK?
HKK
SORRY, WHAT'S THAT? SOUNDS LIKE YER CHOKING.
TOLDJA, GUYS. NOTHING TO WORRY AB--
Heh.
WHA--?
KABOOM

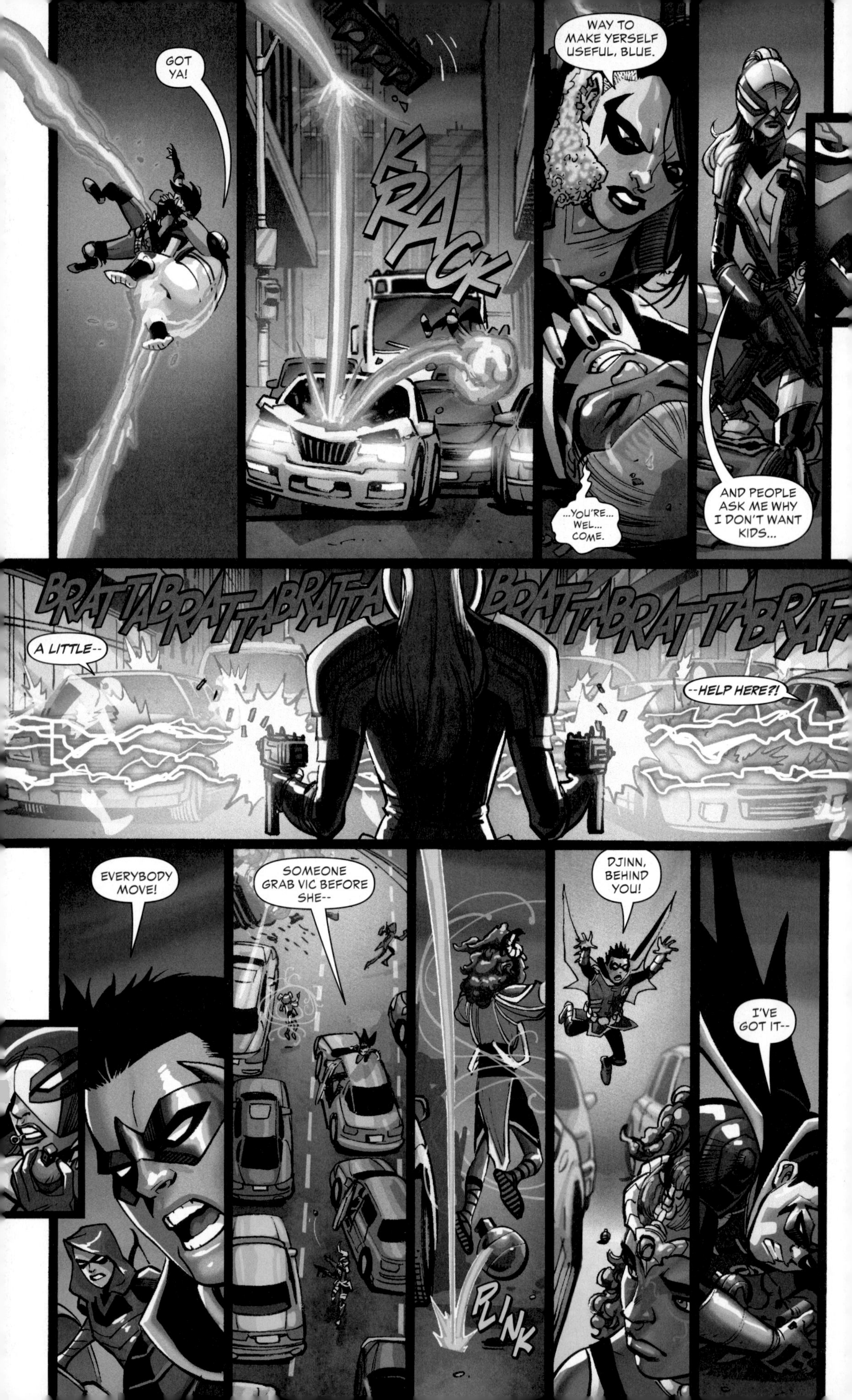
GOT YA!
KRACK
WAY TO MAKE YERSELF USEFUL, BLUE.
...YOU'RE... WEL... COME.
AND PEOPLE ASK ME WHY I DON'T WANT KIDS...
BRATTABRATTABRATTA
BRATTABRATTABRAT
A LITTLE--
--HELP HERE?!
EVERYBODY MOVE!
SOMEONE GRAB VIC BEFORE SHE--
PLINK
DJINN, BEHIND YOU!
I'VE GOT IT--

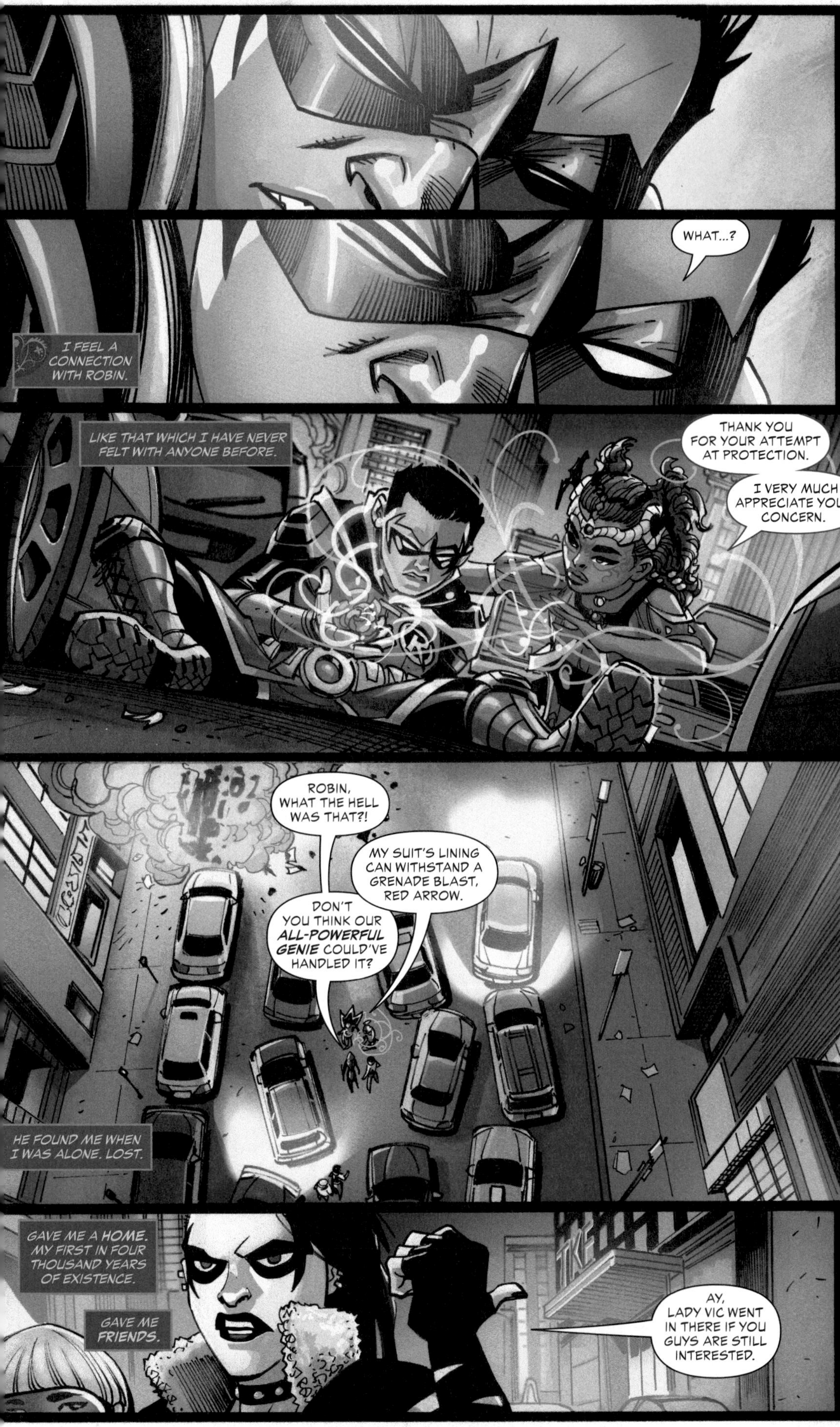
WHAT...?
I FEEL A CONNECTION WITH ROBIN.
LIKE THAT WHICH I HAVE NEVER FELT WITH ANYONE BEFORE.
THANK YOU FOR YOUR ATTEMPT AT PROTECTION.
I VERY MUCH APPRECIATE YOUR CONCERN.
ROBIN, WHAT THE HELL WAS THAT?!
MY SUIT'S LINING CAN WITHSTAND A GRENADE BLAST, RED ARROW.
DON'T YOU THINK OUR ALL-POWERFUL GENIE COULD'VE HANDLED IT?
HE FOUND ME WHEN I WAS ALONE. LOST.
GAVE ME A HOME. MY FIRST IN FOUR THOUSAND YEARS OF EXISTENCE.
GAVE ME FRIENDS.
AY, LADY VIC WENT IN THERE IF YOU GUYS ARE STILL INTERESTED.

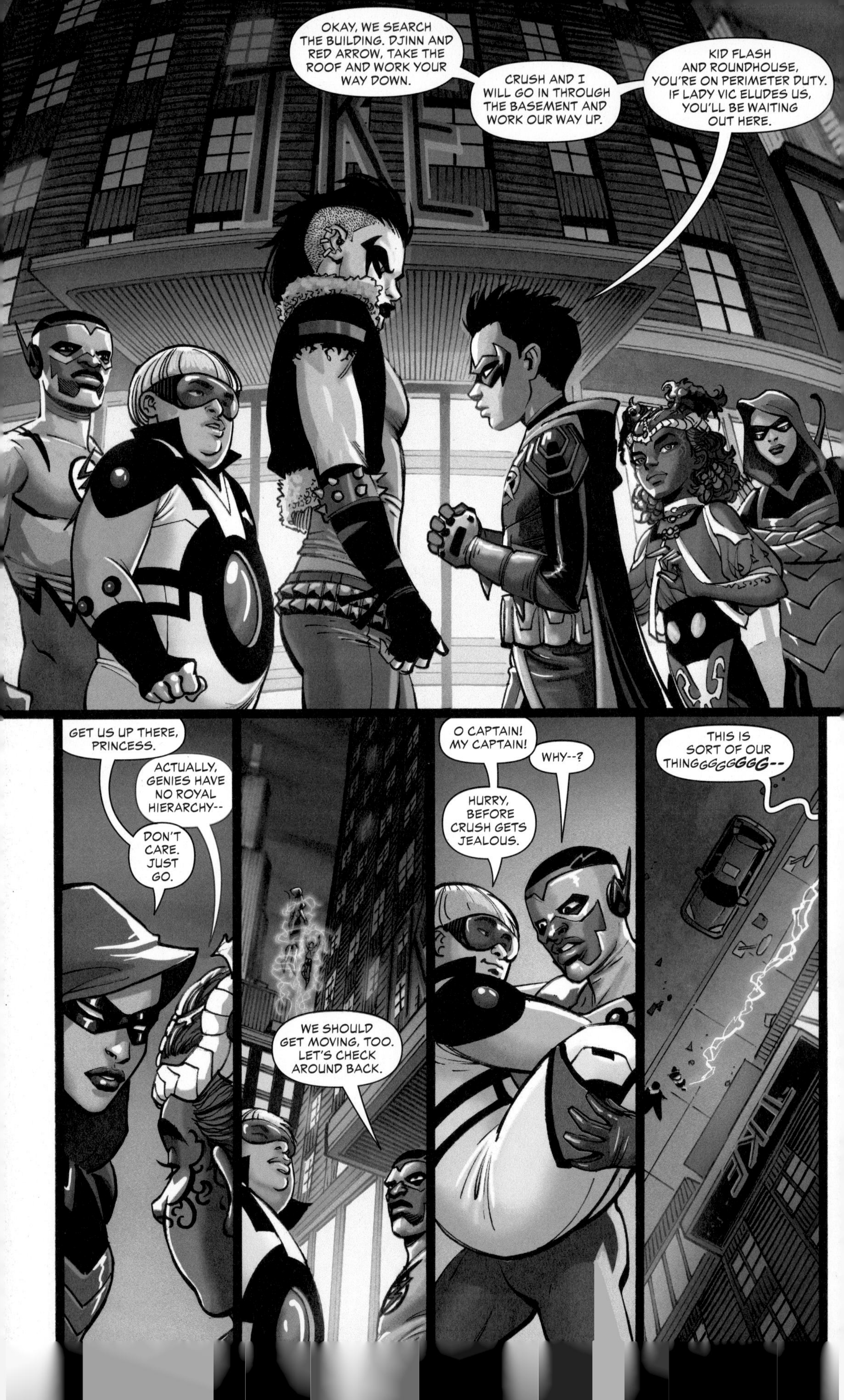
OKAY, WE SEARCH THE BUILDING. DJINN AND RED ARROW, TAKE THE ROOF AND WORK YOUR WAY DOWN.
CRUSH AND I WILL GO IN THROUGH THE BASEMENT AND WORK OUR WAY UP.
KID FLASH AND ROUNDHOUSE, YOU'RE ON PERIMETER DUTY. IF LADY VIC ELUDES US, YOU'LL BE WAITING OUT HERE.
GET US UP THERE, PRINCESS.
ACTUALLY, GENIES HAVE NO ROYAL HIERARCHY--
DON'T CARE. JUST GO.
WE SHOULD GET MOVING, TOO. LET'S CHECK AROUND BACK.
O CAPTAIN! MY CAPTAIN!
WHY--?
HURRY, BEFORE CRUSH GETS JEALOUS.
THIS IS SORT OF OUR THINGGGGGGG--

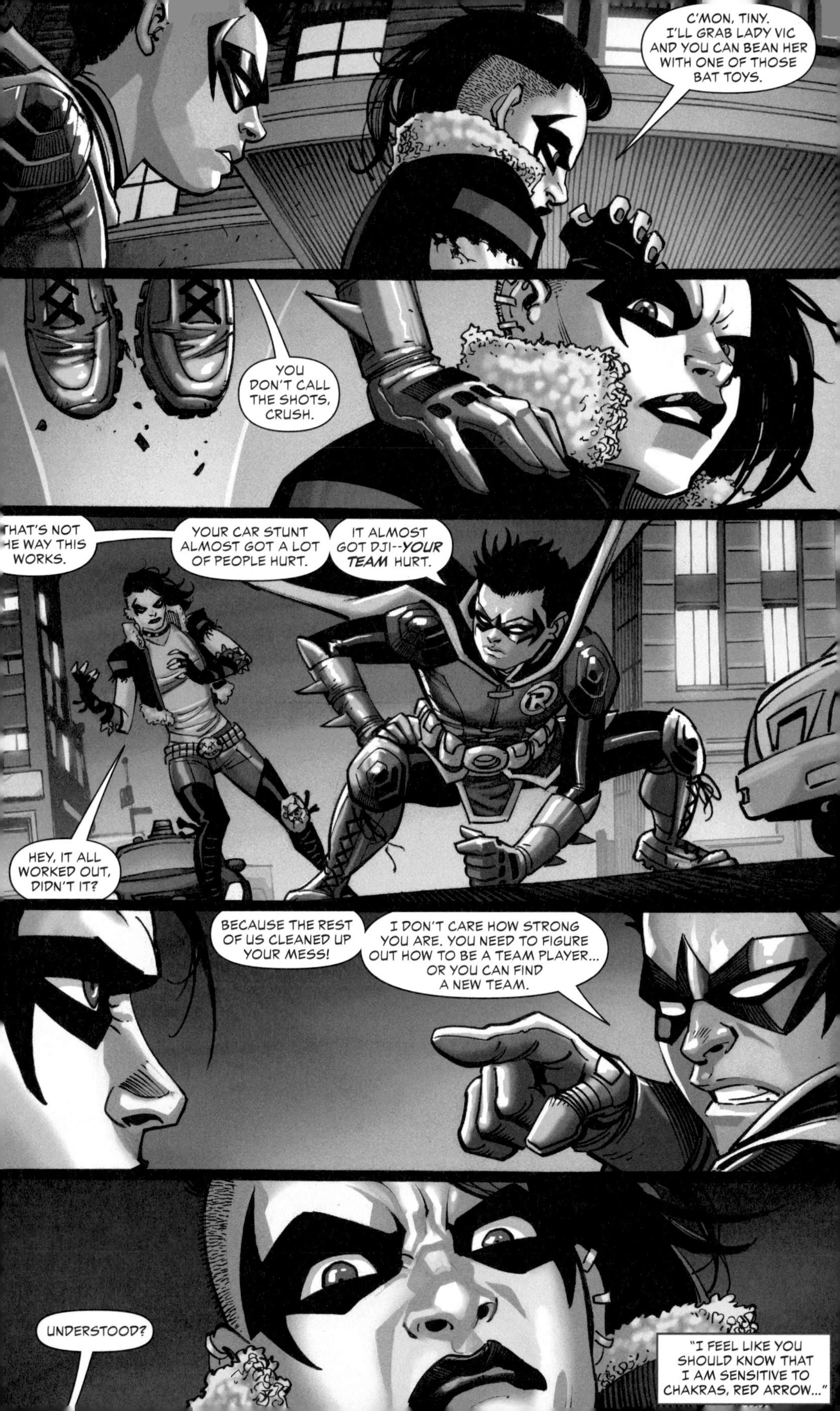
C'MON, TINY. I'LL GRAB LADY VIC AND YOU CAN BEAN HER WITH ONE OF THOSE BAT TOYS.
YOU DON'T CALL THE SHOTS, CRUSH.
THAT'S NOT HE WAY THIS WORKS.
YOUR CAR STUNT ALMOST GOT A LOT OF PEOPLE HURT.
IT ALMOST GOT DJI--*YOUR TEAM* HURT.
HEY, IT ALL WORKED OUT, DIDN'T IT?
BECAUSE THE REST OF US CLEANED UP YOUR MESS!
I DON'T CARE HOW STRONG YOU ARE. YOU NEED TO FIGURE OUT HOW TO BE A TEAM PLAYER... OR YOU CAN FIND A NEW TEAM.
UNDERSTOOD?
"I FEEL LIKE YOU SHOULD KNOW THAT I AM SENSITIVE TO CHAKRAS, RED ARROW..."

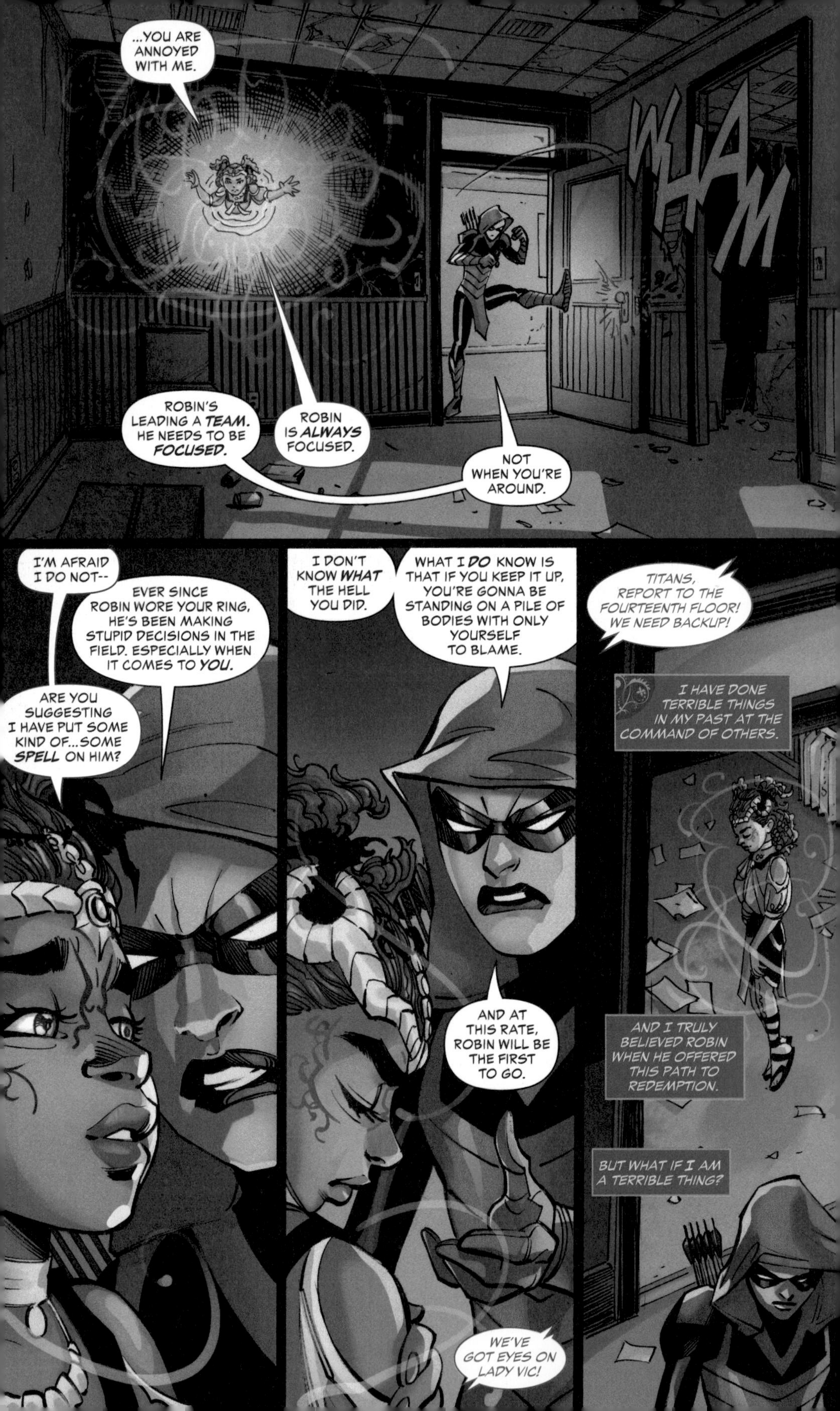
...YOU ARE ANNOYED WITH ME.
WHAM
ROBIN'S LEADING A TEAM. HE NEEDS TO BE FOCUSED.
ROBIN IS ALWAYS FOCUSED.
NOT WHEN YOU'RE AROUND.
I'M AFRAID I DO NOT--
EVER SINCE ROBIN WORE YOUR RING, HE'S BEEN MAKING STUPID DECISIONS IN THE FIELD. ESPECIALLY WHEN IT COMES TO YOU.
ARE YOU SUGGESTING I HAVE PUT SOME KIND OF...SOME SPELL ON HIM?
I DON'T KNOW WHAT THE HELL YOU DID.
WHAT I DO KNOW IS THAT IF YOU KEEP IT UP, YOU'RE GONNA BE STANDING ON A PILE OF BODIES WITH ONLY YOURSELF TO BLAME.
AND AT THIS RATE, ROBIN WILL BE THE FIRST TO GO.
WE'VE GOT EYES ON LADY VIC!
TITANS, REPORT TO THE FOURTEENTH FLOOR! WE NEED BACKUP!
I HAVE DONE TERRIBLE THINGS IN MY PAST AT THE COMMAND OF OTHERS.
AND I TRULY BELIEVED ROBIN WHEN HE OFFERED THIS PATH TO REDEMPTION.
BUT WHAT IF I AM A TERRIBLE THING?

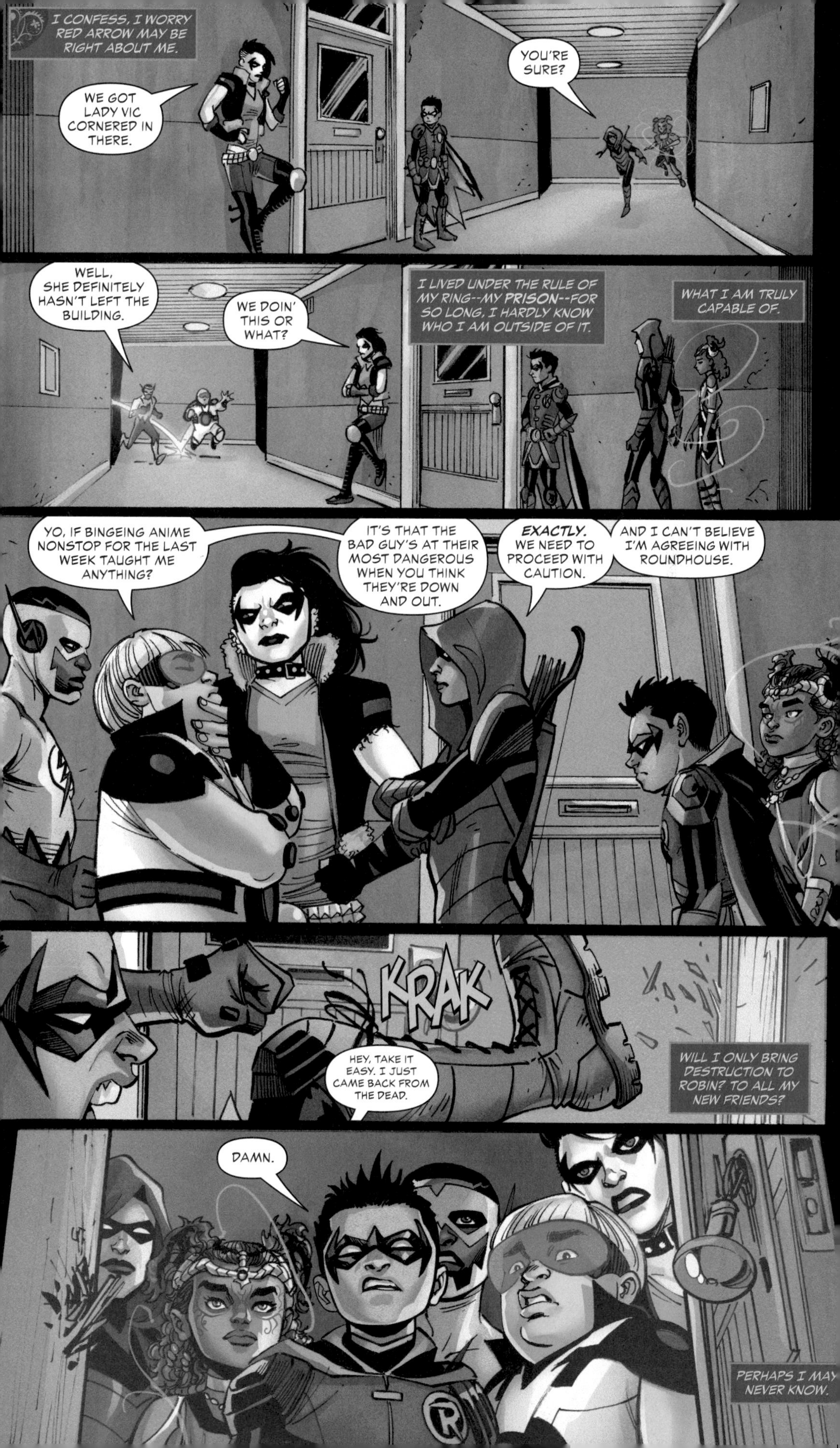
I CONFESS, I WORRY RED ARROW MAY BE RIGHT ABOUT ME.
WE GOT LADY VIC CORNERED IN THERE.
YOU'RE SURE?
WELL, SHE DEFINITELY HASN'T LEFT THE BUILDING.
WE DOIN' THIS OR WHAT?
I LIVED UNDER THE RULE OF MY RING--MY PRISON--FOR SO LONG, I HARDLY KNOW WHO I AM OUTSIDE OF IT.
WHAT I AM TRULY CAPABLE OF.
YO, IF BINGEING ANIME NONSTOP FOR THE LAST WEEK TAUGHT ME ANYTHING?
IT'S THAT THE BAD GUY'S AT THEIR MOST DANGEROUS WHEN YOU THINK THEY'RE DOWN AND OUT.
EXACTLY. WE NEED TO PROCEED WITH CAUTION.
AND I CAN'T BELIEVE I'M AGREEING WITH ROUNDHOUSE.
KRAK
HEY, TAKE IT EASY. I JUST CAME BACK FROM THE DEAD.
WILL I ONLY BRING DESTRUCTION TO ROBIN? TO ALL MY NEW FRIENDS?
DAMN.
PERHAPS I MAY NEVER KNOW.

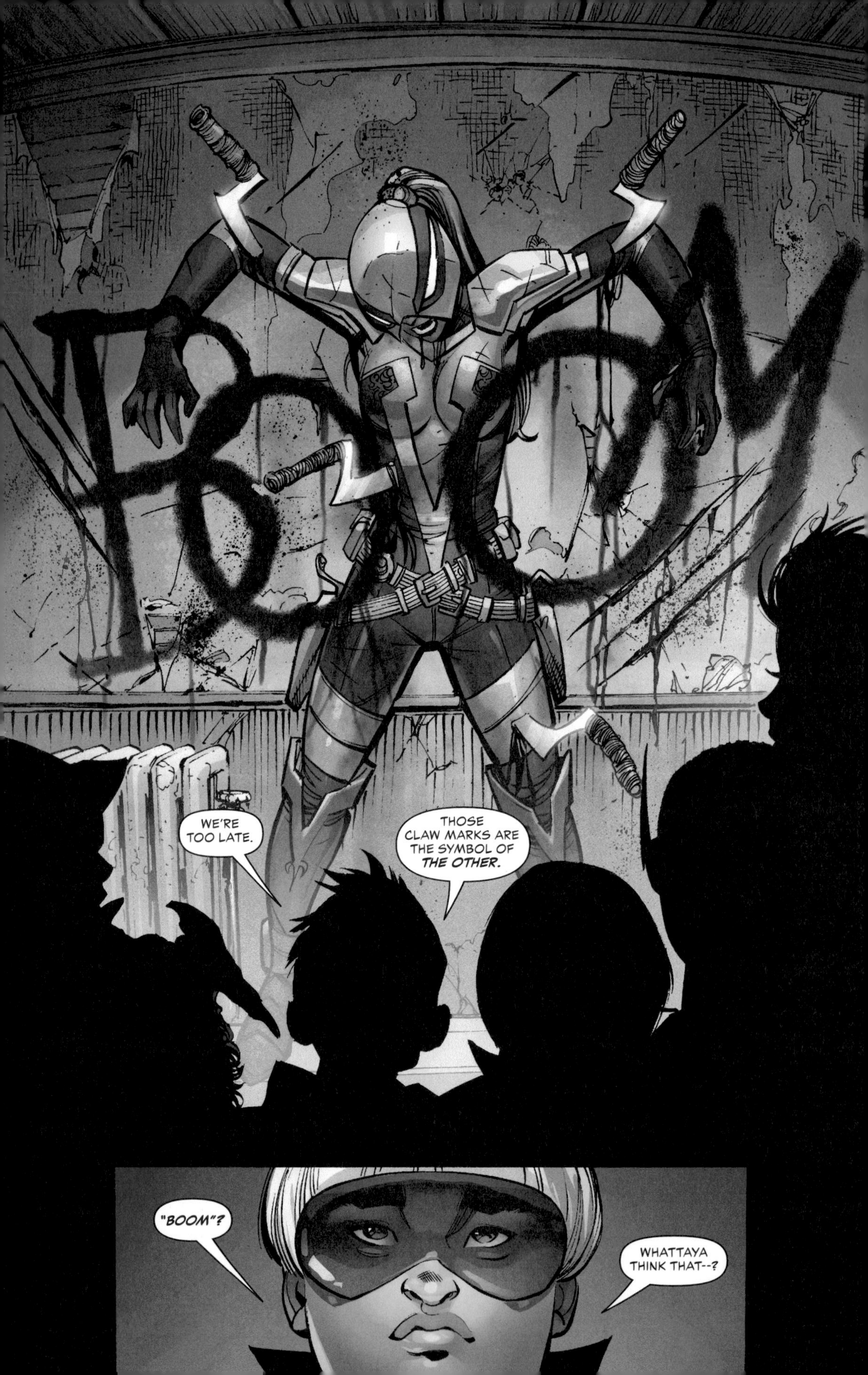
BOOM
WE'RE TOO LATE.
THOSE CLAW MARKS ARE THE SYMBOL OF *THE OTHER.*
"*BOOM*"?
WHATTAYA THINK THAT--?

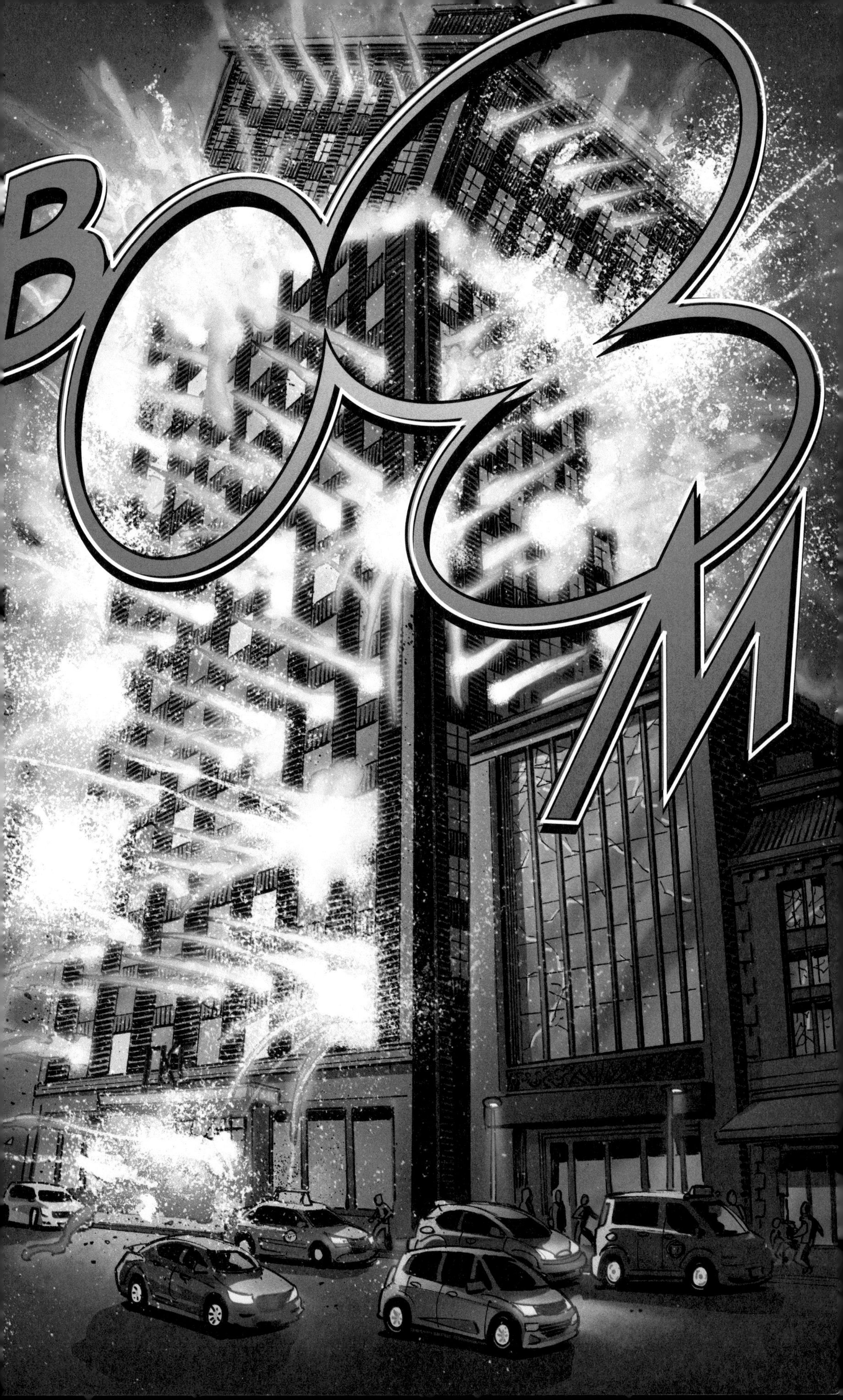
BOOOM

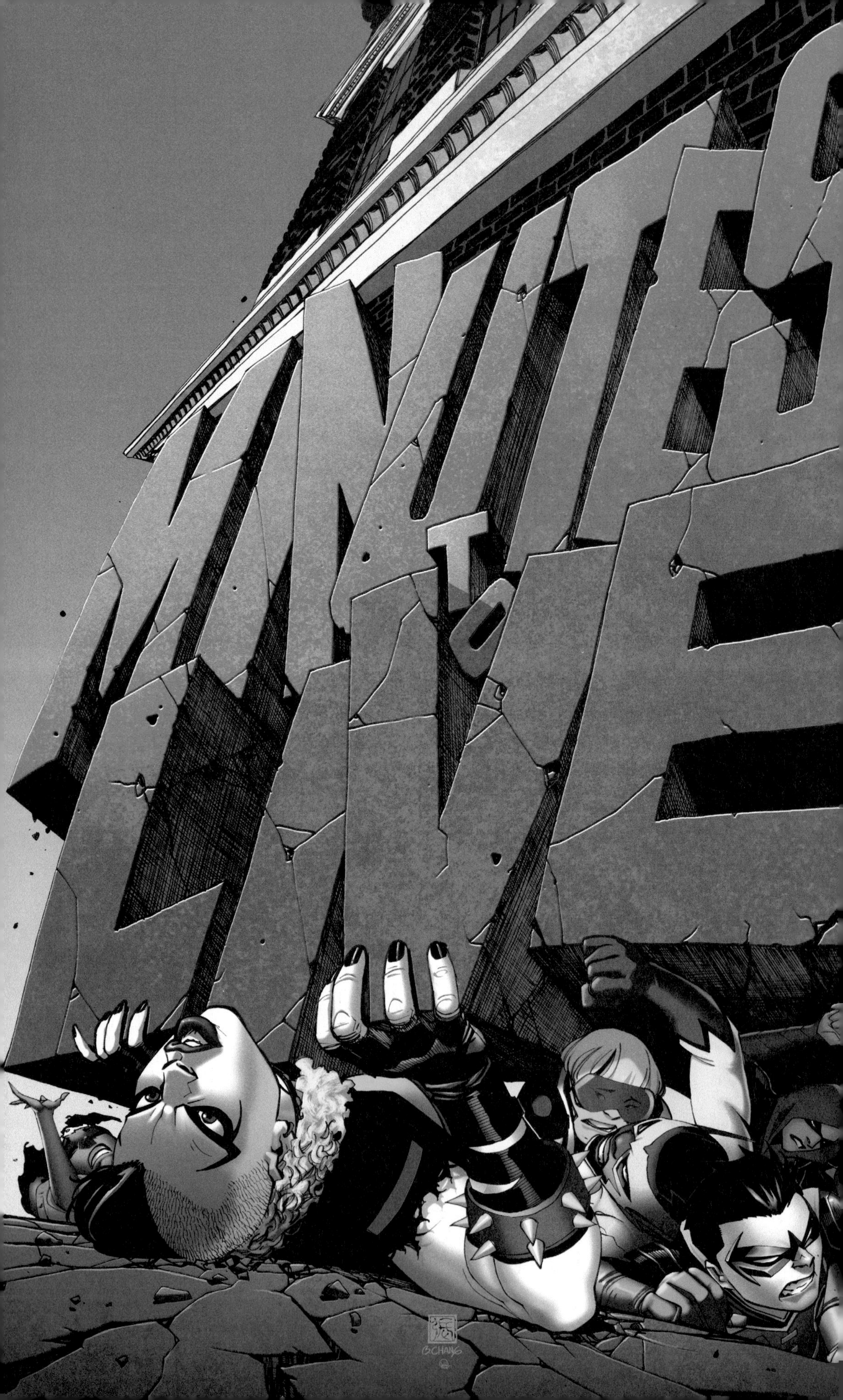
MINUTES
TO
LIVE
B.CHANG

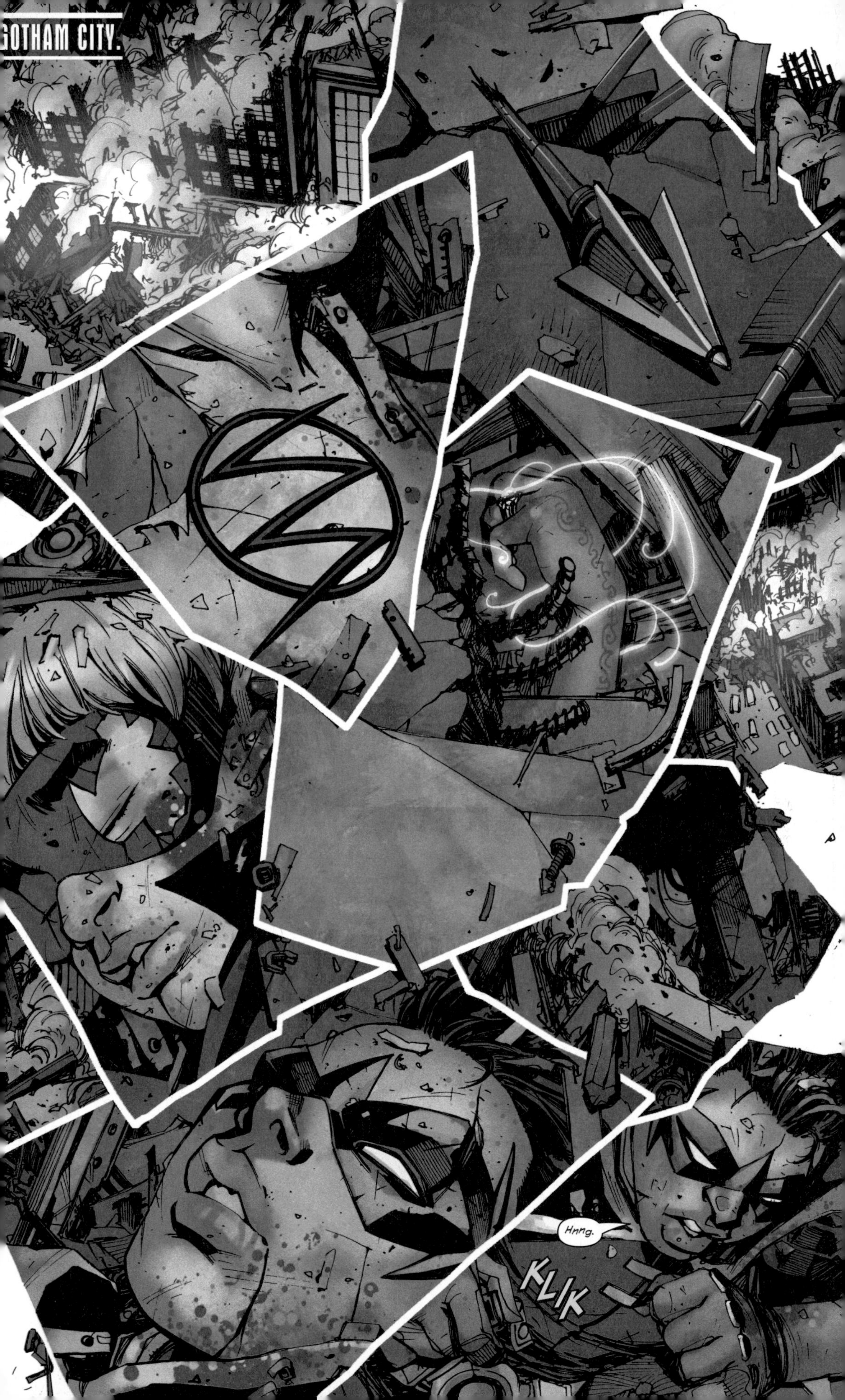
GOTHAM CITY.
Hnng.
KLIK

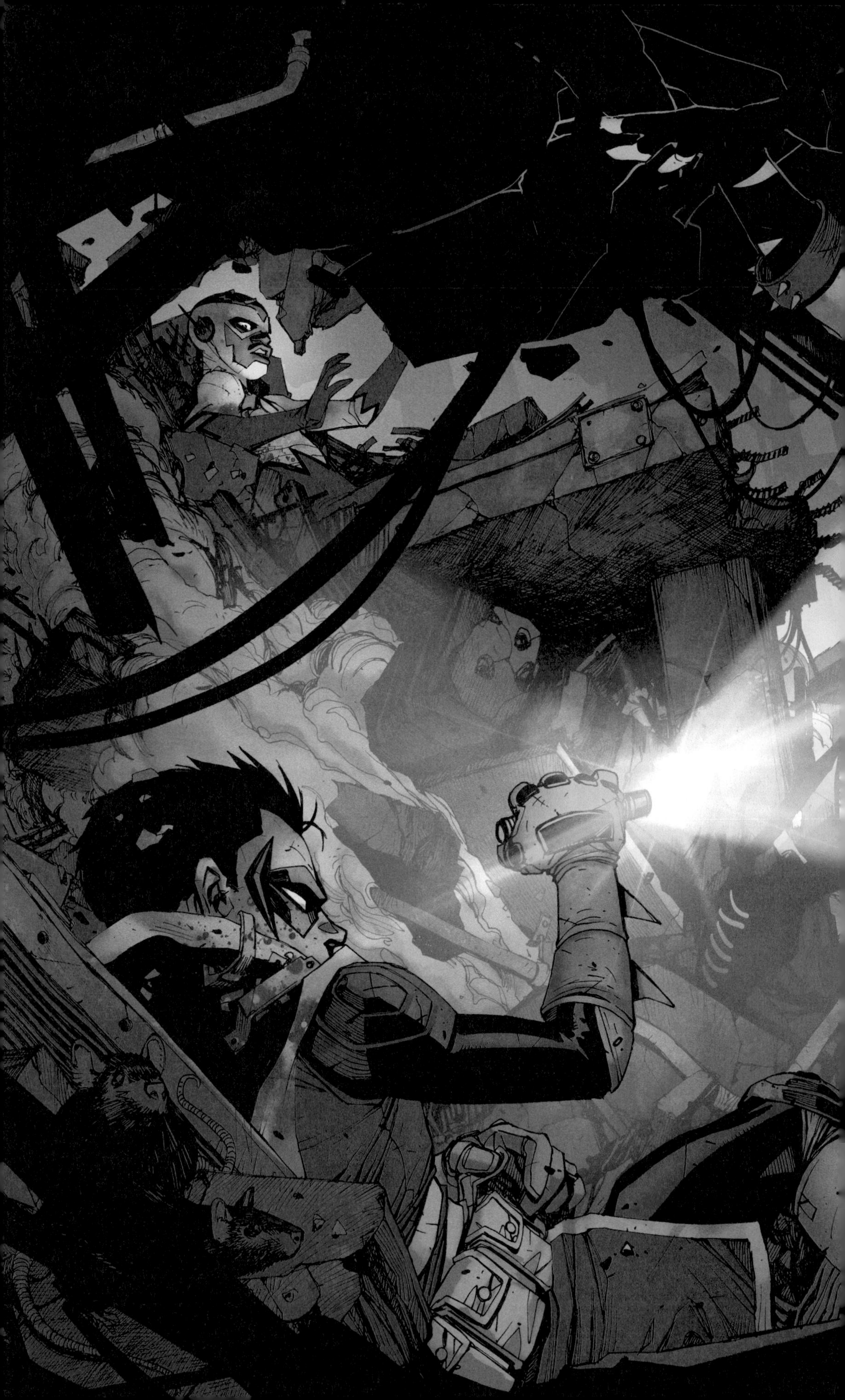

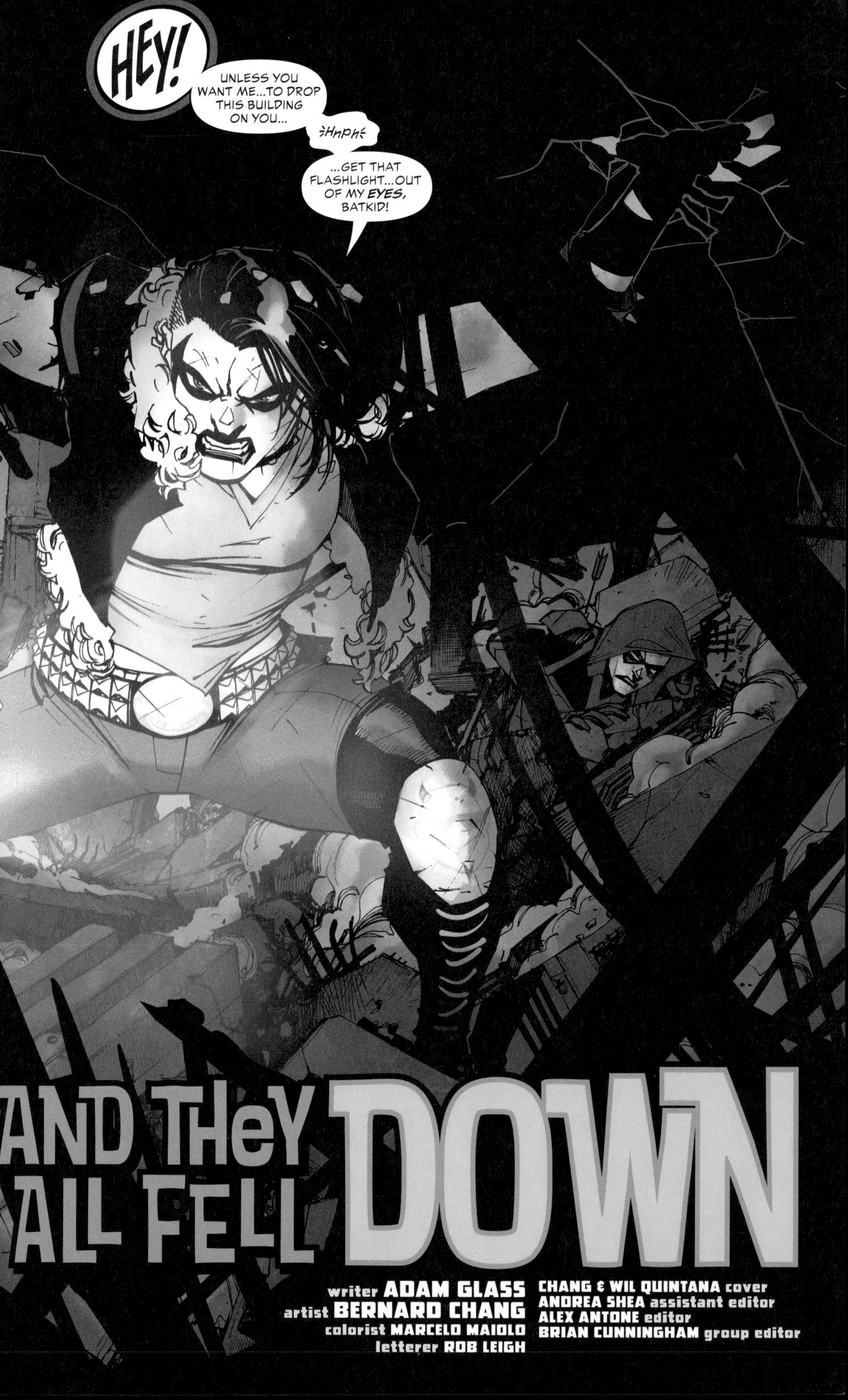
HEY!
UNLESS YOU WANT ME...TO DROP THIS BUILDING ON YOU...
Hnph
...GET THAT FLASHLIGHT...OUT OF MY EYES, BATKID!
AND THEY ALL FELL DOWN
writer ADAM GLASS
artist BERNARD CHANG
colorist MARCELO MAIOLO
letterer ROB LEIGH
CHANG & WIL QUINTANA cover
ANDREA SHEA assistant editor
ALEX ANTONE editor
BRIAN CUNNINGHAM group editor

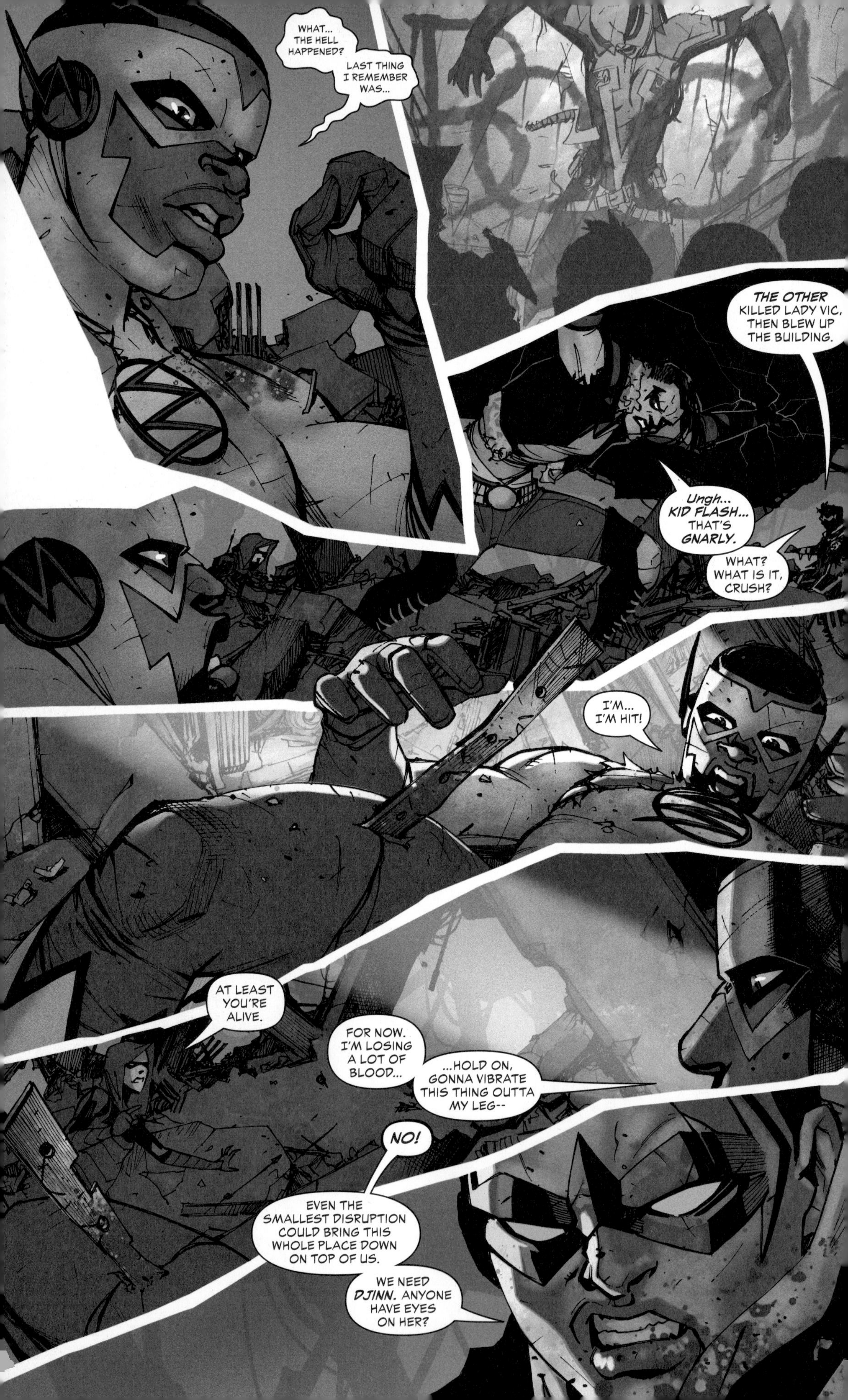
WHAT... THE HELL HAPPENED?
LAST THING I REMEMBER WAS...
THE OTHER KILLED LADY VIC, THEN BLEW UP THE BUILDING.
Ungh... KID FLASH... THAT'S GNARLY.
WHAT? WHAT IS IT, CRUSH?
I'M... I'M HIT!
AT LEAST YOU'RE ALIVE.
FOR NOW. I'M LOSING A LOT OF BLOOD...
...HOLD ON, GONNA VIBRATE THIS THING OUTTA MY LEG--
NO!
EVEN THE SMALLEST DISRUPTION COULD BRING THIS WHOLE PLACE DOWN ON TOP OF US.
WE NEED DJINN. ANYONE HAVE EYES ON HER?

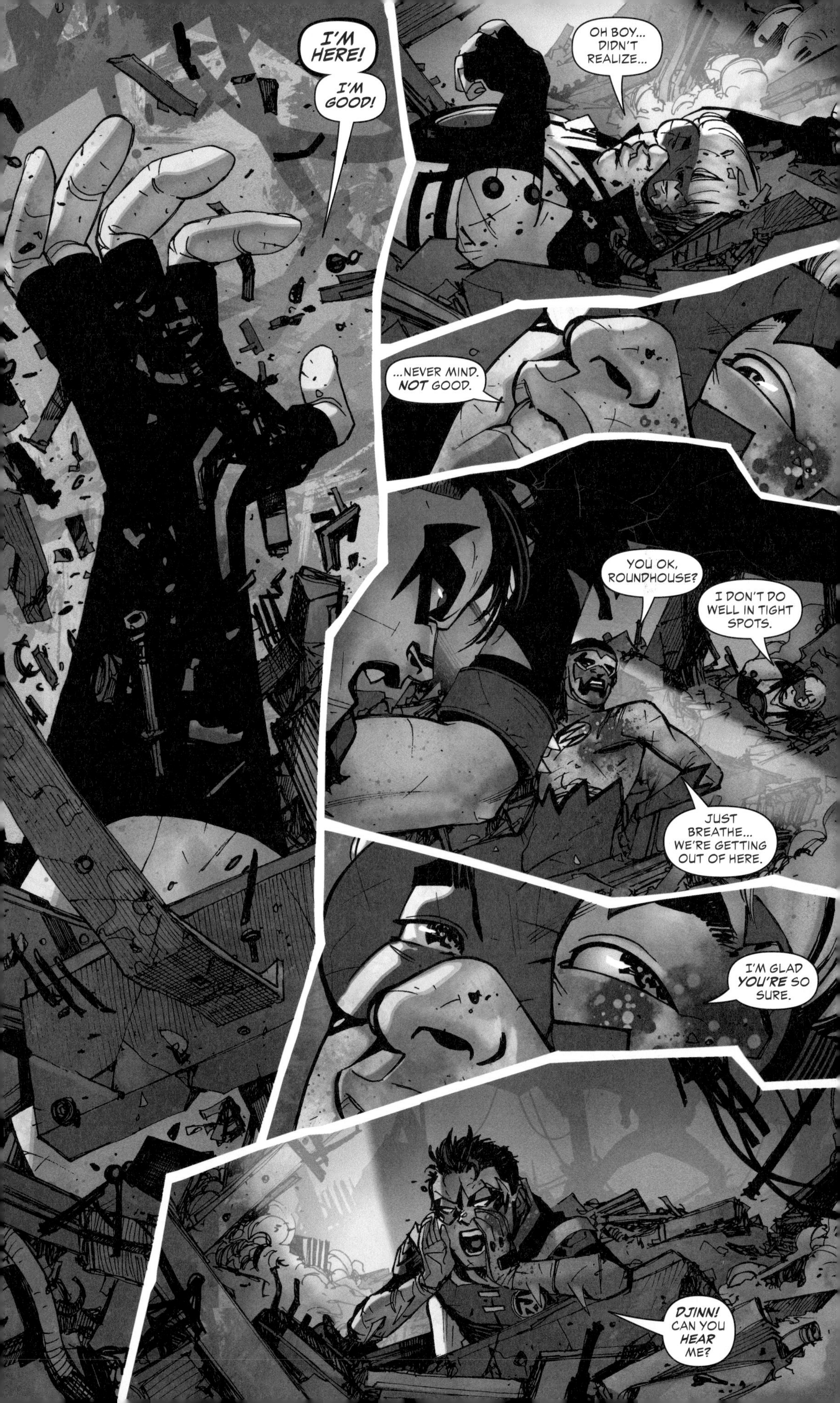
I'M HERE!
I'M GOOD!
OH BOY... DIDN'T REALIZE...
...NEVER MIND. NOT GOOD.
YOU OK, ROUNDHOUSE?
I DON'T DO WELL IN TIGHT SPOTS.
JUST BREATHE... WE'RE GETTING OUT OF HERE.
I'M GLAD YOU'RE SO SURE.
DJINN! CAN YOU HEAR ME?

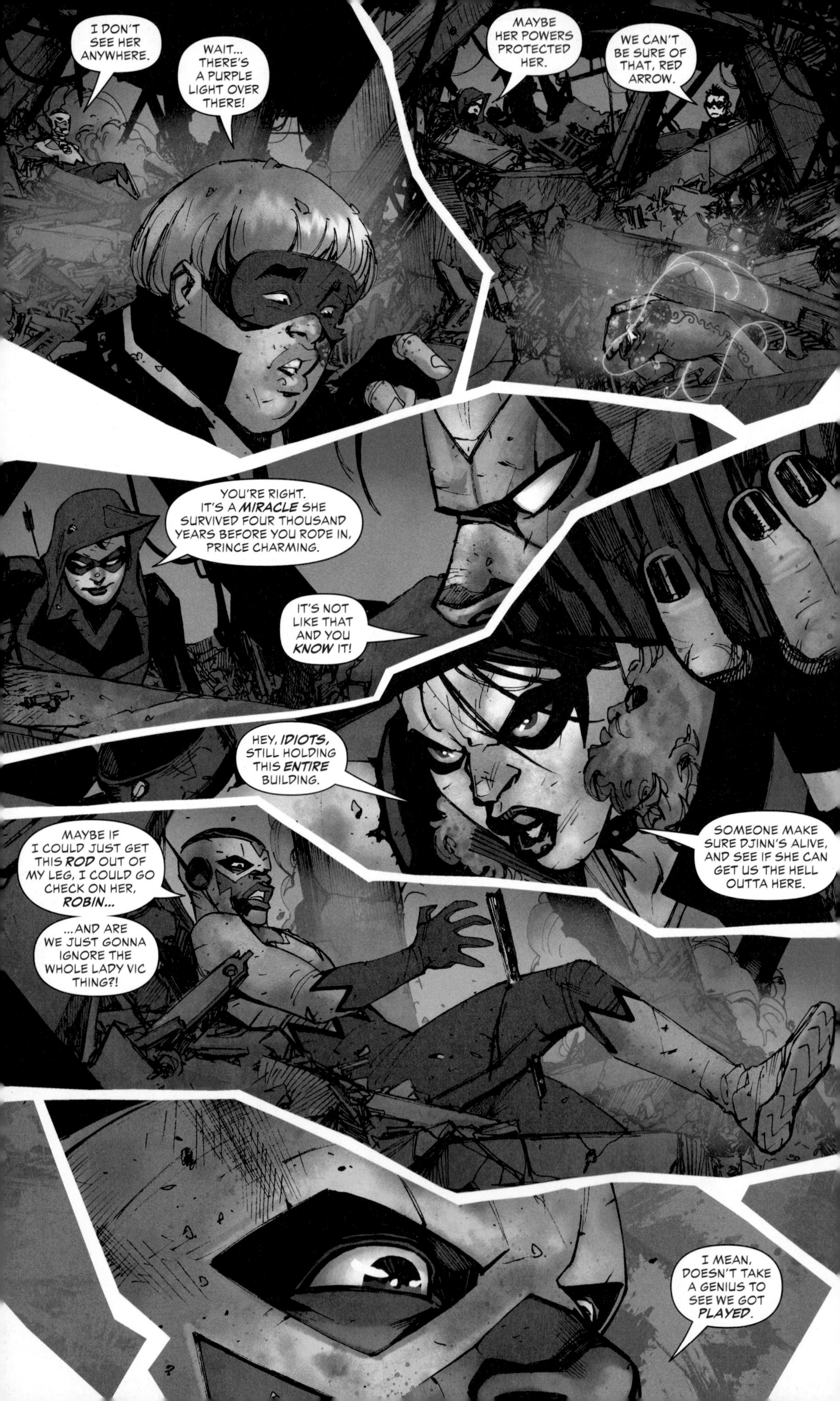
I DON'T SEE HER ANYWHERE.
WAIT... THERE'S A PURPLE LIGHT OVER THERE!
MAYBE HER POWERS PROTECTED HER.
WE CAN'T BE SURE OF THAT, RED ARROW.
YOU'RE RIGHT. IT'S A *MIRACLE* SHE SURVIVED FOUR THOUSAND YEARS BEFORE YOU RODE IN, PRINCE CHARMING.
IT'S NOT LIKE THAT AND YOU *KNOW* IT!
HEY, *IDIOTS,* STILL HOLDING THIS *ENTIRE* BUILDING.
SOMEONE MAKE SURE DJINN'S ALIVE, AND SEE IF SHE CAN GET US THE HELL OUTTA HERE.
MAYBE IF I COULD JUST GET THIS *ROD* OUT OF MY LEG, I COULD GO CHECK ON HER, *ROBIN...*
...AND ARE WE JUST GONNA IGNORE THE WHOLE LADY VIC THING?!
I MEAN, DOESN'T TAKE A GENIUS TO SEE WE GOT *PLAYED*.

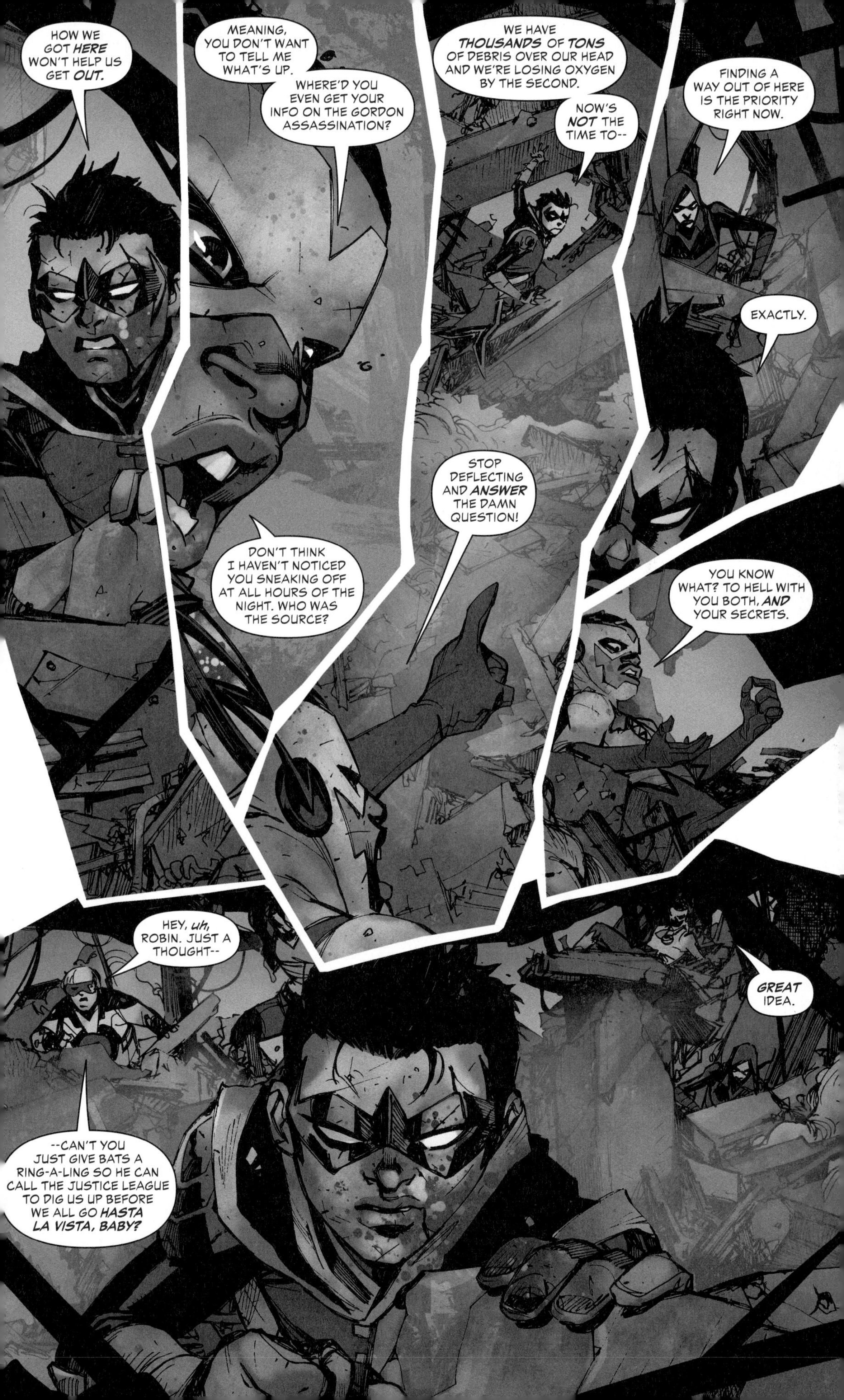
HOW WE GOT HERE WON'T HELP US GET OUT.
MEANING, YOU DON'T WANT TO TELL ME WHAT'S UP.
WHERE'D YOU EVEN GET YOUR INFO ON THE GORDON ASSASSINATION?
WE HAVE THOUSANDS OF TONS OF DEBRIS OVER OUR HEAD AND WE'RE LOSING OXYGEN BY THE SECOND.
NOW'S NOT THE TIME TO--
FINDING A WAY OUT OF HERE IS THE PRIORITY RIGHT NOW.
EXACTLY.
DON'T THINK I HAVEN'T NOTICED YOU SNEAKING OFF AT ALL HOURS OF THE NIGHT. WHO WAS THE SOURCE?
STOP DEFLECTING AND ANSWER THE DAMN QUESTION!
YOU KNOW WHAT? TO HELL WITH YOU BOTH, AND YOUR SECRETS.
HEY, uh, ROBIN. JUST A THOUGHT--
--CAN'T YOU JUST GIVE BATS A RING-A-LING SO HE CAN CALL THE JUSTICE LEAGUE TO DIG US UP BEFORE WE ALL GO HASTA LA VISTA, BABY?
GREAT IDEA.

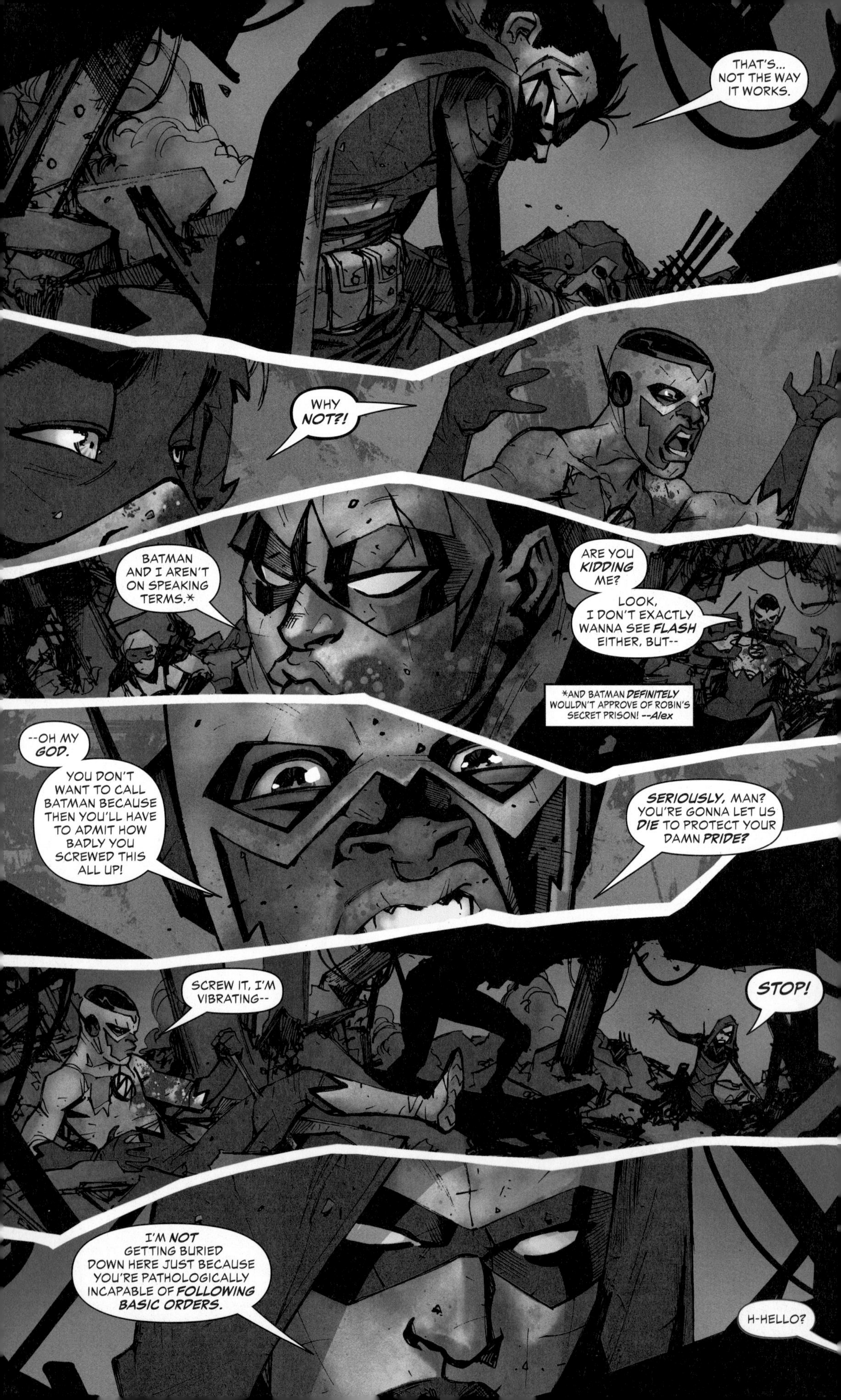
THAT'S... NOT THE WAY IT WORKS.
WHY NOT?!
BATMAN AND I AREN'T ON SPEAKING TERMS.*
ARE YOU KIDDING ME?
LOOK, I DON'T EXACTLY WANNA SEE FLASH EITHER, BUT--
*AND BATMAN DEFINITELY WOULDN'T APPROVE OF ROBIN'S SECRET PRISON! --Alex
--OH MY GOD.
YOU DON'T WANT TO CALL BATMAN BECAUSE THEN YOU'LL HAVE TO ADMIT HOW BADLY YOU SCREWED THIS ALL UP!
SERIOUSLY, MAN? YOU'RE GONNA LET US DIE TO PROTECT YOUR DAMN PRIDE?
SCREW IT, I'M VIBRATING--
STOP!
I'M NOT GETTING BURIED DOWN HERE JUST BECAUSE YOU'RE PATHOLOGICALLY INCAPABLE OF FOLLOWING BASIC ORDERS.
H-HELLO?

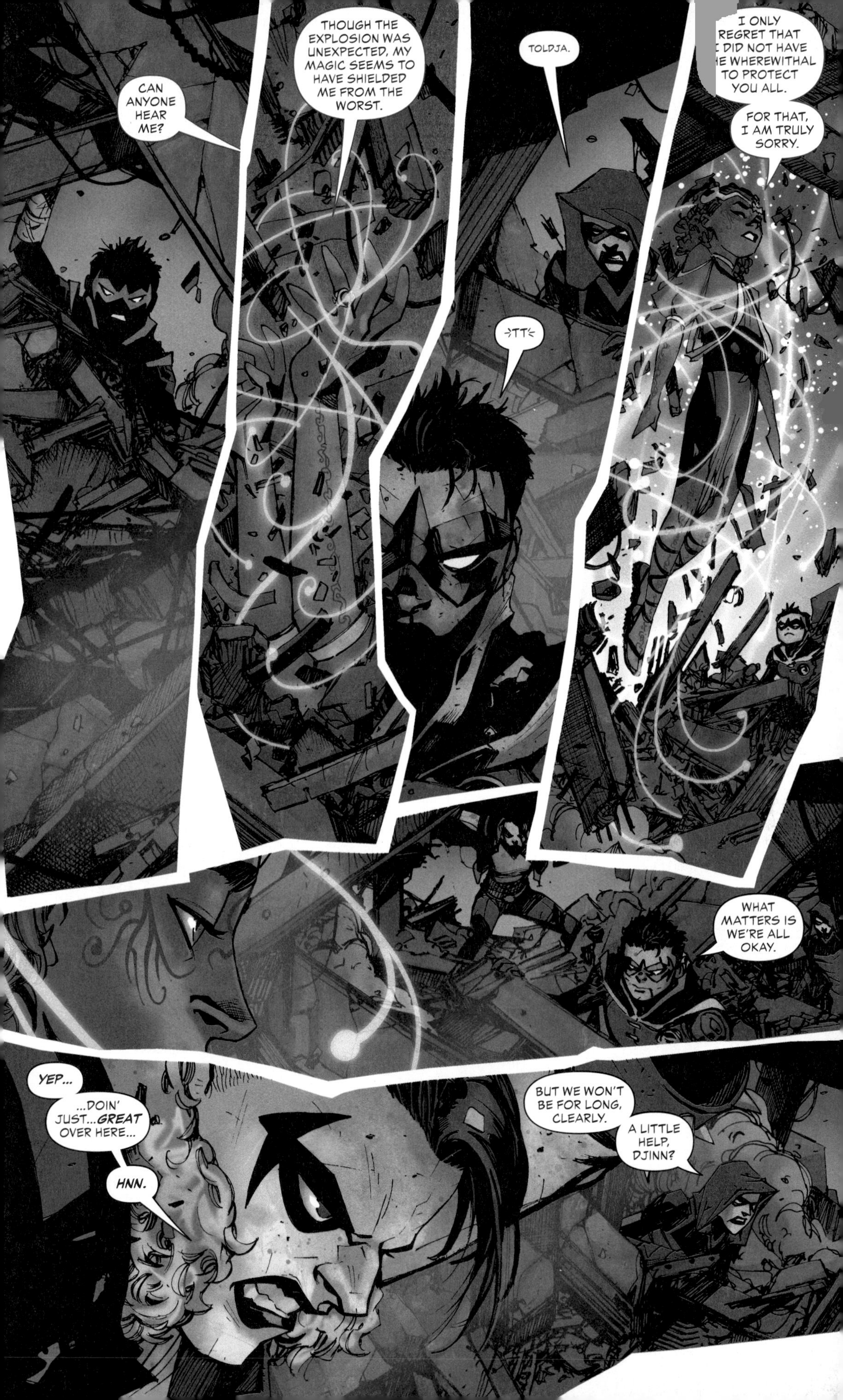
CAN ANYONE HEAR ME?
THOUGH THE EXPLOSION WAS UNEXPECTED, MY MAGIC SEEMS TO HAVE SHIELDED ME FROM THE WORST.
TOLDJA.
-TT-
I ONLY REGRET THAT I DID NOT HAVE THE WHEREWITHAL TO PROTECT YOU ALL.
FOR THAT, I AM TRULY SORRY.
WHAT MATTERS IS WE'RE ALL OKAY.
YEP...
...DOIN' JUST...GREAT OVER HERE...
HNN.
BUT WE WON'T BE FOR LONG, CLEARLY.
A LITTLE HELP, DJINN?

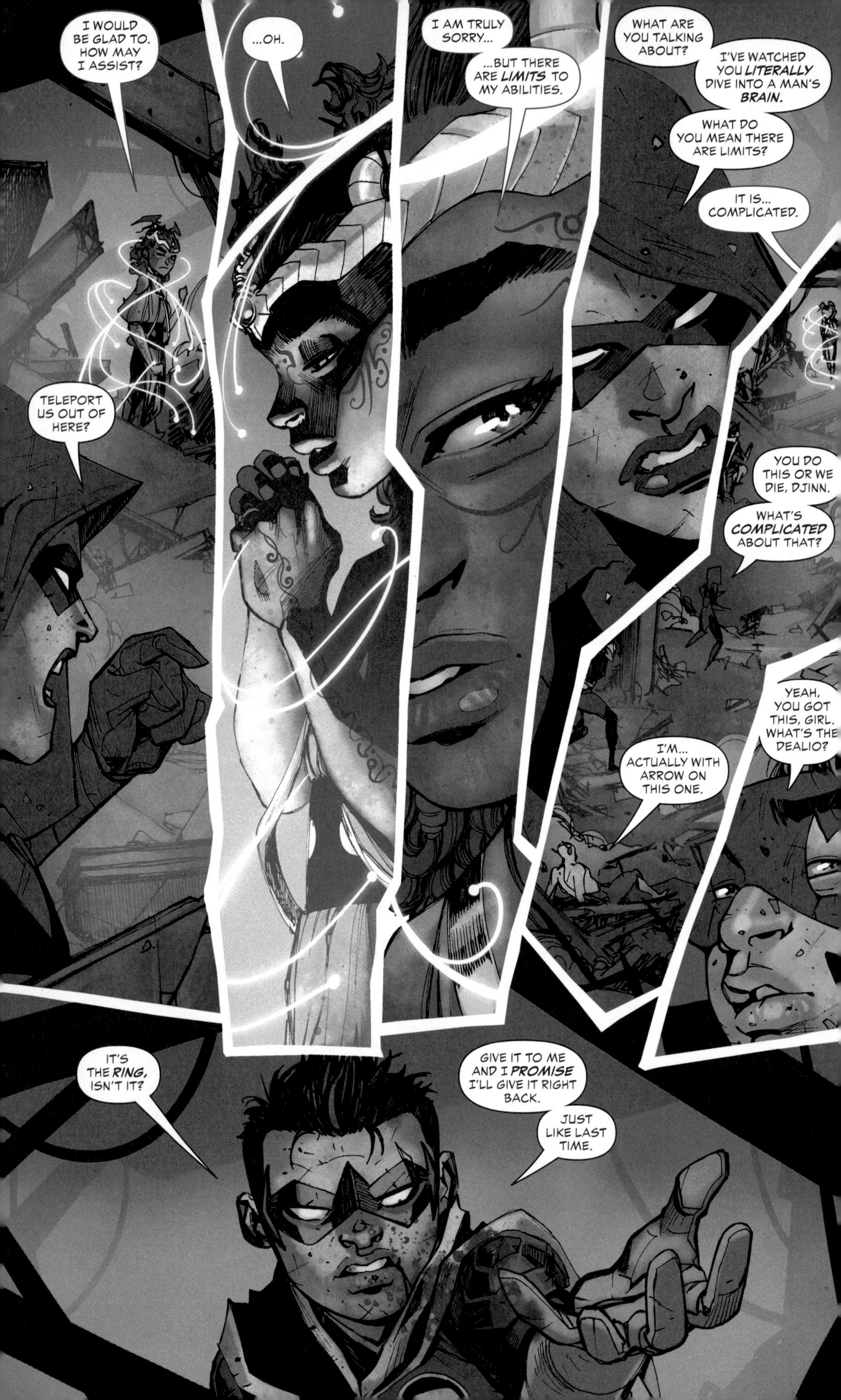
I WOULD BE GLAD TO. HOW MAY I ASSIST?
TELEPORT US OUT OF HERE?
...OH.
I AM TRULY SORRY...
...BUT THERE ARE LIMITS TO MY ABILITIES.
WHAT ARE YOU TALKING ABOUT?
I'VE WATCHED YOU LITERALLY DIVE INTO A MAN'S BRAIN.
WHAT DO YOU MEAN THERE ARE LIMITS?
IT IS... COMPLICATED.
YOU DO THIS OR WE DIE, DJINN.
WHAT'S COMPLICATED ABOUT THAT?
I'M... ACTUALLY WITH ARROW ON THIS ONE.
YEAH, YOU GOT THIS, GIRL. WHAT'S THE DEALIO?
IT'S THE RING, ISN'T IT?
GIVE IT TO ME AND I PROMISE I'LL GIVE IT RIGHT BACK.
JUST LIKE LAST TIME.

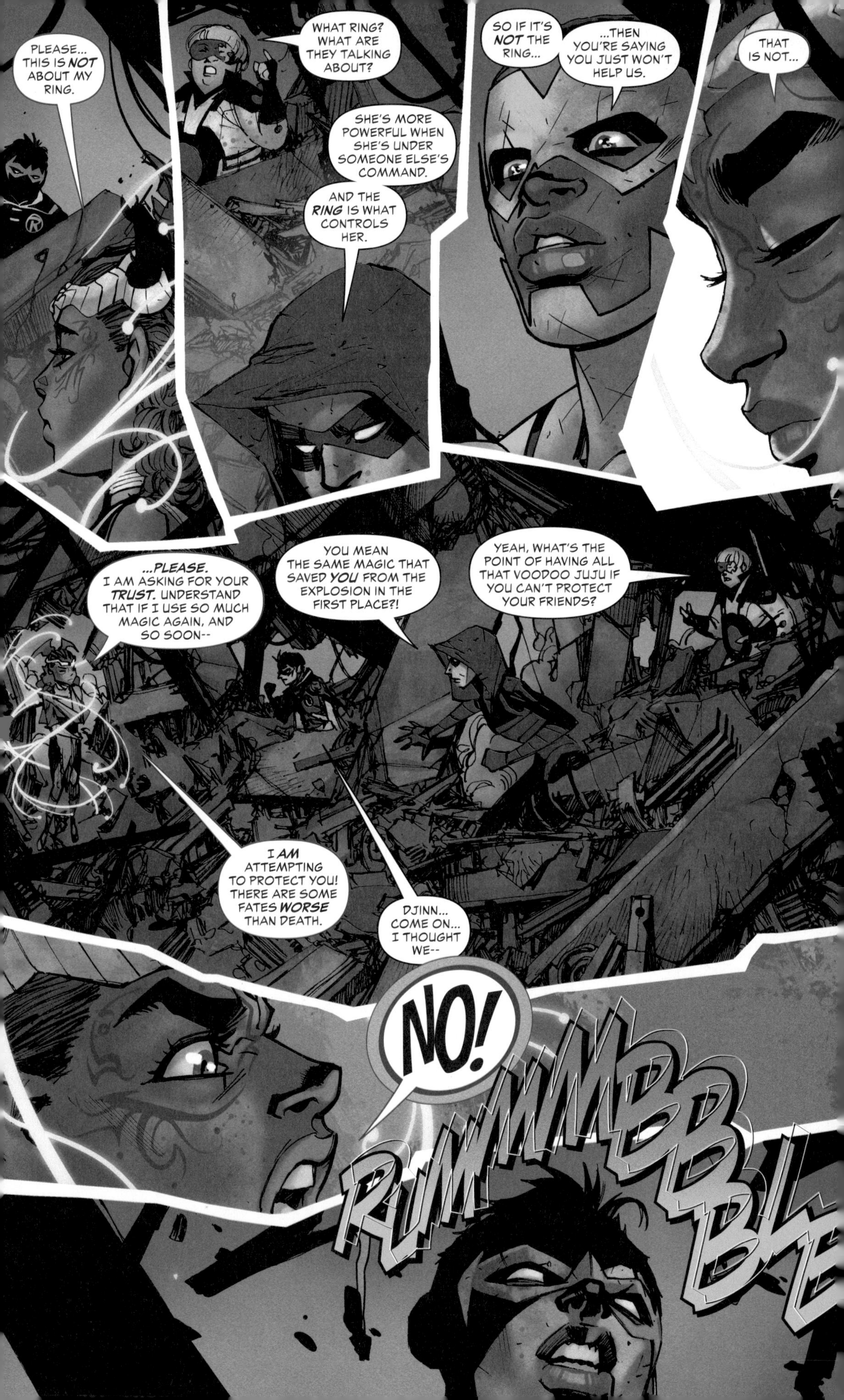
PLEASE... THIS IS NOT ABOUT MY RING.
WHAT RING? WHAT ARE THEY TALKING ABOUT?
SHE'S MORE POWERFUL WHEN SHE'S UNDER SOMEONE ELSE'S COMMAND.
AND THE RING IS WHAT CONTROLS HER.
SO IF IT'S NOT THE RING...
...THEN YOU'RE SAYING YOU JUST WON'T HELP US.
THAT IS NOT...
...PLEASE. I AM ASKING FOR YOUR TRUST. UNDERSTAND THAT IF I USE SO MUCH MAGIC AGAIN, AND SO SOON--
YOU MEAN THE SAME MAGIC THAT SAVED YOU FROM THE EXPLOSION IN THE FIRST PLACE?!
YEAH, WHAT'S THE POINT OF HAVING ALL THAT VOODOO JUJU IF YOU CAN'T PROTECT YOUR FRIENDS?
I AM ATTEMPTING TO PROTECT YOU! THERE ARE SOME FATES WORSE THAN DEATH.
DJINN... COME ON... I THOUGHT WE--
NO!
RUMMMBBLE

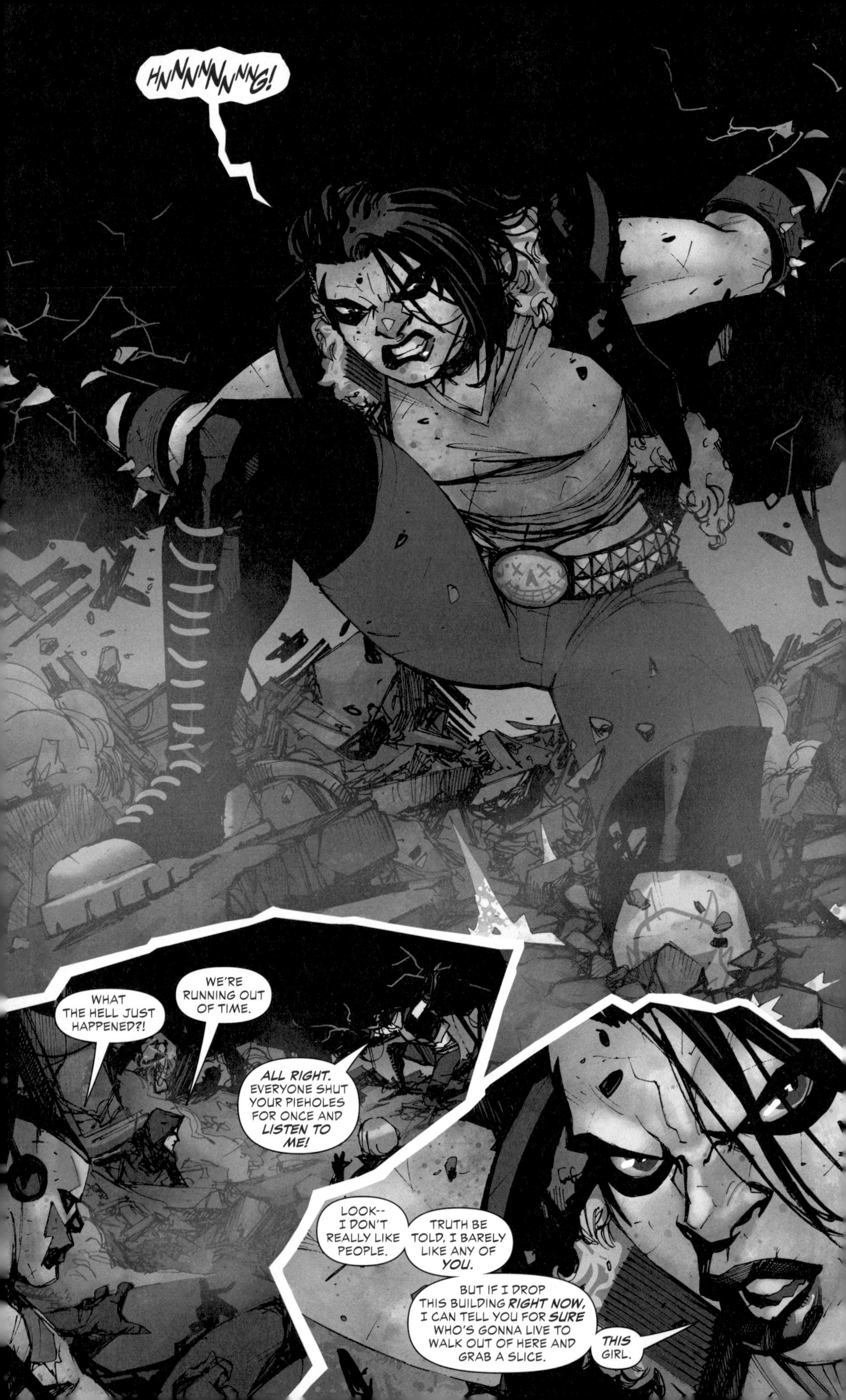
HNNNNNNNG!
WHAT THE HELL JUST HAPPENED?!
WE'RE RUNNING OUT OF TIME.
ALL RIGHT. EVERYONE SHUT YOUR PIEHOLES FOR ONCE AND LISTEN TO ME!
LOOK-- I DON'T REALLY LIKE PEOPLE.
TRUTH BE TOLD, I BARELY LIKE ANY OF YOU.
BUT IF I DROP THIS BUILDING RIGHT NOW, I CAN TELL YOU FOR SURE WHO'S GONNA LIVE TO WALK OUT OF HERE AND GRAB A SLICE.
THIS GIRL.

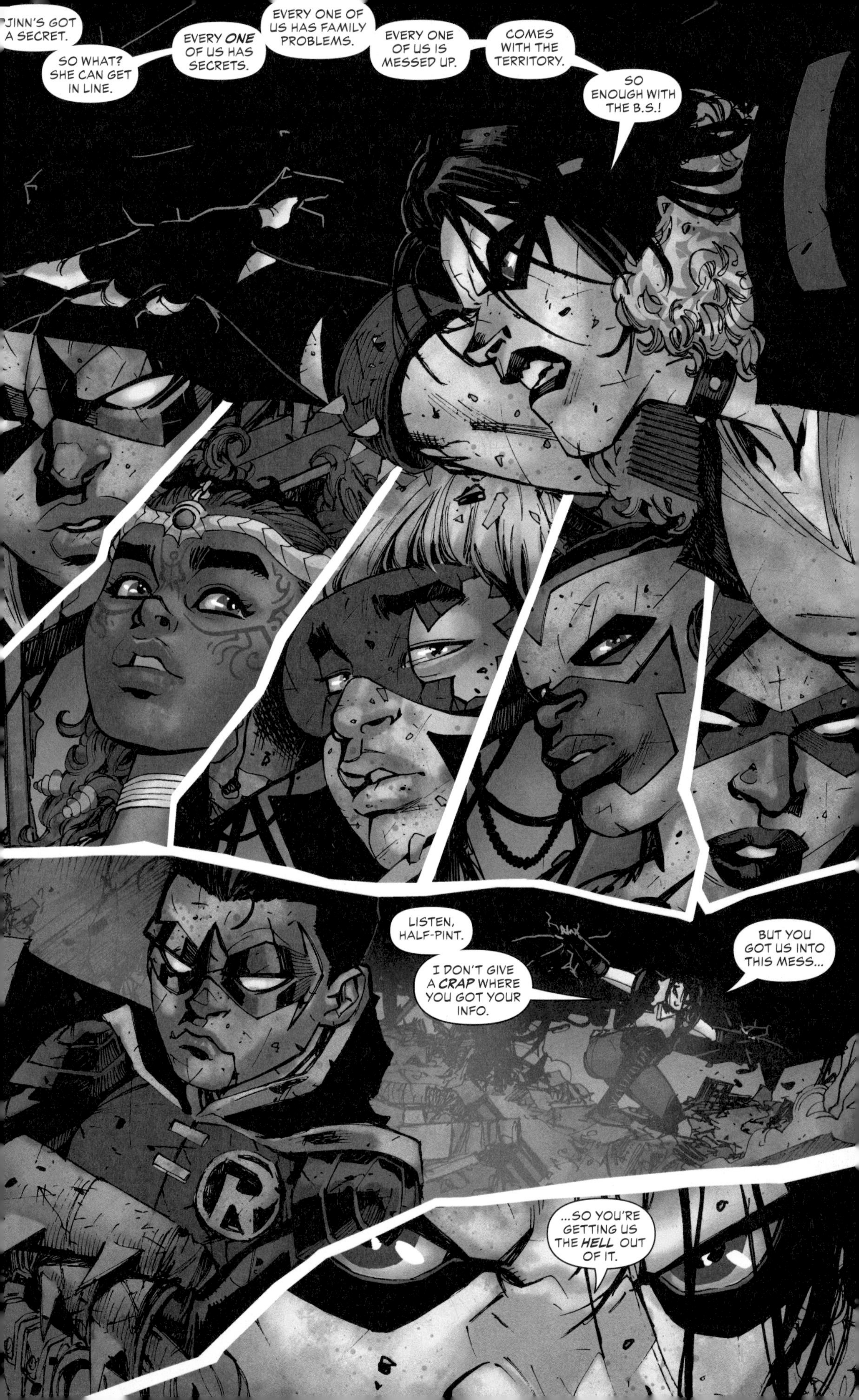
JINN'S GOT A SECRET.
SO WHAT? SHE CAN GET IN LINE.
EVERY ONE OF US HAS SECRETS.
EVERY ONE OF US HAS FAMILY PROBLEMS.
EVERY ONE OF US IS MESSED UP.
COMES WITH THE TERRITORY.
SO ENOUGH WITH THE B.S.!
LISTEN, HALF-PINT.
I DON'T GIVE A CRAP WHERE YOU GOT YOUR INFO.
BUT YOU GOT US INTO THIS MESS...
...SO YOU'RE GETTING US THE HELL OUT OF IT.

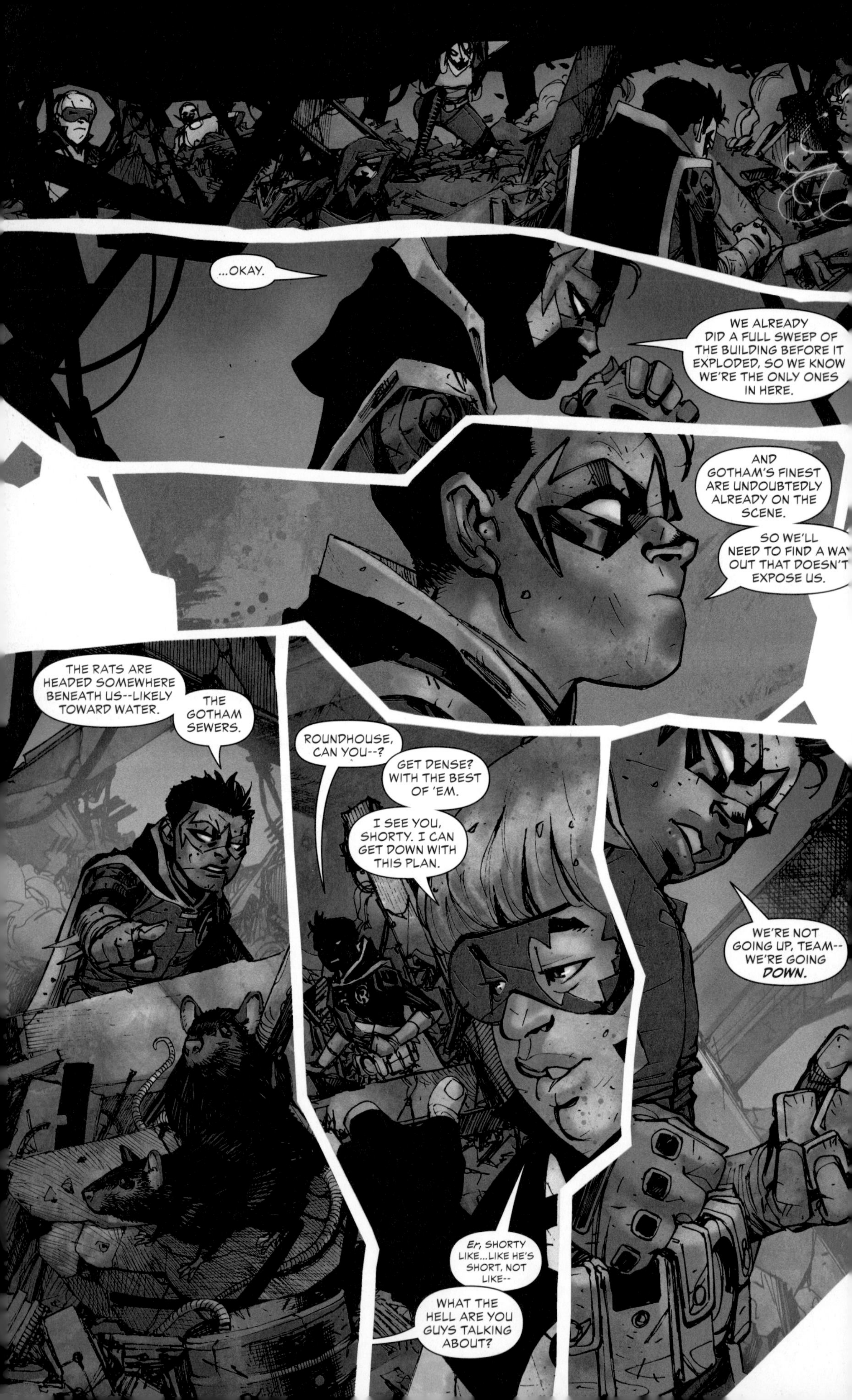
...OKAY.
WE ALREADY DID A FULL SWEEP OF THE BUILDING BEFORE IT EXPLODED, SO WE KNOW WE'RE THE ONLY ONES IN HERE.
AND GOTHAM'S FINEST ARE UNDOUBTEDLY ALREADY ON THE SCENE.
SO WE'LL NEED TO FIND A WAY OUT THAT DOESN'T EXPOSE US.
THE RATS ARE HEADED SOMEWHERE BENEATH US--LIKELY TOWARD WATER.
THE GOTHAM SEWERS.
ROUNDHOUSE, CAN YOU--?
GET DENSE? WITH THE BEST OF 'EM.
I SEE YOU, SHORTY. I CAN GET DOWN WITH THIS PLAN.
WE'RE NOT GOING UP, TEAM--WE'RE GOING *DOWN.*
*Er,* SHORTY LIKE...LIKE HE'S SHORT, NOT LIKE--
WHAT THE HELL ARE YOU GUYS TALKING ABOUT?

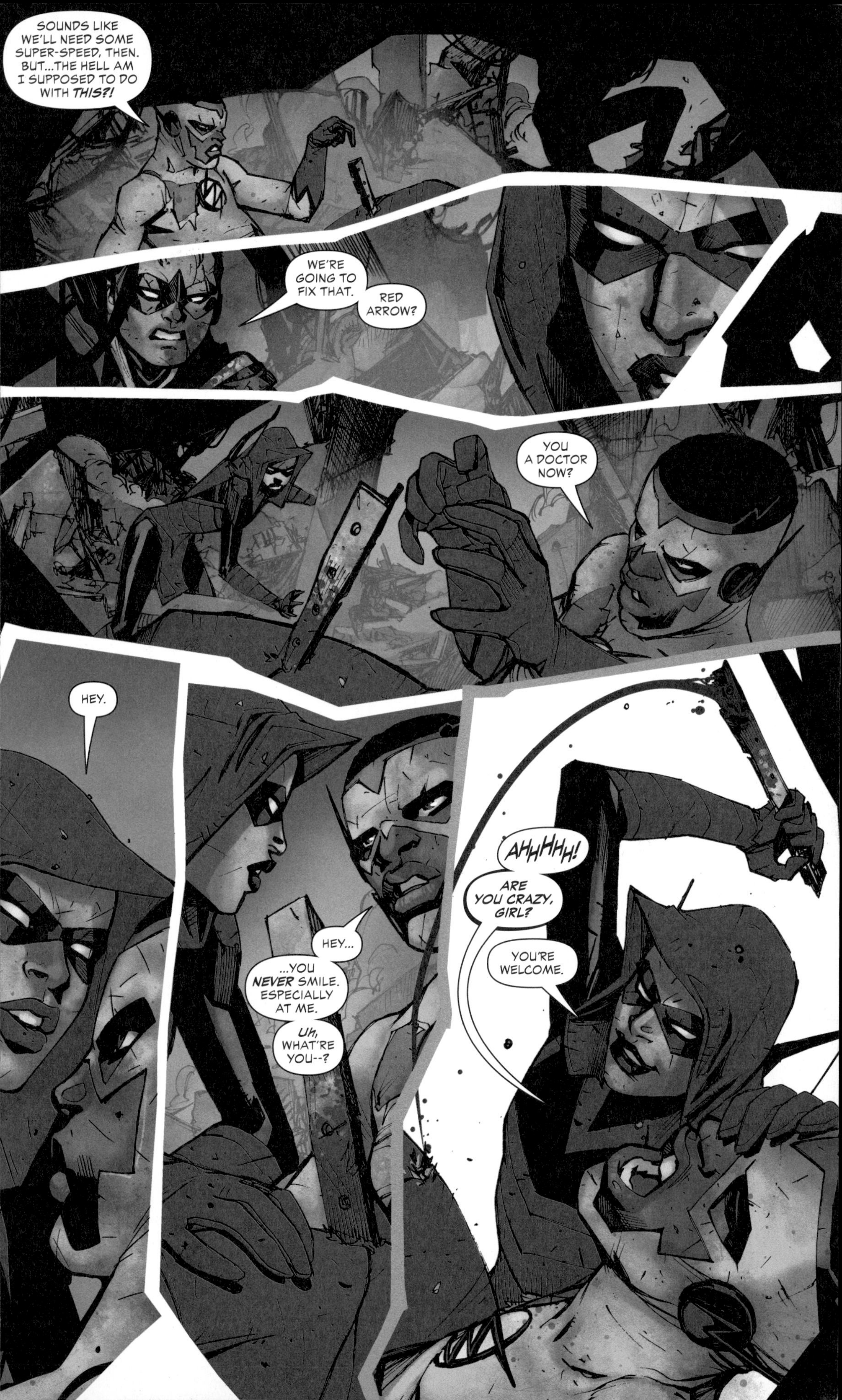

SOUNDS LIKE WE'LL NEED SOME SUPER-SPEED, THEN. BUT...THE HELL AM I SUPPOSED TO DO WITH *THIS?!*
WE'RE GOING TO FIX THAT.
RED ARROW?
YOU A DOCTOR NOW?
HEY.
HEY...
...YOU **NEVER** SMILE. ESPECIALLY AT ME.
*UH,* WHAT'RE YOU--?
AHHHHH!
ARE YOU CRAZY, GIRL?
YOU'RE WELCOME.

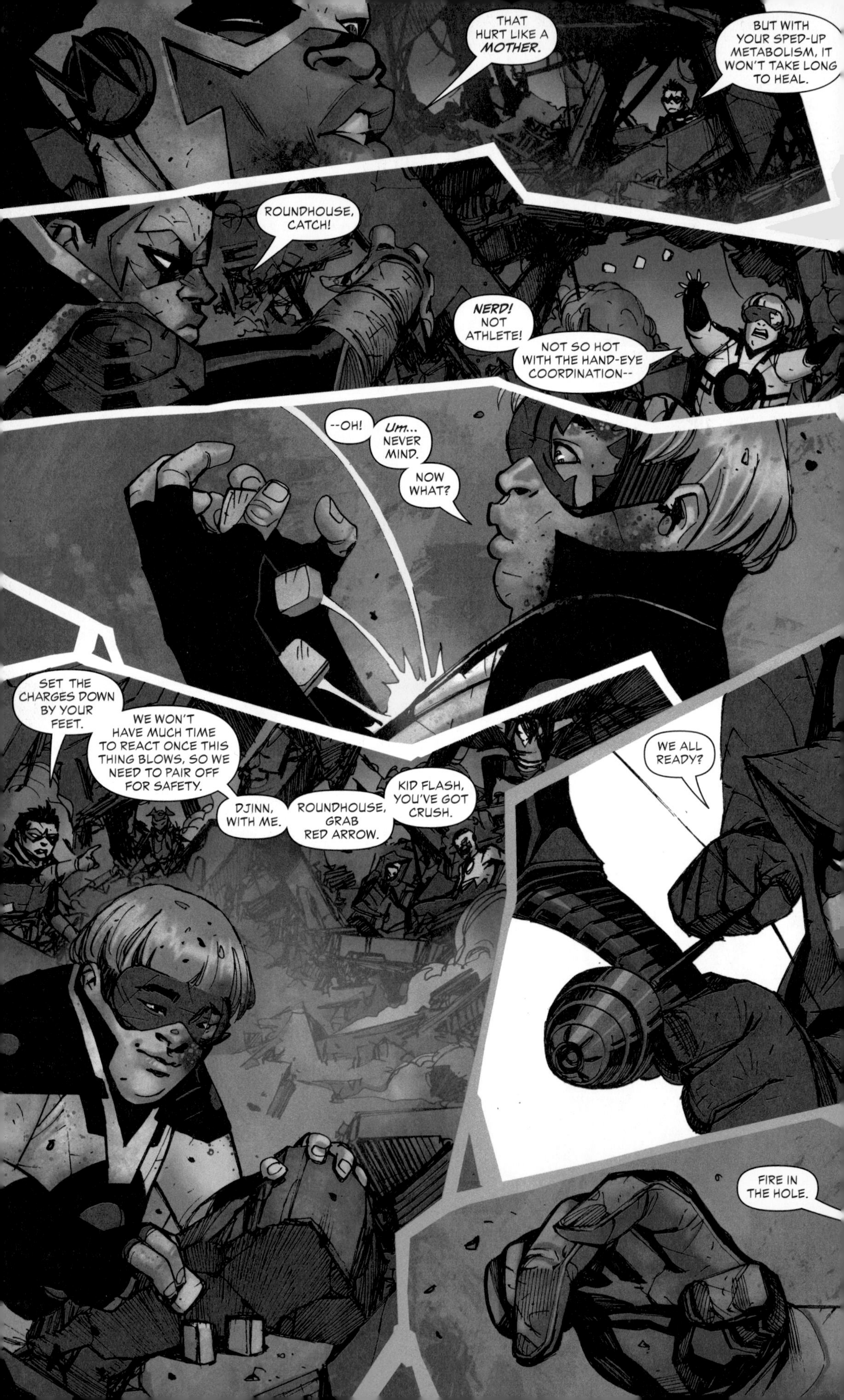

THAT HURT LIKE A *MOTHER*.
BUT WITH YOUR SPED-UP METABOLISM, IT WON'T TAKE LONG TO HEAL.
ROUNDHOUSE, CATCH!
*NERD!* NOT ATHLETE!
NOT SO HOT WITH THE HAND-EYE COORDINATION--
--OH!
*Um...* NEVER MIND.
NOW WHAT?
SET THE CHARGES DOWN BY YOUR FEET.
WE WON'T HAVE MUCH TIME TO REACT ONCE THIS THING BLOWS, SO WE NEED TO PAIR OFF FOR SAFETY.
DJINN, WITH ME.
ROUNDHOUSE, GRAB RED ARROW.
KID FLASH, YOU'VE GOT CRUSH.
WE ALL READY?
FIRE IN THE HOLE.

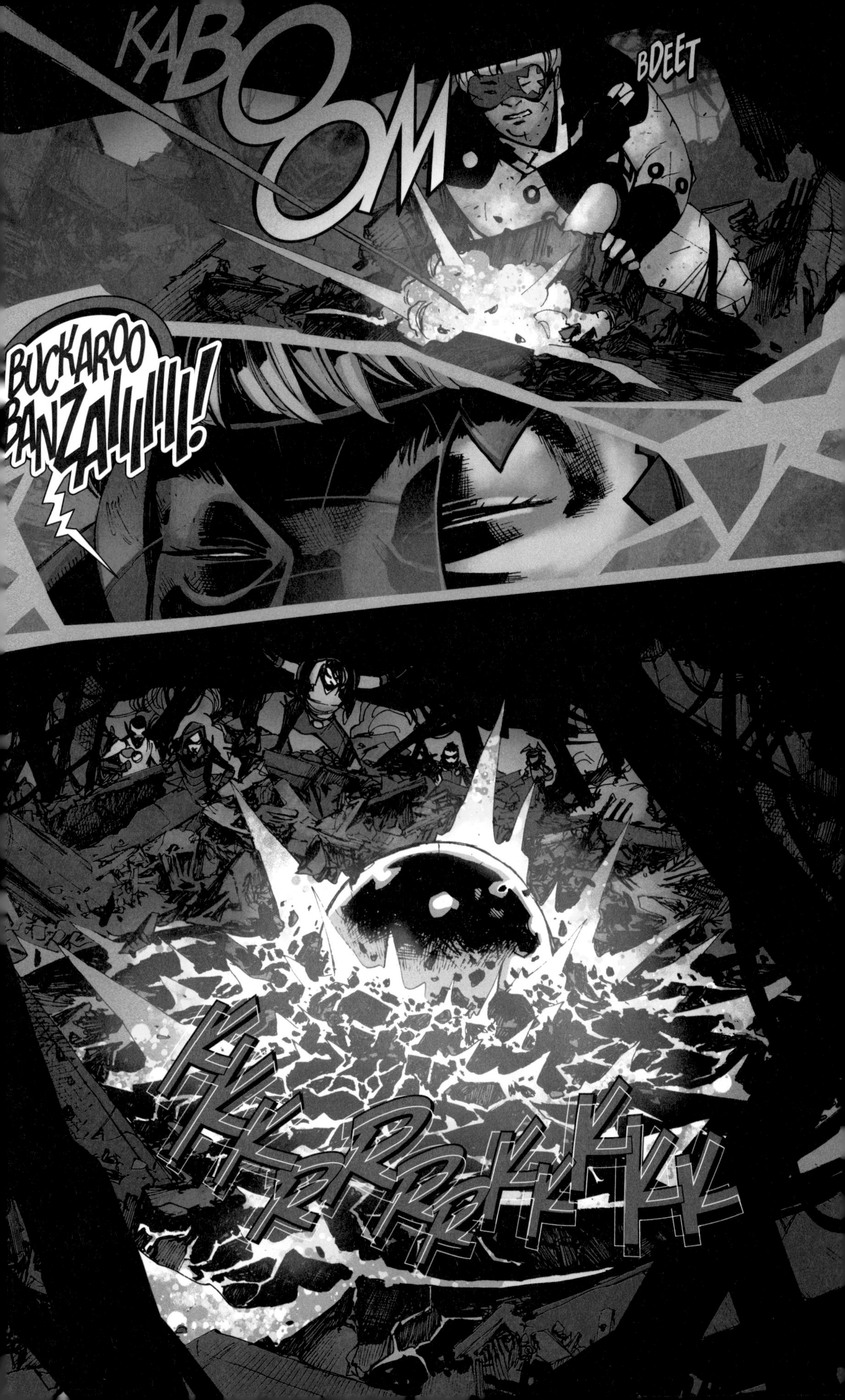
KABOOM
BDEET
BUCKAROO BANZAIIIIIII!
KKKRRRKKKKK

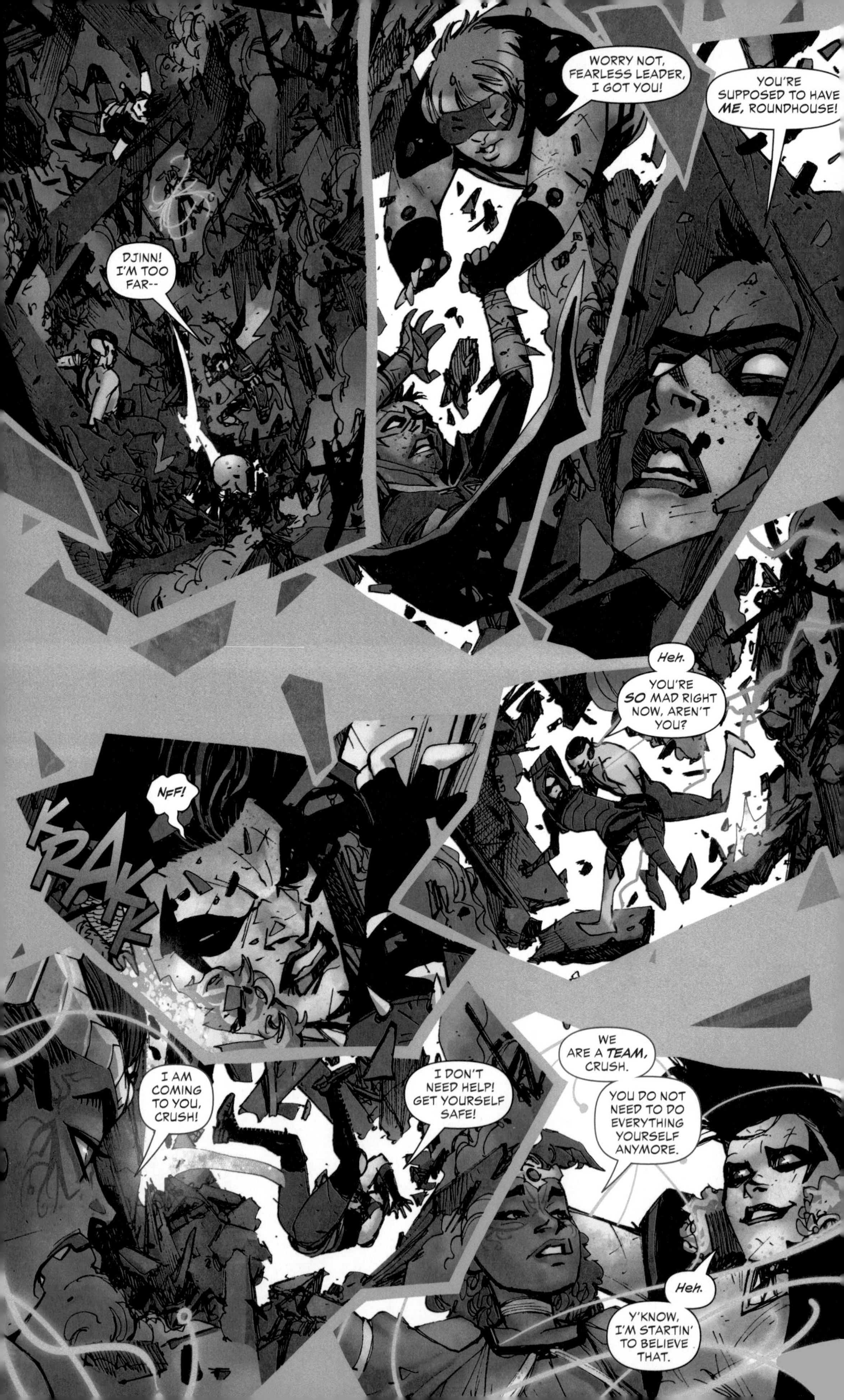
DJINN! I'M TOO FAR--
WORRY NOT, FEARLESS LEADER, I GOT YOU!
YOU'RE SUPPOSED TO HAVE ME, ROUNDHOUSE!
Heh.
YOU'RE SO MAD RIGHT NOW, AREN'T YOU?
NFF!
KRAK
I AM COMING TO YOU, CRUSH!
I DON'T NEED HELP! GET YOURSELF SAFE!
WE ARE A TEAM, CRUSH.
YOU DO NOT NEED TO DO EVERYTHING YOURSELF ANYMORE.
Heh.
Y'KNOW, I'M STARTIN' TO BELIEVE THAT.

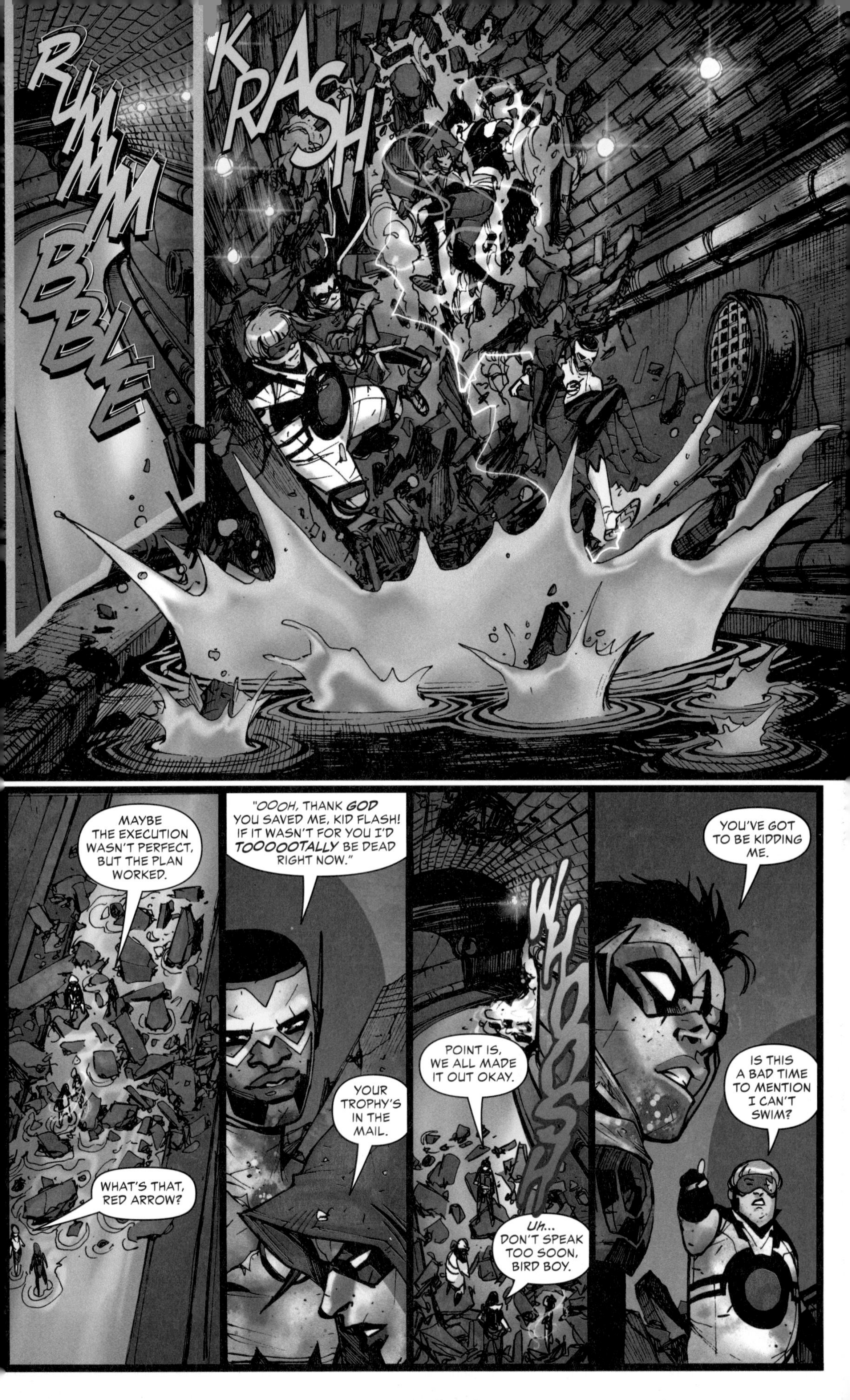
RUMMMBBLE
KRASH
MAYBE THE EXECUTION WASN'T PERFECT, BUT THE PLAN WORKED.
WHAT'S THAT, RED ARROW?
"OOOH, THANK *GOD* YOU SAVED ME, KID FLASH! IF IT WASN'T FOR YOU I'D *TOOOOOTALLY* BE DEAD RIGHT NOW."
YOUR TROPHY'S IN THE MAIL.
POINT IS, WE ALL MADE IT OUT OKAY.
*Uh...* DON'T SPEAK TOO SOON, BIRD BOY.
WHOOSH
YOU'VE GOT TO BE KIDDING ME.
IS THIS A BAD TIME TO MENTION I CAN'T SWIM?

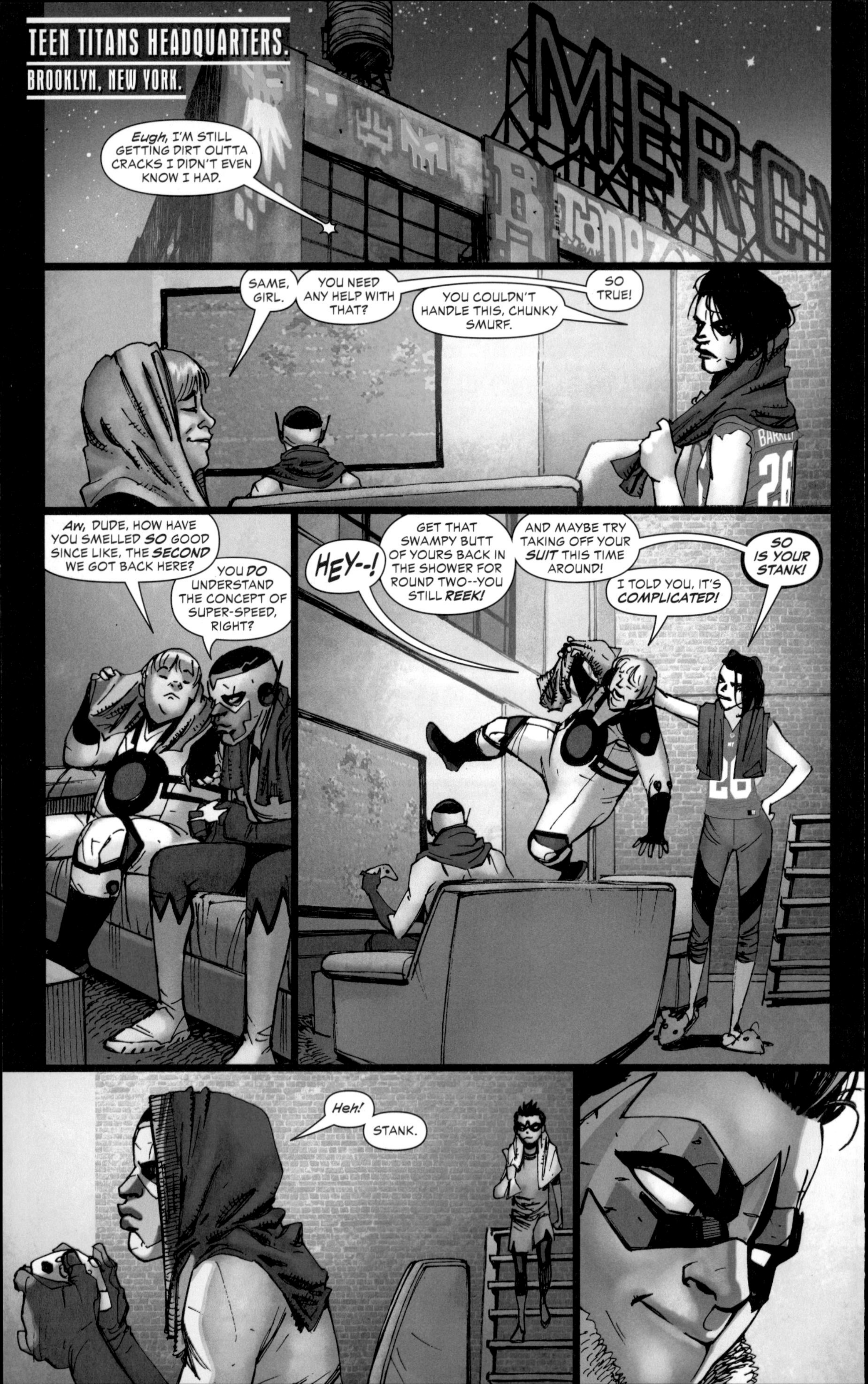
TEEN TITANS HEADQUARTERS.
BROOKLYN, NEW YORK.
Eugh, I'M STILL GETTING DIRT OUTTA CRACKS I DIDN'T EVEN KNOW I HAD.
SAME, GIRL.
YOU NEED ANY HELP WITH THAT?
SO TRUE!
YOU COULDN'T HANDLE THIS, CHUNKY SMURF.
Aw, DUDE, HOW HAVE YOU SMELLED SO GOOD SINCE LIKE, THE SECOND WE GOT BACK HERE?
YOU DO UNDERSTAND THE CONCEPT OF SUPER-SPEED, RIGHT?
HEY--!
GET THAT SWAMPY BUTT OF YOURS BACK IN THE SHOWER FOR ROUND TWO--YOU STILL REEK!
AND MAYBE TRY TAKING OFF YOUR SUIT THIS TIME AROUND!
I TOLD YOU, IT'S COMPLICATED!
SO IS YOUR STANK!
Heh!
STANK.

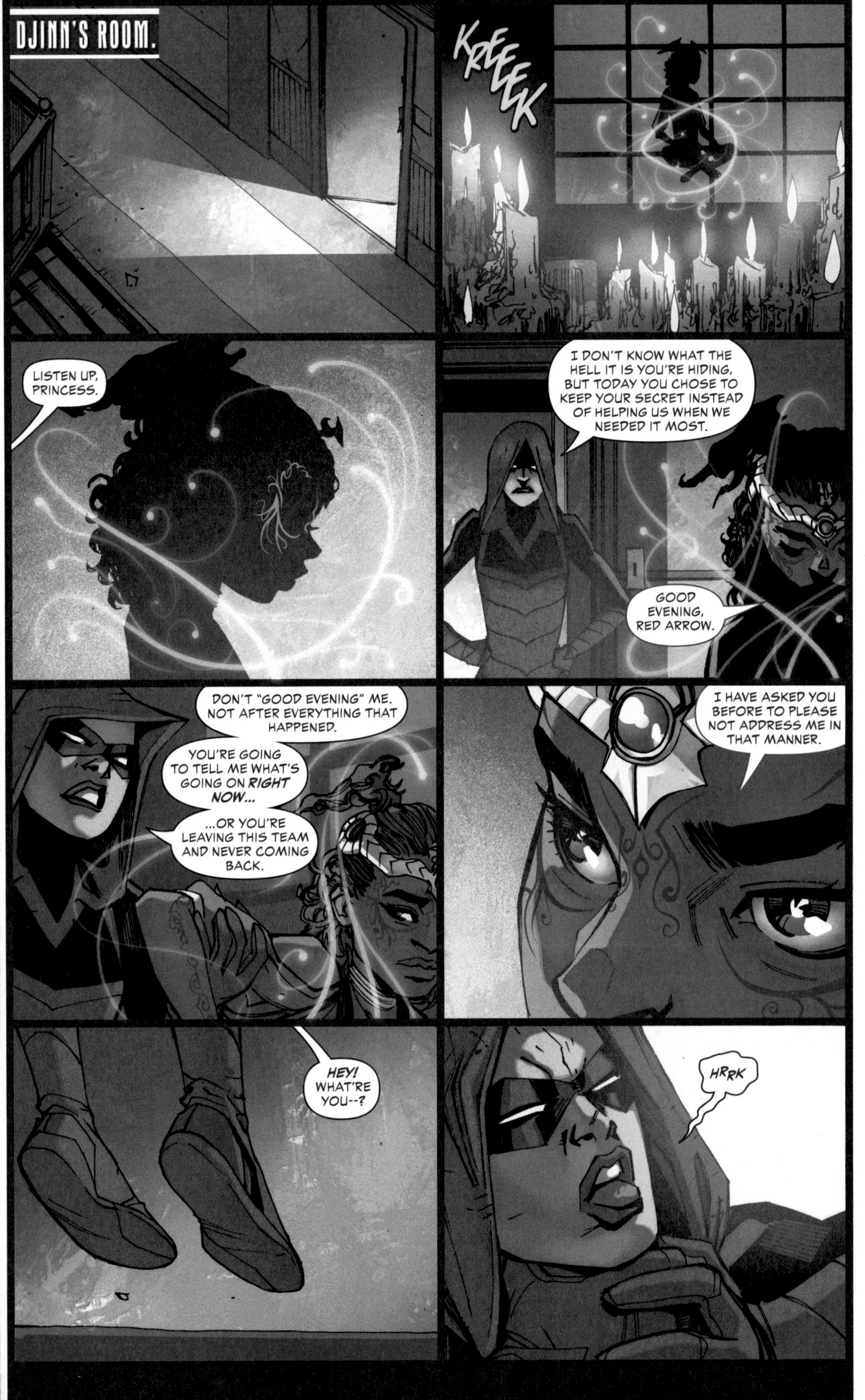
DJINN'S ROOM.
KREEEEK
LISTEN UP, PRINCESS.
I DON'T KNOW WHAT THE HELL IT IS YOU'RE HIDING, BUT TODAY YOU CHOSE TO KEEP YOUR SECRET INSTEAD OF HELPING US WHEN WE NEEDED IT MOST.
GOOD EVENING, RED ARROW.
DON'T "GOOD EVENING" ME. NOT AFTER EVERYTHING THAT HAPPENED.
YOU'RE GOING TO TELL ME WHAT'S GOING ON *RIGHT NOW...*
...OR YOU'RE LEAVING THIS TEAM AND NEVER COMING BACK.
I HAVE ASKED YOU BEFORE TO PLEASE NOT ADDRESS ME IN THAT MANNER.
*HEY!* WHAT'RE YOU--?
*HRRK*

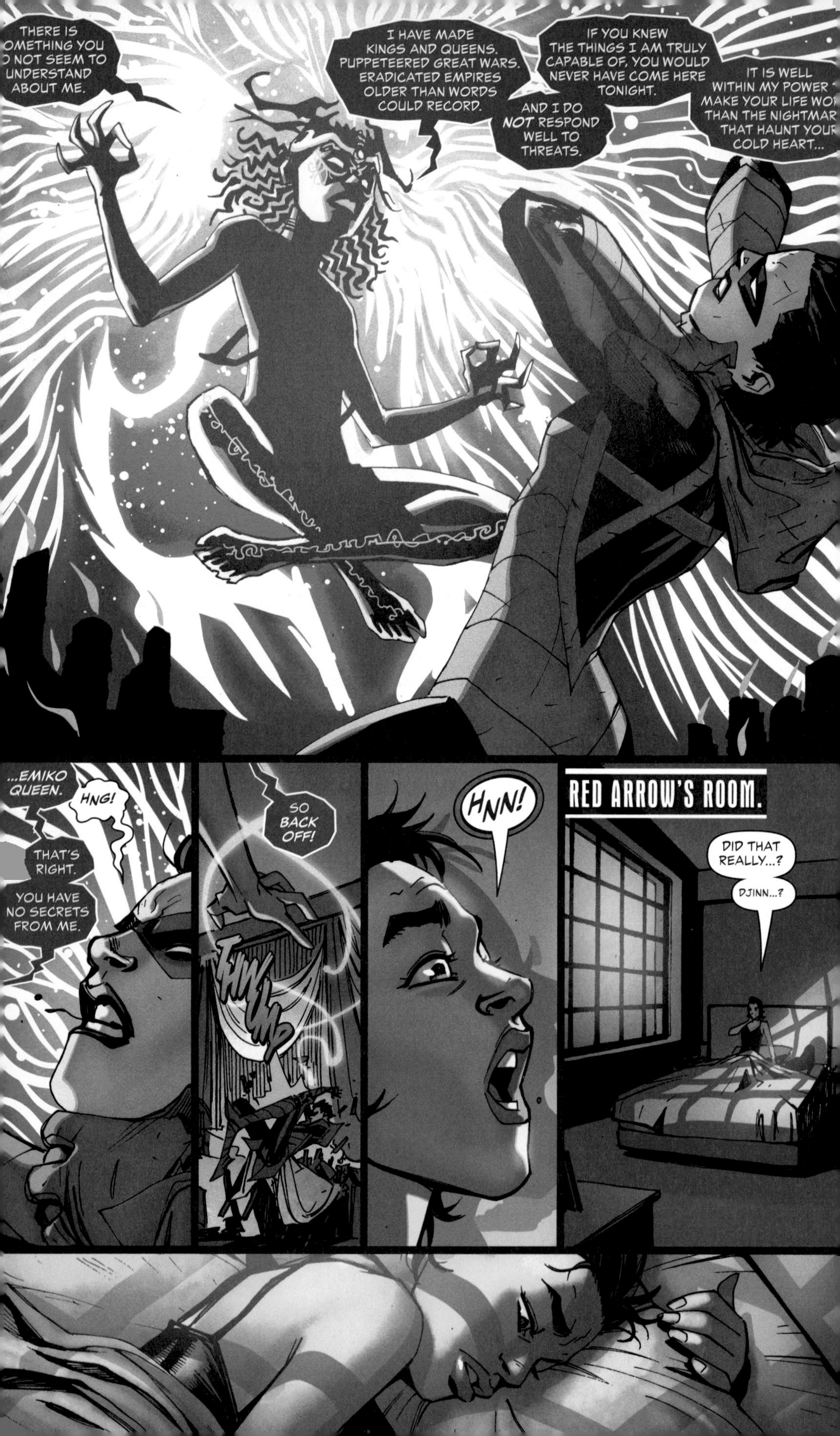
THERE IS OMETHING YOU O NOT SEEM TO UNDERSTAND ABOUT ME.
I HAVE MADE KINGS AND QUEENS. PUPPETEERED GREAT WARS. ERADICATED EMPIRES OLDER THAN WORDS COULD RECORD.
IF YOU KNEW THE THINGS I AM TRULY CAPABLE OF, YOU WOULD NEVER HAVE COME HERE TONIGHT.
AND I DO *NOT* RESPOND WELL TO THREATS.
IT IS WELL WITHIN MY POWER T MAKE YOUR LIFE WO THAN THE NIGHTMAR THAT HAUNT YOUR COLD HEART...
...EMIKO QUEEN.
HNG!
THAT'S RIGHT.
YOU HAVE NO SECRETS FROM ME.
SO BACK OFF!
THWUMP
HNN!
RED ARROW'S ROOM.
DID THAT REALLY...?
DJINN...?

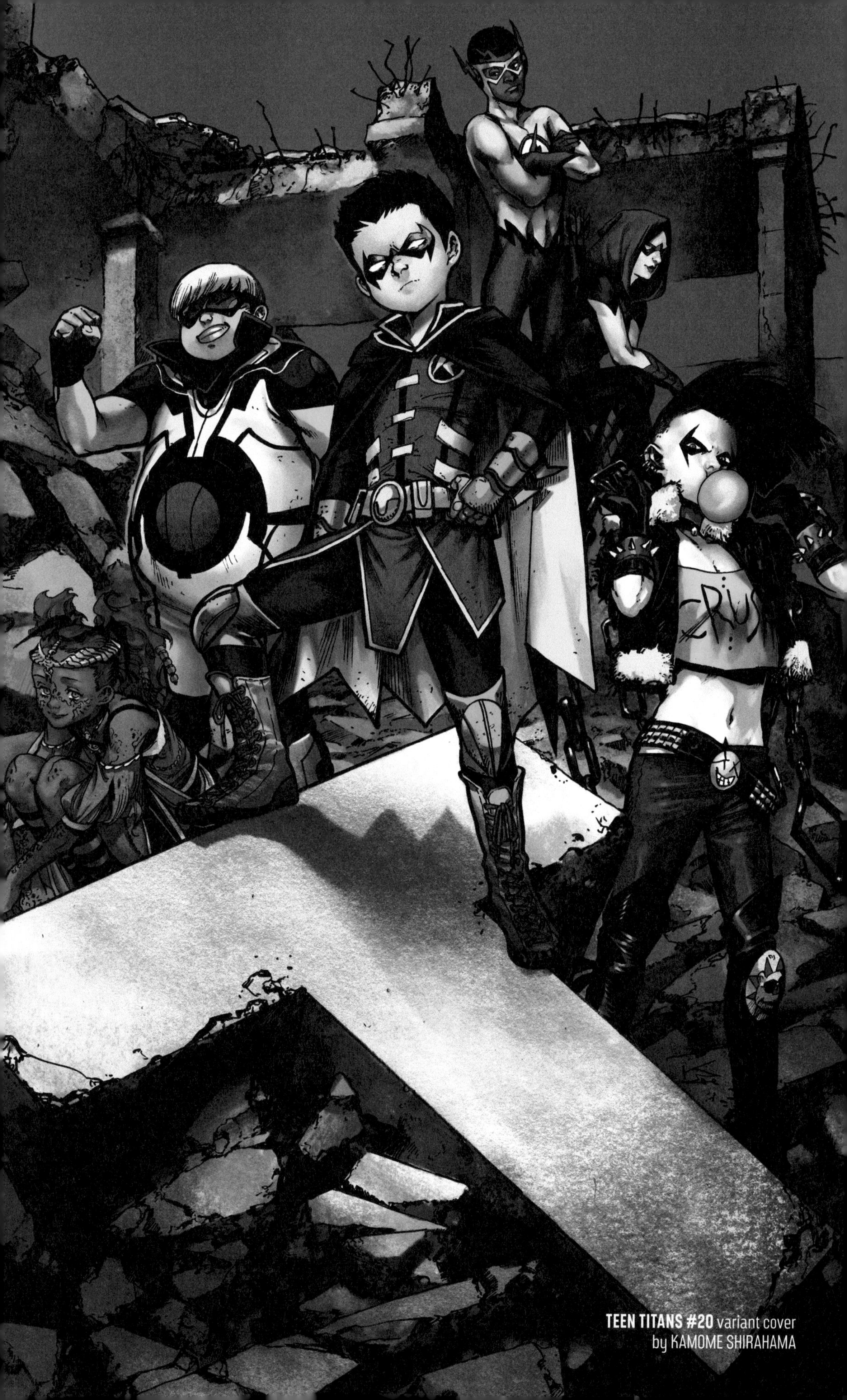

**TEEN TITANS #20** variant cover
by KAMOME SHIRAHAMA

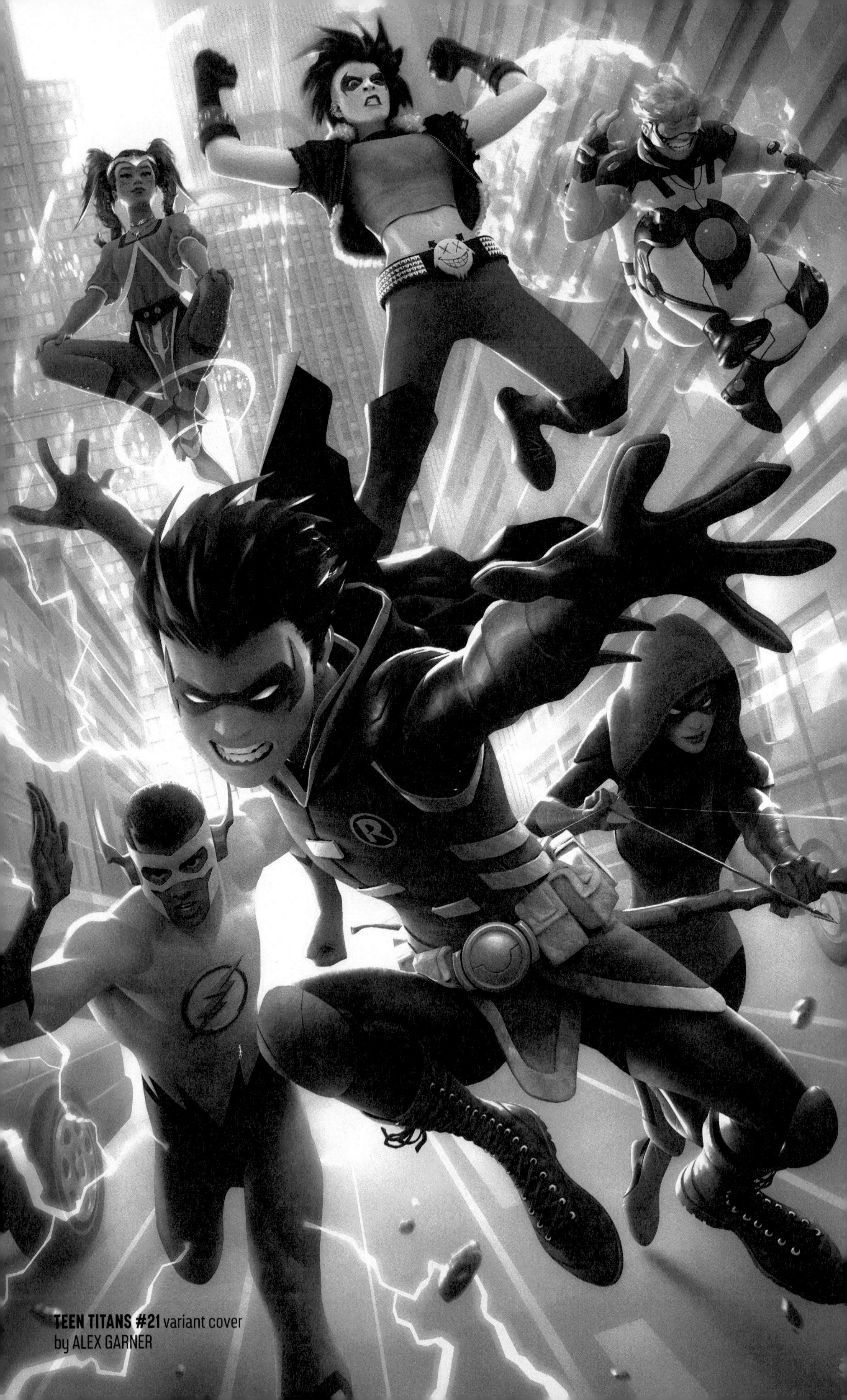

**TEEN TITANS #21** variant cover
by ALEX GARNER

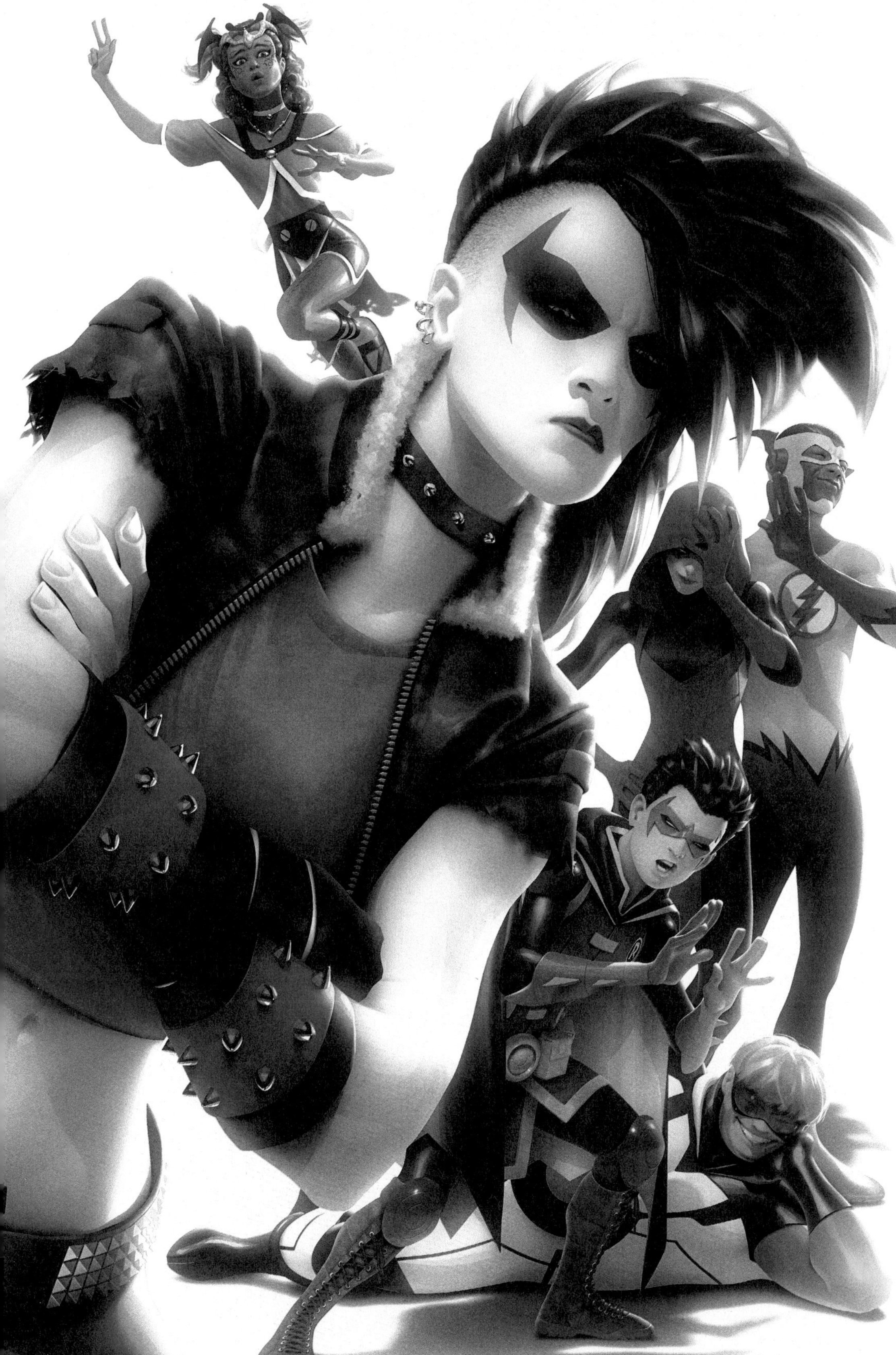

**TEEN TITANS #22** variant cover
by ALEX GARNER

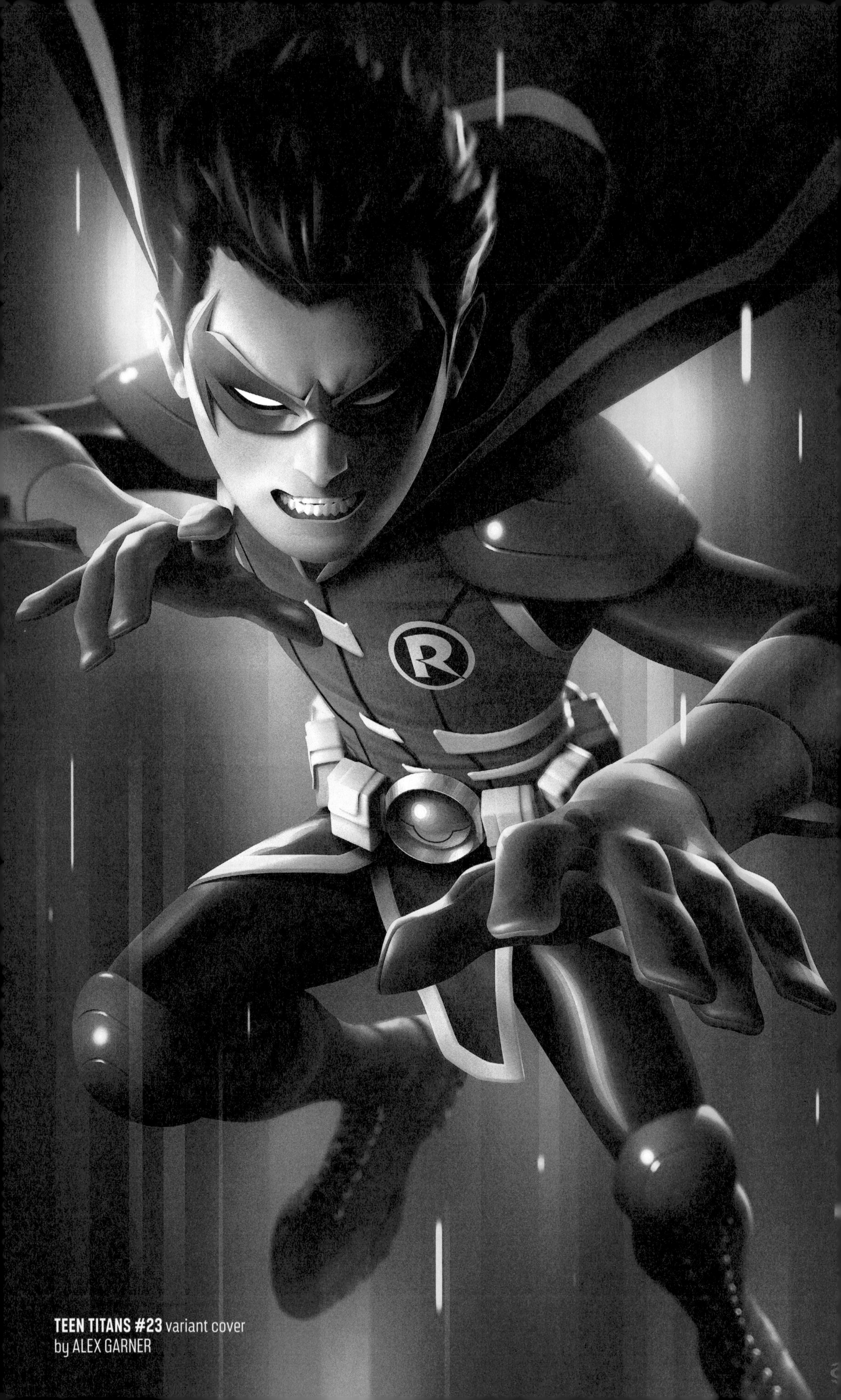
R

**TEEN TITANS #23** variant cover
by ALEX GARNER

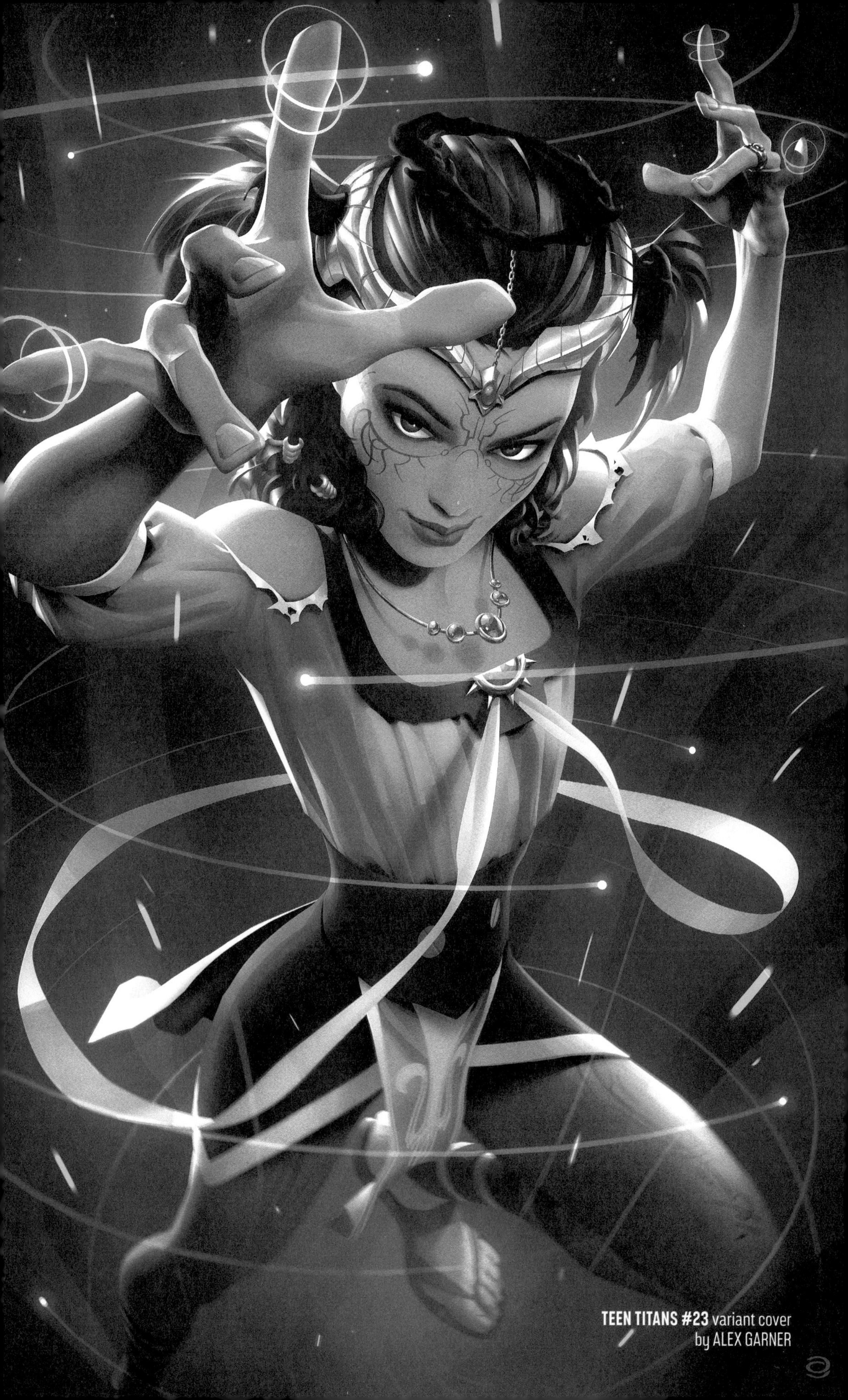

**TEEN TITANS #23** variant cover
by ALEX GARNER

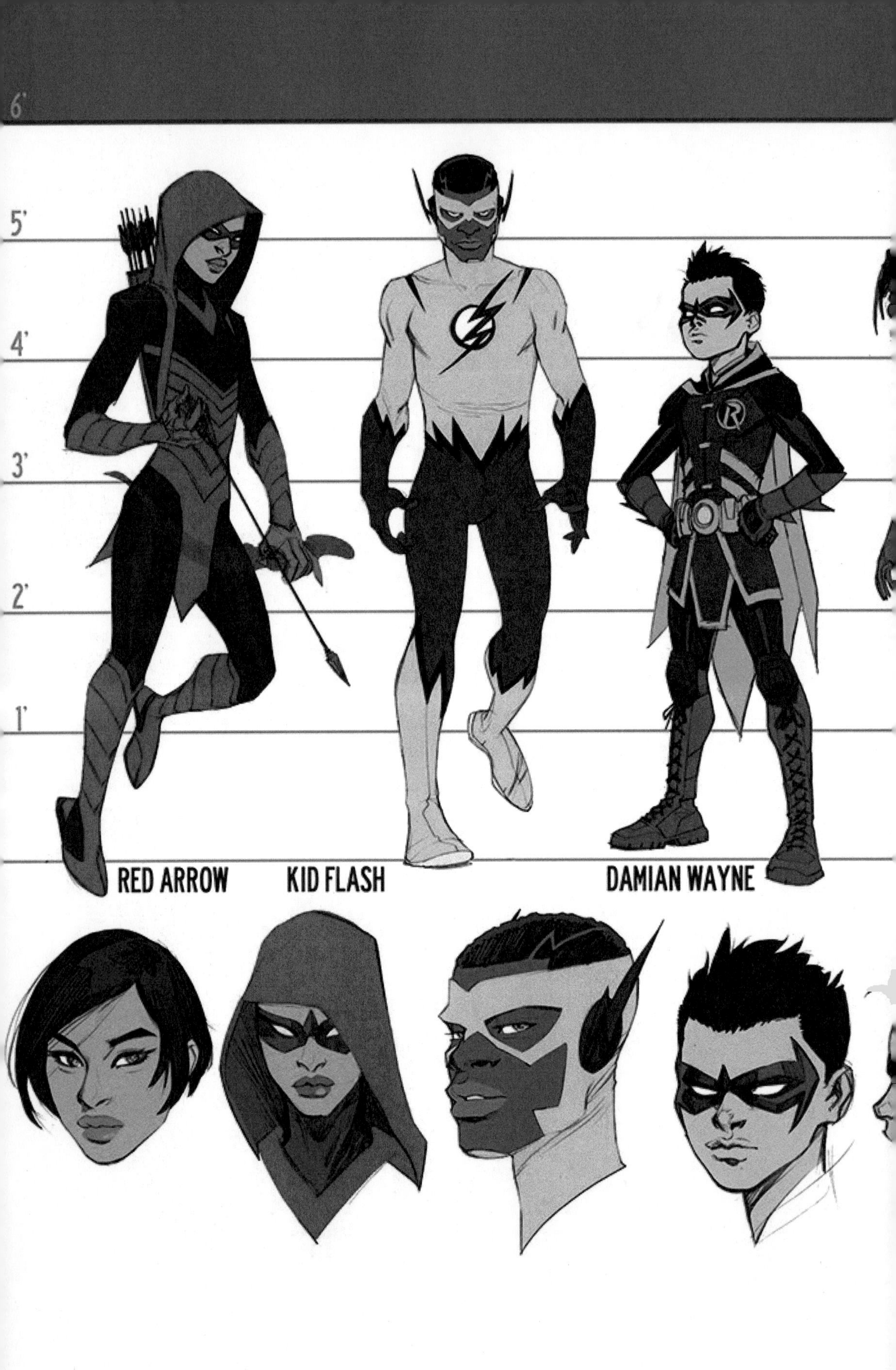
6'
5'
4'
3'
2'
1'
RED ARROW
KID FLASH
DAMIAN WAYNE

**TEEN TITANS** lineup by BERNARD CHANG

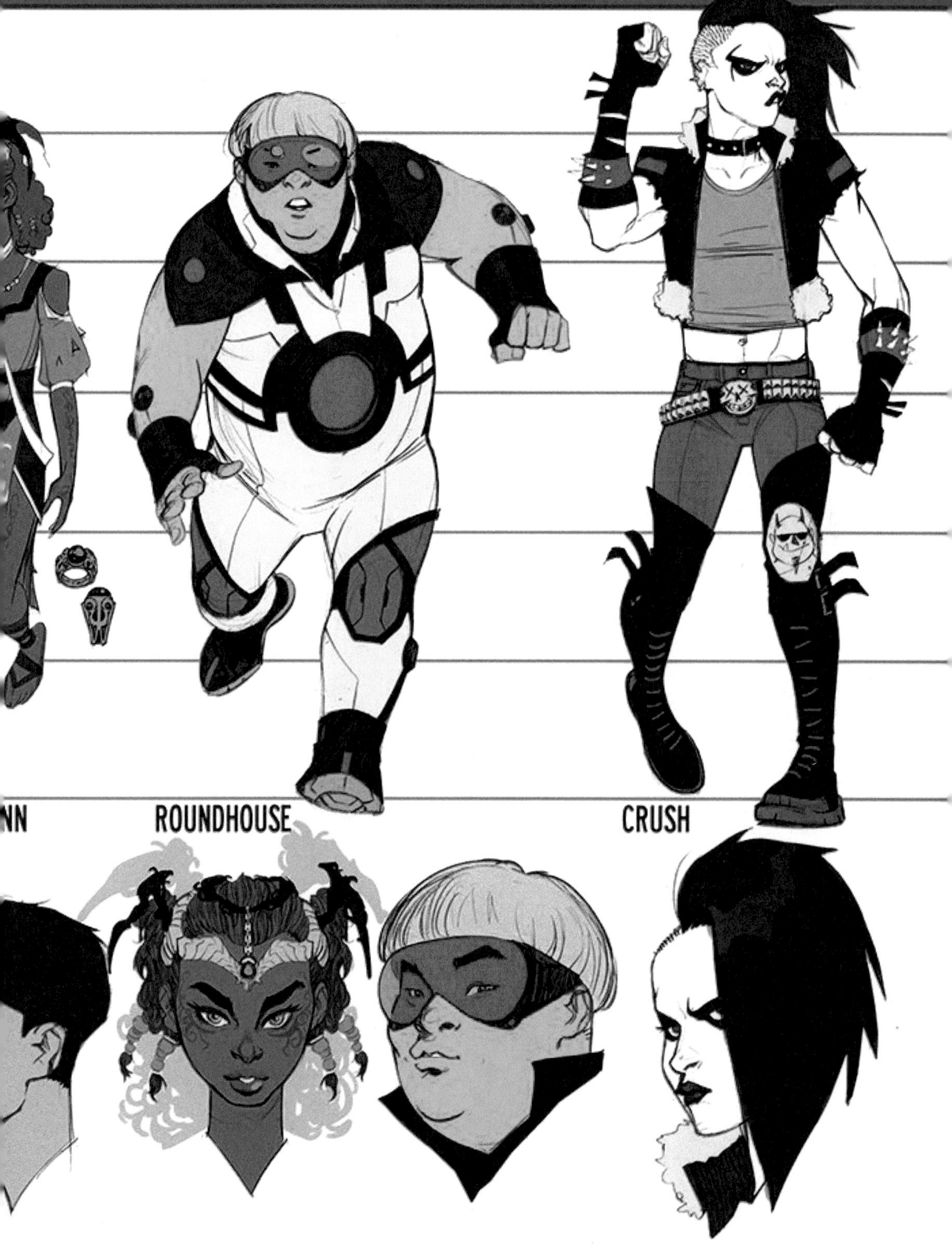
NN
ROUNDHOUSE
CRUSH

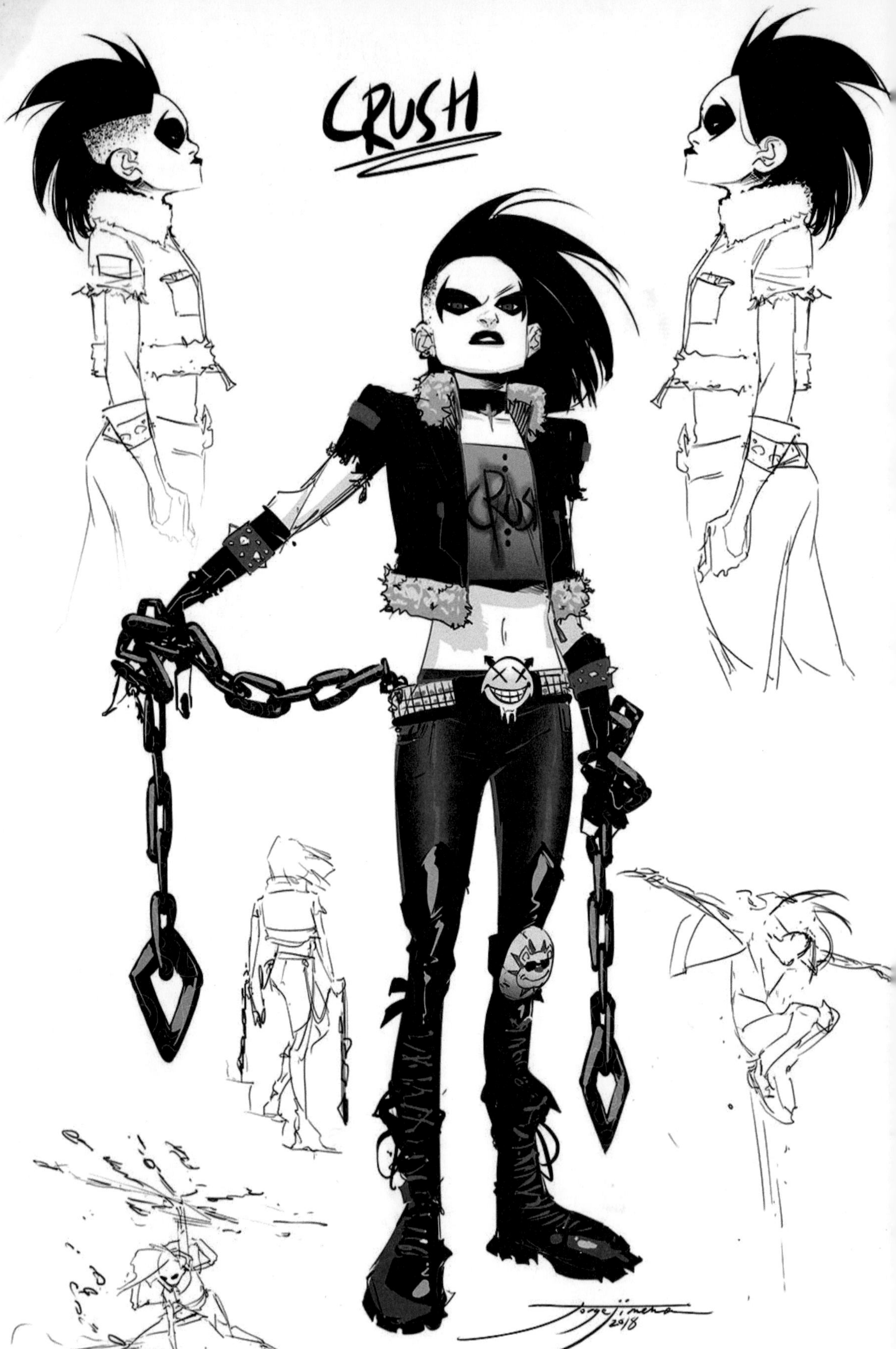
CRUSH
CRUSH
Jorge Jiménez
2018

**CRUSH** by JORGE JIMÉNEZ

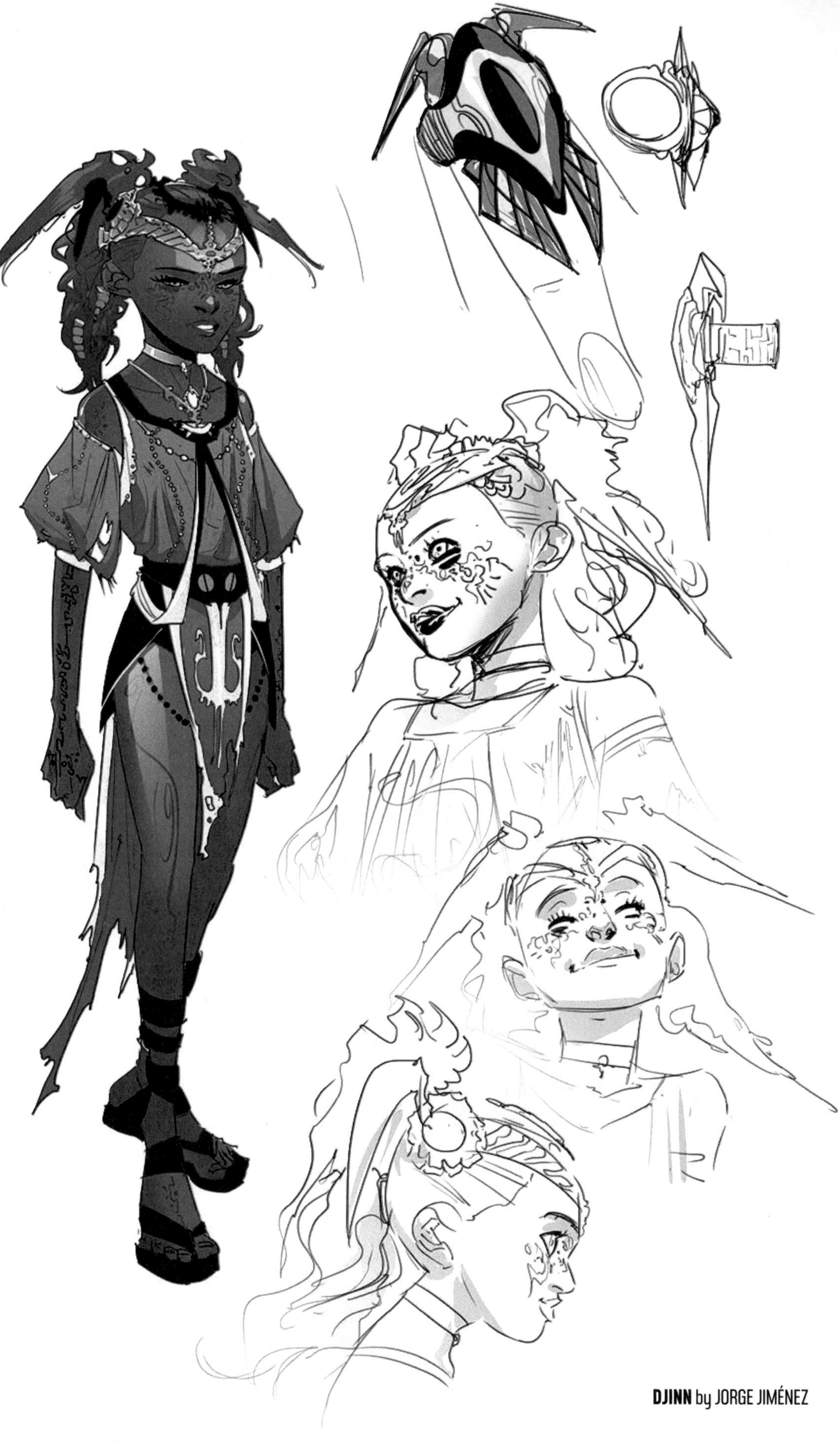

**DJINN** by JORGE JIMÉNEZ

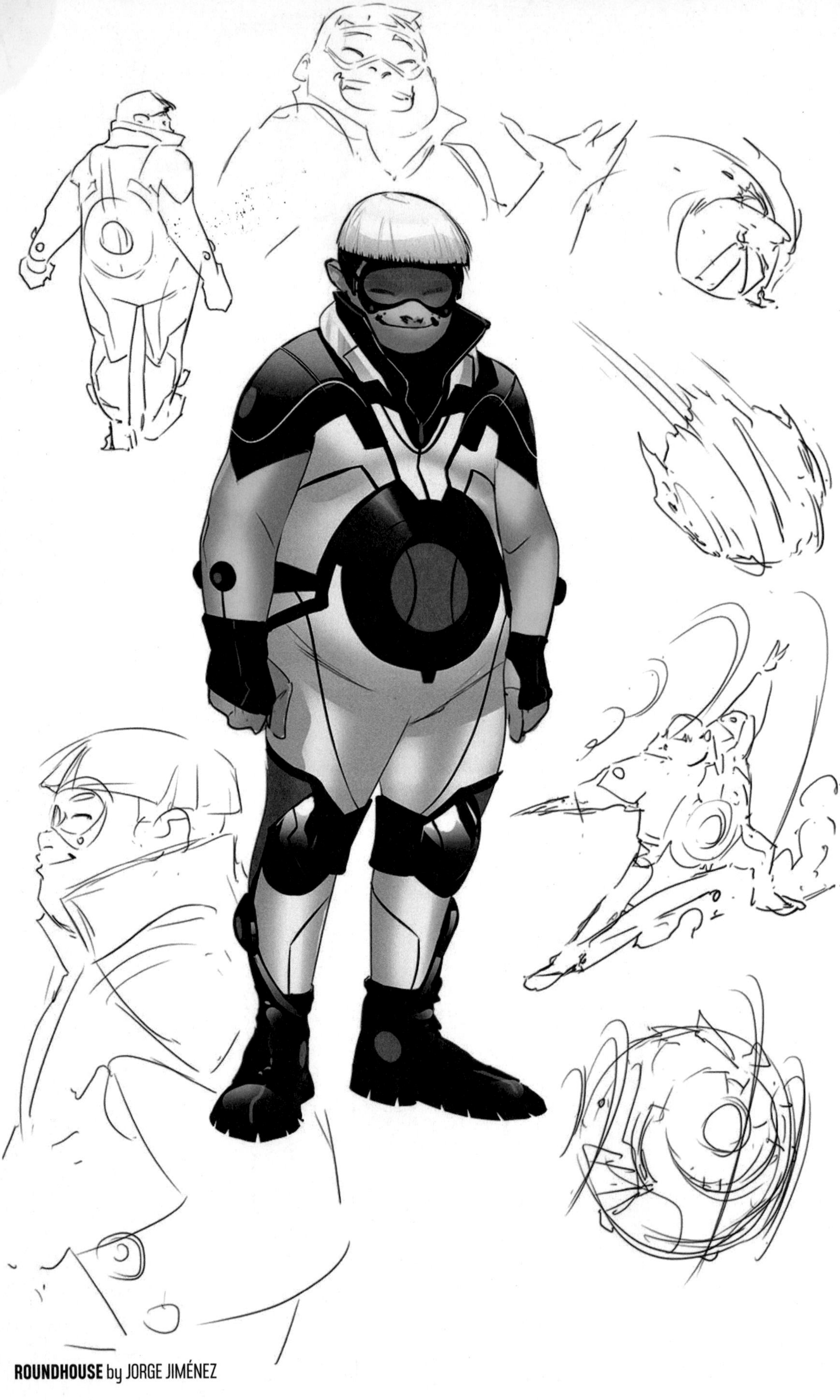

**ROUNDHOUSE** by JORGE JIMÉNEZ